POLK

The Diary of a President

1845-1849

POLK

The Diary of a President

1845-1849

*Covering the Mexican War, the Acquisition
of Oregon, and the Conquest of California
and the Southwest*

EDITED BY
ALLAN NEVINS

LONGMANS, GREEN AND CO.
LONDON · NEW YORK · TORONTO
1952

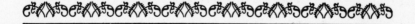

LONGMANS, GREEN AND CO., INC.
55 FIFTH AVENUE, NEW YORK 3

LONGMANS, GREEN AND CO. LTD.
6 & 7 CLIFFORD STREET, LONDON W I

LONGMANS, GREEN AND CO.
215 VICTORIA STREET, TORONTO I

POLK, THE DIARY OF A PRESIDENT, 1845-1849
COPYRIGHT 1929, 1952
BY LONGMANS, GREEN & CO., INC.

Printed in the United States of America

PREFACE

THIS VOLUME is a selection from "The Diary of James K. Polk During His Presidency, 1845 to 1849," edited and annotated by Milo Milton Quaife, and published in four volumes in 1910 by A. C. McClurg & Company of Chicago for the Chicago Historical Society, in whose collections the original manuscript rests. Having been printed in an edition of but five hundred copies, the work is unfortunately but little known to the general public. The editor has attempted to select from it the portions most interesting and valuable to ordinary students and readers, and to knit them together by a full body of notes. Every effort has been made to preserve textual accuracy and to print the diary as Polk wrote it; but the punctuation and capitalization have been rendered uniform, misspellings have been corrected, and a few inadvertent omissions which the original editor, Dr. Quaife, supplied in brackets, have been inserted without them. The Chicago Historical Society and Dr. Quaife have generously given permission for the publication.

CONTENTS

INTRODUCTION

W HO IS James K. Polk?" derisively asked the Whigs when the Democratic Convention of 1844 at Baltimore nominated the first "dark horse" in our political history. The cry had some warrant, for if Polk's name was well known, his personality and views were mysteries to the public. He had been a member of the House of Representatives for seven successive terms, from 1825 to 1839, and Governor of Tennessee after that; he had been Speaker during two years, and was known as an earnest and skilful leader of the Jacksonian Democracy in Jackson's own State. But his name had never been connected with any great measure, he was unknown as an orator or thinker, and he was a distinctly secondary figure in the field of politics. He came on the national stage under strange circumstances. That such a man, colorless, methodical, plodding, narrow, should become President of the United States was itself remarkable. That he should defeat the magnetic Clay, "Harry of the West," a born leader of men, brilliant, dashing, and generous, whose star when the campaign opened seemed rising to certain victory, was astonishing. But for James G. Birney and his Liberty Party, which took from Henry Clay more than twice the 5,000 votes which gave Polk his plurality in New York, Clay would have been elected. Because Polk had defeated the cherished idol of the Whigs, his opponents, rallied by Webster with the ringing quotation, "What though the field be lost, all is not lost," regarded him with added dislike, suspicion, and condescension.

For decades after he left the Presidency Polk was misunderstood and belittled by those who accepted the Whig and

anti-slavery interpretation of the Mexican War. So late
as 1881 the historian Hermann Von Holst could speak of
the conflict as "the war of Polk the Mendacious." The
accusation against him was that he had led Congress to declare war against Mexico by a tissue of perversions, am-
biguities, and suppressions of fact, and that his whole policy
in foreign affairs was "tortuous and sordid." The majority
of the Whigs believed that he and his Southern advisers had
schemed a war of conquest partly to provide new territory
for the expansion of slavery, and partly for other reasons,
and that he entered office deliberately intending to attack
Mexico. Among the motives variously alleged for the aggressions upon our southern neighbor were Polk's desire for
personal glory, for the perpetuation of Democratic ascend-
ancy and his own reëlection, and for obscuring the humiliat-
ing result of the Oregon negotiations. Having made up his
mind, according to his critics, Polk carried out his program
with Machiavellian adroitness. Without a word of warning
to the country, without a conference with Congressional leaders, he ordered Zachary Taylor to advance from the Nueces
to the east bank of the Rio Grande — a wanton and warlike
invasion of territory colonized by Mexico, to which Texas
(it was said) had no shadow of legal right. "To provoke
this feeble sister republic to hostilities, at the same time putting on her the offence of shedding the first blood," writes
Schouler, "was the step predetermined if she would not sign
away her domain for gold."

A fairer perspective, the decay of old sectional and party
prejudices, and a fuller research, have enabled us to correct
the injustice of these views. Polk's career was from first
to last that of an honest, conscientious, and limited man, who
was incapable perhaps of the highest moral elevation, but
was certainly also incapable of deceit and double-dealing.
He rose from step to step by a combination of plodding, careful industry, and strict integrity. Born in Mecklenburg
County, North Carolina (Nov. 2, 1795), of Scotch and

Scotch-Irish ancestry, the son of an enterprising farmer who removed west to become one of the pioneers of the Cumberland Valley, he grew up in Tennessee. At the University of North Carolina he gained a good classical education, he studied law in the office of Judge Felix Grundy, and he went from law into politics. When not quite thirty he entered Congress as a disciple of Jefferson and adherent of Jackson. Devoid of all personal magnetism, cold, formal, and precise in manner, able to make but few friends, he pushed his way forward by his close attention to business and his party zeal.

He bore a prominent and arduous part in Jackson's war against the United States Bank, winning the complete confidence of the old general, and bringing to the discussion of finance an exhaustive preparation and closely logical argument. By sheer hard work he won promotion to the Speakership. Leaving Washington in an unselfish effort to regain the State of Tennessee for the Democratic party, he was once elected Governor and twice defeated. Actuated by principle, he refused a place in Tyler's Cabinet. But though absent from the capital, his staunch adherence to Jacksonian doctrines, his insistence on the annexation of Texas, and his evident "safeness," made him a prominent aspirant in 1844 for the Vice-Presidential nomination; and when the Van Buren faction and the Calhoun faction of the Democratic party came to a deadlock, he was a figure on whom both groups could unite. He was not yet fifty years old, and the youngest of our Presidents to that date, when amid a downpour of rain he stood on the steps of the Capitol and received the oath of office from Chief Justice Taney.

He was not "Polk the Mendacious," as has been wisely observed, but "Polk the Mediocre." In the sense that Rutherford B. Hayes and Calvin Coolidge were mediocre — a comparative sense only — that term may well be applied to Polk. He was a man to command respect, but neither liking nor awe. In person he was spare, of middle height, angular in his movements, with a small head, long grizzled hair brushed stiffly back behind his ears, penetrating and rather chilly grey eyes, and a stern mouth. His countenance was usually sad, but sometimes lightened by a genial smile. His long training as Congressman and Governor had taught him to deal expeditiously with public business, and had increased his natural seriousness and caution; but he had never learned how to share his burdens with others. He was intense, laborious, humorless, pedestrian, immensely aware at all times of the responsibilities which he bore, and inclined to make everyone with whom he came in contact aware of them. He was methodical to a degree, and of a patience which enabled him to listen at length to the petitions of all who came to him for patronage or other favors. Their confidence he seldom repaid in kind, and even his closest official associates were often unaware of his real thoughts or intentions; much of his undeserved reputation for duplicity sprang merely from his taciturnity, which permitted men to deceive themselves. He was what the Yankees of his day called "cute," and what men now would term calculating, yet by his lights he was eminently truthful and upright.

No man can keep a full diary week after week, month after month, for four years, without revealing himself in it; and all of Polk's salient traits appear in these pages. They show us a man who labored at his desk day by day to the point of exhaustion, and who unquestionably impaired his health and shortened his life by his heavy labors. Ben: Perley Poore tells us that "before his term of office had half expired his friends were pained to witness his shortened and enfeebled step, and the air of languor and exhaustion which sat upon him." He survived his Presidency by only a few months, dying on June 15, 1849, and his record plainly reveals the reason. We see in these entries a man too serious and burdened ever to unbend. When a sleight of hand performer appeared in the White House, his mind was too full of the Oregon question and other state affairs to find, as he himself says, any diversion in the juggling. Once he tells us of lying on a sofa and listening to a trusted friend talk all Sunday afternoon; repeatedly he took a horseback ride for relaxation; and he seems really to have enjoyed some of the White House receptions, though visitors found him formal and preoccupied. But the element of play or fun was singularly lacking in his life, and his efficiency was seldom if ever leavened by gusto or enthusiasm.

His range of interests also was remarkably limited, and his mind strikes us as rather arid and inelastic. Did he ever read a novel in his life, or attend a nineteenth century play, or read any modern poetry? If so, the evidence is not here. Did he know anything of art, of music, or of nature, or care to know anything about them? From his diary and other papers no one would suspect that he did. We are told that Mrs. Polk, an attractive woman of great dignity and a strict Presbyterian (Polk himself belonged to no church and preferred the Methodist denomination), shunned what she looked upon as "the vanities of the world," and that she would not permit dancing in the White House. We are told also that on gala occasions callers at the White House were herded rapidly through the rooms, where Polk shook hands systematically and joylessly with the guests as fast as they could be introduced, while above the music of the Marine Band in the corridor could be heard the voice of an attendant repeating in a steady monotone, "Gentlemen-who-have-been-presented-will-please-walk-into-the-East-Room-don't-block-up-the-passage." Twice during his Presidency, and only twice, Polk took time to enjoy what might be called a brief vacation, going the first time to visit his alma mater, and the second to make a brief tour into New England; while once he also appeared briefly at a watering-place in Pennsylvania. But the activity and even gaiety which Van Buren had shown in the White House, the versatile occupations which Jefferson and J. Q. Adams had pursued there, the varied displays of Jackson's energy—these had no counterpart during his four years.

Because he was deficient in imagination, in soul, in vision, we are likely to do him something less than justice. He was uninspired and uninspiring. But he did possess an intellectual acuteness and energy which impressed his associates and served the nation well. He was a sound administrator, who fixed his eyes clearly on his goals and pursued them with undeviating resolution, and who knew how to be master in his Cabinet. Though some of his Secretaries were men of first-rate abilities, George Bancroft has recorded his conviction that Polk was the best of the group. When late in life Bancroft went through the Polk papers for historical purposes, he paid another tribute to his old chief. "His character," wrote Bancroft, "shines out in them just exactly as the man he was, prudent, far-sighted, bold, excelling any Democrat of his day in undeviatingly correct exposition of his democratic principles; and in short, as I think, judging of him as I knew him, and judging of him by the results of his administration, one of the very foremost of our public men, and one of the very best and most honest and most successful Presidents the country ever had." He was unswervingly true to principle. Those who, like James Russell Lowell, abused him as a tool of the slavery interests, little realized that he refused firmly to support the extreme Southern program, that he angrily denounced John C. Calhoun for his use of the slavery question, and that he wished to extend the Missouri Compromise line to the Pacific. He noted without the slightest regret that it seemed impossible that slavery should ever exist in any part of the territory acquired from Mexico. The same firmness and patriotism appear in his handling of the Oregon question, and his adherence to a uniform and moderate course appears in striking contrast to the wabbling of Buchanan, and the demand of Lewis Cass and other Northwestern leaders for 54° 40′ or a fight.

Sometimes the mediocre man makes a better President than the great man; Rutherford B. Hayes was a far more successful executive than Grant, and Polk was a decidedly more effective head of the nation than J. Q. Adams. Few Presidents have seen more distinctly the objects they wished to achieve, or been more successful in attaining their aims. Soon after his administration began, Polk announced to Secretary Bancroft that " There are four great measures " — and he struck his thigh forcibly for emphasis as he spoke — " which are to be the measures of my administration: one, a reduction of the tariff; another, the independent treasury; a third, the settlement of the Oregon boundary question; and, lastly, the acquisition of California." He became President with the inflexible determination to carry these measures into effect, and when he left the Presidency he had accomplished them all. It required courage and energy to obtain the passage of the Walker Tariff, which hung in so close a balance that but two votes in the Senate would have defeated it; it required constancy and adroitness to settle the Oregon question. If he had not faced John Bull firmly, as he put it, the issue might have been less fortunate. Even if the annexation of Texas and the movements of Taylor's army had not brought on war with Mexico, Polk's intelligent measures might have given us California; and when war came, he hastened to make sure of that rich province.

It may be claimed for Polk that his policy of expansion added more than 500,000 square miles to the territory of the United States, an acquisition second only to Jefferson's purchase of the Louisiana Territory; that his tariff of 1846 was our boldest approach to a free-trade policy, and yet the country was entirely prosperous under it; that his independent treasury system adequately served the national government until the Civil War placed an immense new strain upon our financial structure; and that his antagonism to internal improvements at the expense of the federal government was a wise policy. To his utterances in opposition to European interference in American affairs — as when in his message of Dec. 2, 1845, he told Congress that the United States "can not in silence permit any European interference on the North American continent, and should any such interference be attempted will be ready to resist it at any and all hazards" — the name of the "Polk Doctrine" has been given. The doctrine has been criticized, but there can be no question that it has been since maintained and approved by the American people. If he was not a statesman of the first order, Polk may certainly be called a constructive statesman; no President ever labored harder for patriotic ends, and none with less thought of personal considerations. Successful though he was, he, alone of all our Presidents except Hayes, from beginning to end of his term firmly repelled the suggestion that he be renominated.

A man of such intense singleness of purpose, who found his only happiness in duty well-performed, would be certain to take a rather severe view of most contemporaries in public life. The reader of the diary must guard himself against accepting too literally Polk's opinions of those who at various times crossed his path. When he says that Andrew Johnson was "very vindictive and perverse in his temper and conduct," he was making a shrewd observation, but one also tinged with political dislike. The first half of the diary, when Thomas Hart Benton was with him, gives us a very likable impression of Benton; the second half, when Benton was in opposition to him, shows the Missouri Senator as a peevish, small-souled, and intensely selfish person. Such Northern opponents as Webster were largely beyond Polk's comprehension, and it is just as well that he says little of them. Of Calhoun he offers us a decidedly striking portrait; and while it also is subject to discount, it unquestionably displays great insight. Polk perceived, and states plainly in his diary, that Calhoun in 1849 did not really wish to settle or quiet the slavery question; that he wished to awaken and exploit a sectional antagonism of the South for the North. Whether his motive in this was selfish or patriotic was, as Polk dryly says, "not difficult to determine." The deep repugnance he felt for Calhoun's disposition to foment violence and disunion was essentially the same repugnance which he felt for the Wilmot Proviso and its supporters; he shrank from any agitation threatening the national unity as " wicked."

Polk's official family, who appear constantly in his diary, are almost as interesting as himself. James Buchanan, an old-school Democrat, several years older than Polk and of long experience as Representative and Senator, was given his first taste of executive labor as Polk's Secretary of State. His massive frame, courtly manners, and scrupulously neat attire led an English critic to remark that he resembled a British nobleman of the past generation; but beneath that dignified and imposing exterior discerning men saw that there was a lack of substance. His capacity for being first on one side of a question, and then on another, caused Polk great perplexity. First he badgered the President to settle the Oregon boundary on the line of 49°, and the moment there was a strong probability that this would be done he swung sharply around to demand 54° 40'. First he was for acquiring no Mexican territory whatever, or at least none below California and New Mexico; and later he was perversely demanding that we annex the larger part of the republic. He blew hot and cold as regarded a seat on the Supreme Court bench. Serving Polk faithfully, he never forgot, with engaging modesty, to do all that he could to advance his claims to succeed his chief. There is something of the Chadband in Secretary Buchanan, and we can better understand his failure as a President from Polk's intimate view of his foibles.

William L. Marcy, the Secretary of War, was fortunately a man of more solidity and resolution. A New Englander of farm stock, almost wholly self-educated, he had climbed the political ladder in New York with indomitable energy. He was shrewd, broad-minded, and practical. He knew men, and in a trying position, for the Mexican War developed an extraordinary amount of personal friction among army commanders, he played his part well. Heavy, sluggish of body and mind, and willing to take counsel from the right quarters, he was slow in reaching a conclusion, but his conclusion was usually right. He was accustomed to work at home over his dispatches and other papers, going at noon to the War Department to growl at office-seekers and attend to routine business. Another New Englander, George Bancroft, already distinguished as editor and author, remained only a short time in the Cabinet as Secretary of the Navy, but while there paid special attention to operations in California, and performed a memorable service in founding the Naval Academy at Annapolis. Robert J. Walker, a Mississippian, accepted the Treasury when Silas Wright of New York declined that post, and gave his name to the tariff legislation. He was a shrewd man, who worked hard and who sustained the credit of the government ably during the war, but who was held suspect by many, including Andrew Jackson himself, because of his speculations in Texas scrip and his loose handling of his private finances. Cave Johnson, a thorough-going politician, was given that advantageous political seat, the Postmaster-Generalship; and John Y. Mason of Virginia, who had been Polk's classmate in college, and needed the money as much as he liked the dignity, was held over from Tyler's Cabinet as Attorney-General.

With this Cabinet, which certainly needed his strong directing hand, Polk managed the Mexican War with signal address and without failure or scandal. The story of no other of our conflicts contains such closely-woven strands of the heroic and the mock-heroic, of the glorious and the ludicrous, as this. There is something which stirs the blood in the American repulse of Santa Anna's charging hosts at Buena Vista, and in the storming of the fortress of Chapultepec; there are few more gallant episodes in our military history than the long march of Kearny and his Army of the West from Missouri to Santa Fé and Los Angeles, or the exploit of Frémont and Stockton in conquering California before he arrived. Yet as a foil against these achievements we have some almost incredible instances of jealousy, pettiness, and bickering. The spectacle of President Polk filled with bitter distrust of both his generals, Zachary Taylor and Winfield Scott, while they regard him with resentful suspicion; the strange incident of Polk's attempt to place Senator Benton in supreme command of the armies of the United States; the explosion which occurred the moment Gen. Scott and Polk's peace commissioner, Nicholas P. Trist, came into contact; the quarrel between Stockton and Frémont on the one hand and Kearny on the other; and the whole series of court-martials which threatened to grow out of the quarrels of Scott with his officers — these make a strange narrative. In the background we see rising blackly and ominously the cloud of the slavery contest, and our spectacular victory over Mexico is like a short-lived rainbow bent in front of an approaching storm.

There is much else in the diary which deserves comment. It shows us, for example, some sides of the Presidency which seem strange to later eyes. This was a period when the Chief Magistrate was supposed to be accessible to any office-hunter or money-beggar, any impostor or freak, who chose to call, and when he was subject to any and every kind of demand. In the midst of his war duties Polk was harassed to desperation by a multitude of selfish applicants for one trifling favor or another, against whom he had almost no protection. In still other ways his office lacked the dignity it has since acquired, and more than once he had to endure insolence and even insult. The White House yet lay completely under the tradition of Jeffersonian simplicity and democracy, and Polk could not have erected adequate defences for his dignity and strength without arousing angry complaints that he was imitating the exclusiveness and ostentation of European courts. He learned to detest the office-seekers, and express this detestation vehemently. Yet, a

convinced adherent of the spoils system, he strangely failed
to connect this plague of job-hunters with the operation of
the spoils principle, or to argue from it the need of any constructive reform.   Again, it is noteworthy in this diary that
while he was much concerned about the management of publicity for his administration, and had his own newspaper organ, the *Union,* under the editorship of Ritchie, he made
almost no public addresses.   Indeed, his public appearanc
were few and far between.   Though he carried an important
war to a successful conclusion, he took part in no military
pageantry of any kind.   It may be noted, again, how few
were the intellectual contacts of the man shut inside the
White House at this period, and how seldom he saw anyone
of prominence except politicians.   This conscientious document, the only full diary except those of J. Q. Adams and
Rutherford B. Hayes ever kept by an occupant of the White
House, brings before us both a great deal that is quaint and
picturesque and a great deal that is historically important.

THE POLK ADMINISTRATION:
A CHRONOLOGY

I. The Road to the White House.

April 22, 1844. President Tyler sends the Senate a treaty for the annexation of Texas.

April 27, 1844. Martin Van Buren, till then regarded as the inevitable nominee of the Democrats for the presidency, publishes a letter declaring that annexation of Texas without the consent of Mexico would probably mean war, and that he therefore opposes it.

May 6, 1844. Polk publishes in the Washington *Globe* a letter calling for the annexation both of Texas and of Oregon Territory.

May 13-14, 1844. Andrew Jackson, summoning Polk to the Hermitage, tells him that Van Buren's Texas letter is political suicide, that the Democratic Party must have a Southwestern leader committed to annexation, and that Polk is the man.

May 27-29, 1844. The Democratic Convention meets in Baltimore; a determined Southern minority blocks the nomination of Van Buren, who during four ballots leads the field; Lewis Cass, who then takes the lead, similarly fails; and on the ninth ballot Polk is chosen.

November, 1844. Polk is elected President over Henry Clay by a vote of 170 to 105 in the electoral college, and 1,337,243 to 1,299,062 in the popular totals. As James G. Birney, receiving a popular vote of 62,300 on the Liberty Party (Abolitionist) ticket, costs Clay the 41 electors of New York and Michigan, Polk owes his victory to this small body of Northern extremists.

March 1, 1845. Congress by joint resolution offers Texas annexation.

March 4, 1845. Polk is inaugurated as the youngest man who has yet occupied the Presidential chair — he is forty-nine; George Mifflin Dallas inaugurated as Vice-President.

II. Oregon and the Walker Tariff.

March, 1845. Polk tells George Bancroft, his Secretary of the Navy: "There are four great measures which are to be the measures

xxiii

of my administration: one, a reduction of the tariff; another, the independent treasury; a third, the settlement of the Oregon boundary question; and lastly, the acquisition of California."

April, 1845.   To the grief of the dying Andrew Jackson, Polk rejects Francis P. Blair's Washington *Globe* as organ of the Administration, and fills its place by the Washington *Union* under Thomas Ritchie. This, according to Thomas Hart Benton, is to fulfill a campaign pledge to Calhoun and Tyler, who had made their full support of Polk contingent upon his promise to get rid of Blair.

July 12, 1845.   Secretary of State Buchanan tells the British Minister, Richard Pakenham, that the United States is willing to divide Oregon along the 49th parallel. Pakenham flatly rejects this proposal without referring it to the Foreign Office.

August 26-30, 1845.   Polk, acting through Secretary Buchanan, withdraws the offer, and declares for retention of Oregon to the 54° 40′ line. "The only way to treat John Bull is to look him straight in the eye," he records. Actually his mood is far from uncompromising, and this is stage-thunder.

September-November, 1845.   The American Minister in England writes that the British Government would offer to take the 49th parallel line, with the whole of Vancouver Island, if sure the United States would accept that solution.

December, 1845.   Polk in his annual message asserts that the United States will maintain its claim to the whole of Oregon, and recommends giving Britain the required year's notice for ending joint occupation. This is shortly authorized by Congress (April 27, 1846).

¹anuary-May, 1846.   Lord Aberdeen as Foreign Minister conducts a campaign in the press to reconcile British opinion to the division of Oregon.

June 6, 1846.   Buchanan receives Lord Aberdeen's offer to draw the boundary along the 49th parallel, Great Britain retaining all Vancouver Island.

June 15, 1846.   The treaty for the boundary line is formally signed; and (June 17) ratified by the Senate, 37 to 12.

July 30, 1846.   Polk signs a tariff bill, framed in large part by his Secretary of the Treasury, Robert J. Walker of Mississippi. Reducing duties to a low level, it is supported by the agricultural interests of the South and West, opposed by the industrial interests of the Middle Atlantic States and New England.

August 6, 1846. Polk signs the act reestablishing the sub-treasury system as a means of handling the Treasury receipts, thus keeping the government totally divorced from the banking business.

III. The Effort to Maintain Peace with Mexico.

March 6, 1845. The Mexican minister in Washington, outraged by the annexation of Texas, asks for his passports.

March 20, 1845. The State Department appoints W. S. Parrott as confidential agent in Mexico, ordering him to state that although the annexation of Texas is irrevocable, all other differences will be settled "in a most liberal and friendly spirit."

August 29, 1845. Parrott reports that he believes Mexico will warmly welcome the appointment of an American minister.

November 10, 1845. Polk commissions John Slidell as minister to Mexico, with instructions to fix the Texas boundary on the Rio Grande, prevent any cession of California to Britain or France, and if possible purchase at least the northern portion of that province.

December, 1845-March, 1846. The Mexican Government under Herrera refuses to receive Slidell or consider his proposals. Slidell writes Polk: "Be assured that nothing is to be done with these people until they shall have been chastised."

January 13, 1846. Polk orders General Zachary Taylor, who has a force of nearly 4,000 men on the Nueces, to occupy the disputed area between that river and the Rio Grande. The American troops wait there expecting a Mexican attack.

May 8, 1846. Slidell returns to Washington with news of a violent war fever in Mexico City; and next day Polk tells his Cabinet that he has decided to recommend war to Congress. That night news reaches Washington that a Mexican force had crossed the Rio Grande on April 25 and killed or wounded sixteen Americans.

May 13, 1846. Congress, in response to an inflammatory message from Polk dated May 11, declares war, authorizes an army of 50,000, and appropriates ten millions. Sentiment in the United States at once proves highly divided. The Northeastern States are largely opposed to the conflict, which the Massachusetts legislature stigmatizes as "hateful" and "wanton, unjust, and unconstitutional." In the South and West most people support the War, though such Whigs as Tom Corwin and Abraham Lincoln denounce it.

IV. Taylor, Kearny, Frémont

May 8, 1846. Taylor defeats Mexican troops in the hard-fought border battles of Palo Alto and Resaca de la Palma, driving them back across the Rio Grande.

June 10, 1846. Discontented American settlers in the upper Sacramento Valley, encouraged by John C. Frémont at the head of a government exploring party, begin the Bear Flag revolt against Mexican authority.

July 4, 1846. Frémont at Sonoma urges the California settlers to drive the Mexican military commander, General José Castro, from the region, and leads them in a march southward.

July 7, 1846. Commodore John D. Sloat, commanding the Pacific squadron, seizes the port of Monterey. Frémont and Sloat occupy all of Northern California.

June 30, 1846. Colonel Stephen W. Kearny, with about 1,600 men in the "Army of the West," leaves Fort Leavenworth on his 800-mile march to Santa Fe.

August 18, 1846. Assisted by the quasi-diplomatic activities of the rich trader James Magoffin, Kearny takes possession of Santa Fe without fighting. On September 25, Kearny with three hundred dragoons leaves for California.

August 13, 1846. Frémont and Commodore Robert F. Stockton enter Los Angeles, making possible Stockton's proclamation (August 17) of the formal annexation of California, with Frémont as military governor.

September, 1846-January, 1847. Revolts break out first in Southern California and later in New Mexico, both being quelled without great trouble or loss. A quarrel ensues between Kearny and Stockton as to the chief command in California.

February, 1847. Kearny installed as governor of California; Frémont, who has been appointed civil governor by Stockton, temporarily declines to obey Kearny's harshly-administered orders. The ensuing controversy and the court-martial of Frémont give Polk great anxiety and trouble.

August 19, 1846. General Taylor begins the invasion of Mexico, seizes Matamoras, and after three days of hard fighting (September 21-23) occupies Monterey. His willingness to let the Mexican forces evacuate and march away disgusts Polk.

February 22-23, 1847. At Buena Vista Taylor's army is attacked by a far more powerful Mexican force under Santa Anna, but by superior morale and tenacity wins a spectacular victory. The way is now open to Mexico City from the north—but Polk gives precedence to an attack from the coast.

V. Winfield Scott and the Last Campaign.

March 9, 1847. General Scott's army lands at Vera Cruz, which surrenders after an eighteen-day siege.

April 17-18, 1847. The Mexicans are disastrously defeated at Cerro Gordo when Captain Robert E. Lee finds a flanking route around that fortified pass.

May 15, 1847. Puebla, more than halfway to Mexico City, is occupied by Scott's army. Scott cuts himself loose from his supply lines with the coast and drives ahead with his army of 10,000 subsisting on the country.

September 13, 1847. After victories at Contreras and Cherubusco, Scott's army storms the towering and apparently impregnable hill of Chapultepec, at the very gates of the capital.

September 17, 1847. With Santa Anna in flight, Scott completes the occupation of Mexico City. The United States is in a position to dictate its terms—though the possibility of protracted guerrilla warfare makes an agreement desirable. Many American voices clamor for the annexation of all Mexico.

March 2, 1847. Meanwhile, Colonel A. W. Doniphan, moving south from New Mexico, has defeated small Mexican forces and seized Chihuahua.

VI. Peace and Its Problems.

August 8, 1846. Polk requests $2,000,000 of Congress with which to make peace. Thereupon David Wilmot of Pennsylvania introduces his resolution declaring that if any part of Mexico is annexed, "neither slavery nor involuntary servitude shall ever exist in any part of said territory." The House passes but the Senate rejects the measure. In the next two years, Polk advocates extending the Missouri Compromise line to the Pacific as a solution of the sectional problem.

April, 1847. Nicholas P. Trist, chief clerk of the State Department, is sent to Scott's headquarters in Mexico with instructions to gain a treaty ceding New Mexico and both California and Lower California.

May-July, 1847. Trist and General Scott first quarrel fiercely and then become warm friends and allies.

October 6, 1847. Trist, eager to conclude peace, sends Polk a letter so "arrogant, impudent, and very insulting" that the President orders his recall; but the strong-willed envoy ignores the order.

February 2, 1848. At a suburb of Mexico City named Guadelupe Hidalgo, Trist signs a treaty by which Mexico acknowledges the American title to Texas, California, New Mexico, and Arizona, while the United States renounces its old damage claims and pays fifteen millions in gold.

February 22, 1848. After a Cabinet debate in which Buchanan and Walker oppose Trist's arrangement, and the other members support it, Polk sends it to the Senate.

March 10, 1848. The Senate ratifies the treaty 38 to 14.

June 12, 1848. American forces evacuate Mexico City.

September, 1848. The East learns that gold had been discovered in California the previous January, and that a rush from California ports to the mines had begun in March.

November, 1848. Zachary Taylor elected the second Whig President over Lewis Cass, Democrat, and Martin Van Buren, Free-Soiler, by a small majority (Taylor 163, Cass 127) in the electoral college.

March 4, 1849. Polk, in a state of grave physical exhaustion, quits the White House.

DRAMATIS PERSONAE

BANCROFT, George. 1800-1891. As a good Jacksonian Democrat and a leader in the nomination of Polk, the eminent historian merited recognition; and the President made him first Secretary of the Navy and later minister to England. In spite of Bancroft's reluctance to see war declared against Mexico (*p. 82*) their relations were highly harmonious. In his old age Bancroft planned a biography of Polk, never executed.

BENTON, Thomas Hart. 1782-1858. Now friends, now foes, Polk and Benton actually had in common a fundamental moderation. Though he disliked the Mexican War as one of "speculation and intrigue" and a "great blot" on American history, Benton supported the Administration once it began. He also approved Polk's compromise on the Oregon boundary. The President for his part would have made Benton general-in-chief had he possessed the power. But they came to a bitter parting of the ways over the Frémont court-martial, and Polk condemned Benton's "violent passions" (*p. 274*).

BUCHANAN, James. 1791-1868. Fussy, timid, and changeable, the Secretary of State sometimes irritated Polk beyond measure (*pp. 113, 114*). He had his eye on the Presidency, and wanted to annex all of Mexico in order to please the expansionist South. For the same reason he was eager to acquire Cuba. But he handled various international matters well, and was responsible for Polk's reiteration of the Monroe Dictrine in 1848. Making a wager on a diplomatic point, Polk won a basket of champagne from him (*p. 253*).

BUTLER, William O. 1791-1880. This Kentucky veteran of the War of 1812 had real military talent; he was with Taylor at Monterey and Scott at the capture of Mexico City, and Polk made him chief commander when Scott was recalled (*p. 290*).

CALHOUN, John C. 1782-1850. The South Carolinian, now an extreme sectionalist, opposed war with Mexico as leading to governmental centralization and likely to do the South more harm than good. He opposed Polk on other matters. The President for his part wrote that he lacked words to express his contempt for Calhoun's utter want of principle (*p. 214*). "He is wholly selfish and I am satisfied has no patriotism," exploded Polk.

CASS, Lewis. 1782-1866. The Michigan Democrat, an ardent expansionist, wanted to annex Texas, take all of Oregon, and seize most or all of Mexico. He was one of the inventors of the popular sovereignty doctrine. When nominated for President in 1848 "he was in a fine humor" (*p. 325*), but his defeat was decisive.

CLAY, Henry. 1777-1852. Defeated by Polk for the presidency, Clay deplored war with Mexico (in which he lost a son), and opposed the annexation of that country. Out of office throughout the Administration, he visited the White House on his eastern tour of 1848, and paid Mrs. Polk a gracious compliment (*pp. 299, 300*).

CLIFFORD, Nathan. 1803-1881. This former Congressman from Maine, appointed Attorney-General by Polk, lost his nerve and tried to resign, but Polk insisted that he stay. Clifford loyally supported all Polk's policies, and was rewarded with a diplomatic mission to Mexico as the war closed. A painstaking, conscientious, and conservative man, he later (1858) became justice of the Supreme Court.

CRITTENDEN, John J. 1787-1863. Clay's able Kentucky lieutenant thought the war with Mexico a great calamity; but Polk freely divulged his plans and ideas to the Senator as "an honorable gentleman" (*p. 189*). Though hoping for an early and generous peace, Crittenden voted troops and money for the conflict.

DALLAS, George Mifflin. 1792-1864. As a loyal Pennsylvanian, the Vice-President was pained by the low duties of the Walker Tariff. Polk had little patience with his views or with the "capitalists and monopolists" who espoused the demand for higher rates (*p. 134*).

DOUGLAS, Stephen A.. 1813-1861. First in the House, then in the Senate, the impetuous Illinoisan wanted all of Oregon, desired most of Mexico, and was anxious to acquire Cuba. He cooperated cordially with Polk in nearly all his measures. Such was his influence that when the Mexican peace treaty was before the Senate, Polk held a special conference with him (*p. 310*).

FRÉMONT, John C. 1813-1890. The hardy explorer, married to Senator Benton's vivacious daughter Jessie, had just completed his second great Western expedition when Polk was elected. Soon departing for the third, he was in California with sixty armed men when the war clouds threatened—and he knew that the government ardently desired to obtain California. In 1846-47 he played a prominent part in the seizure of the province. Then he became involved in the angry quarrel of Stockton and Kearny over their title to authority in California; was sent home for court-martial; and had Benton and public sentiment on his side as he faced a panel of jealous superiors. Polk upheld the court-martial verdict— "a painful and responsible duty" (*p. 303*).

GAINES, General Edmund Pendleton. 1777-1849. The aged Virginia soldier was center of another of the numerous military squabbles which marked the Administration. He had an old quarrel with Winfield Scott, and in 1846 he opened a new one with Zachary Taylor. He was court-martialed for calling out troops in four Southern States without authority, but excused on the ground of his patriotic motives. Polk believed that he had "cost the Treasury many hundreds of thousands of dollars."

HOUSTON, Samuel. 1793-1863. The hero of the Texan revolution arrived in Washington in March, 1846, to serve almost fourteen years as Senator from the newly admitted State. Having his eye on new military laurels and on the Presidency, he was disappointed by the Administration's refusal to push him forward; but Polk did offer him a major-general's commission, which he declined. Houston was righteously eager to see all Mexico given the blessings of American government.

INGERSOLL, Charles J. 1782-1862. Few public men had more quarrels than the Philadelphia attorney and Congressman, who carried on violent rows with John Quincy Adams, Daniel Webster, and others. An expansionist who had helped push the annexation of Texas, he disliked both extreme antislavery and extreme proslavery men. He quarreled with Polk because the President did not try to ram him down the throat of the protesting Senate as minister to France (*p. 266*).

JOHNSON, Cave. 1793-1866. Polk and his wife had a genuine affection for the sagacious Tennesseean, who as Postmaster-General not only improved the mail services but was a constant and judicious adviser of the President.

KEARNY, Stephen Watts. 1794-1848. An able, energetic frontier soldier, who entered the Mexican War a colonel and emerged a brevet major-general, Kearny immortalized himself by his magnificent march with the Army of the West from Fort Leavenworth to Santa Fe, and his later operations in California. "A good officer and an intelligent gentleman," wrote Polk (*p. 264*). But in his dealings with Frémont he showed his grave faults of temper— "grasping, jealous, domineering, and harsh," writes Justin H.

merited his arrest by that general. Restored to service, he became
head of the department of Texas, and soon died of cholera there.
WILMOT, David. 1814-1868. Though a Jacksonian Democrat,
and at first a warm supporter of the Polk Administration, this
Pennsylvania Representative became convinced that the President
was indifferent to Northern interests, that the South was growing
in power and arrogance, and that the new Southwestern acquisitions must be kept free soil. His Proviso gave him fame; he
became one of the founders of the Republican Party, and Lincoln
offered him a Cabinet post. Polk thought his measure unfair and
unfortunate. Actually it was a well-justified warning that the
North was making up its mind to keep the abomination of slavery
out of the territories.

POLK

The Diary of a President

CHAPTER I

Aug. 25, 1845 — Dec. 6, 1845

BUCHANAN AND THE OREGON QUESTION — TAYLOR AND
THE MEXICAN ARMY — REVOLUTION IN MEXICO CITY — SLI-
DELL APPOINTED MINISTER — BENTON AND THE OREGON
TRAIL — FIRST ANNUAL MESSAGE

Tuesday, 26th August, 1845. — Memorandum of a conversation in Cabinet, Mr. Mason, the Attorney-General, being absent on a visit to Virginia.

The President inquired of Mr. Buchanan at what time his
reply to the official note of Mr. Pakenham, the British Minister, on the subject of the pending Oregon negotiation,
dated 29th July, 1845, would be ready to be submitted to
the Cabinet.[1] Mr. Buchanan replied that when he was sent
for by the President to attend the Cabinet meeting that
morning, he was engaged in preparing his reply, and could
finish the first rough draft in ten minutes: except the conclu-

---

[1] The Democratic platform of 1844, on which Polk was elected, declared
that the re-occupation of Oregon and the re-annexation of Texas " are great
American measures, which the convention recommends to the cordial support
of the Democracy of the Union." On July 12, 1844, Secretary of State
Buchanan made an offer to the British Minister, Sir Richard Pakenham, of a
division of the Oregon country along the 49th parallel, but without the free
navigation of the Columbia River for the British. Pakenham rejected this
offer in rather rough terms on July 29, without referring it to his government.
The situation was thus left somewhat ominous. A withdrawal of the American
offer would bring war within the range of possibility.

I

sion, which would contain the final action of the President, which was most important.

Other matters then came up for consideration, the principal of which related to our army under the command of General Taylor in Texas, and the proper means of defending that territory against the threatened invasion by Mexico.

The President again called up the Oregon question. He remarked that he had at different times communicated to the several members of the Cabinet the settled decision to which his mind had come. He proceeded briefly to repeat his decision, in substance as follows, *viz.*, that Mr. Buchanan's note in reply to Mr. Pakenham should assert and enforce our right to the whole Oregon territory from 42° to 54° 40′ north latitude; that he should distinctly state that the proposition which had been made to compromise on the 49th parallel of north latitude had been made, first in deference to what had been done by our predecessors, and second, with an anxious desire to preserve peace between the two countries. That this proposition, made as it was for the reasons stated and in a liberal spirit of compromise, had been rejected by the British Minister in language, to say the least of it, scarcely courteous or respectful, and that, too, without submitting any counter proposition on his part, was now withdrawn by the United States, and should no longer be considered as pending for the consideration of the British Government. The President said, in summing the reasons which he assigned for this decision, let the argument of our title to the whole country be full, let the proposition to compromise at latitude 49° be withdrawn, and then let the matter rest, unless the British Minister chose to continue the negotiation. Mr. Buchanan said that he assented to the views of the President as the argument of title and withdrawal of our proposition to compromise at 49° were concerned, but that he thought a paragraph should be inserted to the effect that any further proposition which the British Minister might submit would be deliberately considered by

the United States. To this the President objected upon the
ground that our proposition for 49° had been rejected flatly,
without even a reference by the British Minister to his Government. . . Any proposition less favorable than 49° the
President said he would promptly reject. Why then invite
a proposition which cannot for a moment be entertained?
Let our proposition be absolutely withdrawn and then let
the British Minister take his own course. If he chooses to
close the negotiation he can do so. If he chooses to make
a proposition he can as well do it without our invitation as
with it. Let him take the one course or the other, the United
States will stand in the right in the eyes of the whole civi-
lized world, and if war was the consequence England would
be in the wrong. The President further remarked that he
had reflected much on this subject; that it had occupied his
thoughts more than any and all others during his Administration, and that though he had given his assent to the proposition to compromise at 49°, he must say he did not regret that
it had been rejected by the British Minister. We had shown
by it our anxious desire to do full justice to Great Britain and
to preserve peace, but it having been rejected he felt no
longer bound by it, and would not be now willing to compromise on that boundary. Mr. Buchanan then intimated
that if the President's views were carried out, we would have
war. To which the President replied, if we do have war it
will not be our fault. Mr. Buchanan said that war would
probably be the result ultimately, but he expressed the opinion that the people of the United States would not be willing to sustain a war for the country north of 49°, and that if
we were to have war he would like it to be for some better
cause, for some of our rights of person or property or of national honor violated. The President differed with Mr.
Buchanan as to the popular sentiment, and he thought we
had the strongest evidence that was to be anywhere seen
that the people would be prompt and ready to sustain the
government in the course which he proposed to pursue.

Mr. Buchanan then had allusion to our difficulties with Mexico, and thought his reply to Mr. Pakenham ought to be postponed until we could know whether we would have actual war with that country or not. The President said he saw no necessary connection between the two questions; that the settlement of the one was not dependent on the other; that we should do our duty towards both Mexico and Great Britain and firmly maintain our rights, and leave the rest to God and the country. Mr. Buchanan said he thought God would not have much to do in justifying us in a war for the country north of 49°. Mr. Buchanan then suggested that his reply should be postponed until late in September. The President objected to this. He said that a postponement would carry the idea to Great Britain, as well as to our own people, of hesitancy and indecision on our part, which so far as his opinions were concerned would be an erroneous inference. . .[2]

The conversation took a somewhat extended range, viewing the question in the different aspects which it presented, but upon the main points in substance as stated above. The Secretary of the Treasury (Mr. Walker) made some observations in substance sustaining the views taken by the President. The Secretary of War (Mr. Marcy) made a few remarks in the course of the conversation, but expressed no distinct opinion. The Secretary of the Navy (Mr. Bancroft) and the Postmaster-General (Mr. Johnson) said nothing.

Wednesday, 27th August, 1845. — A special meeting of the Cabinet was held at twelve o'clock, Mr. Mason, the Attorney-General, being absent. The Secretary of State

[2] Ex-President Jackson had on May 2, 1845, written Polk a characteristically vigorous letter urging him to resist the British pretensions to Oregon by an uncompromising policy. " The subject," wrote Jackson, " is intended to try your energy — dash from your lips the council of the times on this question, base your acts upon the firm basis of asking nothing but what is right and permitting nothing that is wrong — war is a blessing compared with national degredation. . . To prevent war with England a bold and undaunted front must be exposed. England with all her boast dare not go to war."

(Mr. Buchanan) read the letter which he had prepared in answer to the note of the British Minister of the 29th July, 1845, on the Oregon question. When the reading was concluded the President expressed the opinion that it was an able and admirable paper, and that the argument in support of the American title was conclusive and unanswerable. In this opinion all the members of the Cabinet concurred. The Postmaster-General remarked that if he had heard that argument before the compromise at 49° was proposed he would not have agreed to it. . .

The same evening the President and Secretary of the Navy rode out on horseback. The Secretary in the course of the ride said he admired the President's firmness and added: " I will now go with you, I believe you are right."

Friday, 29th August, 1845. — The President called a special meeting of the Cabinet at twelve o'clock, all the members present except Mr. Mason. The President brought up for consideration our relations with Mexico, and the threatened invasion of Texas with that power.[3] He submitted the following propositions which were unanimously agreed to as follows, *viz.,* If Mexico should declare war or actual hostilities should be commenced by that power, orders to be issued to General Taylor to attack and drive her back across the Del Norte. General Taylor shall be instructed that the crossing the Del Norte by a Mexican army in force shall be

---

[3] Congress in February, 1845, just preceding Polk's inauguration, had passed a resolution for the annexation of Texas; and a Texas Convention which met on July 4 accepted annexation with a single dissenting vote. The Mexican Government broke off diplomatic relations with the United States on March 28. Two decrees passed by the Mexican Congress early in June and signed by President Herrera provided for an increase of the army to resist the incorporation of Texas in the United States, and on July 20 the Mexican executive recommended to Congress a declaration of war against the United States as soon as it was learned that annexation had been concluded, or that Texas had been invaded. Hostilities were clearly unavoidable. General Zachary Taylor was ordered on June 15 to advance into Texas, with its western boundary as its ultimate destination. He did so the following month, and in August established his headquarters on the west bank of the Nueces River, near Corpus Christi, but about 150 miles from the Rio Grande, or, as Polk calls it, the Del Norte.

regarded as an act of war on her part, and in that event General Taylor to be ordered, if he shall deem it advisable, not to wait to be attacked but to attack her army first. General Taylor in case of invasion by Mexico to be ordered not only to drive the invading army back to the west of the Del Norte, but to dislodge and drive back in like manner the Mexican post now stationed at Santiago. General Taylor to be vested with discretionary authority to pursue the Mexican army to the west of the Del Norte, and take Matamoras or any other Spanish post west of that river but not to penetrate any great distance into the interior of the Mexican territory. . .

Mr. Buchanan stated to the President in the course of the meeting that he had added two paragraphs to his letter to Mr. Pakenham, since it had been submitted to the President in Cabinet: the first was, that though the United States had refused to yield the free navigation of the Columbia River to Great Britain, yet they had offered her a free port on the extreme southern point of Vancouver's Island: the second stated the fact, that a recent globe published in England represented the northern boundary of the United States west of the Rocky Mountains as extending to the 54th parallel of north latitude. The President approved both the alterations.

Saturday, 30th August, 1845. — The Cabinet met today, the Attorney-General still absent. The Secretary of State came in at half past twelve o'clock. He stated that he had just delivered his letter in answer to that of the British Minister of the 29th July, 1845, to Mr. Bidwell, the secretary of the British legation. . . Mr. Buchanan said; "Well, the deed is done," but that he did not think it was the part of wise statesmanship to deliver such a paper in the existing state of our relations with Mexico. The President said he was glad it was delivered, that it was right in itself, and he saw no reason for delaying it because of our relations with Mexico.

Monday, 1st September, 1845. — Senator Bagby of Alabama called today and held a long conversation with the President. The President asked his opinion as to the necessity or propriety of calling Congress, in the event of a declaration of war or an invasion of Texas by Mexico. Mr. Bagby gave it as his clear opinion that Congress should not be called, and assigned his reasons at some length. . . Mr. Senator Archer of Virginia called the same day and paid his respects to the President in his office. The subject of the existing relations with Mexico was spoken of. Mr. Archer expressed the opinion that Mexico would neither declare war nor invade Texas. The military and naval preparations which had been made by the Administration were spoken of, and Mr. Archer concurred in an opinion, expressed by the President, that the appearance of our land and naval forces on the borders of Mexico and in the Gulf would probably deter and prevent Mexico from either declaring war or invading Texas.

Tuesday, 2nd September, 1845. — A regular meeting of the Cabinet was held today, all the members present except the Attorney-General. The Secretary of War stated that the United States troops which had been ordered from the eastern posts for Texas had arrived at New York on Saturday, the 30th August, and were detained at that city waiting for the store-ship *Lexington* to be ready to sail.

Wednesday, 10th September, 1845. — Mr. O'Sullivan, editor of the *Democratic Review* and the New York *News,* called today in company with Mr. Buchanan at the President's office. Mr. O'Sullivan read a paper, the object of which was to form a central committee at Washington, to raise by subscription a sum of $100,000 or more for the erection of a monument to the memory of General Jackson. It was proposed that this committee should consist of the President, the Vice President, the members of the Cabinet, and certain citizens who were named, numbering in all fifteen. The President approved the object and said he would most cheeerfully contribute the maximum sum allowed to be subscribed by any one individual, which was $100. Mr. Buchanan approved the proposition, and it was suggested that the gentlemen named should meet to confer on the subject at half-past two o'clock this day, and as the President could not with propriety attend a meeting elsewhere, that the meeting be held at his office. This was agreed to about eleven o'clock A.M. Afterwards Mr. Bancroft, Mr. Marcy, and Judge Mason happening at the President's office on other business, the subject was mentioned. Judge Mason stated some reasons why the President and his Cabinet should not be prominent in the matter, one of which was that it might be attributed to a desire on their part to appropriate the great popularity of General Jackson for the benefit of the Administration and for party purposes. In this view Mr. Bancroft and Mr. Marcy concurred, as did the President.

Friday, 12th September, 1845. — The " Old Defenders of Baltimore," men who were engaged in the defence of that city on the 12th September, 1814, called at the President's mansion to pay their respects. The President, accompanied by his Cabinet and the Hon. Mr. Levy of the Senate of the United States, received them in the circular parlor. An address on their behalf was delivered to the President by Mr. Pressman, in which touching allusion was made to the battle at Baltimore. . .

Saturday, 13th September, 1845. — Judge Mason and the Postmaster-General being with the President in his office today after the Cabinet adjourned, Judge Mason informed the President that Gov. Pierce M. Butler of South Carolina had mentioned to him that morning that Baily Peyton [4] was in the city, and that Mr. Peyton had expressed to him a desire to call and pay his respects to the President, but that he was restrained from doing so, not knowing how the Presi-

[4] Bailie Peyton, 1803–1878, a Tennesseean and later a Louisianian, served on the staff of General Worth in the Mexican War.

dent would receive him. Gov. Butler had said, as Judge
Mason stated, that Mr. Peyton said he had never had any
personal difficulty or misunderstanding with the President,
that in politics he had differed with him, that in the political
discussions in Tennessee he had used strong language towards him, but not stronger than was usual towards political
opponents in that State. The President said that Mr. Peyton had stated the relations between them as he understood
them. He said that for several years past he had had no
personal intercourse with Mr. Peyton in consequence of the
violence of party feeling which had separated them, but
that he had no personal unkind feeling towards Mr. Peyton,
and that if he called upon him he would receive and treat him
courteously and respectfully.

Tuesday, 16th September, 1845. — The Cabinet met today, all the members present. Despatches were read from
Dr. Parrott, the confidential agent of the United States in
Mexico, giving an account of another threatened revolution,
etc., and of the refusal of Paredes to march his army to
Texas.[5] Dr. Parrott's latest despatch was of date 29th
August, 1845. He gives it as his opinion that there will be
no declaration of war against the United States and no invasion of Texas; that the government will be kept employed to
keep down another revolution which was threatened. He is
also of opinion that the government is desirous to re-estab-
lish diplomatic relations with the United States, and that a
Minister from the United States would be received. In
these opinions Mr. Black, the United States consul at Mexico, of date 23d August, and Mr. Dimond, United States
consul at Vera Cruz, of date 30th August, concurred. After
much consultation it was agreed unanimously that it was ex-

[5] Paredes, the eminent Mexican general who commanded the main body of the
army, represented the church and the aristocracy, and was hostile to President
Herrera. As Herrera's administration sank in efficiency and prestige, he was
awaiting his opportunity to revolt. He refused to obey Herrera's orders,
and was plotting a revolution. Herrera meanwhile became genuinely eager
to escape from the public action he had shortly before taken looking toward
war with the United States.

pedient to reopen diplomatic relations with Mexico; but that it was to be kept a profound secret that such a step was contemplated, for the reason mainly that if it was known in advance in the United States that a Minister had been sent to Mexico, it would, of course, be known to the British, French, and other foreign Ministers at Washington, who might take measures to thwart or defeat the objects of the mission.[6] The President, in consultation with the Cabinet, agreed that the Hon. John Slidell of New Orleans, who spoke the Spanish language and was otherwise well qualified, should be tendered the mission. It was agreed that Mr. Slidell, if he accepted, should leave Pensacola in a national armed vessel and proceed to Vera Cruz, without disclosing or making known his official character. One great object of the mission, as stated by the President, would be to adjust a permanent boundary between Mexico and the United States, and that in doing this the Minister would be instructed to purchase for a pecuniary consideration Upper California and New Mexico. He said that a better boundary would be the Del Norte from its mouth to the Passo,[7] in latitude about 32° north, and thence west to the Pacific Ocean, Mexico ceding to the United States all the country east and north of these lines. The President said that for such a boundary the amount of pecuniary consideration to be paid would be of small importance. He supposed it might be had for fifteen or twenty millions, but he was ready to pay forty millions for it, if it could not be had for less. In these views the Cabinet agreed with the President unanimously.

Wednesday, 17th September, 1845. — The President called a special meeting of the Cabinet at twelve o'clock this

[6] England and France were deeply resentful of the American annexation of Texas; and the London *Times* proposed that a Spanish prince be placed on a new Mexican throne, supported by the European Powers as a bulwark against the United States.

[7] By " the Passo " Polk means El Paso, the pass lying south of the Franklin Mountains in latitude 31° 45'. The town of El Paso here is of course now on the boundary between Mexico and New Mexico.

day; all the members present. His object was to consult
further on the subject of the proposed mission to Mexico.
From publications in the New Orleans papers, which had
been brought to his notice by Mr. Buchanan since the meeting on yesterday, it appeared that the President of Mexico
as late as the 21st August had issued a circular to the army,
through his Secretary of War, breathing a war spirit, and
that General Bustamente had been appointed commander-
in-chief of the Mexican army. From these it was left uncertain whether Dr. Parrott and the United States consuls
at Mexico and Vera Cruz may not have been mistaken in
regard to the willingness of Mexico to receive a Minister
from the United States, and the President said his object
in calling the Cabinet meeting today was to consider whether
we should not delay sending a Minister until the next arrival
from Vera Cruz, which might be expected in a few days by
one of our armed vessels, and which might bring more definite and certain intelligence of the dispositions of Mexico.
This suggestion was agreed to by the Cabinet unanimously,
as the more prudent course, and especially to guard against
the danger of having our Minister rejected or not received
by Mexico.

Saturday, 20th September, 1845. — Andrew J. Donelson,
Esquire, late *chargé d'affaires* to Texas, visited the Presi-
dent today and spent some time in conversation with the
President and Cabinet on Texan and Mexican affairs. Mr.
Donelson [8] was in feeble health, and on the President's invi-
tation took a room in the President's mansion.

Sunday, 21st September, 1845. — The President and
Mrs. Polk attended the 1st Presbyterian Church today.
Mr. Donelson was quite ill today; was confined to his chamber all day; sent for Dr. Miller in the afternoon, who prescribed for him.

Friday, 26th September, 1845. — Intelligence was re-

---

[8] Andrew Jackson Donelson, 1800–1871, who had just been *chargé
d'affaires* to Texas, was soon after this entry appointed Minister to Berlin.

ceived today that the convention of Texas had formed a State Constitution and had adjourned on the 28th August, 1845.

Monday, 29th September, 1845.— At eight o'clock P.M. Mr. Buchanan called and held a conversation with me in relation to a rumor which had been put in circulation, that he was to be, or desired to be, appointed a judge of the Supreme Court of the United States in place of Judge Baldwin deceased.[9] He said he had not put the rumor in circulation or given any countenance to it. He stated it was true that he had long desired to have a seat on the bench of the Supreme Court, that he had once or twice had the opportunity to obtain the appointment, but not under circumstances that he was willing to accept it. He said that having heard that such a rumor was abroad and that others had mentioned it to me, he thought it proper to come and have a frank conversation with me on the subject. He said that he had become satisfied that he could not have any influence in controlling the course of the Democratic portion of the Pennsylvania delegation in the next Congress on the subject of the tariff; that from what he could learn the whole Pennsylvania delegation would oppose any reduction of the tariff act of 1842, so as to bring it to the revenue principles avowed in my Kane letter and inaugural address, principles which he fully and heartily approved. He said if he remained in the Cabinet, the opposition of the Democratic members from Pennsylvania to a reduction of the tariff to the revenue standard would be calculated to cast distrust over the sincerity of the Administration in proposing such a reduction. He said his own position would be an awkward one. For these reasons he might desire at the meeting of Congress to relieve the administration from the imputation of want of sincerity on the subject of the tariff, by being transferred from the De-

---

[9] Henry Baldwin of Connecticut, 1780–1844, had been Justice of the Supreme Court since 1830. He had died in 1844, and Tyler had in vain sent several nominations to the Senate. Tyler had also offered Buchanan the place, but Buchanan had refused.

partment of State to the Supreme Court bench. . . In the
event of war or the danger of war he would be willing and
desirous to remain in his present position of Secretary of
State, and perhaps at some future period an opportunity
might be afforded him to go on the bench.

The President expressed himself as being entirely satisfied
with Mr. Buchanan as Secretary of State, and spoke of the
great difficulty he would have in supplying his place in that
office if he was transferred to the bench. After a conversation of some length on the subject, in which the best feeling
prevailed and was mutually expressed, the President said it
was not necessary to decide or act now, to which Mr. Buchanan replied, certainly not. . .

Shortly after Mr. Buchanan retired Mr. Bancroft came
in, and Mr. Donelson came in shortly afterwards. A conversation occurred in relation to General Jackson's papers
and his biography. Major Donelson and the President expressed their earnest desire that Mr. Bancroft should have
charge of his papers and write his life. Mr. Bancroft was
willing to do so. Major Donelson said he had seen Mr.
F. P. Blair, to whom the papers were entrusted by General
Jackson's will, and that Mr. Blair desired to pass the papers
over to Mr. Bancroft that he might prepare his biography.

Friday, 10th October, 1845. — Closed my doors today
until evening to enable me to transact business of importance
on my table, and saw no one but some of the heads of departments and a few gentlemen whom they introduced.

Tuesday, 14th October, 1845. — The Hon. Nathaniel P.
Tallmadge,[10] who had been recently removed by the President as Governor of Wisconsin, called and held a long and
friendly conversation with the President. He said he did
not come to complain of his removal, but desired to state

---

[10] Nathaniel P. Tallmadge, 1795–1869, had been a Whig Senator from
New York 1833–1844. He had joined the " Conservative " ranks, opposed
to Van Buren, in 1837, and Philip Hone states that in 1838 he " labored
harder than any man perhaps in the State to bring about the late Whig victory." Polk naturally felt no political liking for him.

some facts and explain his position. He then gave a history of his political course, his separation from Mr. Van Buren's Administration on the independent treasury question, his appointment without solicitation on his part as Governor of Wisconsin, and that he was now and always had been in principle a Democrat. He stated, among other things, that when he took his ground against the independent treasury scheme, he consulted with Gov. Marcy, who was then Governor of New York, who concurred with him in opinion, but that the Governor afterwards endorsed the scheme in his message to the legislature of New York, and that he was left by many of those leading Democrats in New York who had at first approved his course, to stand alone. . . He said since his removal he had told all his friends that the President was not to blame, and that he had no doubt he had been influenced in his course from a desire to do what he considered justice to Gov. Dodge by restoring him to the office from which he had been improperly removed. The President said to him that in this he was right; that the view he had taken of the case was this: Gov. Dodge was a pioneer in the West and an old Indian fighter, a man of high character, and the half-brother of the late Senator, Dr. Lynn of Missouri, who had been removed from the office of governor by the late Administration, and Mr. Dotey appointed on political grounds solely; that from the papers before him, including the recommendation of the legislative assembly, it appeared to be the popular sentiment of the Democracy in Wisconsin that justice should be done him by restoring him to the office from which he had been removed without cause. The President added that he had not acted from any feeling of hostility to Gov. Tallmadge.

Friday, 17th October, 1845. — Kept my doors closed today, and was engaged in writing off a rough draft of parts of my message to be delivered to Congress at their meeting in December.

Tuesday, 21st October, 1845. — The Cabinet held a regular meeting today, all the members present. An important dispatch under date of Oct. 3d, 1845, was read from Mr. McLane, United States Minister to London. Mr. McLane gave an account of an interview which he had held with Lord Aberdeen at the Foreign Office on the subject of the Oregon negotiations.[11] Lord Aberdeen expressed his regret (as stated in Mr. McLane's dispatch) that Mr. Pakenham had rejected the American proposition of compromise. He condemned Mr. Pakenham's course, and intimated the willingness on the part of the British Government to agree to a modified proposition, and desired to be informed whether the President of the United States would negotiate further on the subject, after he had withdrawn the American proposition. Mr. Buchanan expressed an opinion, formed on the tenor of Mr. McLane's despatch, that the British Government would be willing and desirous to resume the negotiation by making another proposition on their part. He said he had no doubt Mr. Pakenham had received instructions from his Government by the same vessel that brought Mr. McLane's dispatch, that he thought it probable he would call upon him in a day or two to converse on the subject, and if he did so, he desired to know precisely what he should say to him. He would probably desire to know whether the United States would receive another proposition, and to ascertain what modification of the American proposition would be accepted by us. The President said our course was a plain one. We had made a proposition which had been rejected, in terms not very courteous. The British had afterwards been informed, in the note of Mr. Buchanan of the 30th of August, that our proposition was withdrawn and no longer to be considered as pending. In the close of that note, the

[11] Sir Robert Peel had become Prime Minister and Lord Aberdeen Foreign Secretary in 1841. Their reform Ministry, which was now sweeping away the Corn Laws and was interested in the promotion of peace, was one with which Polk found it comparatively easy to deal. For their part, they were pleased by Polk's advances toward free trade in favoring a downward revision of the tariff.

door of further negotiation was left open. If the British Minister, therefore, called on Mr. Buchanan, and made the inquiries suggested, all that could be said to him was, that if he had any further proposition to make on his part, it would be received and considered. This was all that could with propriety be said to him. . .

Mr. Buchanan thought we ought not to precipitate a crisis between the two countries, and that by delay we might secure the Oregon territory, but by strong measures hastily taken we would have war and might lose it. The President said he was satisfied with the state of the negotiation as it stood; and went on to state what he proposed to communicate to Congress in his first message. He would maintain all our rights, would take bold and strong ground, and reaffirm Mr. Monroe's ground against permitting any European power to plant or establish any new colony on the North American continent.

Thursday, 23d October, 1845. — Mr. Buchanan called and reported that he had held a conversation of two hours in length with Mr. Pakenham at the State Department on the subject of the Oregon negotiation. Mr. Pakenham regretted that the American proposition had been withdrawn, as it might have formed the basis of further negotiation. Much conversation, Mr. Buchanan reported to me, occurred on that point, which resulted in a declaration by Mr. Buchanan that what had occurred could not be changed. Mr. Pakenham said that a protocol might be signed which would open the negotiation again, though he did not propose this formally. Mr. Buchanan told him that if the British Government thought proper to make another proposition it would be respectfully considered, and this was the extent to which he went.

Friday, 24th October, 1845. — Received today a letter from Andrew Jackson, Jr., enclosing to me a letter from General Andrew Jackson written on the 6th June, 1845, two days before his death, and the last letter which he ever wrote.

This letter breathes the most ardent friendship to me personally and for the success of my Administration. It is marked " confidential," and communicates information touching the official conduct of a person high in office, in reference to which General Jackson in his dying moments thought it proper to put me on my guard. As it is highly confidential, its contents will never be disclosed by me or with my permission. It will be preserved as a highly prized memorial of the friendship of the dying patriot, a friendship which had never for a moment been broken, from my early youth till the day of his death. Andrew Jackson, Jr., in his letter enclosing it to me, explains the circumstances under which it had been accidentally mislaid among other papers on his table in. his dying room, and had not been discovered until recently before he enclosed it to me.[12] The latter letter I will also preserve. . .

My private secretary . . . informed me that Col. Benton would call on me at one o'clock P.M. today. He accordingly called at that hour. His manner and conversation were altogether pleasant and friendly, and such as they had always been in former years when I was in Congress with him.

After a few minutes of desultory conversation on commonplace subjects I adverted to the fact that the correspondence in relation to Oregon had been submitted to him with my approbation, and that I desired to have a conversation with him on the subject, and to have his views if he had no objection to give them.

He entered into the conversation very cheerfully. I told him that there was no probability that the subject could be adjusted by a negotiation, and that it was a matter of the gravest importance what course the government should take

---

[12] This letter of Jackson's warned Polk that certain rumored measures taken by Secretary of the Treasury Walker, in conjunction with land speculators, might " blow you and your administration sky high." Jackson regarded Polk as his friend and protégé; and the feeling which Polk had for the ex-President is expressed in a letter in which he speaks of him as " the greatest man of the age in which he lived — a man whose confidence and friendship I was so happy as to have enjoyed from my youth to the latest."

at the meeting of Congress.   He remarked that he approved what had been done on the part of the United States, and that he had told Mr. Buchanan last spring that he would support the settlement of the question at the parallel of 49° of north latitude.   I told him that I had reluctantly yielded my assent to make the proposition for that parallel, which had been made and rejected by the British Minister. . . The conversation continued, and without recording it at length as it occurred, we agreed in the following views, *viz.*:

1st. That the twelve months notice for the abrogation of the Convention of 1827 should be given.[13]

2nd. That our laws and jurisdiction should be extended over our citizens in Oregon, to the same extent that the British laws had been extended over British subjects by the act of Parliament of 1821.

3d. That block-houses or stockade forts should be erected on the route from the United States to Oregon, and that two or three regiments of mounted riflemen should be raised, for the protection of emigrants on their route to Oregon.

4th. That our Indian policy should be extended to Oregon.

All these things, we agreed, could be done without a violation of the Convention of 1827, and without giving just cause of offence to Great Britain.   I remarked that I was in favor of making grants of land to the emigrants, but I had some doubts whether this could be done until after the expiration of the year's notice, without a violation of the Treaty of 1827.   Of this Col. Benton also had some doubts, and did not seem to be clear.

I told Col. Benton that I was strongly inclined to reaffirm Mr. Monroe's doctrine against permitting foreign colonization, at least so far as this continent was concerned.   At this point, without denying the general proposition, Col. Benton

---

[13] The Convention of 1827 with Great Britain, establishing a joint occupation of Oregon, had provided that it might be terminated by either party at a year's notice.

remarked that Great Britain possessed the same kind of title to Fraser's River, by discovery, exploration, and settlement, that the United States did to the Columbia River. I remarked that we claimed it under the Spanish title, to which Col. Benton said the Spaniards had occupied and had a good title to Vancouver's Island, but had known nothing of the existence of such a river as Fraser's River; that we were entitled to the coast under the Spanish title. To this I said it would depend on the public law of nations, how far the discovery and possession of the coast would give Spain a title to the adjoining country in the interior.

The conversation then turned on California, on which I remarked that Great Britain had her eye on that country and intended to possess it if she could, but that the people of the United States would not willingly permit California to pass into the possession of any new colony planted by Great Britain or any foreign monarchy, and that in reasserting Mr. Monroe's doctrine I had California and the fine bay of San Francisco as much in view as Oregon. Col. Benton agreed that no foreign power ought to be permitted to colonize California, any more than they would be to colonize Cuba. As long as Cuba remained in the possession of the present government we would not object, but if a powerful foreign power was about to possess it, we would not permit it. On the same footing we would place California.

Col. Benton in the course of the conversation stated the fact that the British Hudson's Bay Company had now twenty forts on Fraser's River.

Some conversation occurred concerning Capt. Frémont's expedition,[14] and his intention to visit California before his return. Col. Benton expressed the opinion that Americans would settle on the Sacramento River and ultimately hold the country.

[14] John C. Frémont, Benton's son-in-law, had set out on his third expedition to the West in the summer of 1845, taking with him sixty men, and intending to visit both the Oregon country and California.

Monday, 27th October, 1845. — Mr. T. W. Ward of Boston called on me today. He told me that he was the agent of Baring Brothers & Co. in London; that he was my political friend and the friend of my Administration. From his conversation I soon discovered that the object of his visit was to obtain information in relation to the intentions of the government of the United States on the Oregon question. I remained silent whilst he continued to speak at some length on that subject. He spoke of the prosperous condition of the two countries, and of the great interest which both nations had in preserving peace. He said the Barings & Co. were largely engaged in business all over the world, and it was of great interest to them to know whether there was to be peace or war. He said he had constantly assured them that there was no danger of war, but that he had heard in New York, as coming directly from Washington, that I had determined to claim the whole of Oregon territory, and he intimated, without saying so in direct terms, if that was the case that there was danger of war. He said he did not expect me to communicate to him anything which was improper, but that perhaps I would feel at liberty to say in general terms that the existing relations of peace would not be changed, that he might know how to make his commercial arrangements. He said his mercantile friends had often consulted him of late to know whether it would be safe to enter into commercial arrangements which it would be unsafe to enter into if there was a probability of war between the United States and Great Britain about the Oregon question. After he had made his statement I said to him, in substance, that our general policy had always been peace; I said also that when I commenced my administration I found the Oregon negotiation pending, that I had given my attention to the subject, and that all it would be proper for me to say was that the negotiation was still pending. I declined giving any opinion of its probable result. I said to him that no one but myself and my Cabinet could know what had occurred or was likely to occur, and that until the negotiation was terminated it would be contrary to all usages of diplomacy for either party to communicate what had transpired.   I said in conclusion that if Lord Aberdeen were to disclose to the public what had transpired, in the present state of the negotiation, I would think very strange of it.   He learned nothing, and after apologizing for making the inquiry, he retired. The conversation took place about two o'clock P.M.   Whilst I was at dinner about four o'clock Mr. Buchanan sent in to me by my porter an official note from Mr. Pakenham on the subject of Oregon dated 25th inst. which Mr. Buchanan had not received when he called at my office at half past twelve o'clock today.

I have a strong suspicion that Mr. Ward called at the instance of Baring Brothers & Co., and that Mr. Pakenham was advised to his call, and probably held back his note of the 25th inst. until after he learned the result of Mr. Ward's interview with me.

Tuesday, 28th October, 1845.—The Cabinet held a regular meeting today. . .   The only subject of interest discussed was what was the proper answer to the note of the British Minister of the 25th inst. delivered to Mr. Buchanan on the 27th.   Mr. Buchanan read a draft of an answer which he had prepared.   Several suggestions of amendment and alteration were made by the members of the Cabinet and myself.   Mr. Buchanan was desirous to leave the door open for further negotiation; the draft of his note was conciliatory and, as I thought, conceded too much.   Mr. Buchanan repeated what he had often before said, that he was willing to settle the question at 49° north latitude, yielding the cape of Vancouver's Island to Great Britain but not the free navigation of the Columbia River.   My own view as expressed was, that our proposition of 49° had been rejected and had been subsequently withdrawn by us; that it would not be renewed, and that no other proposition would be made by us; that if Great Britain chose to make a proposition we would, of course, consider it; but that I was satisfied that no proposition would be made by Great Britain which we could accept.

Wednesday, 29th October, 1845. — . . . The Cabinet assembled at nine o'clock A.M., the hour which was appointed on yesterday, the Secretary of the Navy being still absent. I submitted the proposed modifications, which were discussed and with some modifications agreed to. Mr. Buchanan made a new draft conformably to them. I declined in the answer to renew the proposition which had been rejected, or to make any new proposition, but left the British Minister to take his own course. I declined to invite him to make any proposition, or to give any intimation what our decision on any proposition he might make would be.

Thursday, 30th October, 1845. — At twelve o'clock to-day I received in my office the chiefs of the Pottawatomie tribe of Indians, who were on a visit to Washington on the business of their nation. There were seven or eight of them painted and in full Indian costume; others were in citizen's dress. They held a talk with me through an interpreter in the presence of the Secretary of War, the Commissioner of Indian Affairs, and many other persons, who had been attracted to the President's Mansion by their approach. They retired apparently well satisfied at the manner in which I received them and with what I said to them. They were informed that the Secretary of War would confer further with them on the subject of their business.

I held a confidential conversation with Lieut. Gillespie of the Marine Corps, about eight o'clock P.M., on the subject of the secret mission on which he was about to go to California. His secret instructions and the letter to Mr. Larkin, United States consul at Monterey, in the Department of State, will explain the object of his mission.

Saturday, 1st November, 1845. — After conversing on other public subjects I read to the Cabinet what I had written for my message to Congress, on the subject of the tariff, and the establishment of a Constitutional Treasury, and the separation of the moneys of the public from banks.

There was a concurrence in my views on these subjects by all the members of the Cabinet, except Mr. Buchanan on one point in reference to the tariff. That point was this. I had recommended, among other things in the paper which I read, the abolition of the minimum principle and specific duties and the substitution in their place of *ad valorem* duties. Mr. Buchanan approved of the abolition of the minimum principle, and generally of the *ad valorem* principle, but thought there were some articles such as iron, coal, sugar, and a few others, which could be weighed or measured, on which his opinion was there should be a specific duty.

Sunday, 2d November, 1845.— Attended the Methodist church (called the Foundry Church) today, in company with my private secretary, J. Knox Walker. It was an inclement day, there being rain from an early hour in the morning; and Mrs. Polk and the ladies of my household did not attend church today. Mrs. Polk being a member of the Presbyterian Church I generally attend that church with her, though my opinions and predilections are in favor of the Methodist Church.

This day my birthday, being fifty years old, having been born according to the family register in the family Bible, corroborated by the account given me by my mother, on the 2d of November, 1795.

The text today was from the Acts of the Apostles, Ch. 15, v.31 — "Because he hath appointed a day, in the which he will judge the world in righteousness, by the man whom he hath ordained." It was communion day in the church, and the sermon was solemn and forcible. It awakened the reflection that I had lived fifty years, and that before fifty years more would expire, I would be sleeping with the generations which have gone before me. I thought of the vanity of this world's honors, how little they would profit me half a century hence, and that it was time for me to be " putting my house in order."

Monday, 3d November, 1845. — The facts about the mission to Spain are these. Sometime after Mr. Blair retired from the *Globe* [15] and Mr. Ritchie had taken charge of it, and when Mr. Blair having retired professing good feeling and friendship for the Administration and had made a manly publication to that effect in the Globe before he retired, Mr. Buchanan held a conversation with me in relation to the good feeling with which we both supposed Blair had retired, that he deserved credit for it, etc. Mr. Buchanan suggested that he would be a suitable person to fill the mission, and he thought he would be pleased with it. I concurred with Mr. Buchanan that he was well qualified, and intimated a willingness if on further consideration it should be deemed proper, to appoint him to that station if he desired. I did not authorize Mr. Buchanan to offer the mission to him, and he did not so understand me, as he afterwards informed me. Sometime afterwards Mr. Buchanan told me he had received a note from Blair declining the mission to Spain, and I think read the note to me. Mr. Buchanan expressed surprise at receiving the note, as he had not been authorized by me to offer him the mission, and had not in fact offered it to him.

Tuesday, 4th November, 1845. — Mr. Buchanan returned to me today my draft of my message to Congress on the subject of Oregon, with a condensed draft of his own modifying and softening the tone of mine. I prefer the bold ground which I have taken in my draft, but will further examine the subject before I revise my own draft.

Wednesday, 5th November, 1845. — Saw but few persons today. The Secretary of State introduced Christopher

[15] Francis P. Blair, whom Jackson had brought to Washington when President to edit his Administration organ, the *Globe*, had long been a political enemy to Polk. President Polk refused to accept him as editor for the new Administration; and the result was that Blair and his partner Rives sold the *Globe* to Thomas Ritchie of the Richmond *Enquirer*, and John P. Heiss, formerly of the Nashville *Union*. A new journal, the Washington *Union*, succeeded the *Globe*, with Ritchie as its editor.

Hughes, late *chargé d'affaires* to the Netherlands, and
Dabney S. Carr, Esq., Minister resident at Constantinople,
who was on a visit to the United States on leave of absence.
I suppose they called to pay their respects. After the ordinary salutations, however, they engaged in conversation between themselves on the fine arts, Powers's Eve, Fisherman
Boy, and Greek Slave; and about the distinguished persons
they had seen abroad. They seemed to be well satisfied with
themselves, and it was very clear that they had a good opinion of themselves. Their conduct was scarcely respectful to
me, though I suppose they did not intend to be disrespectful.
Altogether their deportment was highly impolite. They
said not a word in reference to their respective missions, or
public affairs abroad, and were so busily engaged in their
conversation with each other that they gave me no opportunity to make a single inquiry.

Thursday, 6th November, 1845.—Saw Mr. Buchanan
and referred in conversation with him to the conduct of
Messrs. Hughes and Carr, on their visit to me on yesterday,
and inquired of him if he observed it. He said he did, and
he thought they had acted very impolitely, but he had no
idea that they intended it. I gave him my opinion of their
vain conduct, in which he entirely concurred. I remarked
that they had been long enough abroad to have their heads
turned, that I had been, up to the visit, a good friend of Mr.
Carr, but that I thought it was almost time for him to remain at home, and let some other take his place.

At ten o'clock tonight Mr. Bancroft, the Secretary of the
Navy, called with dispatches from Commodore Conner commanding the home squadron in the Gulf of Mexico, to the
effect that the government of Mexico were willing to renew
diplomatic relations, and to receive a Minister from the
United States.

Monday, 10*th November,* 1845.— Saw and had a full conversation with Dr. Parrott, who had been in Mexico as a confidential agent of the United States for some months, and

who arrived at Washington last night. He confirmed the opinion I had entertained that Mexico was anxious to settle the pending difficulties between the two countries, including those of boundary. I informed Dr. Parrott that I wished him to return to Mexico as secretary of legation to the Minister whom I intended to appoint this day, and told him the Hon. John Slidell [16] of New Orleans was the person I intended to appoint as Minister. He was not anxious to accept the office of secretary of legation, but agreed to do so, and said he would be ready to leave in about ten days. At ten o'clock P.M., the instructions and all the documents referred to being copied, I signed the commission of the Hon. John Slidell as Envoy Extraordinary and Minister Plenipotentiary to Mexico.

Tuesday, 11th November, 1845.—The Cabinet held a regular meeting today, all the members present. I read to the Cabinet the passages of my message which I had prepared relating to Mexico. The Secretary of the Treasury read to the Cabinet that portion of his annual report to Congress on the finances, which related to the tariff and reduction of duties.[17] Mr. Buchanan expressed his objections to the doctrine which it contained. He remarked that it was a strong free trade document, and was in its doctrine opposed to his whole course on the subject during his whole public life. He objected especially to that part of it which recom-

[16] John Slidell, 1793–1871, famous chiefly for the Mason and Slidell case, had been a member of Congress from Louisiana 1843–1845. He was an able lawyer, an excellent Spanish scholar, and a suave and tactful diplomatist.

[17] The Democratic platform of 1844 had declared against fostering "one branch of industry to the detriment of another," a statement which in view of the clear struggle of the period between the agricultural and manufacturing interests meant a marked tariff reduction. In his inaugural address Polk had given special attention to the tariff, declaring for a revenue tariff rather than a protective schedule. He intended in his first message to Congress to reiterate and expand his views. Robert J. Walker's report to Congress — here under discussion — was an able review of the whole question of the tariff, and was in line with Polk's own opinions. Both men believed in substituting *ad valorem* for specific duties, the latter being unreasonably rated for the benefit of special industries. Buchanan spoke for the coal, iron, and other industries of Pennsylvania.

mended the abolition of pecific duties and the substitution of *ad valorem* duties in their stead.

Wednesday, 19th November, 1845. — Mr. Buchanan . . . informed me that he had made up his mind not to ask the vacant judgeship on the bench of the Supreme Court of the United States, but to remain in the Cabinet. I told him I was gratified to hear it as I was entirely satisfied with him and would have parted with him reluctantly. Though Mr. Buchanan differs with me on some points, on the Oregon question and on the tariff, yet he had not in consequence of such difference embarrassed me but had shown a willingness to carry out my views instead of his own, and I was desirous to retain him in my Cabinet. Mr. Buchanan, after announcing his determination to remain in the Cabinet, stated that he preferred a place on the Supreme Bench to any other under the Government; that he would rather be Chief Justice of that court than to be President of the United States. He said he did not desire to be President and never had; and now that he remained in the Cabinet he did not wish it, but would do all in his power to prevent his friends in Pennsylvania from presenting his name for that office. . . I told him he knew my position; that I retired at the end of my present term; that I would take no part in selecting the candidate of my party to succeed me, but would leave that to my political friends; I stated further my belief that no man would ever be elected President who was prominently before the public for that office for two or three years or a longer time before the nomination.

Thursday, 27th November, 1845. — About nine o'clock tonight Mr. Robert McLane of Baltimore called on me in my office, and stated that he had come from Baltimore to Washington in the cars this evening in company with John Van Buren (son of the late President).[18] He related to me

---

[18] "Prince" John Van Buren, as debonair and almost as able as his father, was so nicknamed because on a visit to England he had danced with Queen Victoria. The New York Democracy was split into two factions: Martin

a conversation which had taken place between them, which
he said had occupied more than an hour. I shall not attempt
to give it in detail. Among other things he said that Mr.
Van Buren had professed the belief that I was bestowing the
patronage and administering the government with a view to
be a candidate for a second term. On being asked to point
out the evidence of this he did not do so, but thought Gov.
Wright and the party in New York had not been well
treated. . . Mr. Van Buren then expressed the opinion that
Mr. Buchanan, the Secretary of State, or Mr. Walker, Secretary of the Treasury, were aspirants to the Presidency. He
spoke in very unfriendly terms of Gov. Marcy (the Secretary of War) and from the whole conversation as related to
me by Mr. McLane it is very clear that Mr. John Van
Buren is bitterly opposed to my administration. Mr. Mc-
Lane thinks his visit to Washington is to ascertain the tone
of public sentiment towards the administration. My own
opinion is, that if he finds the administration strong among
the members of Congress, he and his friends in New York
will not venture to make open opposition to it, but my firm
conviction is that neither he nor his special friends in New
York are friendly to it. The truth is they are looking to the
next Presidential election, and nothing could satisfy them
unless I were to identify myself with them, and proscribe all
other branches of the Democratic party. . . I will adhere
sternly to my principles without identifying myself with any
faction or clique of the Democratic party.

Friday, 28th November, 1845. — Among other visitors
today was Mr. John Van Buren of New York. (See diary
of yesterday.) He was polite and apparently friendly. I
was courteous toward him but not familiar, treating him with
the respect due to all gentlemen who call on me to pay their

Van Buren and Silas Wright headed the Barnburner faction, opposed to the
annexation of Texas and the spread of slavery, and William L. Marcy and
B. F. Butler headed the Hunker group, friendly to slavery. Polk wisely
refused to align himself in any positive way with either faction, though as
time went on he more and more sympathized with the Hunkers.

respects. What conversation occurred was of a general character, in the course of which I enquired for the health of his father and for Gov. Wright.

About eight o'clock this evening Vice-President Dallas called by appointment. I read to him that portion of my message which relates to Oregon, the tariff, and constitutional treasury. I informed him what had been done in reference to Mexico. He expressed himself not only satisfied but highly delighted with my course on Oregon and in relation to Mexico, and approved in unqualified terms what had been done in reference to these powers. He approved also my views on the tariff and constitutional treasury. Just before leaving he remarked to me, you have made me very happy tonight, I will go home and sleep sound.

Saturday, 29th November, 1845. — The Cabinet held a regular meeting today. . . In speaking of the Oregon question, Mr. Buchanan remarked that he thought from what he had heard from the members of Congress who had spoken to him, that they would be favorable to a settlement of the question on the parallel of 49° of north latitude. I told him that his channels of information were very different from mine; that there was not one in ten of the members whom I had seen who were not roused on the Oregon question and were going the whole length. Mr. Buchanan expressed the opinion with some earnestness that the country would not justify a war for the country north of 49°, and that my greatest danger would be that I would be attacked for holding a warlike tone. I told him that my greatest danger was that I would be attacked for having yielded to what had been done by my predecessors and in deference alone, as he knew, to their acts and commitments, and for having agreed to offer the compromise of 49°. I told him that if that proposition had been accepted by the British Minister my course would have met with great opposition, and in my opinion would have gone far to overthrow the administration; that, had it been accepted, as we came in on Texas the probability was that we would have gone out on Oregon.

Tuesday, 2nd December, 1845. — At half past twelve o'clock today a joint committee of the two houses of Congress waited on me and informed me that their respective houses had organized and were ready to receive any communication which I might have to make. I returned for answer that I would make to the two houses of Congress a communication in writing forthwith. The committee having retired my private secretary left my office with the message and delivered it at one o'clock P.M.

In the evening a number of members of Congress called, all of whom expressed their approbation of the message in strong and decided terms; among them were General Cass, who expressed his entire concurrence in every part of the message. He was delighted with that part of it relating to Oregon, Mexico, and Texas; and in reference to that part relating to the tariff he said to me, " You have struck out the true doctrine, you have cut the Gordian Knot." Mr. Holmes of South Carolina called, he said, to return to me his thanks for the doctrines of the message, and especially in reference to the tariff, and said that he was authorized by Mr. McDuffie to express his hearty approval of it, and especially in reference to the tariff, and that if his health had permitted he would have called in person to have expressed the same thing to me. Mr. Wilmot of Pennsylvania expressed his approval of the whole message and added, the doctrines on the tariff were the true doctrines and he would support them. Mr. Cameron [19] of Pennsylvania (of the Senate) pleasantly said: " We Pennsylvanians may scratch a little

[19] The men named are Lewis Cass, Senator from Michigan 1844–1857; Isaac E. Holmes, Representative from South Carolina 1839–1851; George McDuffie, Senator from South Carolina 1843–1846; David Wilmot, Representative from Pennsylvania 1845–1851; and Simon Cameron, Senator from Pennsylvania 1845–1849. Wilmot was the future author of the famous Proviso to exclude slavery from the territory acquired from Mexico. Cameron was destined to sit in Lincoln's Cabinet.

about the tariff but we will not quarrel about it," and added, " we are well pleased with all the rest of the message." Several other members expressed unqualified approbation of the message.

Friday, 5th December, 1845. — A great number of members of Congress, many of them of the Whig party, called to see me today. Among them was Mr. Archer of Virginia, who expressed his gratification at the message, and especially that part of it relating to Oregon.[20] He spoke in very friendly terms and said he had, on the day the message was read in the Senate, written to a Whig member of the Virginia legislature that he believed he was half a Polk man. He intimated that on the tariff we did not exactly agree. He admired, he said, the frankness and plainness of the message, that it was not ambiguous in any of its parts but that everyone knew where to find me.

Saturday, 6th December, 1845. — Many members of Congress called today, chiefly Whigs. Among others Col. Benton called, and after the usual salutations said, in presence of Judge Mason who was in my office, " Well! You have sent us the message," and " I think we can all go it as we understand it." I pleasantly replied that he had very high authority for saying, " as we understand it," alluding to a remark of General Jackson that he administered the government according to the Constitution " as he understood it "; and I added, I endeavored to write it in plain English, and thought no part of it could be misunderstood. Col. Benton was in a very pleasant humor, and remarked that he thought the British title to that part of Oregon which lay on Fraser's River was as good as ours to that on the Columbia River, but he said he had said nothing about that.

[20] William S. Archer, Senator from Virginia 1841–1847, was chairman of the Committee on Foreign Relations.

CHAPTER II
Dec. 14, 1845 – April 24, 1846

JOHN QUINCY ADAMS — NATIONAL DEFENCE — THE JOINT
OCCUPATION OF OREGON — ATOCHA AND SANTA ANNA —
A POSSIBLE PURCHASE OF CALIFORNIA — SLIDELL REJECTED
AND WAR LIKELY

Sunday, 14th December, 1845. — This was a very inclement day; during the greater part of the day it rained and sleeted, the pavements and streets being covered with ice. I was indisposed from the effects of cold, and the excessive fatigues of the last week and remained quietly at home; the family did not attend church as was usual with them.

Wednesday, 17th December, 1845. — Received company until twelve o'clock today. At that hour left my office and in company with the Secretary of the Navy visited the Navy Yard at Washington; went on board the vessel called the *Spitfire* and witnessed Mr. Taylor descend into the water with his diving bell, and remain under water for half an hour. Returned to my office about one o'clock P.M., and was engaged until dinner in disposing of the official business on my table.

Friday, 19th December, 1845. — Had a large number of visitors today. After they had left Mr. Lester, United States consul at Genoa, called. He had much conversation. I heard him, but I cannot say with patience, for I had much business on my table which I was anxious to dispose of. Among other things he adverted to the fact that he was a

32

writer for the New York *Herald,* and asked me how I was pleased with the course of the *Herald.* I told him I had but little opportunity to read newspapers, and could at no time do more than glance hastily over them.

Monday, 22d December, 1845. — Some days ago Mr. Bancroft, the Secretary of the Navy, and myself held a conversation, in which I expressed a willingness to extend to Mr. John Quincy Adams,[1] ex-President of the United States, an invitation to dine with me.   Though we had always differed widely in politics, and there were many acts of his public life which I disapproved, Mr. Bancroft agreed with me in opinion that it would be proper for me as President of the United States in consideration of his age and the high stations which he had held to extend to him such an invitation, provided it was ascertained that it would be agreeable to him.   After some further conversation I authorized Mr. Bancroft to intimate to him my disposition to invite him to dinner, if it should be agreeable to him to accept.

This morning Mr. Bancroft called at my office, and informed me that he had just had a conversation with Mr. Adams, and had intimated to him what I had authorized him to do.   Mr. Adams, he informed me, said that a similar communication had been made to him by General Jackson while he was President of the United States through a common friend (Col. Richard M. Johnson) and that he had declined it.   Mr. Adams, as Mr. Bancroft informed me, said further that his personal relations with me had always been good, and while in Congress together, though we had voted differently on almost every public question, that yet our personal relations had never been disturbed.   He expressed his determination to support my administration on the Oregon question, and that he would take an early occasion to make known his views in the House.   Mr. Adams, as Mr.

---

[1] Adams tells us in his *Memoirs* that the election of Polk was " the victory of the slavery element in the constitution of the United States." He declined to attend Polk's inauguration, to which he received a special invitation. He was of course bitterly opposed to the annexation of Texas.

Bancroft informed me, then alluded to the controversy which he had had with General Jackson, Mr. Charles J. Ingersoll of Pennsylvania, and Gov. Brown of Tennessee, in relation to the boundary fixed by the Florida Treaty of 1819, in which there had been an attempt by these persons to make it appear that he had accepted a less favorable boundary for the United States than he could have obtained, and had thereby lost Texas to the United States. He said that I had written a letter to the same effect and that I would know what letter it was.[2] He said that he had made a speech in Massachusetts in which he had spoken of that letter, and intimated that some explanation of my statements in that letter would be necessary before he could accept an invitation to dinner. Mr. Bancroft said he left him in a good humor. I told Mr. Bancroft that it was a matter of no consequence whether he was invited to dinner or not, and that certainly I had no explanations to make. At first I was at some loss to recollect to what letter of mine he alluded. Upon a little reflection I remarked that he must have alluded to my letter to a committee of citizens of Cincinnati in April, 1844, on the subject of the annexation of Texas. I told Mr. Bancroft that my statements in that letter were correct, and were sustained by the public records of the country, and that I had no explanations concerning it to make. I told him further that I had never read Mr. Adams's speech in Massachusetts, in which, Mr. Adams had informed him, he had referred to it. I told Mr. Buchanan to let the matter rest where it was, and that I would not think of inviting him to dinner. . .

Mr. John C. Calhoun of South Carolina called on me

[2] Polk had written this letter April 22, 1844, in answer to Ohioans who inquired his attitude toward the annexation of Texas. He argued in it that Texas had belonged to the United States as part of the Louisiana Purchase from 1803 to 1819, when John Quincy Adams, as Secretary of State, had unwisely ceded it to Spain in the treaty of 1819. It was on the basis of this doctrine that Polk and other Democrats spoke of the " reannexation " of Texas. Polk's letter is to be found in John S. Jenkins, *The Life of James Knox Polk* (1850), 120 ff. Polk and Adams could not have made cordial dinner companions.

this morning, having arrived in the city on Saturday night last. He appeared to be in a fine humour. He introduced the subject of Oregon, and expressed his desire to assert our rights in that Territory. He declared himself, however, opposed to giving the year's notice for the termination of the treaty of joint occupancy of 1827, as recommended in my message. That point was discussed in a conversation of a few minutes' length in which we differed in opinion. Mr. Calhoun expressed himself as being strongly in favor of peace. I told him I was in favour of peace, but at the same time all our just rights must be maintained. I went on to speak of the recommendations of my message and to enforce them. Mr. Calhoun then said that he feared, or rather that the greatest danger of disturbing the peace between the two countries, would grow out of the hasty action of Congress and the debates which would arise. He expressed strong desire for delay on the subject, and said the Executive should confer with the proper committees of Congress and restrain them from taking rash or warlike measures. I became satisfied from the whole conversation that he would not support the views of the message. He said a few words on the tariff part of my message, the substance of which was that he approved part of my views on that subject but not the whole, or, as I inferred, that I had not gone to the extent that he would have done. Upon the whole the conversation was not a satisfactory one, and the impression left on my mind is very strong that Mr. Calhoun will be very soon in opposition to my Administration.[3]

[3] Calhoun loved peace, while war with England did not fit his ambitions. He was bent on gaining the Presidency; and he hoped to do so by a combination of the South and West against the Northeast. He feared that war would upset this political alignment; that by draining the treasury, it would make impossible the reduction of the tariff or the expenditure of large sums on internal improvements to please the West; and looking forward to the possibility of ultimate Southern secession, he did not wish the Southern States to expend their manpower in conflict to add territory to the North. If Oregon had been situated south of Mason and Dixon's Line, Calhoun might have refused to accept a division or compromise. As it was, he was glad to see the territory divided along the line of the 49th parallel. As Secretary of State under Tyler, he had proposed and labored for this boundary, which he believed fair.

Tuesday, 23d December, 1845. — The Cabinet held a regular meeting today; all the members present except the Attorney-General, who was officially engaged in the Supreme Court of the United States. A grave discussion took place in view of the contingency of war with Great Britain, growing out of the present critical state of the Oregon question. Mr. Buchanan expressed himself decidedly in favor of making vigorous preparations for defence, and said it was his conviction that the next two weeks would decide the issue of peace or war. I expressed my concurrence with Mr. Buchanan that the country should be put in a state of defence without delay; that if peace continued the expenditure would not be lost, and if war came such preparation would be indispensable. . . The opinion was then expressed by Mr. Buchanan that the British Minister here would probably very soon propose arbitration as an ultimatum. All agreed that this was probable, and also that we could not agree to arbitration, first, because the question of a compromise of territorial limits was not a fit subject for such reference, and second, because in the existing state of the principal powers of the world an impartial umpire could not be found. Mr. Buchanan . . . desired to know if he could inform the British Minister that any new proposition he would make would be respectfully considered. He desired to know also, if the British Minister should offer the 49th degree of north latitude as the boundary from the Rocky Mountains to the Straits of Fuca, leaving the southern cape of Vancouver's Island to the British, whether I would submit such a proposition to the Senate for their previous advice. In relation to the latter inquiry I told him if an equivalent, by granting to the United States free ports north of 49° on the sea and the Straits of Fuca should also be offered, I would consult confidentially three or four Senators from different parts of the Union, and might submit it to the Senate for their previous advice.

Wednesday, 24th December, 1845. — Mr. Horn was in

conversation with me on the subject of his nomination to
the Senate as Collector of Philadelphia, when Mr. Buchanan called in and after shaking hands with Mr. Horn
and myself immediately retired, although invited to take
a seat. He went into my private secretary's room. Mr.
Horn left in a few minutes when my private secretary informed me that Mr. Buchanan had left. My private secretary informed me that Mr. Buchanan seemed to be in a
pet, and asked him how long Mr. Horn would probably
remain; to which he replied that he did not know how
long it would take him to get through his grievances. Mr.
Buchanan said he had some grievances too. The truth
is Mr. Buchanan has been for some days, when I saw
him, taciturn, with a careworn countenance and apparently in trouble. I know of no cause for it but the difference between us on the Oregon question, which has
existed from the time he entered on the negotiation;
and the appointment of a judge of the Supreme Court
of the United States for Pennsylvania and New Jersey,
in place of Judge Baldwin, deceased. . . He was most
anxious to have Mr. John M. Read of Philadelphia
appointed. Mr. Read, I learned, was until ten or twelve
years ago a leading Federalist, and a Representative of
that party in the legislature. . . I have never known
an instance of a Federalist who had after arriving at the
age of thirty professed to change his opinions, who was to
be relied on in his constitutional opinions. All of them
who have been appointed to the Supreme Court bench, after
having secured a place for life became very soon broadly
Federal and latitudinarian in all their decisions involving
questions of Constitutional power. General Jackson had
been most unfortunate in his appointments to that bench
in this respect. I resolved to appoint no man who was not
an original Democrat and strict constructionist, and who
would be less likely to relapse into the broad Federal doctrines of Judge Marshall and Judge Story. . . On yester-

day I nominated Mr. Woodward to the Senate, and in so doing greatly disappointed and as I suppose dissatisfied Mr. Buchanan.[4] . .

Hopkins L. Turney of the Senate from Tennessee called about six o'clock P.M., having previously written to me that he desired to see me on the subject of the Oregon question. . . He said shortly after he reached Washington Mr. Benton had a conversation with him, and that he was well satisfied that Mr. Benton entertained no friendly feelings toward me or my administration. He informed me that Col. Benton asked him if there was not a combination among my friends in Tennessee to defeat Mr. Van Buren and to run me for a second term, to which he said he replied that he had never heard such a suggestion in the State. Col. Benton spoke, he said, of the Baltimore Convention of 1844, and charged corruption and fraud upon them. Mr. Turney said he told him that after Mr. Van Buren's letter on Texas came out in the spring of 1844, and the people were all against his views, that my name had not been mentioned for the Presidency except conjecturally among a few friends, as a possible event if a new candidate should be nominated. Mr. Turney expressed the distinct opinion that Col. Benton would oppose my administration, whenever a fair pretext to do so occurred. He said however that his opposition would amount to nothing more than his own single vote in the Senate. Mr. Calhoun, he said, could take some Southern strength with him, and the two combined might give me trouble.[5]

[4] Buchanan, as Polk says, supported John Meredith Read of Pennsylvania (whom Tyler had vainly nominated) for the vacant place on the Supreme Court bench; but Polk, on the recommendation of George M. Dallas, the Vice President, nominated George W. Woodward, of the Pennsylvania inferior courts. Woodward was an able man, but he was opposed by Senator Simon Cameron of Pennsylvania, and was obnoxious to many Pennsylvania Democrats because of his alleged " Native American sentiments." Polk was even more determined than Tyler never to appoint a Federal Judge " of the school of Kent."

[5] Benton had supported Calhoun's efforts in the Tyler Administration to divide Oregon by the line of 49°. He never abetted the cry of the North-

I remark, on this information thus communicated to me, that I have no doubt both Mr. Benton and Mr. Calhoun apprehend that I may be a candidate for reëlection, for which there is not the slightest foundation. My mind has been made up from the time I accepted the Baltimore nomination, and is still so, to serve but one term and not to be a candidate for reëlection.

Thursday, 25th December, 1845. — This being Christmas Day no company called, with a very few exceptions, who remained but for a short time. Congress had adjourned over, the public offices were closed, and no public business was transacted. After night Mr. Buchanan called. His manner was one of some agitation and care. He made known the object of his visit by saying he wished to converse with me on a subject which had caused him to spend two sleepless nights. He said that I had a right to nominate Judge Woodward to the Supreme Bench of the United States, but that I should have done so as I had done on Tuesday last without informing him of it was what he complained of. I promptly answered that as President of the United States I was responsible for my appointments, and that I had a perfect right to make them without consulting my Cabinet, unless I desired their advice. Mr. Buchanan said it had been done by all my predecessors. I told him I did not so understand it. . . I told him that I had not intended to mortify him by concealing the nomination from him. He said reverse the case; suppose I had

---

western Democrats for the line of 54° 40′, and was totally unwilling to risk war for such a line. In the end the combination of the Whigs with the Southern Democrats under Benton and Calhoun resulted — in spite of the frantic opposition of the Northwestern Democrats — in the adoption of the treaty for the line of 49°.

As this entry indicates, Benton had expected and hoped for the nomination of Van Buren in 1844; he had regarded the Baltimore Convention of that year — "a motley assemblage called Democratic," largely under the influence of "Texas land and scrip speculators" — as recreant to its trust in nominating Polk; and he was particularly outraged by the "intrigue" which had resulted in the annexation of Texas. His opinions are forcibly expressed in chapter 136 of the second volume of his *Thirty Years' View*.

been President and you Secretary of State, and I had been about to appoint a judge from Tennessee, would you not have thought you ought to have been consulted by me before I made the nomination? I told him I had once conversed with him fully, that I knew Mr. Read was his choice, that I thought Mr. Woodward the preferable man; but that perhaps it would have been better to have mentioned it to him again, but that as I knew no further conversation I could have had with him could have changed my mind, I had not thought it necessary to do so. I told him that if I had supposed that he would have taken the view of it he had, I certainly should have mentioned it to him again before I made the nomination; and that I regretted that anything had occurred to give him pain. He then said that the impression was becoming general among his friends in Pennsylvania that the patronage of the government here was being wielded against him. I told him that he knew that nothing was more unfounded, and after a long conversation, in which the appointments which had been made in Pennsylvania were discussed, he expressed himself as entirely satisfied.

Saturday, 27th December, 1845. — At ten P.M. Mr. Buchanan and Mr. Bancroft called, and the former informed me that immediately after he left the Cabinet he met Mr. Pakenham at the State Department, who submitted a proposition to refer to arbitration the Oregon question. The despatch was read. It proposed to refer the question not of *title* but to *divide* the Oregon Territory, to the arbitrament of some friendly power. I instantly said it must be rejected, in which decision Mr. Buchanan and Mr. Bancroft both agreed.

Thursday, 1st January, 1846. — This being the first day of a new year, the President's Mansion was open for the reception of company according to custom. At a few minutes after eleven o'clock A.M. the members of the Cabinet and the ladies of their families, with a few friends began to assemble. At half past eleven o'clock the Diplomatic

Corps, in full court dress, with the ladies of their families came in and paid their respects. At twelve o'clock all the halls, parlours, and the East Room were crowded with visitors, ladies and gentlemen, and persons of all ages and sexes, without distinction of rank or condition in life. I shook hands with thousands of them and interchanged salutations with them. The day passed off pleasantly and at about half past two o'clock P.M. the company began to retire, and before half past three o'clock they had with few exceptions retired. The most perfect order prevailed.

Friday, 2d January, 1846. — I find that I will be compelled to refuse company absolutely, at twelve o'clock each day, in order to be enabled to discharge promptly my public duties.

Saturday, 3d January, 1846. — Mr. Cameron, I have learned from Mr. Westcott of the Senate and other sources, is active in his exertions to have Mr. Woodward's nomination as judge of the Supreme Court of the United States rejected. I hope my suspicions may be wrong, but facts and circumstances which have come to my knowledge, I think justify me in indulging them, that Mr. Buchanan has given countenance to these movements of opposition on the part of Mr. Cameron. It will be deeply painful to me, if I ascertain that my suspicions are correct, but if I do so ascertain, I will act with promptness and energy towards Mr. Buchanan, whatever the consequences to myself or my administration may be.

Sunday, 4th January, 1846. — Mr. Black, who is a member of the House of Representatives from South Carolina . . . introduced the Oregon question, and expressed his apprehension and belief that the question of the notice to terminate the joint occupation under the Convention of 1827, would produce a serious split in the Democratic party in Congress. He said the Northwestern members were for the notice, were excited, and he feared would act rashly and imprudently, and that Mr. Calhoun and a portion of

the Southern Senators were against the notice. He said he
had been endeavoring to harmonize them and bring them
together on some common ground; that for this purpose he
had seen Mr. Senator Semple of Illinois and Mr. Senator
Atchison of Missouri, that he thought they would agree
not to press the notice if the South would unite with them
in supporting all the other recommendations of my message, including grants of land to emigrants to Oregon, with
this provision, that if any of the settlers in Oregon should
locate themselves on the British side of the line which by any
future arrangement between the two governments might
be established as a boundary between them, they should
have floats and land titles to be located elsewhere. He said
he had seen Mr. Calhoun and he thought, though he was
not authorized to say positively, that he would agree to
this proposition; that he doubted about granting floats to
settlers, etc. He said in the present excited state of the
House of Representatives, he apprehended that the question
of notice would be forced to a vote under the operation
of the previous question. . . I told him that my opinions
were contained in my message, that they had been well considered, and that I had not changed them; that I had recommended the notice and thought it ought to be given. I remarked to him that the only way to treat John Bull was
to look him straight in the eye; that I considered a bold
and firm course on our part the pacific one; that if Congress
faltered or hesitated in their course, John Bull would immediately become arrogant and more grasping in his demands;
and that such had been the history of the British nation in
all their contests with other powers for the last two hundred years.

  Friday, 9th January, 1846. — Saw company until six
o'clock today; had an unusual number of visitors in my
office, male and female, to call on visits of ceremony. Had
also the calls of many office seekers, but having learned
to say No! with a good grace, I soon disposed of them.

Unfortunately a portion of our people, and I must say not the most meritorious, seem to have concluded that the chief end of government is office. They are most importunate in their demands, and I have learned that the only way to treat them is to be decided and stern.

Saturday, 10th January, 1846. — Mr. Senator Calhoun of South Carolina called this morning. . . He said he desired to pursue the course most likely to preserve peace, and desired to know if I had any information beyond what had been communicated to Congress on the probable course of the British Government. I told him I had reason to believe, judging from the conversation of Mr. Pakenham with Mr. Buchanan, and from the information communicated by Mr. McLane at London, that Lord Aberdeen and Sir Robert Peel would be averse to going to war, but that no new proposition to compromise the dispute had been made. I expressed the strong conviction that the notice should be given, that it was pacific, being expressly provided for by the convention of 1827, and that until it was done and the American government boldly faced the British power and asserted their rights, that the latter would yield nothing of her pretensions. . . Mr. Calhoun said that the members of Congress who were in favour of giving the notice would so vote from very different motives. The larger portion of them would vote for the notice from the belief that it would prevent any compromise, and in the event the notice was given and no compromise followed, in his opinion war was certain and inevitable. Another portion of members who would vote for the notice would do so believing that when the question was brought to this crisis, it would lead to a compromise and settlement of the question.

Thursday, 15th January, 1846. —Saw company as usual in my office until twelve o'clock today. At one o'clock P.M. Mr. Healy, the French artist, sent to the United States by the King of the French to take the portraits of General Jackson and other distinguished persons, called and exhib-

ited the original portraits of General Jackson, Mr. John
Quincy Adams, and Mr. Henry Clay. They were exhibited
in the parlour below stairs in the presence of the ladies of
the family, and some company who had called. I thought
the portrait of General Jackson, which was completed only
four days before his death, very good. Those of Mr.
Adams and Mr. Clay were fair likenesses.

Monday, 19th January, 1846. — Mr. Senator Cass of
Michigan called in shortly after Mr. Chalmers left, and
held a conversation with me in relation to the news received today, of the dissolution of the English Ministry,
and its probable effect upon our relations with that country.
He expressed himself strongly in favour of vigorous preparations for defence, in which I concurred with him.

Thursday, 22nd January, 1846. — About half past five
o'clock Mr. Shields, the Commissioner of the General Land
Office, called and informed me that he had seen General
Cass of the Senate, who informed him that the Senate had
rejected the nomination of George W. Woodward as Asso-
ciate Justice of the Supreme Court of the United States.[6]
Judge Shields advised the appointment of Mr. Buchanan,
the Secretary of State, and said that General Cass advised
the same thing. I had some conversation with Judge Shields
on the subject, who among other things told me that he had
conversed with Mr. Buchanan on yesterday, and that he
knew he was anxious to have the appointment. I thought
it strange that Mr. Buchanan should have expressed such
a wish to anyone pending the nomination of Mr. Woodward
before the Senate.

Friday, 23d January, 1846. — Among others Mr. Speight
of Mississippi called, and spoke very indignantly and
strongly of the course of the six Democratic Senators who

[6] The nomination of Woodward was defeated by a vote of 29 to 20. All
the Whig members voted against him, and among others, the Democratic
Senators from Virginia, who wished to see Buchanan placed in the Supreme
Court in the hope that Andrew Stevenson of Virginia (former Speaker and
Minister to England) might become Secretary of State.

had united with the Whig Senators on yesterday, and rejected the nomination of Mr. Woodward as judge of the
Supreme Court. I said nothing, except to give general and
evasive answers. He expressed the confident opinion that
Mr. Buchanan had controlled, if not directly at all events
indirectly, the votes of Mr. Sevier, Cameron, and Westcott,
and this without the slightest intimation indicating such
a suspicion on my part. He said he boarded near Mr.
Sevier and Mr. Thompson of Mississippi, and that they
were very intimate with Mr. Buchanan, and visited him
at least three times a week, and to use his own words, he
said Sevier and Thompson almost lived at Buchanan's, and
with an oath he expressed the opinion that Sevier, if Mr.
Buchanan had given him the slightest intimation, would
have voted as he desired. To all this I replied that I hoped
he was mistaken.

Saturday, 24th January, 1846. — I learned from my
private secretary, Mr. Walker, and from others today that
it was the common talk at Mr. Buchanan's ball last night
that he (Mr. Buchanan) was to go on the bench of the
Supreme Court, in place of Mr. Woodward rejected. I
learned, too, that there is another rumour in the streets that
Mr. Buchanan will soon leave the Cabinet. These rumours
are strange to me. . . His greatest weakness is his great
sensitiveness about appointments to office. He has repeatedly seemed to be troubled, and taken it greatly to heart
when I have differed with him about appointments and
made my own selections. Being responsible for my appointments, I cannot surrender the appointing power to anyone
else, and if, because I will not do so, Mr. Buchanan chooses
to retire from my Cabinet I shall not regret it. I have
heard of his talking and complaining to others of my self-
will in making my appointments. His opposition to my
nomination of Mr. Woodward was, I understand, a matter
publicly known in the streets.

Wednesday, 28th January, 1846. — Mr. Wilmot, a

member of the House of Representatives from Pennsylvania, informed me today that his colleague, Mr. Garvin of the House, had informed him that he had called at the lodgings of Mr. Cameron, Senator from Pennsylvania, on Sunday last. . . Mr. Garvin informed him that General Cameron on that occasion in speaking of my nomination of Mr. Woodward and his rejection by the Senate, said that Mr. Westcott, one of the Senators from Florida, had remarked and applied the remark to me and my course in nominating Mr. Woodward, that "the only way to treat an ugly negro who was unruly, was to give him a d—d drubbing at the start, and he would learn to behave himself." The drubbing given to me, according to the low and vulgar language of Mr. Westcott, was the rejection of Mr. Woodward by himself and five other professed Democrats united with the whole Whig vote in the Senate. . .[7] I cannot express my contempt for a Senator who could be capable of such coarseness and vulgarity. This Mr. Westcott, too, was elected as a Democrat by the Democratic Legislature of Florida. While Mr. Wilmot was in my office, where he related to me the foregoing conversation as communicated to him by Mr. Garvin, Mr. Cameron came in and introduced a friend. He put on a smiling and hypocritical air, and acted as though he had been one of my friends. I of course treated him civilly in my own office, but I felt great contempt for him.

Mr. Wilmot had no hesitation in avowing his opinion that Mr. Buchanan had controlled both Cameron and Westcott, and had been the cause of Mr. Woodward's rejection.

[7] William S. Garvin, who reported this insolent remark, was a Pennsylvania Representative 1845–1847; James D. Westcott was a Senator in Congress from the admission of Florida in 1845 until 1849. He was a Virginian by birth, and had been appointed Secretary of the Territory of Florida by Jackson. On the day following this diary-entry, Wilmot sent a note to Polk explaining that it was really Cameron, and not Westcott, who had applied this offensive remark about "drubbing a negro" to President Polk. Simon Cameron had entered the Senate from Pennsylvania as a Democrat in 1845. He was interested in railroads, banking, and manufacturing, and resented Polk's low-tariff policies.

Saturday, 31st January, 1846.—After night Senator Semple called and held a conversation with me in relation to the intended emigration of the Mormons of Illinois to Oregon. I had examined Gov. Ford's letter on the subject, which he had delivered to me on the 30th instant, and which I have placed on file, and informed him that as President of the United States I possessed no power to prevent or check their emigration; that the right of emigration or expatriation was one which any citizen possessed. I told him that I could not interfere with them on the ground of their religious faith, however absurd it might be considered to be; that if I could interfere with the Mormons, I could with the Baptists, or any other religious sect; and that by the Constitution any citizen had a right to adopt his own religious faith.[8]

Monday, 2d February, 1846.—Among others General Cass called and enquired of me if I cared anything about the nomination by the Senate of Gov. Morton as Collector of Boston, remarking that he might vote against him on account of his abolition tendencies. I told him he was no abolitionist, and asked him if he had seen a letter written by Gov. Morton to Mr. Bancroft denying the charge. . .

Tuesday, 3d February, 1846.—Held a regular Cabinet meeting today; all the members present except the Attorney-General. Mr. Buchanan read the draft which he had prepared of an answer to Mr. Pakenham's second proposal to refer the Oregon question to arbitration. All concurred in the conclusion that the offer to refer to arbitration should be rejected.

[8] On June 27, 1844, the leaders of the Mormon community at Nauvoo, Illinois, Joseph and Hyrum Smith, had been murdered by a mob at Carthage. During 1845 the anti-Mormon element in Illinois instituted a campaign for the purpose of driving the sect from its prosperous settlement. There were renewed mob outrages, and in October the Mormons offered to remove if the " gentiles " would assist them in selling or renting their property. During the winter of 1845–1846 Nauvoo was turned into a busy camp preparing for a great emigration westward, the men all making wagons and the women tents, clothing, and bedding. On Feb. 10, 1846, the first teams crossed the Mississippi.

Friday, 6th February, 1846. — The young ladies of my household and some other young persons, having obtained Mrs. Polk's assent, had arranged it that Herr Alexander, the juggler or performer of tricks of sleight of hand, should visit the President's Mansion and exhibit before a select company. They mentioned it at dinner today at four o'clock P.M. About eight o'clock P.M. I was in my office with Mr. Senator Allen when Mr. Bancroft and Mrs. Judge Catron came to my office and said they were deputed by the company in the parlour below to come up and bring me down. I went down, and found some forty or fifty ladies and gentlemen, before whom Mr. Alexander exhibited his art greatly to their wonder and amusement, but as I think not much to their edification or profit. It was, however, innocent in itself, but I thought the time unprofitably spent. I, however, was thinking more about the Oregon and other public questions which bear on my mind than the tricks of the juggler, and perhaps on that account the majority of the company might think my opinions entitled to but little weight.

Tuesday, 10*th February,* 1846. — This evening Martin, my porter, delivered to me a sealed letter which, on breaking the seal, was found to be from Henry H. Gilbert, dated at New Hartford, February 6, 1846, which he stated was delivered today while the Cabinet were in session by the Hon. John Quincy Adams, who informed the porter that he was requested to hand it to me in person. Mr. Adams, as the porter informed me, drove to my door, but did not get out of his carriage.

Wednesday, 11*th February,* 1846. — Saw company as usual until twelve o'clock today. Mr. Cameron of the Senate remained in my office after the balance of the company had retired. He said he wished to have a conversation with me. I told him I would hear him. He commenced by professing friendship for the administration. He said he had opposed the nomination of George W. Woodward as judge of the Supreme Court of the United States and went on to assign his reasons, which were unsatisfactory, though I did not deem it to be necessary to tell him so; indeed, I did not think they were the real reasons. . . I told him as he had sought the conversation I would talk frankly to him. He said he desired that I should. I then told him that the public understood that there was a Democratic majority of six in the Senate, and that the effect of rejecting my principal nominations at the commencement of my administration, and especially as the Senate sat with closed doors and the public could not know the reason of the rejection, was calculated to weaken my administration, and destroy or impair my power and influence in carrying out the measures of my administration. The truth is Mr. Woodward's rejection was factious, Mr. Cameron and five other professed Democrats having united with the whole Whig party to effect it. And now those by whose votes he was rejected refuse, as the Executive Journal proves, to remove the injunction of secrecy, so that the public may know by whose votes he was rejected. I told Mr. Cameron that since the rejection it had been communicated to me that a coarse and vulgar remark had been made and applied to me, in reference to his nomination, by a professed Democrat, at which I had felt indignant, and that remark was, applying it to me for having nominated Judge Woodward, in substance: that the way to treat an ugly or stubborn negro when you first got him, was to give him a d—d drubbing at the start and he would learn how to behave himself. He immediately denied that he had used such language, although I had not said that he was the person who used such language. He showed in his manner some confusion. I told him that the first use of these vulgar terms had not been attributed to him; but that afterwards they had been familiarly repeated among members of Congress and others as applied to me. I told him I had done nothing to merit such epithets of reproach; that I had exercised my constitutional power in making the nomination of Judge Woodward, and the Senate had a right to reject him, but that no man had a right to use such terms. In the after part of the conversation on this point, with a countenance and manner still confused and embarrassed, he admitted that such language had been used, but did not say by whom, but denied that it had been applied to me.

Friday, 13th February, 1846. — Saw company today until twelve o'clock. Among others who called was Col. Atocha, who called on me in June last. He is a Spaniard by birth but says he has become a naturalized citizen of the United States. He has lived at New Orleans and spent many years in Mexico. He was with Santa Anna when his government was overthrown last year; was himself arrested, but it being made known that he was a naturalized citizen of the United States he was ordered out of the country. He called on me in June last to present claims which he had against the government of Mexico, with a view to have their payment urged by the government of the United States.

Col. Atocha stated this morning that since he saw me in June last he had visited General Santa Anna in his exile at Havana, and that he had left him a month ago.[9] His conversation with me, he said, he desired to be confidential. He represented that Santa Anna was in constant communication with his friends in Mexico, and received by every vessel that left Vera Cruz hundreds of letters. He inti-

[9] A. J. Atocha, a naturalized American citizen, had been an intimate friend and tool of Santa Anna in Mexico City. Polk was highly distrustful of him, but willing to make use of what information he could bring. Santa Anna, long the principal military chieftain in Mexico, had become dictator in October, 1841, and under a new constitution, President in January, 1844. His regime had been to the last degree arbitrary and corrupt, and the people had finally revolted against his exactions. Driven from the capital in January, 1845, he was captured and later in the year was banished. Now he was waiting in Havana for his chance to regain control. The foremost Mexican of his time, and apparently extraordinary in his versatile energy, " in reality he was a charlatan." (J. H. Smith, *The War With Mexico*, I, 54.) He was of course eager to impose upon and betray Polk.

mated that the recent revolution headed by Paredes met
Santa Anna's sanction, and that Santa Anna might soon be
in power again in Mexico. He said that Santa Anna was in
favor of a treaty with the United States, and that in adjusting a boundary between the two countries the Del Norte
should be the western Texas line, and the Colorado of the
West down through the Bay of San Francisco to the sea
should be the Mexican line on the north, and that Mexico
should cede all east and north of these natural boundaries
to the United States for a pecuniary consideration, and
mentioned thirty millions of dollars as the sum. This sum
he said Santa Anna believed would pay the most pressing
debts of Mexico, support the army until the condition of the
finances could be improved, and enable the government to
be placed on a permanent footing. Col. Atocha said that
Santa Anna was surprised that the United States naval
force had been withdrawn from Vera Cruz last fall, and
that General Taylor's army was kept at Corpus Christi
instead of being stationed on the Del Norte; and that the
United States would never be able to treat with Mexico,
without the presence of an imposing force by land and sea,
and this, Col. Atocha added was his own opinion. Col.
Atocha did not say that he was sent by Santa Anna to hold
this conversation with me, but I think it probable he was
so. . .

Mr. Buchanan called, and said, contrary to his rule, he
was urged by Mr. Flenniken of Uniontown, Pa., to see me
about an office. He read a letter to himself from Mr.
Flenniken. I told him I had been and was desirous to bestow some office on Mr. Flenniken, and was disposed to do
so as soon as an opportunity offered and I could do so with
propriety. I note the fact of Mr. Buchanan's call because
it is the first on the subject of office since the rejection by
the Senate of Mr. Woodward's nomination as Judge of the
Supreme Court of the United States. Since that time Mr.
Buchanan has never called except on official business, and

has been entirely formal in his intercourse with me. His manner indicates that he has been in a dissatisfied mood.

Gave a dinner party today to about forty persons. Among the guests were Mrs. General Alexander Hamilton, now in her eighty-eighth year, and George Washington Parke Custis,[10] who is the relative of Mrs. General Washington. . . Mrs. General Hamilton, upon whom I waited at table, is a very remarkable person. She retains her intellect and memory perfectly, and my conversation with her was highly interesting.

Monday, 16th February, 1846. — At precisely half-past two o'clock P.M. Col. Atocha called, when I gave him a further audience of more than an hour. He had a long conversation with me about the present condition of Mexico, and the relations of the United States with that government. . . He repeated that General Santa Anna was in favor of a treaty between Mexico and the United States by which the former should, for a pecuniary consideration, cede to the United States all the country east of the Del Norte and north of the Colorado of the West, and had named thirty millions of dollars as the sum that would be satisfactory. I then remarked that Mexico must satisfy the claims of American citizens, and that if the government of Mexico had any proposition to make, such as was suggested, it would be considered when made; to which Col. Atocha said no government or administration in Mexico dared to make such a proposition, for if they did so there would be another revolution by which they would be overthrown. He said they must appear to be forced to agree to such a proposition. He went on to give his own opinion and, as he said, that of General Santa Anna, that the United

[10] George Washington Parke Custis was a grandson of Mrs. George Washington, and was the builder of Arlington on the Potomac opposite Washington. Elizabeth Schuyler Hamilton, daughter of General Philip Schuyler, had married Alexander Hamilton in 1780, and outlived him by half a century, dying in 1854. Mrs. Hugh White's letters tell us that she went to Washington parties at the age of 88, and " dressed in the style of fifty years ago and looked comical enough."

States should take strong measures before any settlement could be effected. He said our army should be marched at once from Corpus Christi to the Del Norte, and a strong naval force assembled at Vera Cruz, that Mr. Slidell, the United States Minister, should withdraw from Jalappa, and go on board one of our ships of war at Vera Cruz, and in that position demand the payment of the amount due our citizens; that it was well known the Mexican Government was unable to pay in money, and that when they saw a strong force ready to strike on their coasts and border they would, he had no doubt, feel their danger and agree to the boundary suggested. He said that Paredes, Almonte, and General Santa Anna were all willing for such an arrangement, but that they dare not make it until it was made apparent to the Archbishop of Mexico and the people generally that it was necessary to save their country from the United States. He said the last words which General Santa Anna said to him when he was leaving Havana a month ago was, "when you see the President, tell him to take strong measures, and such a treaty can be made and I will sustain it." Col. Atocha said the government of Mexico was indebted to the Archbishop half a million of dollars, and he would be reconciled by an assurance by the Mexican Government that he would be paid, when the consideration should be paid by the United States. . . Col. Atocha is a person to whom I would not give my confidence. He is evidently a man of talents and education, but his whole manner and conversation impressed me with a belief that he was not reliable, and that he would betray any confidence reposed in him, when it was his interest to do so. I therefore heard all he said but communicated nothing to him.

Tuesday, 17th February, 1846.— Mr. Buchanan was manifestly in a bad mood, as he has been since Judge Woodward's nomination to the bench of the Supreme Court of the United States, and since he has discovered that he cannot control me in the dispensation of the public patronage. For several weeks past he has not been pleasant in his intercourse with me; has not heartily coöperated with me, but has been disposed to differ with me, as I think unnecessarily. He is, I am told, deeply mortified that I refused to appoint him judge of the Supreme Court of the United States, after Mr. Woodward's rejection by the Senate. I suspect he is seeking some public ground to break with my administration. . . I will be careful to give him no other ground of complaint.

Thursday, 19th February, 1846. — Saw company as usual until twelve o'clock today. Among others who called was the Rev. Mr. Dean, who had been many years a Christian missionary in China. He had with him a native Chinese man, who had been converted to the Christian religion. He spoke but little English. He was about twenty-three years of age, and appeared to be intelligent. On taking leave of him, and while shaking hands, he expressed in his own language, which was interpreted by Mr. Dean, that he had seen the King of this country, and said he would tell it to his countrymen when he got home. I told him through Mr. Dean there was no king in this country, but that he had seen a citizen who had been chosen by the people to manage the government for a limited time.

Saturday, 21st February, 1846. — About nine o'clock P.M. Mr. Buchanan sent to me a despatch received by this evening's mail from Mr. McLane, the United States Minister at London. The information communicated by Mr. McLane was not altogether of so pacific a character as the accounts given in the English newspapers had led me to believe.

Monday, 23d February, 1846. — At one o'clock Mr. Bancroft called in and a few minutes afterward Mr. Buchanan came in, the latter by appointment. Mr. McLane's despatch was carefully read over, and the question considered whether in view of the additional information communicated of the warlike preparations making by Great Britain, it would be proper for me to send a message to Congress recommending similar preparations on our part. After a free conversation on this point, all agreed it was proper to postpone any decision until the meeting of the Cabinet on tomorrow.

Tuesday, 24th February, 1846.—The Cabinet held a regular meeting today; all the members present. Mr. McLane's despatch of the 3d instant was read. Mr. Buchanan declared his opinion to be that an answer should be forwarded to Mr. McLane by the packet which will leave Boston on the first proximo, in substance to the following effect, *viz.*: That Mr. McLane be instructed to inform Lord Aberdeen in conversation that the door was not closed by anything which had heretofore occurred on the Oregon question against any further proposition of compromise which that government might wish to make; he proposed that Mr. McLane should be informed also that if the British Government made a proposition for the 49th parallel of latitude, reserving for a limited term of 7 or 10 years, as suggested by Mr. McLane in his despatch, the free navigation of the Columbia, and the occupation of their establishments for a like term of years, that such a proposition would be submitted by the President to the Senate in executive session for their previous advice. The proposition was discussed at length by the Cabinet. I called upon each member of the Cabinet individually for his advice before I expressed any opinion of my own. All of them except Mr. Johnson, the Postmaster-General, concurred with Mr. Buchanan that such a despatch should be forwarded to Mr. McLane. . . Mr. Buchanan finally remarked that he thought he could prepare a despatch which would harmonize the opinions of the Cabinet, and not be objected to by the Cabinet. It was agreed that he should prepare a draft of a despatch, and that the Cabinet would hold a special meeting to consider it at eight o'clock tomorrow night. . .

After night Mr. Senator Haywood called and informed me that there was a scheme on foot on the part of Mr. McDuffie, Mr. Calhoun, and perhaps other Senators to bring forward a resolution in executive session of the Senate advising the President to reopen the negotiation on the Oregon question, and settle it by compromise. He informed me that Col. Benton, to whom it had been made known, had declared to him (Mr. Haywood) that he would oppose it upon the ground that it would be taking the question out of the President's hands, and that those who moved in it wished to have the credit of settling it. Mr. Haywood told me that Mr. Calhoun and those who followed him would be willing to settle it upon any terms, even if all Great Britain demanded was yielded to her, whilst Mr. Senator Allen and others from the Northwest would be satisfied with nothing less than our extreme demand of 54° 40′, and he thought each of these sets of gentlemen had their ulterior or personal objects to accomplish, and were endeavoring to make political capital for themselves in the next Presidential election.[11]

Wednesday, 25th February, 1846. — Mr. Calhoun handed me a letter marked Private, from Mr. McDuffie, which I opened and read. In the letter he regrets that the state of the weather (there being a snowstorm) prevents him from calling on me this morning. It relates to the

---

[11] Polk in his annual message to Congress at the close of 1845 had stated that " all efforts at compromise having failed " in the Oregon question, it was for Congress to determine what course to pursue; but that he was in favor of giving notice of the termination of the joint occupancy, of building forts on the way to Oregon to protect our settlers, and of granting these settlers lands as soon as the joint occupation ended. The danger of war seemed great. The House on Feb. 10, 1846, passed resolutions directing the President to give notice terminating the joint occupation, but adding that they did not wish to interfere with negotiations. These and other resolutions came up in the Senate on Feb. 25, and the result was what Ritchie called a " Monster Debate." Calhoun opposed notice in any peremptory or offensive form, and wished it only as a step toward a compromise with Great Britain. In the end, much to the indignation of Northwestern expansionists, he triumphed. George McDuffie had been elected Senator from South Carolina in 1842, and was an ardent co-worker of Calhoun's.

present state of the Oregon question and his opinions on the subject. It is an important letter and I have placed it in my files.

Mr. Calhoun, as soon as I had read the letter, opened a conversation on the Oregon question. He said he thought it important that some action of a pacific character should go out to England by the steamer of the first *proximo,* and he asked my opinion of the policy of the Senate in executive session passing a resolution advising the President to re-open negotiations on the basis of the 49th degree of north latitude. He said Mr. McDuffie was very anxious to pre-sent such a resolution, and went on to advocate the policy of such a movement. I told him that there were many members of the Senate of more age and experience in public affairs than I possessed, and of course they would act upon their own views, but that as he had called on me for my opinion I must frankly say that I could not in the present state of the question advise such a course. For this opinion I assigned my reasons, and asked him if he knew that such a resolution as Mr. McDuffie proposed to offer would com-mand a vote of two thirds of the Senate, and pointed out to him the fatal consequences of bringing forward such a reso-lution if it should receive a smaller vote. I told him that though the proceeding proposed would be in executive ses-sion with closed doors, we all knew that it would be known in the streets and to the British Minister in less than twenty-four hours. . . Mr. Calhoun continued the conversation on the Oregon question, and intimated that I could, without national dishonor, repropose the 49° as the basis of com-promise. I told him I would not do so, and that if a further proposition was made it must come from the British Gov-ernment. The free navigation of the Columbia River was spoken of, and I repeated to him what I had said in my an-nual message, that I would not yield it.

Friday, 27th February, 1846. — Saw an unusually large number of visitors today. Many called to pay their respects, and many to annoy me about office. The pressure upon me for office has not in any degree abated. It is one of the most painful of my duties to hear these applications, and especially when I have no offices to bestow. There is at present an unusual number of office-seekers in the city, who are so patriotic as to desire to serve their country by getting into fat offices. The truth is I have become greatly disgusted with the passion for office, which seems to be increasing.

Saturday, 28th February, 1846. — The Cabinet held a regular meeting today; all the members present. Several public matters of minor importance were considered and disposed of. Our relations with Mexico were also the subject of conversation. The state of the Oregon question was the one of chief deliberation. Mr. Buchanan brought up for consideration the propriety of sending a message to Congress recommending as a precautionary measure that they should make provision for the public defence. I told him I inclined to the opinion that it should be done, and added that I would be pleased to have the opinion and advice of the Cabinet. No distinct vote was taken or opinion expressed, but enough was said to satisfy me that the members of the Cabinet were inclined to favor the suggestion, unless it was Mr. Bancroft and Mr. Mason, who appeared to doubt the policy of such a message. I remarked that the Secretary of War and Secretary of the Navy had with my concurrence made communications to the Military and Naval Committees of both houses of Congress asking additional appropriations to put the country in a better state of defence, and I had hoped that Congress would have done so in a quiet way, without alarming the country at home or attracting unnecessary attention abroad. I added that the state of our relations both with Mexico and England required that it should be done. It appeared, however, that it would not be done unless Congress were roused by a special message, and yet I saw if such a message were sent in to

Congress, it would be calculated to produce a panic in the country. . .

Being greatly exhausted by constant confinement and labour, I directed my porter to admit no more company tonight. There was a heavy snowstorm and it was a very inclement evening. I needed rest, and was rejoiced at the opportunity to be relieved from company.

Wednesday, 4th March, 1846. — I venture the remark in reference to the feverish excitement of members of the Senate on the question of notice [of termination of the joint occupation] on the Oregon question, that it all proceeds from the ambitious aspirations of certain leading members of that body. For example, Mr. Calhoun probably thought by opposing the notice at the early part of the session, that he would best advance his views upon the Presidency, by placing himself at the head of the peace party in the country. He now finds his mistake and is struggling to extricate himself from his embarrassment. By his influence he induced sixteen Democrats in Virginia and South Carolina in the House to vote against the Notice, and now that he is probably convinced of his mistake, and finds that he will not be sustained by either party in the country, he feels bound not to desert those friends in the House whom he has caused by their votes to commit the same mistake. Mr. Allen,[12] on the other hand, will hear to no compromise under any circumstances, and will probably prefer war to peace, because it might subserve his ambitious views. Mr. Cass takes the same view that Mr. Allen does, as probably his best chance of reaching the Presidency, and therefore he acts with Mr. Allen, but is not so ultra or ardent. Col. Benton feels that he lost caste with Democracy on the Texas question, and feels sore and dissatisfied with his position. In the midst of these factions of the Democratic party I am left without any certain or reliable support in Congress, and especially

[12] William Allen, a native of North Carolina, was a Senator from Ohio from 1837 to 1849.

in the Senate. Each leader looks to his own advancement more than he does to the success of my measures. I am fortunately no candidate for reëlection, and will appeal to the people for support. If the notice is defeated it will be by the war between these factions.

Thursday, 5th March, 1846. — Saw company as usual until twelve o'clock today. Among others Gov. Anderson of Maine called, and in the course of a long conversation expressed his conviction that the party would be so divided and distracted in 1848 that I would be compelled to stand again as a candidate for the Presidency, and that the Democracy would demand it of me. I told him that it was not to be thought of; that I desired to harmonize the party if possible, and carry out my measures, but that I was sincere in the declaration which I had often made that I would not be a candidate for re-election. . .

Mr. McKay, chairman of the Committee of Ways and Means, called by appointment. I had a long conversation with him about the tariff, and urged him in reporting a bill to the House to preserve the *ad valorem* principle. I had heard that the committee were about to introduce specific duties on iron and a few other articles; it was for that reason that I had requested an interview with him. He agreed to report the bill retaining the *ad valorem* principle.

Friday, 6th March, 1846. — Had company today as usual until twelve o'clock. Shortly after twelve o'clock Mr. McDuffie of South Carolina and Mr. Burt of South Carolina called, and as Mr. McDuffie walked with difficulty, I met them in the parlor below. . . The debate in the Senate on yesterday on the Oregon question was spoken of. Mr. McDuffie regretted it. I expressed myself as I had done to General Cass on last evening and to others on the subject, and repeated that no one in the Senate was authorized to speak for me any other opinions or sentiments than were contained in the message. I urged the importance of harmony in the Democratic party and of giving the notice.   Some further conversation took place on the Oregon question and the tariff.

Sunday, 8th March, 1846. — At three o'clock P.M. Senator Allen called according to the appointment made last night.   The subject of the debate in the Senate on Thursday last on the Oregon question was renewed by him.   He was still much excited towards Mr. Haywood and avowed his intention to vindicate his own honour and reputation in the floor of the Senate.   The whole matter was again talked over, as it was last night, in the conversation detailed in yesterday's diary, with himself and Mr. Hannegan and Mr. Atchison, I repeating to him that no one was authorized to speak by authority from me, except from the message and published documents.   Mr. Allen took from his hat a written paper which he had prepared, containing what he proposed to say in the Senate.   He read it, and as well as I can remember from hearing it a single time it was in substance that he was authorized to say that I had asserted the United States title to Oregon up to 54° 40', and that I had not changed my opinion, and had not authorized Mr. Haywood to express any other opinion.   He read it for the purpose of obtaining my assent to it.   I told him I could give no authority to him or anyone else to say anything in the Senate; that I had given no such authority to Mr. Haywood and I would give none such to him; that I did not wish to be involved in the matter and that what he said he must say on his own responsibility.   I told him that his statement as read embraced only a part of what I had said in the message, and that all I had said in that paper was necessary to a full understanding of my position and opinions.   I told him he could say what he pleased on his own responsibility, but not on mine or by my authority. . .

This whole excitement in the Senate has grown out of the aspirations of Senators and their friends for the Presidency. Mr. Allen has such aspirations himself.   Mr. Haywood probably prefers Gov. Wright of New York.   General

Cass has aspirations but is more prudent than some others. Mr. Calhoun has aspirations. My fear is that these factions looking to the election of my successor in 1848 will so divide and weaken the Democratic party by their feuds as to defeat my measures and render my administration unsuccessful and useless.

Wednesday, 11th March, 1846. — In the course of the morning Col. Benton called and introduced his brother-in-law, Gov. McDowell, of Virginia. . . He said he would support a treaty dividing the country on the 49th parallel of latitude, or some settlement which would make the 49° the basis. I told him in the present state of the matter I would make no proposition, but I would say to him confidentially that if the parallel of 49° was offered, or that parallel with perhaps a modification surrendering the Southern cape of Vancouver's Island to Great Britain, my present impression was that it would be my duty to submit it to the Senate for their previous advice before I acted on it. This he decidedly approved. I told him if Great Britain offered 49° and insisted on the perpetual free navigation of the Columbia River, I would reject it without submitting it to the Senate.

Friday, 20th March, 1846. — Saw company today until about eleven o'clock, when I learned from Mr. Heiss, one of the proprietors of the *Union,* that he had received by express the European news by the steamer which had just arrived. He handed to me *Welmer & Smith's European Times* of the 4th of March, 1846. I closed my office in a few minutes and read to the Attorney-General and Secretary of State the news contained in the paper. At two o'clock P.M. I gave Mr. Healy and Mr. Debousier another sitting for my portrait and miniature.

At eight o'clock received visitors informally in the parlour. Forty or fifty persons, ladies and gentlemen, called; among them the Russian Minister, the Secretary of State and the Secretary of the Navy, and several members of

Congress. These informal reception evenings twice a week (on Tuesdays and Fridays) are very pleasant, and afford me moreover an opportunity to devote the other evenings of the week to business.

Saturday, 21st March, 1846. — I saw at different times today and tonight Mr. Douglas[13] of Illinois, Mr. Tibbatts of Kentucky, Mr. Stanton, and Mr. Chase of Tennessee, and urged upon all of them the great importance of acting promptly upon the recommendations of my annual message in relation to Oregon. I called to their recollection that the Democratic party were in a decided majority in both houses of Congress, that nearly four months of the session had expired, that very little had been done, and that the Democratic party would be held responsible by the country for the delay, and for the failure by Congress to act upon these and the recommendations of the message on other subjects.

Sunday, 22d March, 1846. — Between seven and eight o'clock P.M. the members of the Cabinet came in, agreeably to the understanding on yesterday. The subject of the message to the Senate in answer to their resolution of the 17th instant, being that on which they had convened, was taken up. . . Mr. Buchanan seemed wholly to have changed the tone he had held during the whole of last year on the Oregon question. Up to within a recent period he had been most anxious to settle the dispute on the parallel of 49°, and had often declared that he would take the whole responsibility of such a settlement. Some of the discussions showing this fact are recorded in this diary, and will be remembered by the whole Cabinet. His dread of war and anxiety to avoid it by a compromise has been often expressed to me, in and out of the Cabinet. He recently mentioned to

[13] Stephen A. Douglas of Illinois served in the House of Representatives 1843–1847, and was elected a Senator in December, 1847, serving in the upper chamber until his death in 1861. It is to be noted that while Polk's *Diary,* like J. Q. Adams's, makes frequent mention of Douglas, neither contains a single reference to another Illinois Congressman 1847–1849 — Abraham Lincoln.

me that General Cass, he thought, was making political capital by insisting on our extreme rights on the question and by his course in favour of warlike preparations. Within a few days past it is pretty manifest to me that Mr. Buchanan has manifested a decided change of his position, and a disposition to be warlike. His object, I think, is to supersede General Cass before the country, and to this motive I attribute his change of tone and the warlike character of his draft of my proposed message. I think he is governed by his own views of his chances for the Presidency. It is a great misfortune that a member of the Cabinet should be an aspirant for the Presidency, because I cannot rely upon his honest and disinterested advice, and the instance before me is clear evidence of this.

Among other things which Mr. Buchanan and Mr. Walker (and the latter has probably Presidential aspirations) desired to have inserted in the message was an implied but strong censure of the Senate for not having passed the notice. This paragraph was opposed by Mr. Bancroft and Mr. Mason. I expressed myself against it as not within the scope of the call of the Senate, as unnecessary, and as bringing me in collision with the Senate. I agreed that the delay to pass the Notice was censurable, and had embarrassed the question, but thought it was not my duty or my province to lecture the Senate for it.

Wednesday, 25th March, 1846. — Saw a large number of visitors today. Among them was John Ross, and a delegation of Cherokees who called on the business of their tribe. I held a few minutes conversation with them, and received from them certain papers which they delivered to me relating to the existing difficulties among the Cherokees. In a short time after they retired, the Secretary of War and the Commissioner of Indian Affairs called and consulted me in reference to the Cherokee difficulties. The Commissioner informed me that he would have his report on the subject prepared and ready to submit to me in a few days.[14]. .

Four Englishmen who were of the Society of Friends called. They were intelligent men and informed me that they had just returned from a tour through Indiana and some other of the Western States and that they would soon return to England. They expressed their great desire that peace should be preserved between the United States and Great Britain. They said they spoke as Christians and not as Englishmen or partisans or politicians. They urged the great importance of suppressing the African slave trade, and one of them had commenced speaking on the subject of slavery as it existed in this country, but was interrupted by company coming in. I treated them courteously.

Saturday, 28th March, 1846. — The Cabinet held a regular meeting today; all the members present. After some unimportant matters of business were disposed of, I brought before the Cabinet the state of our relations with Mexico. Despatches received from Mr. Slidell rendered it probable that he would very soon be received by the existing government of Mexico in his character of Minister of the United States. I stated to the Cabinet that I apprehended that the greatest obstacle to the conclusion of a treaty of boundary, such as he had been instructed if practicable to procure, would be the want of authority to make a prompt payment of money at the time of signing it. The government of General Paredes, having recently overthrown that of President Herrera, was a military government and depended for its continuance in power upon the allegiance of the army under his command, and by which he had been enabled to

---

[14] John Ross, 1790–1866, a man of Scotch-Indian descent, was principal chief of the Cherokee tribe from 1828 to his death. He and the majority of the Cherokees asked in 1835 a payment of $20,000,000 from the United States for their lands in Georgia; a sub-chief, John Ridge, with a minority of the tribe behind him, made a treaty selling the lands for $5,000,000. The whole nation was removed to the west of the Mississippi, Ross and the last of the Cherokees departing in 1838. Despite Ross's moderate policy and statesmanlike qualities, factional troubles in the tribe continued.

effect the late revolution. It was known that the government of Paredes was in great need of money, and that in
consequence of the deficiencies in the treasury and the de-
ranged state of the finances, the army upon whose support
General Paredes depended to uphold him in power, being
badly fed and clothed and without pay, might and probably
would soon desert him, unless money could be obtained to
supply their wants. I stated that if our Minister could be
authorized upon the *signing* of the treaty to pay down a
half a million or a million of dollars, it would enable General Paredes to pay, feed, and clothe the army, and maintain
himself in power until the treaty could be ratified by the
United States and the subsequent instalments which might
be stipulated in the treaty be paid. Indeed, I thought that
the prompt payment of such a sum might induce him to
make a treaty, which he would not otherwise venture to
make. In these views there seemed to be a concurrence.
The question followed how an appropriation could be obtained from Congress without exposing to the public and
to foreign governments its object. That object, as may
be seen from Mr. Slidell's instructions, would be in adjusting a boundary to procure a cession of New Mexico and
California, and if possible all north of latitude 32 from the
Passo on the Del Norte and west to the Pacific Ocean; or if
that precise boundary cannot be obtained, then the next
best boundary which might be practicable so as at all events
to include all the country east of the Del Norte and the Bay
of San Francisco. For the boundary desired, see Mr.
Slidell's instructions. The Cabinet thought it important
that Mr. Slidell should have the command of the money
to make a prompt payment on the signature of the treaty.
Mr. Buchanan thought it impracticable to procure such an
appropriation from Congress, and was disinclined to favor
any effort to obtain it. I suggested that in informal consultations with leading Senators it could be ascertained
whether such an appropriation could pass that body, and

expressed the opinion that if it could pass the Senate, it
could be passed through the House of Representatives. I
called their attention to an act appropriating two millions
which had been passed in 1806 in Mr. Jefferson's Administration. I afterwards learned that this appropriation had
been passed to enable Mr. Jefferson to purchase the Floridas. Mr. Buchanan had still no confidence in the success
of such a movement; but finally agreed, as did all the other
members of the Cabinet, that I should consult Col. Benton,
Mr. Allen, General Cass, and if I chose, other Senators on
the subject. As soon as the Cabinet adjourned I sent my
private secretary to request Col. Benton to call on me at
eight o'clock this evening. At that hour Col. Benton called
and I explained to him fully my views and object. He at
once concurred with me in the importance of obtaining if
practicable such a boundary as I proposed, and in the propriety of such an appropriation by Congress to enable me
to do it. I suggested to him that it might be proper, if the
subject was brought forward in the Senate, that it should be
first considered in executive session of the Senate, and if it
was deemed proper by the Senate, it should be afterwards
moved in open session and passed without debate. In this
he also concurred. . .

I showed Col. Benton an endorsement made by General
Scott of the army on a letter from General Worth on the
subject of brevet rank and my order of the 12th instant.
Col. Benton thought as I did, that General Scott's endorsement on the letter was highly exceptionable and amounted
to insubordination. The letter and the endorsement made
on it by General Scott was laid by him before the Secretary
of War, and by the Secretary of War communicated to me.
Col. Benton said there was no use for the commander-in-
chief of the army at Washington, and he advised that he
should be forthwith ordered to some post on the northern
frontier, as a merited rebuke to his resistance to my order
of the 12th instant, and other exceptionable matter in his

endorsement on General Worth's letter. This he thought would be the mildest punishment which should be inflicted.

Sunday, 29th March, 1846. — At six o'clock this evening General Samuel Houston, late President of Texas and now a Senator in Congress, called. I was much pleased to see him, having been with him in Congress twenty years ago and always his friend. I found him thoroughly Democratic and fully determined to support my administration.

At eight o'clock Mr. Senator Allen called and I consulted him fully in relation to our Mexican policy, and especially in reference to the adjustment of a boundary. I explained to him my views fully, as I had done to Col. Benton on last evening (see diary of yesterday). He fully concurred with Col. Benton and myself. He entered fully into the importance of procuring from Congress the appropriation suggested of one or two millions, to be placed at my disposal for the purpose of enabling Mr. Slidell to negotiate such a treaty if it was practicable.

Monday, 30th March, 1846. — Saw company until twelve o'clock today as usual. Among others I saw and had a free conversation with General Cass on the subject of our relations with Mexico, in substance of the same import with the conversation I had held with Col. Benton on Saturday and Mr. Allen on yesterday. He fully concurred with me and with them on the importance of procuring an appropriation from Congress. . .

. . . At seven o'clock . . . Mr. Calhoun called, and I explained to him as I had done to Col. Benton, Mr. Allen, and General Cass the object which I had in view, and asked his confidential opinion on the subject. He concurred with me in the great importance of procuring by a treaty with Mexico such a boundary as would include California. . . I pointed him to the precedents in 1803 and 1806, and asked his advice on the subject. He said with the utmost care to prevent it the object of the appropriation would become public, and he apprehended it would embarrass the settlement of the Oregon question. Much conversation on the subject occurred, the result of which was that he did not yield his assent to the movement to procure the appropriation from Congress, but said he would reflect upon the subject and turn it over in his mind. He said if I had no objection he would consult with Mr. McDuffie confidentially on the subject. I told him I had no objection to his doing so. Mr. Calhoun several times in the course of the consultation turned the conversation on the Oregon question, and was much disposed to dwell on that subject. He insisted that the two governments ought to settle it, and that they could do it on the basis of 49°. He said that a question of etiquette ought not to prevent either from reopening the negotiations by a new proposition. I told him I could make no proposition.

Wednesday, 1st April, 1846. — Mrs. Polk and myself paid a visit this evening at seven o'clock to Mr. Johnson, the Postmaster-General, and sat an hour with the family. It is the first visit of the kind which I have made since I have been President, except to call on Mrs. Madison and on Mr. Attorney-General Mason when he was sick last summer, and to dine with Mr. Bancroft the past winter. My time has been wholly occupied in my office, in the discharge of my public duties. My confinement to my office has been constant and unceasing, and my labours very great.

Tuesday, 7th April, 1846. — The Cabinet held a regular meeting today; all the members present except the Secretary of State, who is still absent on a visit to his residence in Pennsylvania. A despatch was received by last night's mail from our consul at Vera Cruz, which renders it probable that Mr. Slidell, our Minister to Mexico, will not be received by that government and will return to the United States. The despatch was read, and I stated that in the event Mr. Slidell was not accredited, and returned to the United States my opinion was that I should make a communication to Congress recommending that legislative measures be adopted, to take the remedy for the injuries and wrongs we had suffered into our own hands. In this there seemed to be a concurrence on the part of the Cabinet, no one dissenting. Several other subjects of minor importance were considered and disposed of. . .

This being reception evening between fifty and one hundred persons, ladies and gentlemen, called. These informal reception evenings are very pleasant. Members of Congress, strangers, and others call without ceremony and without invitation, and retire when they are disposed to do so. By setting apart two evenings in the week (Tuesdays and Fridays), I can devote the balance of the evenings of the week to business in my office.

Received despatches from Mr. Slidell, United States Minister to Mexico, tonight, announcing that the Mexican authorities had refused to receive him and that he had demanded his passports.[15]

Thursday, 9th April, 1846. — At eight P.M. Col. Benton called according to his appointment. . . We had a full

[15] The refusal of Mexico to receive Slidell meant, as Polk's ominous statement on the subject under the date of April 7 indicates, that war was probably near. While Slidell waited at Jalapa, the Mexican Minister of Foreign Relations told him that the annexation of Texas had always been regarded by Mexico as a *casus belli,* that it was still so regarded, and that he could not be accepted as an envoy. Mexico, it was added, had agreed to receive an American commissioner, but instead the United States had sent a Minister Plenipotentiary, who was expected to take up his residence. The Mexican Government warned Slidell that if the United States continued in its present course, Mexico would " call upon all her citizens to fulfill the sacred duty of defending their country." Of course Slidell at once asked for his passports and set out on his return. " The appeal to reason had failed, and now there remained only the appeal to arms." (G. P. Garrison, *Westward Expansion,* 225.) Mexico should have received Slidell and treated with him. It would have done so but that the new Paredes government was insecure in its tenure, dependent upon an excited popular feeling, and fearful that it would be thrown out of power if it consented to negotiate.

Slidell reported to the United States that this might be the chief reason for the refusal of Mexico to negotiate. He also reported that the chief reason might be that Mexico relied upon foreign intervention. The American consul in Mexico City wrote that Paredes was paying confidential visits to the British Minister; and this explains Polk's references below to the possibility the British were playing a sinister part.

conversation in reference to our relations with Mexico, and
the steps proper to be taken, and especially if the principal
powers of Europe should attempt to force a foreign prince
on a throne in Mexico. In the course of the conversation
Col. Benton remarked that his opinion was that our ablest
men should be Ministers to the South American states; that
we should cultivate their friendship and stand with them
as the crowned heads of Europe stood together. He considered the missions to Europe less important than those
to South America, and incidentally he stated a fact of which
I had never heard before. It was that General Jackson
had offered him the first mission to Europe, which he had
declined. He did not mention to which of the courts he had
been offered the mission.

Col. Benton spoke throughout in the most friendly terms,
and the interview was a pleasant one. I told him as he was
about to leave that I would send for him when I next heard
from Mexico.

Saturday, 18th April, 1846. — Mr. Calhoun called.
After speaking to me about some appointments and among
others of his son, who is in the army and whom he desired
to have promoted in the new regiment about to be authorized by Congress, he inquired about the state of our relations with Mexico. I told him that Mr. Slidell had, on
being rejected as Minister of the United States, returned,
and that our relations with Mexico had reached a point
where we could not stand still but must assert our rights
firmly; that we must treat all nations whether weak or
strong alike, and that I saw no alternative but strong
measures towards Mexico. Mr. Calhoun deprecated war
and expressed a hope that the Oregon question would be
first settled, and then we would have no difficulty in adjusting our difficulties with Mexico. He thought the British
Government desired to prevent a war between the United
States and Mexico, and would exert its influence to prevent
it. I told him I had reason to believe that the British Min-

ister in Mexico had exerted his influence to prevent Mr.
Slidell from being received by the Mexican Government.
He said the British Government desired to prevent a war,
but did not desire a settlement between the United States
and Mexico until the Oregon question was settled. He then
expressed an earnest desire to have the Oregon question
settled. I told him that as long as Congress hesitated and
refused to give the notice he need not expect a settlement of
the Oregon question; that until Congress authorized the
notice Great Britain would calculate largely on our divisions, and would make no proposition. I expressed the
opinion also that if Congress had given the notice in the
early part of the session and had shown that we were united
and firm, I thought it probable the question would have
been settled before this time.

Tuesday, 21st April, 1846. — I learned tonight that the
Senate by the votes of Mr. Calhoun and his wing of the
Democratic party united with the whole Whig party had
rejected the nomination of Dr. Amos Nourse as collector at
Bath in Maine. This is, in addition to other evidence, a
pretty clear indication that Mr. Calhoun intends to oppose
my administration. He has embarrassed the administration on the Oregon question. He is playing a game to make
himself President, and his motives of action are wholly
selfish. I will observe his future course and treat him
accordingly.

Wednesday, 22d April, 1846. — Saw company until
eleven o'clock today; at which hour the English mail which
left Liverpool on the 4th instant was brought in. I closed
my doors and shortly afterwards the Secretary of State
called. A despatch received from Mr. McLane was read.
He communicated his opinion that no step would be taken
by the British Government on the Oregon question until the
decision of the Senate on the question of notice was known.
The long delay in the Senate and our divided councils in Congress have added greatly to the embarrassments of the ques-

tion. Had the notice been authorized in December the question would either have been settled or it would have been ascertained that it cannot be settled before this time. The speeches of Mr. Webster, Mr. Calhoun, and others in the Senate advocating peace and the British title to a large portion of the country, have made the British Government and people more arrogant in their tone and more grasping in their demands. If war should be the result, these peace gentlemen and advocates of British pretensions over those of their own country will have done more to produce it than any others.

The truth is that in all this Oregon discussion in the Senate, too many Democratic Senators have been more concerned about the Presidential election in '48 than they have been about settling Oregon either at 49° or 54° 40′. "Forty-eight" has been with them the great question, and hence the divisions in the Democratic party.[16] I cannot but observe the fact, and for the sake of the country I deeply deplore it. I will however do my duty whatever may happen. I will rise above the interested factions in Congress and appeal confidently to the people for support.

Thursday, 23rd April, 1846. — Mr. Buchanan called about two o'clock on business; and shortly afterward Mr. Walker, the Secretary of the Treasury, came in. Montgomery Blair and Martin Van Buren, Jr. sent up their cards

[16] This is one of the rare glints of humor in Polk's Diary. But he fails to do justice to Webster and other "peace gentlemen," many of whom were thoroughly patriotic in their policy. To Webster, indeed, belongs much of the credit for the preservation of peace. He made a speech in Faneuil Hall speaking of the necessity of peace, and the fairness of an adjustment on the 49th parallel. In a letter to a friend in Glasgow he suggested that the British Government would do well to accept this boundary, and this letter was shown to Lord Aberdeen. Meanwhile in the Senate he opposed a brusque notice of termination of the joint occupation. There is no evidence that Webster's and Calhoun's speeches made the British Government "more arrogant." The hotheads, like Senator Hannegan of Indiana, who charged the South with being indifferent to Oregon now that they had Texas, and who said that if Polk was willing to take the 49th parallel, then "James K. Polk has spoken words of falsehood, and with the tongue of a serpent," would have precipitated war between the two countries.

and I directed them to be shown in. The Secretary of the Treasury had been to the Capitol and stated the fact that the committee of conference between the two houses on the disagreeing votes on the question of notice on the Oregon question had reported an agreement which had been concurred in by both Houses by large majorities, there being but 10 dissenting votes in the Senate and 46 in the House. I would have preferred a naked notice without a preamble, and think it unfortunate that such a notice had not been authorized early in the session of Congress. After all, however, Congress by authorizing the notice have sustained the first great measure of my administration, though not in a form that is altogether satisfactory or one that was preferred.[17]

Friday, 24th April, 1846.—Saw company today until twelve o'clock. Shortly after that hour Senator McDuffie of South Carolina called. I met him in the parlour below stairs, the decrepit state of his health being such as to make it inconvenient for him to ascend the stairs and see me in my office. His object was, as he said, to express to me his own opinion freely on the Oregon question, without asking me to declare what course I intended to take. He proceeded to say that in his opinion it would be wise for me when I gave the Notice to accompany it with a renewal of the American offer of 49° made last summer. He thought this would manifest our desire to settle the controversy and to preserve the peace, and that there was no point of honor as the question now stood to prevent me from doing so. After expressing his opinion fully upon these points, I told him I would give the notice as I was authorized to do by the joint resolution of Congress, but that I would not accompany it with any offer on our part. . . I then stated to him

[17] The vote on the question of notice was 42 to 10 in the Senate, 142 to 46 in the House. But it was a much softened form of notice; and the debate had lasted so long that when Polk sent it to the British Government, Peel and Aberdeen had already taken the steps which were to bring an immediate settlement along the line indicated by Webster, Benton, and Calhoun.

confidentially that if Great Britain made an offer of 49°
or what was equivalent to it, or with slight modifications, I
would feel it to be my duty to submit such proposition to
the Senate for their previous advice before I took any action
on it. With this course he appeared to be satisfied.

. . At five o'clock the Attorney-General called with his
carriage and I took a ride with him and Major A. J. Donelson, United States Minister to Prussia, across the Potomac
to see the fishermen drawing the seine. On our return I
spent half an hour at Judge Mason's residence. . .

The Postmaster-General called on me early this morning
and expressed apprehensions that the article in last evening's
Union on the question of the passing of the notice resolutions in Congress would give dissatisfaction to some of the
Democratic members. I told him I had known nothing of
the article until it had appeared in the paper, and upon a
casual reading of it this morning there were portions of it
which I did not approve. Mr. Ritchie called afterwards
and I told him the article I thought was exceptionable. He
was much concerned about it and said it had been prepared
in hurry and confusion at a late hour of the night. Mr. Buchanan afterwards called and informed me that there was
extensive dissatisfaction among some of the Democratic
members of Congress whom he had seen. Mr. Buchanan
said if Blair could be associated with Ritchie in conducting
the paper it would be a strong paper; and that Blair would
whip in Democrats from Congress, who were disposed to
fly off from their party and join the Whigs. I told him that
such an arrangement would never do, for that neither
Ritchie nor Blair would be willing to yield the conduct of the
paper to the other. I told him also that I had no doubt, if
such a suggestion was made to Mr. Ritchie, that he would
instantly retire from the paper, under the impression that
his management of it was not satisfactory to the administration. I told him Mr. Ritchie meant well, but might occasionally make mistakes, but he was always ready to correct

them when informed of them.   I had on yesterday spoken to Mr. Buchanan to prepare a proper article, on the passage of the notice resolutions, and the proceedings in Congress in relation to them. . Mr. Buchanan now informed me that he had early this morning written part of an article, but that before he finished it the *Union* was brought to him and he was so much dissatisfied with it that he had written no more. I expressed my regret that he had not finished it.   He told me also that he had an article in his pocket written by Judge Shields, which at my request he read.   It was very severe upon Mr. Calhoun and the minority of Democratic Senators who had united with the Whigs and defeated the House resolutions of notice.   I told Mr. Buchanan that though I disapproved the course of Mr. Calhoun and the minority of Democrats who had acted with him, I could not approve the article because I thought it too denunciatory and severe.   Mr. Buchanan on reflection concurred with me that it was so, and ought not to be published.   At my request Mr. Buchanan walked to his office and brought his own unfinished article which he read.   It, too, was harsh and severe upon Mr. Calhoun and the minority who had acted with him.   Mr. Buchanan said he had written it under strong feelings of disapprobation of their course, but on reading it over it would not do and immediately tore it up and threw it into the fire.   I then read the commencement of an explanatory article of that in yesterday's *Union,* which I had hastily sketched during the few minutes Mr. Buchanan had been absent.   Mr. Buchanan approved it and requested me to finish it.   I told him I would do so, and requested him to call at six o'clock.   I finished the article and gave it to Col. Walker, who copied it.   Mr. Ritchie called at dark and talked over the matter, and I gave him the article copied by Col. Walker to make out of it what he pleased.   It is the second or third time since I have been President that I have sketched an article for the paper.   I did so in this instance to allay if possible the excitement which I learned the article

in yesterday's *Union* had produced among the Democratic
members.[18]

[18] The factional dissension in Congress had aroused great bitterness, and
as the attack on the *Union* editorial showed, both sides were ready to find
fault with Polk. The Whig leader John J. Crittenden had written to a
friend on March 9 regarding the situation. "Bitter dissensions are already
manifested among our opponents; they are about equally divided in the Senate.
They quarrel about what the President's sentiments and purposes are in relation to Oregon — each interprets the 'oracle' to suit himself, and each pre-
tends to speak for him, while all are suspicious and jealous of him and of
each other. They know that one side or the other is cheated and to be
cheated, but they can't yet exactly tell which. In the mean time they curse
Polk hypothetically. If he don't settle and make peace at forty-nine or some
other parallel of compromise, the one side curses him; and if he yields an inch
or stops a hair's breadth short of fifty-four degrees forty minutes, the other
side damns him without redemption. Was ever a gentleman in such a fix?"
(Coleman, *Life of John J. Crittenden,* 235). To conduct an administration
newspaper in such times was no easy matter.

CHAPTER III
April 25, 1846 – June 30, 1846

RITCHIE AND THE UNION — THE WAR MESSAGE — HOSTILITIES BEGIN WITH MEXICO — THE WAR AIMS — REASSURING MEXICAN CATHOLICS — THE MANUFACTURERS' FAIR — DIFFICULTIES WITH GENERAL SCOTT — A BRITISH PROPOSAL ON OREGON

Saturday, 25th April, 1846. — Mr. Allen spoke strongly against Mr. Ritchie's course in conducting the *Union,* and said the Democratic party were broken up unless there was a new editor of that paper, and went so far as to say that Mr. Ritchie could not now get five votes for public printer out of the Calhoun faction in either house of Congress. . . He said he ought, if he remained at the head of the paper, to have some bold and strong man associated with him, and suggested Francis P. Blair as the man, as Mr. Buchanan had done yesterday. I told him Mr. Blair would not do; that in addition to public reasons which existed for making it, there were reasons of a personal character which made the change proper when Mr. Ritchie succeeded Blair last year. These reasons were in substance that Mr. Blair's course as editor of the *Globe* for several years had indicated anything rather than personal or political friendship for me. . . I reminded Mr. Allen that when I was defeated for Governor of Tennessee in 1843, the *Globe* coolly laid me on the shelf by stating that when I redeemed my own State the Democratic party would remember me, and this, too, after I had fought three hard battles in Tennessee in sustaining Mr. Van Buren and our principles; and again, in January, 1844, the *Globe* had published a violent article disparaging my claims to the Vice Presidency; I stated to him other facts which satisfied me that Mr. Blair was no friend to my advancement, and I had reason to believe that he would not have given a hearty support to my administration if he had continued to edit the *Globe*.

Thursday, 30th April, 1846. — The principal instructor of an institution in New York for the instruction of the blind, accompanied by his assistant instructors and between 20 and 30 blind pupils, male and female, called on me at half past one o'clock P.M. I received them in the circular parlour, and witnessed an exhibition of the blind in literature. They read from the Bible printed in raised letters with facility. In arithmetic some of them were well educated. They conversed intelligently. The most remarkable person among them was a female named Bridgman who had been taught by signs with the hands and fingers to understand and communicate ideas and to write.[1] She was about 16 years old and was deaf and dumb as well as blind. Altogether it was an interesting exhibition, and impressed me sensibly with the benevolence and great value of the discovery by which these unfortunate persons could be taught to understand and communicate their thoughts.

Sunday, 3rd May, 1846. — Col. Benton called this evening at eight o'clock, having been requested to do so, at my instance, by my private secretary. I consulted him about the measures proper to be taken in relation to Mexico in the present state of our relations with that country, stating to

---

[1] Laura Bridgman, 1829–1889, was already so famous that Polk's impersonal reference to her seems remarkable. The efforts of Dr. S. G. Howe had brought her — the deaf-mute daughter of a New Hampshire farmer — into the Perkins Institution for the Blind at Boston in 1837. After four years' instruction, in 1841 she began to keep a journal to record her daily work and ideas. Dickens, visiting the Institution in 1842, wrote enthusiastically of Dr. Howe's work with her. In 1843 a special teacher was provided for Miss Bridgman, who by this time was learning geography and astronomy. It is probable that it was a delegation from the Boston school, and not a New York school, which called on Polk.

him that I could not permit Congress to adjourn without making a communication to them on the subject. After stating to him the precise state of the existing relations between the two countries, I asked his views. He said he had not made up his mind, that it was a difficult question to decide, but advised delay until the English question concerning Oregon was either settled or had been brought to a crisis, one of which must happen very soon. He expressed a very decided aversion to a war with Mexico if it could be avoided consistently with the honour of the country. I told him we had ample cause of war, but that I was anxious to avoid it if it could be done honourably and consistently with the interests of our injured citizens. I told him I would delay at all events until the arrival of Mr. Slidell, who was expected daily, but that I could not permit Congress to adjourn without bringing the subject before that body.

In reference to the Oregon question I told him that the notice had been sent to England by the steamer of the 1st instant. I repeated to him my purpose, if a proposition of the 49° or substantially that line, was made by Great Britain, I would ask the previous advice of the Senate. I repeated to him also that I could never concede the perpetual navigation of the Columbia River. He thought the downward navigation might be conceded, in which I differed with him.

Wednesday, 6th May, 1846. — After night despatches were received from the army under the command of General Taylor on the Del Norte as late as the 15th ult. Newspaper accounts were also received as late as the 19th ult. No actual collision had taken place, though the probabilities are that hostilities might take place soon. Vice-President Dallas, the Secretary of War, Mr. Cass, and Mr. Buchanan called in the course of the evening, and the Mexican question and the condition of our army were the chief subjects of conversation.

Friday, 8th May, 1846. — Saw company until twelve

o'clock today. Among others the Hon. John Slidell, late United States Minister to Mexico, called in company with the Secretary of State. Mr. Buchanan retired after a few minutes, and Mr. Slidell remained about an hour in conversation concerning his mission and the state of our relations with Mexico. Mr. Slidell's opinion was that but one course towards Mexico was left to the United States, and that was to take the redress of the wrongs and injuries which we had so long borne from Mexico into our own hands, and to act with promptness and energy. In this I agreed with him, and told him it was only a matter of time when I would make a communication to Congress on the subject, and that I had made up my mind to do so very soon.

Saturday, 9th May, 1846. — The Cabinet held a regular meeting today; all the members present. I brought up the Mexican question, and the question of what was the duty of the administration in the present state of our relations with that country. The subject was very fully discussed. All agreed that if the Mexican forces at Matamoras committed any act of hostility on General Taylor's forces I should immediately send a message to Congress recommending an immediate declaration of war. I stated to the Cabinet that up to this time, as we knew, we had heard of no open act of aggression by the Mexican army, but that the danger was imminent that such acts would be committed. I said that in my opinion we had ample cause of war, and that it was impossible that we could stand in *statu quo,* or that I could remain silent much longer; that I thought it was my duty to send a message to Congress very soon and recommend definite measures. I told them that I thought I ought to make such a message by Tuesday next, that the country was excited and impatient on the subject, and if I failed to do so I would not be doing my duty.[2] I

[2] The rejection of Slidell had been greeted by a great part of the American public and press as evidence that forbearance with Mexico was bootless and that drastic action was required. "The indignity to our Minister requires atonement," said the New Orleans *Picayune;* the St. Louis *Republican* declared

then propounded the distinct question to the Cabinet, and took their opinions individually, whether I should make a message to Congress on Tuesday, and whether in that message I should recommend a declaration of war against Mexico. All except the Secretary of the Navy gave their advice in the affirmative. Mr. Bancroft dissented but said if any act of hostility should be committed by the Mexican forces he was then in favour of immediate war. Mr. Buchanan said he would feel better satisfied in his course if the Mexican forces had or should commit any act of hostility, but that as matters stood we had ample cause of war against Mexico, and he gave his assent to the measure. It was agreed that the message should be prepared and submitted to the Cabinet in their meeting on Tuesday. A history of our causes of complaint against Mexico had been at my request previously drawn up by Mr. Buchanan. I stated that what was said in my annual message in December gave that history as succinctly and satisfactorily as Mr. Buchanan's statement, that in truth it was the same history in both, expressed in different language, and that if I repeated that history in a message to Congress now I had better employ the precise language used in my message of December last. Without deciding this point the Cabinet passed to the consideration of some other subjects of minor importance. . .

About six o'clock P.M. General R. Jones, the Adjutant-General of the army, called and handed to me despatches

---

that the United States owed it to her character and dignity " not to suffer so open an insult to her representative to pass unnoticed." The American people outside the Northeastern States felt that a long series of grievances demanded redress. They included insults to our flag, threats to our consuls, imprisonment of our citizens, confiscation of American property, the flouting of just claims, and injuries to our trade. Moreover, many Americans felt that it was dangerous to permit the situation to drift, lest Great Britain, France, and Spain take some action in Mexico to the detriment of American policy. The revolution under Paredes, who overthrew Herrera at the end of 1845, was known to have a definitely anti-American character. Under the circumstances American public opinion, as Polk intimates, was on the whole ready for determined steps.

received from General Taylor by the Southern mail which
had just arrived, giving information that a part of the Mexican army had crossed the Del Norte and attacked and
killed and captured two companies of dragoons of General
Taylor's army consisting of 63 officers and men. The
despatch also stated that he had on that day (26th April)
made a requisition on the Governors of Texas and Louisiana
for four regiments each, to be sent to his relief at the earliest
practicable period.[3] Before I had finished reading the
despatch, the Secretary of War called. I immediately summoned the Cabinet to meet at half past seven o'clock this
evening. The Cabinet accordingly assembled at that hour;
all the members present. The subject of the despatch received this evening from General Taylor, as well as the
state of our relations with Mexico, were fully considered.
The Cabinet were unanimously of opinion, and it was
so agreed, that a message should be sent to Congress on
Monday laying all the information in my possession
before them and recommending vigorous and prompt
measures to enable the executive to prosecute the war.
The Secretary of War and Secretary of State agreed
to put their clerks to work to copy the correspondence
between Mr. Slidell and the Mexican Government and
Secretary of State and the correspondence between the
War Department and General Taylor, to the end that
these documents should be transmitted to Congress
with my message on Monday. The other members of

[3] Zachary Taylor, who had about 3900 troops in Texas, had advanced to
near Matamoras in March, 1846, where he began to construct works that
were later known as Fort Brown. The Mexican forces on the other side of the
Rio Grande were under instructions to attack the Americans. They crossed
the river above Matamoras, surrounded a reconnoitring party of sixty American dragoons, killed and wounded several, and compelled the rest to surrender. " Hostilities may now be considered as commenced," reported Taylor
on April 26, and made a requisition on Texas and Louisiana for 5,000 men.
Polk had not expected or wished the war to begin in this way. He was planning to lay the grievances of the United States before Congress, and apparently did not believe that the Mexicans would so resent Taylor's advance a•
to strike at his army.

the Cabinet tendered the services of their clerks to aid in preparing these copies.

Mr. Senator Houston, Hon. Barclay Martin, and several other members of Congress called in the course of the evening, and were greatly excited at the news brought by the Southern mail from the army. They all approved the steps which had been taken by the administration, and were all of opinion that war with Mexico should now be prosecuted with vigor.

The Cabinet adjourned about ten o'clock and I commenced my message; Mr. Bancroft and Mr. Buchanan, the latter of whom had prepared a history of our causes of complaint against Mexico, agreed to assist me in preparing the message.

Sunday, 10th May, 1846.—As the public excitement in and out of Congress was very naturally very great, and as there was a great public necessity to have the prompt action of Congress on the Mexican question, and therefore an absolute necessity for sending my message to Congress on tomorrow, I resumed this morning the preparation of my message. About half past nine o'clock Mr. Bancroft called, and with his assistance I was engaged in preparing it until eleven o'clock, at which time I suspended my labours in order to attend church. I left the part of the message which had been written to be copied by my private secretary, and accompanied Mrs. Polk, my niece, Miss Rucker, and my nephew, Marshall T. Polk, to church. . . On my return from church about one o'clock P.M. I resumed the preparation of my message. In the course of half an hour Mr. Bancroft and Mr. Buchanan called and the part of the message which had been written was examined and approved. At two o'clock my family dinner was announced. I invited Mr. Buchanan and Mr. Bancroft to dine with me. Mr. Buchanan declined and Mr. Bancroft dined with me. After dinner Mr. Bancroft and myself returned to the preparation of the message. Two confidential clerks . . . were engaged in assisting my private secretary in making two copies of my message, one for the Senate and one for the House.

At five o'clock Mr. Haralson and Mr. Baker called according to the appointment made this morning. They informed me that deeming the present a great emergency they had called the committee on military affairs of the House of Representatives together this morning and that they had unanimously agreed to support a bill appropriating ten millions of dollars, and authorizing the President to raise fifty thousand men to prosecute the war with Mexico. They showed me a copy of the bill which they proposed to pass. I pointed out some defects in it and advised them to consult with the Secretary and officers connected with the War Department, including General Scott and Adjutant-General Jones. They said they would do so. I discovered in the course of the conversation that both Mr. Haralson and Mr. Baker desired to be appointed to high commands in the army of volunteers which their bill proposed to raise. I talked civilly to them but made no promises.

After night and whilst the clerks were still copying my message in my private secretary's office, the Secretaries of State, of the Treasury, of the Navy, the Postmaster-General, and the Attorney-General called, but were not all present at any one time. The Secretary of War was indisposed, as I learned, and did not call during the day. Senator Houston and Barclay Martin and Ch. J. Ingersoll called to consult me on the Mexican question, and to learn what I intended to recommend in my message. The two former had retired before Mr. Ingersoll called. I addressed notes to Senator Allen, chairman of the Committee of Foreign Affairs of the Senate, and Mr. McKay of North Carolina, chairman of the Committee of Ways and Means of the House of Representatives, requesting them to call at my office tonight. In the course of half an hour they called, and the message being copied, I read it to them and Mr.

Ingersoll in presence of some of the members of the Cabinet who had remained. They all approved it.

At half past ten o'clock the company left and I retired to rest. It was a day of great anxiety to me, and I regretted the necessity which had existed to make it necessary for me to spend the Sabbath in the manner I have.

Monday, 11th May, 1846. — I refused to see company generally this morning. I carefully revised my message on the Mexican question, but had no time to read the copies of the correspondence furnished by the War and State Departments which was to accompany it. I had read the original correspondence and presume the copies are correct.

I addressed notes to Senators Cass and Benton this morning requesting them to call. General Cass called first. The message was read to him and he highly approved it. Col. Benton called before General Cass left, and I gave him the copy of the message and he retired to an adjoining room and read it. After he had read it I had a conversation with him alone. I found he did not approve it in all its parts. He was willing to vote men and money for defence of our territory, but was not prepared to make aggressive war on Mexico. He disapproved the marching of the army from Corpus Christi to the left bank of the Del Norte, but said he had never said so to the public. I had a full conversation with him, and he left without satisfying me that I could rely upon his support of the measures recommended by the message, further than the mere defence of our territory. I inferred, too, from his conversation that he did not think the territory of the United States extended west of the Nueces River.

At twelve o'clock I sent my message to Congress. It was a day of great anxiety with me. Between five and six o'clock P.M. Mr. Slidell, United States Minister to Mexico, called and informed me that the House of Representatives had passed a bill carrying out all the recommendations of the message by a vote of 173 ayes to 14 noes, and that the Senate had adjourned after a debate without coming to any decision.[4]

My private secretary brought me a note from Col. Benton desiring information as to the number of men and amount of money required to defend the country. There was nothing in his note to commit him to any course of policy beyond what he had intimated in his conversation this morning. My private secretary informed me that Col. Benton would call for an answer at eight o'clock this evening. I immediately sent his note to the Secretary of War and requested him to call at that hour. The Secretaries of War and State called a few minutes before eight o'clock but before I had consulted the former in relation to Col. Benton's note, Col. Benton came in. I told Col. Benton that the Secretary of War had just come in and that I had no opportunity to consult him on the subject of his note. I told him that my own opinion was that it was at present impossible to say what number of troops would be wanted, and that until Congress acted I could not tell what authority would be given to the executive; but that if the bill which had passed the House today should also pass the Senate, no more men would be called out and no more money expended than would be absolutely necessary to bring the present state of hostilities to an end. I told him if the war was recognized by Congress, that with a large force on land and sea I thought it could be speedily terminated. Col. Benton said that the House of Representatives had passed a bill today declaring war in two hours, and that one and a half hours of that time had been occupied in reading the documents which accompanied my message, and that in his

[4] Polk's "war message" sent to Congress this day declared that "after repeated menaces, Mexico has passed the boundary of the United States, has invaded our territory, and shed American blood upon the American soil." He asserted that as war "exists by the act of Mexico herself," the United States was called upon to vindicate its honor and rights, and he recommended prompt and energetic measures for bringing the conflict to a triumphant conclusion. The House at once passed a bill authorizing the Executive to raise a military force not to exceed 50,000, and to take other military and naval steps.

opinion in the nineteenth century war should not be declared without full discussion and much more consideration than had been given to it in the House of Representatives. Mr. Buchanan then remarked that war already existed by the act of Mexico herself and therefore it did not require much deliberation to satisfy all that we ought promptly and vigorously to meet it. Mr. Marcy and Mr. Buchanan discussed the subject for some time with Mr. Benton, but without any change of the opinions which he had expressed to me in conversation this morning. I saw it was useless to debate the subject further with him and therefore I abstained from engaging further in the conversation. After remaining near an hour Col. Benton left. Mr. Buchanan, Mr. Marcy, and myself were perfectly satisfied that he would oppose the bill which had passed the House today, and that if the Whigs on party grounds acted with him the bill might be defeated.

Gov. Yell of Arkansas, Senator Houston, and other members of Congress called in the course of the evening, and were highly gratified at the action of the House in passing the bill by so overwhelming a majority. The part taken by Mr. Calhoun in the Senate today satisfies me that he too will oppose the bill passed by the House today if he thinks he can do so safely in reference to public opinion. The Whigs in the Senate will oppose it on party grounds probably, if they can get Mr. Calhoun, Mr. Benton, and two or three other Senators professing to belong to the Democratic party to join them, so as to make a majority against the bill. Should the bill be defeated by such a combination, the professed Democratic members who by their votes aid in rejecting it will owe a heavy responsibility not only to their party but to the country. I am fully satisfied that all that can save the bill in the Senate is the fear of the people by the few Democratic Senators who wish it defeated.

Tuesday, 12th May, 1846. — The Cabinet held a regular meeting today. . . The Mexican question was the subject of conversation, and all had doubts whether the bill which passed the House on yesterday would pass the Senate today. Should it pass, the course of operations was considered. . .

At seven o'clock P.M. my private secretary returned from the Capitol and announced to me that the bill which passed the House of Representatives on yesterday, making a formal declaration of war against Mexico, had passed the Senate by a vote of 42 ayes to 2 noes, with some immaterial amendment in its details. He represented to me that the debate in the Senate today was most animating and thrilling, and that Mr. Calhoun, who spoke in opposition to the bill, but finally did not vote, had suffered much in the discussion.[5] Mr. Crittenden and other Whigs, he informed me, had made speeches against portions of the bill and made indirect opposition to it, but had finally voted for it. He represented the whole debate as a great triumph for the administration. The Senate, he informed me, adjourned as soon as the bill was passed.

Wednesday, 13th May, 1846. — A very large number of visitors called on me this morning, consisting of Senators, Representatives, citizens, and strangers. All took a deep interest and many were excited at the declaration of war which passed Congress on yesterday, and now only awaited my approval to become law. All approved the acts. Many members of Congress, especially from the Western States, desired that volunteers under the law should be accepted from their respective States.

[5] Calhoun showed great courage in stemming the fever for war, which he thought might easily have been avoided. He was ready to vote the men and munitions at once, but objected vehemently to the preamble fastening the blame for the war upon Mexico. " It was just as impossible for him," he said, " to vote for that preamble as it was for him to plunge a dagger into his own heart, and more so." A motion to strike out the preamble was lost, 28 to 18. As Polk states, Calhoun was silent on the final vote. But he remained out of sympathy with the war, fearing, for one reason, that a war of conquest would result in centralizing and consolidating tendencies in the government, and interfere with State rights. He also foresaw a sectional struggle over the conquered territory.

About one o'clock P.M. a committee of Congress waited on me and presented the act declaring war against Mexico for my approval. I read it in their presence and approved and signed it.

General Scott, commander in chief of the United States army, called in company with the Secretary of War. I had requested the Secretary to invite General Scott to call. I held a conference with them in relation to the execution of the act declaring war against Mexico. General Scott presented a project of the number and disposition among the States of the number of troops required. It was incomplete and after giving him my views I requested him to make a more formal report to me during the day. I tendered to General Scott the command of the army to be raised. He accepted and retired. Though I did not consider him in all respects suited to such an important command, yet being commander-in-chief of the army, his position entitled him to it if he desired it.

Most of the Cabinet were in attendance, though no Cabinet meeting had been called. A proclamation announcing the existence of the war was prepared and signed by me. This was done in pursuance of the precedent of Mr. Madison in 1812. . .

Mr. Buchanan read the draft of a despatch which he had prepared to our Ministers at London, Paris, and other foreign courts, announcing the declaration of war against Mexico, with a statement of the causes and objects of the war, with a view that they should communicate its substance to the respective governments to which they are accredited. Among other things Mr. Buchanan had stated that our object was not to dismember Mexico or to make conquests, and that the Del Norte was the boundary to which we claimed; or rather that in going to war we did not do so with a view to acquire either California or New Mexico or any other portion of the Mexican territory. I told Mr. Buchanan that I thought such a declaration to foreign governments un-

necessary and improper; that the causes of the war as set
forth in my message to Congress and the accompanying
documents were altogether satisfactory. I told him that
though we had not gone to war for conquest, yet it was
clear that in making peace we would if practicable obtain
California and such other portion of the Mexican territory
as would be sufficient to indemnify our claimants on Mexico,
and to defray the expense of the war which that power by
her long continued wrongs and injuries had forced us to
wage. I told him it was well known that the Mexican Government had no other means of indemnifying us. Mr.
Buchanan said if when Mr. McLane announced to Lord
Aberdeen the existence of the war with Mexico the latter
should demand of Mr. McLane to know if we intended to
acquire California or any other part of the Mexican territory
and no satisfactory answer was given, he thought it almost
certain that both England and France would join with
Mexico in the war against us. I told him that the war with
Mexico was an affair with which neither England, France,
nor any other power had any concern; that such an inquiry
would be insulting to our government, and if made I would
not answer it, even if the consequence should be a war with
all of them. I told him I would not tie up my hands or
make any pledge to any foreign power as to the terms on
which I would ultimately make peace with Mexico. I told
him no foreign power had any right to demand any such
assurance, and that I would make none such let the consequences be what they might. Then, said Mr. Buchanan,
you will have war with England as well as Mexico, and
probably with France also, for neither of these powers will
ever stand by and see California annexed to the United
States. I told him that before I would make the pledge
which he proposed, I would meet the war which either England or France or all the Powers of Christendom might
wage, and that I would stand and fight until the last man
among us fell in the conflict. I told him that neither as a

citizen nor as President would I permit or tolerate any intermeddling of any European Powers on this continent. Mr. Buchanan said if my views were carried out, we would not settle the Oregon question and we would have war with England. I told him there was no connection between the Oregon and Mexican questions, and that sooner than give the pledge he proposed that we would not if we could fairly and honorably acquire California or any other part of the Mexican Territory which we desired, I would let the war which he apprehended with England come and would take the whole responsibility. The Secretary of the Treasury engaged warmly and even in an excited manner against the proposition of Mr. Buchanan in his draft of his despatch. The Secretary of the Navy, the Attorney-General, and the Postmaster-General in succession expressed similar opinions. Mr. Buchanan stood alone in the Cabinet, but was very earnest in expressing his views and enforcing them. Towards the close of the discussion, which lasted for more than two hours, I stepped to my table and wrote a paragraph to be substituted for all that part of Mr. Buchanan's proposed despatch which spoke of dismembering Mexico, of acquiring California, or of the Del Norte as the ultimate boundary beyond which we would not claim or desire to go. I strongly expressed to Mr. Buchanan that these paragraphs in his despatch must be struck out. Mr. Buchanan made no reply, but before he left took up his own draft and the paragraphs which I had written and took them away with him. I was much astonished at the views expressed by Mr. Buchanan on the subject. The discussion tonight was one of the most earnest and interesting which has ever occurred in my Cabinet.[6]

[6] In view of Buchanan's opinions, it is to be noted that in May, 1846, just before war began, the President of Mexico offered to transfer California to Great Britain in return for financial assistance; but Palmerston replied that "Her Majesty's Government would not at present feel disposed to enter into any treaty for the acquisition of California." It was understood in London that any such treaty would mean war with the United States. This diary-entry shows that Polk had not yet fully resolved on the acquisition of California as an object of the war.

The Cabinet adjourned about eleven o'clock P.M. and I retired to rest much exhausted after a day of incessant application, anxiety, and labour.

Thursday, 14th May, 1846. — Many members of Congress and others called this morning. Great anxiety prevailed to know the number of volunteers I would call to the Mexican frontier, and the States from which they would be taken. All I could say was that probably about 20,000 would be called out, and that they would be taken from the Western and Southwestern States which were nearest the scene of action, but that I had not yet distributed the proportions among these States.

Mr. Buchanan sent over for my approval a revised copy of his despatch to our Ministers abroad, which had been so fully discussed in Cabinet last night. He had struck out of it the parts I had directed to be struck out and had substituted the paragraph I had written. . .

At eight o'clock P.M. the Secretary of War and General Scott of the United States Army called.

I had a long conference with them concerning the plan of conducting the war with Mexico. I gave it as my opinion that the first movement should be to march a competent force into the northern provinces and seize and hold them until peace was made. In this they concurred. The whole field of operations was examined with all the information before us, but it would be tedious to detail all the views and the reasons for them which were expressed.

It was agreed to call out immediately for service 20,000 volunteers, and we proceeded to apportion this force among the States of Texas, Arkansas, Illinois, Missouri, Ohio, Indiana, Kentucky, Tennessee, Alabama, Mississippi, and Georgia. After very full examination of the subject the Secretary of War and General Scott retired between eleven and twelve o'clock P.M. General Scott did not impress me favourably as a military man. He has had experience in his profession, but I thought was rather scientific and visionary in his views. I did not think that so many as 20,000 volunteers besides the regular army was necessary, but I did not express this opinion, not being willing to take the responsibility of any failure of the campaign by refusing to grant to General Scott all he asked.[7]

Friday, 15th May, 1846. — Colonel R. M. Johnson of Kentucky and I had a friendly conversation of an hour. He approves the whole course of my administration, and expressed himself warmly to that effect. He told me there were some of Mr. Calhoun's friends who had come to him and condemned my course on the Mexican question, and had attributed to me as the motive in bringing on the war with Mexico the desire to run a second time for the Presidency. Col. Johnson said he repelled the imputation as unworthy of them and vindicated my course on the Mexican question, and had told them plainly that he would prefer me to any other man spoken of for the Presidency, and if I withheld my assent to be a candidate the people had a right to elect me whether I agreed to it or not. I told him I was no candidate for a second term and would not be; and repeated to him my fixed and unalterable resolution on this subject, from the day I wrote my letter of acceptance of the Baltimore nomination. I told him I had not changed the resolution expressed in that letter and should not do so.

Saturday, 16th May, 1846. — The Cabinet held a regular meeting today; all the members present. The Postmaster-General being much engaged in the business of his office remained but a short time. The chief subject consid-

---

[7] Both the Mexican and European press predicted that the American forces, operating so far from home, might soon fail. The Mexican army numbered 32,000 men, that of the United States 7,200; and the London *Times* remarked sarcastically: " The invasion and conquest of a vast region by a state which is without an army and without credit is a novelty in the history of nations." Polk had a truer estimation of the strength of American troops. Some excellent pages on the heterogeneous, undisciplined, and poorly officered Mexican army, armed with old English muskets and with poor artillery, and on the well-officered and well-equipped American troops, may be found in George Lockhart Rives' *The United States and Mexico, 1821–1848*, II, 148 ff.

ered was the Mexican War. A "confidential circular" to all our consuls abroad stating the causes of the war with Mexico and the views of the government, which had been printed, was presented by the Secretary of State, and met the approbation of the Cabinet. I had before approved it.

The plan of the campaign against Mexico was considered and particularly against the northern provinces. I presented my views to the Cabinet and they were approved. My plan was to march an army of 2,000 men on Santa Fé and near 4,000 men on Chihuahua and at once conquer the northern provinces, leaving General Scott to occupy the country on the lower Del Norte and in the interior. After the Cabinet adjourned I sent for Col. Benton and submitted the plan to him and he approved it.

During the sitting of the Cabinet I submitted to them the distribution among the States of the 50,000 volunteers authorized to be raised. A portion of this force was assigned to each State and Territory in the Union, so as to make each feel an interest in the war. The 20,000 to be called into service immediately were to be taken from the Western and Southwestern States, and the remaining 30,000 to be organized in the other States and Territories and held in readiness subject to the call of the Government. I had constant calls during the latter part of the day by many members of Congress on the subject of the war and the organization of the volunteer force. After night fifteen or twenty members of Congress, chiefly from the Western States, called. The Vice President and the Speaker of the House of Representatives also called. All desired to see me on the subject of the Mexican War. The law passed Congress today to raise a regiment of riflemen to guard our emigrants to Oregon, in pursuance of the recommendation in my annual message. The officers to command this regiment are of course to be appointed soon. Most of the members who called recommended persons to fill these of-

fices. Near twelve o'clock P.M. I retired much fatigued
and exhausted.

Monday, 18th May, 1846. — An unusually large number of visitors called today. A great number of strangers
are in the city to attend the fair to be held by the manufacturers on the 20th instant. Many others have doubtless
been drawn to the city by the recent declaration of war
against Mexico; some of them to tender the services of themselves and others as volunteers, and a very large number to
seek appointments in the regiment of mounted riflemen,
which passed Congress two or three days ago. From these
combined causes I saw a larger number of persons in my
office today than have called on me in my office on any one
day since I have been President. At twelve o'clock I
usually close my office, but when that hour arrived today
so many persons were in desiring to see me that though my
porter closed the door below stairs and prevented others
from entering my time was occupied in conversation until
near my dinner hour.

Tuesday, 19th May, 1846. — I had . . . a long and full
conversation with the Secretaries of War and of the Navy
in relation to the prosecution of the war with Mexico, and
urged upon both the necessity of giving their personal attention to all matters, even of detail, and not confiding in
their subordinates to act without their supervision. I required of them, too, to keep me constantly advised of every
important step that was taken. I urged the most energetic
and prompt action. I told them that I had understood that
General Scott had given out that he would not probably go
to the seat of war on the Del Norte to take command until
about the 1st of September. I remarked to the Secretary
of War that any such delay was not to be permitted, and
that General Scott must proceed very soon to his post, or
that I would supersede him in the command. The Secretary
of War informed me that General Scott was embarrassing
him by his schemes, that he was constantly talking and not

acting. I told the Secretary to take the matter into his own hands; to issue his orders and cause them to be obeyed.

Mr. Buchanan called whilst some of the members of the Cabinet were still in my office and introduced Bishop Hughes of the Catholic church in New York. I requested Bishop Hughes to call with Mr. Buchanan at seven P.M. Bishop Hughes had come to Washington upon an invitation given by Mr. Buchanan upon consultation with me some days ago. Our object was to procure his aid in disabusing the minds of the Catholic priests and people of Mexico in regard to what they most erroneously supposed to be the hostile designs of the government and people of the United States upon the religion and church property of Mexico.[8]

Bishop Hughes called with Mr. Buchanan at seven o'clock. Mr. Buchanan having already conversed with me on the subject retired, and I held a conversation of an hour with him. I fully explained to him the objections which we would probably have to encounter from the prejudices of the Catholic priests in Mexico, and the false impressions they had of the hostile designs of this country on their religion; that the false idea had been industriously circulated by interested partisans in Mexico that our object was to overthrow their religion and rob their churches, and that if they believed this they would make a desperate resistance to our army in the present war. Bishop Hughes fully agreed with me in the opinion I expressed that it was important to remove such impressions. I said to him that the great object of my desiring to have this interview with him was to ask whether some of the priests of the United States who spoke the Spanish language could be induced

---

[8] John Hughes, 1797–1864, born in Ireland and at one time a day-laborer in Pennsylvania, was for twenty-five years bishop and archbishop of New York. He organized more than one hundred churches, and began the erection of St. Patrick's Cathedral. He was an aggressive defender of the doctrines and institutions of the Catholic Church. Besides serving Polk as here recorded, he also served Lincoln, undertaking a special mission to Europe in 1861–1862, and travelling almost a year in France, Italy, and Ireland to counteract the propagandist activities of the Confederacy.

to accompany our army as chaplains and others to visit Mexico in advance of the army, for the purpose of giving assurance to the Catholic clergy in Mexico that under our constitution their religion and church property would be secure, and that so far from being violated, both would be protected by our army, and in this way avoid their active hostility in the pending war. Bishop Hughes at once said he thought such a visit to Mexico and having a few Catholic priests with the army would have a good effect, and expressed his entire willingness to coöperate with our government in giving such aid as was in his power. He said he knew personally the Archbishop of Mexico, and expressed his willingness to visit Mexico himself if the government desired it. I found Bishop Hughes a highly intelligent and agreeable man, and my interview with him was of the most satisfactory character. . .

I was surprised to see Senator Westcott of Florida present in the drawing room this evening. . . Mr. Westcott has acted in most improper manner toward me, as is stated in the previous part of this diary, and I had not seen him for several months. He came up and spoke to me in the crowd, and I treated him as the President should treat any citizen in his own mansion.

Wednesday, 20th May, 1846. — I had a busy day. At six o'clock the Marine Band performed in the grounds south of the President's house. A very large number of persons attended.

Thursday, 21st May, 1846. — A very large crowd of strangers called on me today. The pressure for appointments in the new regiment of riflemen is beyond anything of the kind which I have witnessed since I have been President. There are many hundred applicants, and but 3 field officers, 10 captains, 11 first lieutenants, and 10 second lieutenants to be appointed. Upwards of 100 officers of the army have applied for promotion. Except in the case of Captain Frémont, I have upon full consideration determined to select

the officers from civil life, for the reason that if any of the
officers of the present army are promoted, it will produce
heartburning with all officers of the same grade who have
performed equal service and have equal merit with themselves. Capt. Frémont's is an excepted case. He has made
several explorations to Oregon and California, and his reports show that he is an officer of high merit and peculiarly
fitted for this regiment, which is intended to guard
and protect our emigrants to Oregon. Moreover, it is
peculiarly a Western regiment, and I will give a larger
proportion of officers to that part of the Union than to
any other. . .

    Mr. F. W. Risque of Lynchburg, Va., with whom I had
no acquaintance, called today and sought an interview with
me. His object was to secure the restoration of his brother-
in-law, Captain Hutter, late of the army. . . He handed
me a letter from General Scott to Mr. Archer on the subject
dated 6th February, 1846, which was highly unjust and
disrespectful to the administration and especially to the
President. . . The letter was of a partisan character;
wholly unbecoming to the commander-in-chief of the army,
and highly exceptionable in its tenor and language towards
the President. It proved to me that General Scott was not
only hostile, but recklessly vindictive in his feelings towards
my administration. Whilst I was examining the papers in
Capt. Hutter's case the Secretary of War came in on official
business, and Mr. Risque, to whom I had returned General
Scott's letter, handed it to the Secretary, who read it. Mr.
Risque said the letter was not marked private and he felt at
liberty to use it. After Mr. Risque left, taking the letter
with him, the Secretary of War and myself conversed about
the very offensive and highly exceptionable character of the
letter. After seeing this letter I can have no confidence
in General Scott's disposition to carry out the views of the
administration as commander-in-chief of the army on the
Del Norte, and yet unless Congress shall authorize the ap-

pointment of additional general officers I may be compelled
to continue to entrust the command to him. If I shall be
compelled to do so, it will be with the full conviction of his
hostility to my administration, and that he will reluctantly
do anything to carry out my plans and views in the campaign.

After night the Secretary of War sent to me a letter of
this date addressed to himself by General Scott in relation to
the Mexican campaign, of an exceptionable character, and
going conclusively to prove his bad feelings and hostility
to the administration. I will request the Secretary of War
to preserve this letter. Taken in connection with the letter
shown to me by Mr. Risque today, I am satisfied that the administration will not be safe in intrusting the command of
the army in the Mexican War to General Scott. His bitter
hostility towards the administration is such that I could not
trust him, and will not do so if Congress will pass the bill
now before them, authorizing the appointment of additional major-generals of the army.

Friday, 22d May, 1846. — I learned yesterday and today
that General Scott, General Wool, and Adjutant-General
Jones were using their influence with members of Congress
to prevent the passage of the bill now before the Senate authorizing the appointment of two additional major-generals
and four brigadier-generals. Such conduct is highly censurable. These officers are all Whigs and violent partisans,
and not having the success of my administration at heart
seem disposed to throw every obstacle in the way of my
prosecuting the Mexican War successfully. An end must be
speedily put to this state of things.

Saturday, 23d May, 1846. — I read to the Cabinet a letter
addressed by General Winfield Scott to the Secretary of War
dated 21st instant, which had been communicated to me by
the Secretary. . . This letter of General Scott is foolish
and vindictive toward the administration. Without the
slightest reason for it General Scott makes base and false
insinuations in reference to the administration, as connected

with the command of the army on the Mexican frontier, which I had on the commencement of hostilities requested him to assume. He uses language not only exceptionable but unbecoming an officer. After making false insinuations against the administration, he concludes by using the following language, *viz.*: " My explicit meaning is, that I do not desire to place myself in the most perilous of all positions, a fire upon my rear from Washington and the fire in front from the Mexicans." I repeat this insinuation is wholly false, and proves, as I think, two things; 1st, that General Scott seeks a pretext to avoid going to the Del Norte to take command of our army, and 2d, that his partisan feelings are such that he is unfit to be entrusted with the command.[9] The only reason assigned for making such an insinuation is that in an interview with the Secretary of War a few days ago he had expressed the opinion which he repeats in this letter, that operations on the Del Norte under the late act of Congress authorizing a call for volunteers could

[9] It is the verdict of Justin H. Smith (*The War With Mexico*, II, 318) that Winfield Scott was " a superb general " and " a great man." Polk bore a prejudice against him from the very beginning, tinged strongly with political jealousy. He was acutely aware that Scott was a Whig, and that success in the war was likely to make him President of the United States. Moreover, the two differed radically in their view of the war. Polk believed that it would be short and easy, and as a civilian did not fully appreciate the time required to outfit an army for field service. Scott took the war with the utmost seriousness, and wished to make elaborate and imposing preparations. Without troubling to consult the War Department, Scott, who was working fourteen hours a day, gave notice that he would probably not be ready to leave for the seat of war until the first of September; whereupon the irate Polk informed him through Secretary of War Marcy that unless he soon proceeded to the Rio Grande he would be superseded by another general. This clash led Scott into some extraordinary indiscretions. He told applicants for military positions that the Administration was reserving its places " to give commissions or rather pay to Western Democrats." He replied to Secretary Marcy in a highly offensive and egotistic letter. " I am too old a soldier, and have had too much special experience, not to feel the infinite importance of securing myself against danger (ill-will or pre-condemnation), in my rear, before advancing upon the public enemy," he declared. He added: " My explicit meaning is, that I do not desire to place myself in the most perilous of all positions — *a fire upon my rear from Washington, and the fire in front from the Mexicans.*" Polk and Marcy at once assented to the injustice of placing the apprehensive general in any such position. But some of Polk's observations on Scott are quite unfair.

not commence before the 1st of September, to which the Secretary had informed him that I wished prompt action, and that the delay proposed was unnecessary. This is what General Scott calls "a fire upon my rear from Washington." The facts are that war has been declared against Mexico, twenty thousand volunteers have been called out to take the field as soon as possible, I had designated General Scott, solely because he was commander-in-chief of the army, to take the command; I desired a prompt and energetic movement; whereas General Scott was in favour of remaining in Washington and not assuming the command before the first of September. This as far as I know is the sole cause of his extraordinary and vindictive letter. I submitted to the Cabinet the impropriety, with this letter before us, of continuing him in command. The subject was discussed, the Secretary of the Treasury expressing a decided opinion that he ought not to be intrusted with the command. . .

While the subject was under consideration, a committee of manufacturers accompanied by Mr. Seaton, mayor of Washington, called to accompany me to the manufacturers' fair now holding in this city. The Cabinet suspended the consideration of the subject and adjourned. I visited the fair accompanied by the mayor and committee and the ladies of my family. There were a great variety of manufactured articles collected in a very large temporary building erected for the occasion by the manufacturers. I was informed that the building alone cost over $6,000, and that as soon as the fair was over would be taken down. The specimens of manufacture exhibited are highly creditable to the genius and skill of our countrymen. All must desire that the manufacturing interests should prosper, but none ought to desire that to enable them to do so heavy burthens should be imposed by the government on other branches of industry. The manufacturers have spent many thousands of dollars in getting up this fair, with a view no doubt to operate upon members of Congress to prevent a reduction of the present rates of duty imposed by the oppressive protective tariff act of 1842. . .[10]

The Southern mail this evening brought intelligence of two decided victories obtained by General Taylor's army over the Mexicans on the Del Norte. No official account of these battles was received.

Sunday, 24th May, 1846. — Attended the first Presbyterian church today in company with Mrs. Polk and her niece, Miss Rucker. As we were going out of the door to attend church we were accosted by a young man, much emaciated and very feeble, who said his name was Bledsoe, and that he was the same person who had been a law student with James H. Thomas, Esq. (my law partner) of Columbia, Tenn., in 1844. I remembered that there was such a person in our law office at that time, but he was so changed in his appearance I did not recognize him. He said he had been advised to go to sea for the benefit of his health, that he had done so, and during his absence had been three months in the hospital at Gibraltar, that he had made his way thus far back towards his home in Mississippi, and that he had no money to pay his way at a tavern. His appearance and his story excited my sympathy. I handed him $5 and directed the steward to give him refreshments and then conduct him to a hotel and see that he had comfortable quarters. I told him I would give him further assistance on tomorrow.

Monday, 25th May, 1846. — The Secretary of War, who had shown me the draft of his answer to General Scott's extraordinary letter of the 21st instant, called a few minutes after twelve o'clock and it was carefully examined and revised. It had previously undergone the revision of

[10] The Walker Tariff bill — based on the recommendations of Polk and Secretary Walker — was reported by the Ways and Means Committee on April 14, 1846. Though it sharply reduced the duties of the Tariff Act of 1842, it was far from a free-trade measure; yet the advocates of protection assailed it as ruinous, and a large lobby assembled in Washington to attack it.

the Attorney-General. Deeming it to be a matter of sufficient importance, I called a special meeting of the Cabinet at two o'clock P.M. today, to consider of the answer to General Scott's letter. The Cabinet convened at that hour. Mr. Buchanan suggested and prepared a modification of one of the paragraphs, which was approved, and as thus modified the letter of the Secretary of War was approved unanimously by the Cabinet. I directed the Secretary of War to have it copied and delivered to General Scott today. The conclusion of the letter was to excuse General Scott from the command of the army against Mexico, and to order him to remain in the discharge of his duties at Washington. . .[11]

Official despatches from General Taylor were received this evening, confirming the previous intelligence of the success of the American arms in two engagements with the Mexican forces on the Del Norte on the 8th and 9th days of May, 1846.[12]

Tuesday, 26th May, 1846. — The Cabinet held a regular meeting today; all the members present. The Secretary of War produced a letter from General Scott in reply to the Secretary's letter to him on yesterday. In his letter General Scott disavows that he meant to impute to the President the unworthy motives mentioned in his letter of

[11] Marcy's letter was able and dignified, and was of course a heavy blow to General Scott's pride. The general complained later that as if to add insult to injury, it was handed to him " as I sat down to a hasty plate of soup." In his reply Scott explained that he had feared a rear-fire from Congress and not from the President, but he sneered at Polk's " magnanimity " in not having him court-martialled.

[12] In the battles of Palo Alto and Resaca de la Palma the army under Taylor, May 8 and 9, 1846, drove the Mexicans across the Rio Grande. The engagements showed the decisive superiority of the American troops. The Mexicans relied chiefly upon cavalry and the lance, and the intense artillery fire of the Americans took them by surprise. Taylor had about 2,000 men in these engagements, and the enemy at least twice as many. But the American losses were slight, amounting to 170 killed and wounded, while the Mexicans by their own accounts lost 800 men, and Taylor estimated their losses at probably quite twice as many. The way was at once open for the invasion of Mexico.

the 21st instant, but says he referred to the Secretary of
War and members of Congress who were raising a clamour
and creating a prejudice against him.   There is nothing in
his answer which changes my determination to order General Scott to remain at Washington instead of taking command of the army on the Del Norte.   General Scott's last
letter is in a subdued tone and even passes a high compliment on me.   He now sees his error no doubt, but it is too
late to recall what has been done.   The Secretary of War
read the rough draft of the answer which he had prepared
to General Scott's last letter.   I sent a message to the Senate today nominating General Zachary Taylor of the army
a Major-General by brevet, for his gallant victories obtained over the Mexican forces on the Del Norte on the 8th
and 9th days of this month.

The plan of military operations against Mexico was the
subject of a long conversation in Cabinet.   I proposed that
an expedition be immediately fitted out against Upper California, and after full consideration it was unanimously
agreed that it should be done, if it was ascertained that
there was time for two or three mounted regiments to be
assembled and marched from Independence in Missouri to
the Sacramento before the setting in of winter.

It was agreed that Brigadier General Wool should be
forthwith ordered to proceed west and assist in organizing
the volunteers and march with them to the Del Norte, where
he would assume his command as a brigadier-general of the
United States army.

Wednesday, 27th May, 1846. — A great crowd of persons, male and female, called today.   A greater number
of persons (strangers) are said to be in Washington than
have been at any one time for many years, unless at the
inauguration of a President.   Among others ex-President
Tyler called.   I spent twenty minutes in agreeable conversation with him.   He informed me that he had come to
Washington in obedience to a summons of a committee of

Congress. I told him that I had heard of the summons and
deeply regretted the proceeding, and wholly condemned it.
I had before understood that one of the committees of the
House of Representatives appointed to investigate the quarrel between Mr. Charles J. Ingersoll and Mr. Daniel Webster concerning the secret service fund expended during Mr.
Tyler's administration, had issued such a summons.

Thursday, 28th May, 1846. — Had a conference with
the Secretary of War and General Wool today. Had a
similar conference with them on yesterday. General Wool
was ordered to proceed to the West and see that the volunteers were speedily raised and marched to the Rio Grande
with the least possible delay. General Wool's particular
service in the Mexican War has not yet been determined
upon, viz., whether he is to proceed to the lower Rio Grande
or go in a separate command to the upper provinces.

Saturday, 30th May, 1846. — A plan of the campaign
against Mexico and the manner of prosecuting the war was
fully considered. I brought distinctly to the consideration
of the Cabinet the question of ordering an expedition of
mounted men to California. I stated that if the war should
be protracted for any considerable time, it would in my judgment be very important that the United States should hold
military possession of· California at the time peace was
made, and I declared my purpose to be to acquire for the
United States, California, New Mexico, and perhaps some
others of the Northern Provinces of Mexico whenever a
peace was made. In Mr. Slidell's secret instructions last
autumn these objects were included. Now that we were at
war the prospect of acquiring them was much better, and to
secure that object military possession should with as little
delay as possible be taken of all these provinces. In these
views the Cabinet concurred. The only doubt which remained was whether the season was not too far advanced
to enable an expedition of mounted men from Missouri to
pass the mountains and reach California before the setting

in of winter. In winter, all whom I had consulted agreed
that it was impracticable to make the expedition. Col. Benton had given me his opinion that if the expedition could
leave Independence in Missouri there would be time. Col.
Benton had brought me Frémont's map and book and given
me much detailed information of the route and of the difficulties attending it, but advised the expedition this season
provided it could move from Independence by the first of
August. Col. Benton had written me a note with an outline
of the plan of the expedition, which I read to the Cabinet.
I finally submitted a distinct proposition to the Cabinet.
Col. Kearny of the United States army was as I learned an
experienced officer, and had been with a part of his regiment to the South Pass of the Rocky mountain, and made
an extensive tour in that region last year. Immediately
after the act declaring war against Mexico was passed
(May 13, 1846) orders had been given to Col. Kearny
with his regiment to move to Santa Fé to protect our trad-
ers. A requisition had at the same time been made on the
governor of Missouri for 1,000 mounted volunteers to go
under Col. Kearny's command on the same service. These
troops or a portion of them could be put en route for California three weeks earlier than any new force, which could
be now ordered out. The proposition which I submitted
was that Col. Kearny should be ordered as soon as he
took Santa Fé, if he thought it safe to do so and practicable for him to reach California before winter, to leave
Santa Fé in charge of his Lieutenant-Colonel with a sufficient force to hold it, and proceed towards California with
the balance of his command, including a portion of the 1,000
mounted men who had been ordered out. I proposed further that another 1,000 mounted men should be immediately ordered out from Missouri to proceed to Bent's Fort or
Santa Fé, and a portion of them to follow Col. Kearny towards California or not, as Col. Kearny might leave orders behind him, leaving a large discretion to Col. Kearny

whether he should undertake the California expedition this season or not, but expressing to him the strong wish of the government that he should do so, if he thought it practicable. The Cabinet assented to this proposition. The Cabinet adjourned after a very full discussion of the subject, with the understanding that the Secretary of War would see me again before the orders were issued. After the Cabinet adjourned I sent for Col. Benton, and saw him with the Secretary of War. He approved the general outline of the campaign. He suggested that General Price of the House of Representatives of Missouri should command the 1,000 mounted men now to be called out from Missouri.[13]

Monday, 1st June, 1846. — Being much wearied by my long confinement for several months, I took a ride on horseback with my private secretary in the evening. We visited Judge Mason, the Attorney-General, and found him confined to his bed and quite ill.

Tuesday, 2d June, 1846. — I submitted to the Cabinet that a large number of cannon, small arms, munitions of war, and provisions should be immediately sent from New York to the Pacific for the use of our army. This was unanimously approved by the Cabinet. It was agreed that Col. Kearny should be authorized to take into service any emigrants (American citizens) whom he might find in California or who may go out with these munitions of war and

---

[13] This operation was carried out much as Polk here outlines it. Orders were issued to Kearny on June 3, 1846, to march for upper California by way of Santa Fé. By the end of July his 1800 troops were concentrated at Bent's Fort on the Arkansas River, and from this post he advanced on Santa Fé. An army of 4,000 Mexicans dissolving on his approach, he occupied the city on Aug. 18, 1846, and at once proceeded to organize a temporary government for New Mexico. Taking 300 dragoons with him, he then left on Sept. 25 for California.

Col. Stephen W. Kearny, who was now (June, 1846) made a brevet brigadier-general, was an experienced officer, a harsh disciplinarian, and as we shall see, a man of stiff and jealous temper. He belonged to the well-known New Jersey family. The General Price here mentioned is Sterling Price, who became governor of Missouri 1853–1857, and was famous as a Confederate general in the Civil War.

military stores.   Col. Kearny was also authorized to receive into service as volunteers a few hundred of the Mormons who are now on their way to California, with a view to conciliate them, attach them to our country, and prevent them from taking part against us.[14]   Many other matters of detail connected with the expedition were considered.

Wednesday, 3rd June, 1846. — Closed my doors as usual at twelve o'clock.   A despatch from our Minister (Mr. McLane) at London, dated 18th of May, 1846, was received this morning.   It communicated the substance of the proposition which he had learned from Lord Aberdeen would be made by the British Government through their minister at Washington for the settlement of the Oregon question.   If Mr. McLane is right in the character of the proposition which will be made, it is certain that I cannot accept it, and it is a matter of doubt in my mind whether it will be such as I ought to submit to the Senate for their previous advice before acting upon it.   If I reject it absolutely and make no other proposition the probable result will be war.   If I submit it to the Senate and they should advise its acceptance I should be bound by their advice and yet I should do so reluctantly.   I had a conference on the subject with Mr. Buchanan. . .

Held a conversation with Mr. Amos Kendall and Mr. J. C. Little of Peterborough, N. H., (a Mormon) today. They desired to see me in relation to a large body of Mormon emigrants who are now on their way from Nauvoo and other parts of the United States to California, and to learn the policy of the government towards them.   I told Mr. Little that by our Constitution the Mormons would be treated as all other American citizens were, without regard

[14] The Mormons driven from Nauvoo had gathered at Council Bluffs, Iowa, preparing to emigrate to the West. It was important to conciliate them, and their military assistance might be valuable. Kearny, authorized to accept a body of these emigrants not greater than one-fourth his command, enlisted about five hundred of them in June. This Mormon battalion did excellent service in the conquest of New Mexico.

to the sect to which they belonged or the religious creed
which they professed, and that I had no prejudices toward
them which could induce a different course of treatment.
Mr. Little said that they were Americans in all their feelings, and friends of the United States. I told Mr. Little
that we were at war with Mexico, and asked him if 500 or
more of the Mormons now on the way to California would
be willing on their arrival in that country to volunteer and
enter the United States army in that war, under the command of a United States officer. He said he had no doubt
they would willingly do so. He said if the United States
would receive them into the service he would immediately
proceed and overtake the emigrants now on the way and
make the arrangement with them to do so. I told him I
would see him tomorrow on the subject.

Thursday, 4th June, 1846. — I called a special meeting of
the Cabinet at two o'clock P.M. today to consider of the
English proposition on the Oregon question, the substance
of which as it will probably be made by Mr. Pakenham was
communicated to me in the despatch of Mr. McLane on the
18th ultimo. That proposition will probably be a line of
partition of the Oregon territory by the line of 49° from
the Rocky Mountains to the Straits of Fuca, and thence
through the Straits to the sea, leaving the Straits in their
whole extent around Vancouver's Island an open sea to
both nations; a fee-simple title to British subjects for the
farms and lands they occupy between the Columbia River
and 49°, and the free navigation of the Columbia, not to
British subjects generally but to the Hudson's Bay Company only. I asked the advice of the Cabinet, if such a
proposition was made by Mr. Pakenham what I should do.
Mr. Buchanan said he did not feel prepared without further
reflection to commit himself, but was inclined to the opinion
that I should submit it to the Senate for their previous advice accompanied by a message reiterating my opinions expressed in my annual message of the 2d of December last.

He said if the right of free navigation of the Columbia, which was the objectionable feature of the proposition to his mind, was confined to the duration of the present charter of the Hudson's Bay Company which would expire in 1859, he should be clear it should be submitted to the Senate for their previous advice.   Mr. Bancroft thought such a modification in regard to the navigation of the river should be made, but was clear that the proposition as it was with a recommendation of such modification should be submitted to the Senate before I acted on it.   Mr. Bancroft gave his views at some length in favour of this course.   Mr. Marcy concurred in substance in opinion with Mr. Bancroft. Mr. Johnson inclined to favour the same view. . .   No decision was made, and I expressed no opinion, desiring to hear the opinions of the Cabinet before I did so.

Saturday, 6th June, 1846. — Mr. Buchanan submitted a proposition from the British Government for the settlement of the Oregon question, which he said had just been delivered to him by Mr. Pakenham.   The proposition which was in the form of a convention was read, and also a protocol of the conference which had taken place at the delivery of the proposition.   The proposal is substantially that the Oregon territory shall be divided between the parties by the 49° parallel of latitude from the Rocky Mountains to the Straits of Fuca, thence through the main channel of such straits to the sea, the country south of this line to belong to the United States and that north of it to Great Britain. The proposition also contained two reservations, *viz.,* 1st, that the Hudson's Bay Company and all British subjects in the actual occupancy of their farms and lands used for other purposes shall be secured in their titles to the same, south of 49°, but to be subject to the jurisdiction and sovereignty of the United States; and secondly, that the navigation of the Columbia River shall be free, not to British subjects generally but to the Hudson's Bay company and to British subjects trading with that company.   As the Hudson's Bay

Company will under its present charter cease to exist in the year 1859, a question arose whether if the charter of the company should be extended for an additional term of time this reservation as to the right to navigate the Columbia would extend beyond the life of the present company under the existing charter. . .

I asked the advice of the Cabinet as to what action should be taken on the proposition now submitted. . . Mr. Walker, Mr. Marcy, Mr. Bancroft, and Mr. Johnson advised that it should be submitted to the Senate for their previous advice. Mr. Buchanan held back his opinion and was the last to express himself and not then until I asked his opinion. He said it would depend upon the character of the message whether he would advise its submission to the Senate or not. He said the 54° 40′ men were the true friends of the administration and he wished no backing out on the subject. I felt excited at the remark but suppressed my feelings and was perfectly calm. Mr. Walker made an animated remark in reply, and I interposed and gave the conversation a different direction, for I desired no excitement or division in the Cabinet. All agreed that if the proposition was rejected without submitting it to the Senate that in the present position of the question I could offer no modification of it, or other proposition, and that if it was rejected and no other proposition made, war was almost inevitable. I then remarked to Mr. Buchanan that the substance of my message would be, if I submitted the proposition to the Senate, a reiteration of my opinion as expressed in my annual message of the 2d of December last, but in view of the action of my predecessors and of the debates and proceedings of Congress at its present session, I submitted it to the Senate for their previous advice, accompanied with a distinct statement that if the Senate advised its acceptance with or without modifications I should conform to their advice; but if they declined to express an opinion, or by the constitutional majority to give their advice, I should reject the proposition.   Mr. Buchanan then said that with such a message as that he would advise its submission to the Senate.   I then asked Mr. Buchanan to prepare such a message. He declined to do so, but said if I would prepare a draft of one he would examine it, and make such suggestions as might seem to him to be proper.   I told him I would do so. The Cabinet adjourned, after having considered several questions in relation to the war with Mexico.   Mr. Marcy remained after the other members had retired, on business connected with the military operations.   He remarked to me that Mr. Buchanan's course was a very queer one, for that he had been for a long time the most strenuous advocate of settling the question on the basis of the 49° of north latitude, and had often said in and out of the Cabinet that he would be willing to take the whole responsibility of settling the question on the basis of 49°.   This I remembered distinctly, and it was not till within a short time since that he gave indications of a change of position.   The first indication I had of it was a remark which fell from him incidentally when speaking of the subject, to the purport that General Cass had made character by his course in the Senate on the subject.   General Cass was a 54° 40′ man.

Sunday, 7th June, 1846. — My impression is that Mr. Buchanan intends now to shun all responsibility for the submission of the British proposition to the Senate, but still he may wish it to be done without his agency, so that if the 54° 40′ men shall complain, he may be able to say that my message submitting it did not receive his sanction.   I shall be disappointed if any message which can be drawn will receive his assent.   He will choose to dissent and if it is condemned he will escape all responsibility.   In his dispatches to Mr. McLane I have more than once, and in the presence of the Cabinet, caused paragraphs to be struck out yielding as I thought too much to Great Britain, and now it is most strange that he should take suddenly, and without the assignment of any reason, the opposite extreme, and talk as he did yesterday of "caking out from 54° 40'." His course is one which I cannot approve. Mr. Marcy and Mr. Bancroft both condemned it in decided terms.

Tuesday, 9th June, 1846. — The Cabinet held a regular meeting today, all the members present except the Attorney-General, who is still confined to his house by indisposition. I read my message to the Senate submitting for their advice the British proposition for the adjustment of the Oregon question. . . Mr. Buchanan objected to some portions of it.[15] A discussion ensued between him and other members of the Cabinet. I remained silent. Mr. Bancroft reminded Mr. Buchanan of a remark which he had made in the Cabinet some months ago, that the title of the United States north of 49° was a shackling one. Mr. Buchanan said that remark related to Fraser's River, and that the British Government had never placed their claim to that river on the proper ground. Mr. Bancroft reminded him of several of his own despatches to Mr. McLane strongly in favour of a settlement of the question on the basis of 49°, and hinted intelligibly enough at his recent strange and unaccountable change of position. Several suggestions in way of objection to parts of my message were made by Mr. Buchanan. I at

[15] On the previous day President Polk and Secretary Buchanan had had a sharp interchange on the Oregon question. He declined for a second time to assist Polk in preparing his message to the Senate, and showed reluctance to let Polk send the Senate some of his former correspondence with Minister McLane on the subject. After he had done reading these letters, says Polk, "not deeming it very important whether they were sent to the Senate or not, I told him I left it to him to select what portions of the correspondence, if any, should be sent to the Senate. He then said, Well! when you have done your message I will then prepare such an one as I think ought to be sent in. I felt excited at this remark, as he had on Saturday and on this morning refused to aid me in preparing my message, and I said to him. For what purpose will you prepare a message? You have twice refused, though it is a subject relating to your department, to give me any aid in preparing my message; do you wish, after I have done, to draw up a paper of your own in order to make an issue with me? He became excited and said that remark struck him to the heart, and asked me if I thought him capable of doing such a thing?" From this point, adds Polk, "the conversation became a very painful and unpleasant one, but led to mutual explanations that seemed to be satisfactory." Buchanan reverted to his usual timidity, and retired.

length spoke and said I would yield anything but principle
for the sake of harmony and union in the Cabinet on this important subject. Mr. Buchanan then said if I would give
him my draft of the message he would go into another room
and draw up such a draft as he would approve. I told him
to do so and he took my draft and retired. He was gone
more than an hour and returned with his draft and read it.
I saw at once it would not do, but said nothing. The other
members of the Cabinet each in turn expressed objections to
it. I at length proposed, in order to obtain union of opinion,
to strike out a large part of my draft, leaving only that portion which proposed to submit the British proposition to the
Senate for their advice, the reasons which induced me to ask
that advice, reiterating the opinions expressed in my annual
message and declaring that I would be governed in my
action by the advice which the Senate might give. Mr.
Buchanan and all the other members of the Cabinet agreed
to this, and after a session of more than five hours
the message in this form was agreed to and the Cabinet
adjourned.

Friday, 12th June, 1846. — About six o'clock P.M. the
secretary of the Senate called and delivered to me a resolution of the Senate, passed as stated on its face with the concurrence of two thirds of the Senators present, advising me
" to accept the proposal of the British Government," accompanying my message to the Senate of the 10th instant, " for
the settlement of the Oregon question." About seven
o'clock P.M. the secretary of the Senate sent to me a copy
of the executive journal of this day, from which it appears
that the vote on the resolution advising acceptance of the
British proposition stood ayes 38, noes 12.

Saturday, 13th June, 1846. — Saw Mr. Buchanan early
this morning, and communicated to him the proceedings and
resolutions of the Senate, advising by a vote of ayes 38 to
noes 12 the acceptance of the British proposition for the
settlement of the Oregon question, which was communicated

to the Senate by my message of the 10th instant.[16]   It was agreed that he should see Mr. Pakenham this morning and agree upon a time when the treaty in pursuance of the advice of the Senate should be signed.

Monday, 22d June, 1846. — The two Senators and several of the Representatives from the State of Illinois called today and presented their joint recommendation in writing in favour of persons to fill the staff offices of the Illinois volunteers who have been called into the public service in the war against Mexico. . .   The truth is that Mr. Semple and several other members of Congress who are militia officers in their respective States desire to get commands for themselves, and therefore oppose any amendment of the act of June 18, 1846, which requires me to select the brigadier and major-generals from the officers now in command of the militia in the States.[17]   The passion for office among members of Congress is very great, if not absolutely disreputable, and greatly embarrasses the operations of the government.   They create offices by their own votes and then seek to fill them themselves.   I shall certainly refuse to appoint them, though it be at the almost certain hazard of incurring their displeasure.   I shall do so because their appointment would be most corrupting in its tendency.

Tuesday, 23d June, 1846. — I saw Mr. Douglas of the House of Representatives from Illinois today, and in a long

[16] On June 15, 1846, the treaty was signed, and it was promptly ratified by a vote of 41 to 14. Polk's stiffly uncompromising attitude shows that he was not eager to obtain a settlement simply in order to free the hands of the United States to deal with Mexico. But he was doubtless glad to give way indirectly by the unusual expedient of calling upon the Senate for its previous advice. He had no desire for two wars at once, and he was convinced that the British settlements north of the forty-ninth parallel had given them rights in that country similar to ours south of that line. Much of the credit for the avoidance of war must go to the pacific policy of Great Britain.

[17] James Semple, Senator from Illinois 1843–1847, was an active supporter of the demand for the 54° 40′ boundary in Oregon. He was a brigadier-general of the Illinois militia, and was recommended by the Illinois delegation in Congress to command the militia called out from that State. This delegation also recommended Stephen A. Douglas, who was Representative from Illinois 1843–1847, and Senator 1847–1861, to be brigade-major. Polk expresses a proper indignation at this Congressional thirst for military office.

and friendly conversation advised him to abandon his application for a place in the army and remain in his seat in Congress. I expressed to him my objections to appoint members of Congress to office, and especially to offices created by laws passed by their votes. Mr. Douglas is a sensible man, and he received what I said to him well. In the after part of the day he addressed me a letter withdrawing the application which was made in his behalf by the Illinois delegation on yesterday.

Wednesday, 24th June, 1846. — The secretary of the Senate delivered to me this afternoon a resolution of the Senate rejecting the nomination of Henry Horn as Collector of Philadelphia. . . Messrs. Hannegan, Semple, and Atchison have lashed themselves into a passion because two thirds of the Senate advised the acceptance of the British proposition for the adjustment of the Oregon question, and subsequently voted for the ratification, and have since that time voted and acted with the Whig party. They voted first for Mr. Archer (Whig) and then for Mr. Webster (Whig) for chairman of the committee on foreign affairs, and refused through many ballotings to vote for Senator Sevier, who was the Democratic candidate, and ultimately defeated his election. They now vote against my nominations, as I suppose out of spite. The sooner such party men go into the ranks of the Whig party the better. They oppose, too, and embarrass the military bills for the prosecution of the war against Mexico. They profess to be in a great rage (there is certainly no reason in their course) at the settlement of the Oregon question, and yet they can find no just cause of complaint against me, because my message transmitting the proposal to the Senate, as they know, repeated the doctrines and positions of my annual message of the 2nd December last, which they had over and over again approved. Their course is that of spoiled children.

Tuesday, 30th June, 1846. — This was the regular day of meeting of the Cabinet. . . A discussion arose between Mr.

Buchanan and Mr. Walker in regard to the objects of the war against Mexico, in the course of which Mr. Buchanan expressed himself in favour of acquiring the Rio Grande as our western boundary as high up as the Passo in about latitude 32° of north latitude and thence west to the Pacific. He expressed himself as being opposed to acquiring any territory by treaty with Mexico south of 32° of north latitude. He spoke of the unwillingness of the North to acquire so large a country that would probably become a slaveholding country if attached to the United States. Mr. Walker warmly resisted Mr. Buchanan's views, and insisted that we should if practicable acquire by treaty all the country north of a line drawn from the mouth of the Rio Grande in latitude about 26° west to the Pacific. Mr. Buchanan said . . . that if we attempted to acquire all this territory the opinion of the world would be against us, and especially as it would become a slaveholding country, whereas while it was in possession of Mexico slavery did not exist in it. Mr. Walker remarked that he would be willing to fight the whole world sooner than suffer other Powers to interfere in the matter. I remained silent until the discussion had proceeded to a considerable length, when I spoke and said in substance that the causes and objects of the war were as I supposed well understood, and that when we came to make peace the terms of the peace would be a subject for consideration. As to the boundary which we should establish by a treaty of peace, I remarked that I preferred the 26° to any boundary north of it, but that if it was found that that boundary could not be obtained I was willing to take 32°, but that in any event we must obtain Upper California and New Mexico in any treaty of peace we should make.[18] The other members of the Cabinet expressed no opinions, not being called upon to do so. The discussion between Mr. Buchanan and Mr. Walker was an animated one.

---

[18] A boundary line along the 26th parallel would have given the United States the entire northern third of what is now Mexico.

CHAPTER IV
July 1, 1846 — Sept. 10, 1846

BUCHANAN AND THE SUPREME COURT — TERRITORIAL AIMS
OF THE WAR — THE WALKER TARIFF ENDANGERED —
ITS PASSAGE — THE WILMOT PROVISO — GEN. ZACHARY
TAYLOR'S DEFICIENCIES

Wednesday, 1st July, 1846. — Had a crowd of visitors
until twelve o'clock today. The importunity for office it
would seem will never cease. There were many visitors this
morning upon the patriotic errand of seeking office for themselves. My mind was occupied about more important matters and I gave them no countenance.

About one o'clock Mr. Buchanan called, and I had a full
conversation with him on the subject of his transfer from
the State Department to the Supreme Court bench. I told
him I had received his note of the 28th *ult.* expressing his
preference for the bench. I told him I was satisfied to retain him in the Cabinet, and that I would leave it entirely to
himself to decide whether he remained in the Cabinet or took
the judgeship. He indicated at once his preference for the
bench. I then said to him that I would part with him with
reluctance, but that I knew that he had long desired a seat
on the Supreme Bench, and that if he did not get it now no
other opportunity might occur, and that I would not stand in
the way of his wishes. He then expressed a wish to be nominated immediately. I told him I did not see how I could dis-
pense with his services in the State Department until near
the close of the present session of Congress, and expressed

a desire that he should remain until that time. To this he assented, but with seeming reluctance because of his extreme anxiety to go on the bench. . .[1]

At five o'clock P.M. between forty and fifty chiefs and braves of the Comanche and other bands and tribes of wild Indians from the prairies in the north of Texas, were presented to me by M. G. Lewis, Esq., who had been sent with Gov. Butler last fall to visit these tribes. . . They were afterwards conducted through the East Room and through all the parlours below stairs. The large mirrors in the parlours attracted their attention more than anything else. When they saw themselves at full length, they seemed to be greatly delighted. They came to Washington nearly in a naked state, with little more than a breech clout on them. They were dressed in American costume to visit me, and, as I learned, it was with difficulty some of them could be restrained from tearing their clothes off themselves, and especially the squaws. I was informed that the chief, Santa Anna, had said that he thought before he came to the United States that his nation could whip any nation in the world, but that since he came here he found the white men more numerous than the stars, and that he could not count them. Their visit to the United States will no doubt have a fine effect in impressing them with our numbers and power, and may be the means of preserving peace with them. After going through the parlours below stairs, they passed into the grounds south of the President's House, where the Marine Band were playing (this being the evening for music on the grounds) in the presence of many hundred ladies and gentlemen. The Indians attracted much more attention than the music. Many of the Indians, as I learned, who had on shoes to visit me, took them off and walked barefooted as soon as they got into the grounds.

[1] But Buchanan again changed his mind about the Supreme Court, deciding in August, 1846, as we shall see, to retain the Secretaryship of State. Polk then appointed Robert Cooper Grier, of Pennsylvania, who was confirmed Aug. 4.

Tuesday, 7th July, 1846. — The Cabinet held a regular meeting today; all the members present except the Attorney-General, who was detained at his residence by continued indisposition. Various questions connected with the manner of conducting the war with Mexico were considered. Among other questions which arose was one in relation to the municipal and commercial regulations to be established in any Mexican port or town which should be taken by our navy. After this question was considered, or rather during its consideration, Mr. Buchanan expressed the opinion that our naval forces should be instructed to take and hold Monterey on the Pacific, and the Bay of San Francisco. Farther south than these ports he insisted that we should not take or hold, because as he said we intended to hold California permanently and he was opposed to taking or holding permanently the country south of these places. This was the substance of the reason assigned by him for not being in favour of taking and holding the country south of Monterey on the Pacific. He was opposed, too, to giving to the inhabitants of Tamaulipas or any of the provinces south of New Mexico any encouragement to annex themselves to the United States or that we would receive them. It was clear from the general tenor of his remarks on this, as well as on former occasions, that he was unwilling by treaty with Mexico, or in any manner to acquire any part of the Mexican territory south of New Mexico and Upper California. Mr. Walker discussed the matter with him, differing from him in opinion and insisting upon having a more southerly line of boundary, if it could be obtained. Finally I remarked that if when we came to make a treaty I found that I could obtain a boundary from the mouth of the Rio Grande west to the Pacific by paying a few millions more for it than for the boundary mentioned by Mr. Buchanan, I should certainly make such a treaty, but that if I could do no better I would take the boundary mentioned by him. It was very manifest that Mr. Buchanan desired to avoid acquiring any Southern territory below the boundary indicated by him. I differed with him in my views, and was sorry to find him entertaining opinions so contracted and sectional.

Washington, 8th July, 1846. — Saw company as usual until twelve o'clock today. Nothing of special interest occurred. I had a long interview with the Secretary of War. I submitted to him the draft of instructions to General Taylor in relation to the manner of conducting the Mexican War. A part of this draft was prepared by Col. Benton at my request, and the latter part of it, and that which I regard as most important, was prepared by me. It was in the form of a letter to be addressed by the Secretary of War to General Taylor. The Secretary of War approved it.

Friday, 10*th July,* 1846. — I requested my private secretary to invite Mr. Dix to call on me. Mr. Dix called about six o'clock P.M., when I tendered the mission to England to him. It evidently took him by surprise. He expressed his gratitude for the honour done him by the offer of the mission. He said he would give me an answer in the course of a week or ten days.[2]

Saturday, 11*th July,* 1846. — Great doubt at this moment exists of the passage of . . . the Tariff Bill, or rather the bill to reduce the tariff. Upon the latter bill Senator Semple of Illinois, I learn, expresses opinions which render it doubtful how he will vote. Mr. Semple, I learn, has been for some time dissatisfied with the administration. I know of no cause, unless it be that I did not appoint him a brigadier or major-general of volunteers, which he sought to obtain of me. I learned, too, today that Senator Dickinson of New York is in bad humour with the administration, and that his complaint is that his friends in New York have in his opinion

[2] John A. Dix, Senator from New York 1845–1849, refused the proffered post. He was a Democrat, but came to oppose the policy of the administration. "No doubt," writes his biographer, "there were those at Washington and at Albany who would gladly have got rid of one whose opposition to their designs was foreseen and dreaded." (Morgan Dix, *Memoirs of John A. Dix,* 1, 203.)

been overlooked in appointments to office. Several other members have similar griefs. They have either been disappointed themselves or have not obtained offices for their favourites and friends, and at this moment the great domestic measures of the session are endangered from these causes. I sincerely wish that I had no offices to bestow. I cannot gratify all who apply, and it is certain from my experience that the dispensation of the public patronage is a weakening operation. There is more selfishness among members of Congress which is made to bear upon great public measures, than the people have any knowledge of.

Sunday, 12th July, 1846. — I sent for Mr. Buchanan this evening. He called about eight o'clock P.M. I told him that having made up my mind to appoint Mr. McLane, now at London, his successor in the Department of State, in the event he elected, as he had informed me he would, to go on the bench of the Supreme Court of the United States, I had sent to him for the purpose of saying that if on reflection he had changed his mind the matter was still in his own hands. . . Mr. Buchanan expressed a strong desire to be nominated to the Senate for the appointment of judge of the Supreme Court of the United States immediately. To this I objected, and assigned as my reasons that if he was nominated at this time (a month probably before the adjournment of Congress) it would in my opinion put in jeopardy the reduction of the tariff and all the leading measures now pending before Congress. I told him he saw the want of harmony and the factious spirit which prevailed among the Democratic members of Congress. I told him that the moment it became known that his place as Secretary of State was vacant, that all the factions and sections of the Democratic party in Congress would immediately set to work to press upon me their respective favourites as his successor; that they would probably be getting up petitions signed by members of Congress for this purpose. I told him that I knew that it was impossible to select any man who breathed who would be satisfactory to all the factions of the Democratic party, and that if by any means, by public rumour or otherwise, it became known whom I was likely to appoint, I would be annoyed by protests against him be he whom he might, and that my position would be one of perfect torment and vexation until the close of the session. I told him further that at the present critical moment, when all my leading domestic measures were pending before Congress, it was not difficult to foresee that to change the head of the Cabinet would probably have the effect to defeat them all. Mr. Buchanan said if I believed that such would be the effect I ought not to make the change at this time.

Wednesday, 15th July, 1846. — At five o'clock P.M. my private secretary returned from the Capitol, and reported to me that Senator Semple of Illinois had been absent from the Senate chamber today, and that it was understood that he was packing his trunk to leave for Illinois this evening or tomorrow morning. I immediately sent Col. Walker to see Judge Douglas and Mr. Smith of the Illinois delegation and get them if possible to detain Mr. Semple to vote on the tariff bill. My information is that the fate of that bill in the Senate will depend on a single Democratic vote, and that if Mr. Semple is absent it will probably be lost. After Col. Walker left, the Postmaster-General called and I requested him to go and see Mr. Semple, if he had not left the city, and prevail on him if possible to remain. About sunset I learned that Mr. Semple had been at the railroad depot at the hour of departure of the cars this evening, with his baggage, on his way to Illinois, but had been prevailed upon by Mr. Ficklin of Illinois to remain until tomorrow morning. About the same time the Postmaster-General returned and reported that he had seen Mr. Semple, and requested him to call on me tonight. About eight o'clock P.M. Mr. Semple called. He showed me a letter which he said he had received from Illinois stating that judgments had been recovered against him in the courts of that State for between five and six thousand dollars and that his property would be levied on to satisfy them. I made an earnest appeal to his patriotism and for the sake of the country to remain and vote on the tariff bill. After a conversation of nearly an hour he agreed to remain and to vote for the bill. I can but remark that Mr. Semple has been disappointed in not getting an office in the army, and has been dissatisfied for some time past. (See the notice of him taken in this diary.) The most tremendous efforts I understand are being made by the capitalists who are engaged in manufactures to defeat the bill of the House now before the Senate to reduce and modify the duties imposed by the tariff act of 1842. Scores of them I understand are flocking to Washington for that purpose. The absence of a single Democratic Senator will probably enable them to effect their object.[3]

Thursday, 16th July, 1846. — Had the usual number of visitors this morning; was greatly annoyed by importunities for office and by beggars for money. I am applied to almost daily and sometimes half a dozen times a day for money, by persons who do not ask it for charitable purposes, but by well dressed persons, men and women. They call on me to contribute to build academies, to aid colleges, and for churches in every part of the Union. Except in the District of Columbia I am compelled to decline contributing except for charitable purposes; otherwise I should be utterly bankrupt. The idea seems to prevail with many persons that the President is from his position compelled to contribute to every loafer who applies, provided he represents that the sum he wants is to build a church, an academy, or a college.

[3] The Senate was closely divided politically. It comprised 31 Democrats and 25 Whigs, but both the Democratic Senators from Pennsylvania and one Democratic member from Connecticut were opposed to modifying the tariff of 1842. One of the North Carolina Senators, Haywood, who opposed both Walker's bill and the manner in which it was managed in the Senate, resigned, as Polk here notes, to avoid voting on the measure. On the other hand, Senator Spencer Jarnagin of Tennessee, after speaking against the bill, voted for it under peremptory instructions from the legislature of his State. For days it was seen that the bill hung in the closest balance.

Saturday, 18th July, 1846. — At eleven o'clock A.M. Lieut.-Col. Payne of the United States Army called in company with General Scott and all the principal officers of the army stationed at Washington to exhibit to me several Mexican flags as the trophies of the victory of the 8th and 9th May on the Rio Grande. These flags were captured from the enemy in the battles on those days, and two of them had been perforated by balls in these battles. They had been sent by General Taylor to Washington as trophies of the victories of the American arms. Col. Payne himself was in these battles and had been severely wounded. He walks now on his crutches. The officers of the army who were present today were in full uniform. A number of ladies and citizens were present on the occasion.

Sunday, 19th July, 1846. — I had a conversation with Col. Benton in relation to the probability of the passage of the bill of the House of Representatives through the Senate to reduce and modify the tariff act of 1842. He thought it would pass the Senate by a very close vote, and agreed with me that it would probably depend upon the vote of Senator Haywood of North Carolina. I knew Col. Benton's intimacy with Mr. Haywood and requested him to induce him if practicable to vote for the bill. He said he would do so. In the course of the afternoon I received a note from Col. Benton expressing the opinion in substance that Mr. Haywood would not separate from his political friends but would vote for the bill. . .

At twelve o'clock a delegation of eight or ten persons from Berks County, Pennsylvania, called upon me. Among them were the Hon. E. B. Hubley (former member of Congress), Dr. Muhlenberg (son of the late Henry A. Muhlenberg) and Mr. Saladay. The names of the others I do not remember. They stated that they had come to Washington to see if some compromise on the bill now before Congress in relation to a reduction of the tariff could not be effected. They expressed great alarm, if it passed the Senate in the form it had passed the House, that it would prostrate the iron and coal interests in Pennsylvania and reduce the Democracy of that State to a minority, and they appealed to me to know if such a compromise in relation to iron and coal could not be effected. I told them that my views on the subject of the tariff were before Congress and that these views I had not changed. They asked me if I would give my assent to a compromise in relation to these leading interests in Pennsylvania and thus save the Democratic party in that State from overthrow. I told them that I must leave the matter in the hands of my Democratic friends in Congress, but if they could agree upon a compromise within the principles embraced in my message to Congress on the 2d of December last I would be rejoiced at it. They said all they wished was adequate protection on iron and coal. I asked them what protection they could consider adequate on these articles. They said a reduction of 20 per cent on the present rates of duty, and that $33\frac{1}{3}$ per cent had been mentioned by some of the manufacturers. I told them that this was a matter wholly for the consideration of Congress. They still urged a compromise and said they had been advised to call on me on the subject by some Democratic Senators. I then told them that I was not authorized to speak for any Democratic member of Congress on the subject, but that I would express an opinion on one point. It was this, *viz.*, " that if a proposition such as they suggested was made, it must come from the Pennsylvania Senators, and that if made by them, before it would probably be entertained by the other Democratic members of Congress they must pledge themselves that if the amendment of compromise was adopted they would vote for the bill as amended and that the Pennsylvania Democratic members in the House of Representatives would vote for it also.". . They retired apparently in a good humour.

Tuesday, 21st July, 1846. — Before the hour of assembling of the Cabinet arrived Andrew Johnson, one of the

Representatives from Tennessee, called.[4] He had not been
in my office or at the President's mansion for many weeks, indeed months, except once for a few minutes about two
months ago in company with the Hon. John Blair and some
other East Tennesseeans who called and remained for a
few minutes. . . He said he had held a conversation with
Mr. Cave Johnson (the Postmaster-General) a few days
ago, and was surprised to learn from him that his course in
opposition to the administration, as he said Mr. C. Johnson
informed him, was understood and marked by the administration. He was very much agitated in his manner. He said
he did not wish to be understood as making an apology, and
then went on to say that he was a Democrat and had spent
a great deal of time and money in my support in Tennessee,
and particularly in 1844, and complained that his politics
should now be suspected. . . He left professing to be a
good Democrat and denying that he was opposed to me or
my administration. The truth is that neither Johnson nor
(George W.) Jones have been my personal friends since
1839. They were in the Baltimore Convention in 1844 and
were not my friends then. I doubt whether any two members of that convention were at heart more dissatisfied with
my nomination for the Presidency than they were. This I
learned from members of the convention from Tennessee.
Mr. Johnson, I was informed, said at Baltimore when my
nomination was suggested that it was a " humbug."

  Thursday, 23d July, 1846. — Senator Haywood
called. . . I made an earnest appeal to him in regard to
what was understood to be his intended course on the bill
of the House of Representatives to modify and reduce the
tariff of 1842, and urged him to give it his support. I found
him much opposed to the bill. Indeed, he used the strong
expression, " I would rather die than vote for it." He said

---

[4] Andrew Johnson was a Representative in Congress from Tennessee
1843–1853; he and Polk had a mutual dislike, though Johnson sustained
Polk's policy in the Mexican War.

if the Senate would agree to vote in an amendment to postpone the commencement of its operation from the 1st of
December next until the 4th of March next he would vote
for it. I told him that the principal objection to such an
amendment would be that it might put in jeopardy the fate
of the bill in the House of Representatives. He seemed to
have no other objection to the bill, except that he thought
it would be too sudden a revolution of the existing system.
I told him that the Senate in my opinion had to choose between the bill of the House of Representatives and the act
of 1842, and that if he voted against the House bill he
would be voting in effect to rivet and continue the act of
1842 on the country, which was manifestly oppressive and
unjust. I had a long conversation with him, but it would
be too tedious to repeat the arguments I used to induce
him to vote for the House bill. He left leaving me satisfied
that unless he changed his mind he would vote against the
House bill. After he left I addressed him a note requesting
him to call again, and he did so about nine o'clock P.M., when
I had a further conversation with him on the subject. . .
He was manifestly deeply impressed with the appeal which
I made to him, and left saying he would think of it till the
last moment before he voted. Before he left I told him
I had been informed that a rumour was abroad that he had
spoken of resigning his seat in the Senate, and I begged him
not to do so. I told him if he resigned the effect would be
the same as if he voted against the bill, for it was understood
that if he voted for the bill the Senate would be equally divided and that would enable the Vice-President to give his
casting vote for the bill.

   After Mr. Haywood left about nine-thirty o'clock P.M.
I saw Senators McDuffie and Lewis and General McKay of
North Carolina, and had a full conversation with them about
the prospects of passing the House bill to reduce the tariff.
They agreed that it depended on Mr. Haywood's vote, un-
less Senator Jarnagin of Tennessee voted for the bill, as he

had repeatedly said he would do, in which event the Senate would still be tied even if Mr. Haywood voted against it. The Secretary of the Treasury came in during the conversation and participated in it. All agreed that they would ascertain on tomorrow whether the bill in its present form could pass, and if they ascertained it could not, they would endeavour to effect some compromise with the Pennsylvania Senators, and if possible to pass it in some modified form.

Friday, 24th July, 1846.— This was reception evening. . . After the company retired Vice-President Dallas and the Secretary of the Treasury retired to my office to talk with me about a proposed compromise of the tariff question, which had been suggested by a leading manufacturer to the Secretary of the Treasury. It was to reduce all existing duties one-fourth of the excess above 30 per cent; at the end of five years another fourth, and at the end of ten years to bring the duties down to the rates of the pending bill. Mr. Dallas was in favour of the proposition. I did not encourage it, fearing that it might produce confusion and be the means of losing the bill. Mr. Dallas said if the Democrats did not agree to it he would let them know, if it came to his casting vote they might lose the bill as it was.

Saturday, 25th July, 1846.— After the Cabinet adjourned, and about half past three o'clock, I was astonished to learn that Senator Haywood had today addressed a letter to the Vice-President resigning his seat in the Senate of the United States. It was a great error, and I am sure he will deeply regret it. The fate of the tariff bill will now depend on the vote of Senator Jarnagin. If he votes as he declared he would today, the bill will still pass. I sincerely regret Mr. Haywood's course. I was at college with him and have ever been his friend. I believe him to be an honest and pure man, but a man of great vanity and possessing a good deal of self-esteem. He is, I think, ambitious, and had probably a desire to have some participation or authorship in effecting the contemplated tariff reform. From some feeling of this sort and without due reflection, I conjecture, he took ground against the tariff bill, and having committed himself was of too proud a spirit, when he found himself separated from all his friends, and that none of them would go with him, to recede. He is moreover nervous, and in an excited state, no doubt, tendered his resignation. . .

About six o'clock the Secretary of the Treasury called and informed me that he had just been informed that Mr. Senator Jarnagin had spoken this evening about resigning his seat also. Should he do so, and Mr. Haywood's successor reach here in time, the tariff bill will be lost by one vote. On hearing this I immediately sent for Senator Turney and informed him of it. He left for the purpose of seeing Mr. Jarnagin, but before he did so he informed me of a very important fact. It was this, that a manufacturer who was in the city a few days ago had urged him to vote against the tariff bill and had called to see him on the subject two or three times : that in his last conversation this person (whose name he did not mention) had described the prosperity which would prevail if the pending bill did not pass, and had said to him, Turney, that if it did not pass he could loan to him (Turney) any amount of money which he might want. Turney was indignant at it, and considered it an attempt in this indirect way to induce him to vote against the bill; or in other words an attempt to bribe. Turney expressed the opinion to me that money would be used, if it could be, to defeat the bill. I was shocked at the story, and said nothing but to express my astonishment.

Sunday, 26th July, 1846. — Col. Benton called this evening, having been requested by Mr. Cave Johnson to do so. I read to him a despatch to the Mexican Government proposing to renew negotiations with a view to peace, which Mr. Buchanan had prepared, and asked him his opinion as to the policy of sending it. He approved it and advised that it be sent. I told Col. Benton that if Congress would pass an appropriation of two millions of dollars, such as was passed in 1803 to enable Mr. Jefferson to purchase Louisiana, or in 1806 to enable him to purchase the Floridas, I had but little doubt that by paying the sum in hand at the signature of a treaty we might procure California and such a boundary as we wished, and that in the present impoverished condition of Mexico the knowledge that such a sum would be paid in hand might induce Mexico to treat, when she might not otherwise do so.   Col. Benton approved the suggestion, and advised that I should see some members of the committee of foreign affairs on the subject.

Monday, 27th July, 1846. — About six o'clock P.M. my private secretary returned from the Capitol and informed me that the bill of the House to reduce the tariff had been committed to the committee on finance after a stormy and violent debate by a majority of one vote, Mr. Jarnagin having disregarded his instructions and voted with his Whig friends.   Jarnagin holds the fate of the bill in his hands and there is no reliance to be placed upon him.   He declared on Saturday last in presence of the Cabinet, when he called on me as a member of the committee of enrolled bills to present to me some bills which had passed Congress, that he would vote for the bill, and yet today he voted to embarrass and defeat it.

Tuesday, 28th July, 1846. — About two o'clock I received a note from Senator Bagby informing me that the tariff bill had been ordered to a third reading by the casting vote of the Vice-President, Mr. Jarnagin declining to vote. A slight amendment had been made to the bill.   At five o'clock P.M. Mr. Ritchie called and informed me that the bill had passed its final reading by a majority of one vote, Senator Jarnagin voting for it.   If the amendment be concurred in by the House of Representatives, the bill will only require the approval of the President to become a law.[5]

---

[5] The Walker Tariff Bill passed by a vote of 28 to 27.   If Senator Jarnagin had abstained from voting, Vice President Dallas, though a protectionist and Pennsylvanian, would have given a casting vote in the bill's

This was reception evening, and an unusually large number of persons attended, ladies and gentlemen, among whom were an unusual number of members of Congress, all of them I believe of the Democratic party, who were exchanging congratulations on the passage of the tariff bill in the Senate today. They seemed to be confident that the House of Representatives would concur in the amendment made by the Senate, but I had my doubts and expressed them to several members.

After the company had nearly all retired Mr. Woodworth of New York of the House of Representatives called and informed me that the New York Democratic members of the House of Representatives had held a caucus tonight at which he was present. He informed me that five of them who had voted in favour of the bill, *viz.*, Rathbun, King, Wood, Grover, and Goodyear would, he thought, vote against concurring in the amendment of the Senate to the tariff bill, with a view of defeating the bill by a disagreement between the two houses. This gave me great uneasiness, especially as I learned that the Whigs with the same object in view would vote against it, and that the Democratic portion of the Pennsylvania delegation would unite with them and make great efforts to defeat the bill. Upon hearing this, after the violent struggle which had taken place in the Senate on yesterday and today, I had great fears that there might be a sufficient defection in the House of Representatives to defeat it. The city is swarming with manufacturers who are making tremendous exertions to defeat it.

Wednesday, 29th July, 1846. — About two o'clock P.M. Senator Bagby called and informed me that the House of Representatives had concurred in the amendment of the Senate to the bill to reduce the tariff of duties. The five New York members named in yesterday's journal voted, as I

---

favor. This enactment of 1846 was destined to remain unchanged for eleven years, the longest period during which any tariff act has been in operation; and under it the country was uniformly prosperous.

learn, with the opponents of the bill (the Whigs) upon all the collateral and incidental questions which arose, the vote on some of which was very close, being decided by a single vote in favour of the bill. It is certain from what I learn of the proceedings of the House that Messrs. Grover, Good-year, King, Rathbun, and Wood of the New York delegation desired to defeat the bill, and yet feared upon a direct vote to record their votes against it. This great measure of re-form has been thus successful. It has given rise to an im-mense struggle between the two great political parties of the country. The capitalists and monopolists have not sur-rendered the immense advantages which they possessed, and the enormous profits which they derived under the tariff of 1842, until after a fierce and mighty struggle. This city has swarmed with them for weeks. They have spared no effort within their power to sway and control Congress, but all has proved to be unavailing and they have been at length van-quished. Their effort will probably now be to raise a panic (such as they have already attempted) by means of their combined wealth, so as to induce a repeal of the act. The Pennsylvania Democracy have been placed in a false posi-tion upon this subject. Her public men have not had the moral courage to take bold ground and proclaim the true doctrines of her people. Pennsylvania is essentially an agri-cultural State, and as a community cannot be interested in imposing enormous taxes on the many for the benefit of the few. I do not doubt that Pennsylvania will continue to be Democratic if her public men and presses shall have the independence and moral courage to avow the truth as they know it to exist.

Saturday, 1st August, 1846. — Mr. Buchanan called about six o'clock P.M. and informed me that he had decided to remain in the Cabinet and not to accept the offer which I had made to appoint him judge of the Supreme Court. He said that he did this cheerfully, although he had long de-sired a seat on the bench, and that now he would stick to me and go through my administration with me.

Sunday, 2d August, 1846. — I saw Mr. Bancroft (the Secretary of the Navy) this morning, and informed him that if he preferred the English to the French mission as he had intimated to me some weeks ago that he did, that he could have it, but informed him at the same time that if he accepted it he would have to go out in September. He received the offer I thought favorably, but said he would like to think of it for twenty-four hours. I had previously promised to appoint him Minister to France towards the close of the next session of Congress.[6]

Wednesday, 5th August, 1846. — General Robert Armstrong, special bearer of despatches, arrived this morning from London, bringing with him the exchange of ratifications of the Oregon Treaty. In the course of the day I had a message prepared, and transmitted it with the ratified treaty to Congress, and recommended the establishment of a territorial government in the Oregon Territory.

Friday, 7th August, 1846. — On Tuesday last, the 4th instant, I communicated a confidential message to the Senate in executive session giving them information of the existing state of our relations with Mexico, and of my desire to treat with that Power. For the reasons assigned in that message I recommended, if the Senate approved my policy, that an appropriation might be made by Congress to facilitate negotiations with Mexico. The message will explain itself. On the 6th instant the Senate in executive session passed two resolutions, with a copy of which I was furnished, approving my recommendations. I learned from several Senators that it was expected by the Senate that I would now send in a confidential message to both houses asking the appropriation. I objected to this course as unnecessary, and well calculated to defeat the object I had in view altogether. To send a confidential message to so numerous a body as the House of Representatives, composed as that body un-

---

[6] George Bancroft, who was eager to press on with his historical labors, wished to exchange his post as Secretary of the Navy, in which he had clashed with Congress and not been wholly popular with the service itself, for a diplomatic position. He served as our Minister to England 1846–1849.

fortunately is of so many discordant factions, and expect my
message to be kept a secret, would be as I thought a perfect
farce. No confidential message has been made to the House
for more than a dozen years, and to do it now would excite
universal curiosity in our own country, and ultimately give
the proceeding greater publicity than if a public message
were at once sent in. It would, moreover, excite the jealousy and alarm of foreign Powers as to our designs upon
Mexico. I advised the Senators with whom I conversed, as
the Senate had approved the object in view, to pass the appropriation through the Senate in legislative session without
debate, and I had no doubt by seeing and explaining to a
few leading members of the House of Representatives the
object of the appropriation, it would pass the House also
without arousing much attention. This course I hoped
would have been adopted. I learned last evening and this
morning that certain Whig Senators objected to the appropriation unless I first took the responsibility of recommending it. To this I answered that I had done so in my
confidential message. In order to remove all pretext, however, to resist the appropriation on such grounds, I saw Mr.
Buchanan, and upon consultation with him it was agreed
that he as Secretary of State should address a letter (a mode
not unusual in the intercourse between the executive departments and Congress) to the chairman of the committee of
finance in the Senate and of ways and means in the House
of Representatives, asking the appropriation. He prepared
such a letter accordingly in which he spoke in my name, and
took it to the Capitol to deliver in person.

Saturday, 8th August, 1846. — Early in the day I was
informed by a Senator that the Whig Senators, although
committed by their votes in executive session to vote for the
appropriation which I had asked in my confidential message
to the Senate to enable me to make peace with Mexico, were
now interposing objections, and saying that they would not
do so unless the President took the responsibility of the

measure.[7] . . I expressed the opinion that a message should be immediately sent in to both houses in open session asking for the appropriation, and thus place the responsibility of refusing it, if it was not made, on Congress. Mr. Buchanan agreed to this suggestion. A message was accordingly prepared and sent in to both houses before twelve o'clock today.

At about seven o'clock P.M., I went to the Capitol as is usual on the last nights of the session. This is done for the convenience of Congress, and especially of the committee of enrolled bills. I occupied the Vice-President's room. All my Cabinet were with me. A large number of enrolled bills were presented to me, which I examined, approved, and signed. . . The Senate adjourned about a quarter past eleven P.M.

Great confusion, I learned, prevailed in both houses during this night's session and what is deeply to be regretted several members as I was informed were much excited by drink. Among others I was informed that Senators Webster and Barrow were quite drunk, so much so that the latter gentleman, it was said, was noisy and troublesome. From all I learned it was a most disreputable scene. At half past eleven o'clock I left the Capitol. Both houses adjourned to meet, the House at eight, the Senate at eight-thirty A.M. on Monday next.

Monday, 10th *August,* 1846. — The two Houses had by

[7] Polk had reached the conclusion in the spring of 1846 that the offer of a large sum in cash might induce the Paredes Government in Mexico to conclude a satisfactory treaty, and had consulted with various Senators upon the possibility of obtaining a secret grant of one million dollars. The project was dropped for a time, on the advice of Senator Allen, lest it embarrass the settlement of the Oregon question. Later it was revived, and the sum was increased to two millions. On Aug. 1, 1846, Polk's Cabinet agreed to ask the advice of the Senate in executive session, and the Senate endorsed the plan by a vote of 33 to 19. Several Whigs, including Webster and Thomas Corwin, supported it. Polk then sent a message to both houses on August 8, as is shown here, asking two millions " to facilitate negotiations with Mexico." Chairman McKay of the Ways and Means Committee on the same day introduced a bill making the appropriation. The disappointing fate of the bill is disclosed in the entry for August 10.

a joint resolution agreed to adjourn for the session at twelve o'clock. At precisely that hour by the House clock the Speaker adjourned the House. . . The appropriation for $2,000,000 to enable the President to negotiate a peace with Mexico came up in the Senate some 30 or 40 minutes before twelve o'clock. Senator Davis of Massachusetts took the floor and spoke until the time had expired, so as to defeat action on it. . .

Late in the evening of Saturday the 8th, I learned that after an exciting debate in the House a bill passed that body, but with a mischievous and foolish amendment to the effect that no territory which might be acquired by treaty from Mexico should ever be a slaveholding country. What connection slavery had with making peace with Mexico it is difficult to conceive. This amendment was voted on to the bill by the opponents of the measure, and when voted on, the original friends of the bill voted against it, but it was passed by the Whigs and Northern Democrats, who had been opposed to making the appropriation. In this form it had gone to the Senate. Had there been time, there is but little doubt the Senate would have struck out the slavery proviso and that the House would have concurred.[8]

Thursday, 13th *August,* 1846. — About one o'clock, the Cherokee chiefs, including those of the Ross party, the Treaty party, and the Old Settlers, called in a body to take

---

[8] Polk of course refers to the Wilmot Proviso, attached to the two-million-dollar bill, and offered by David Wilmot, a Pennsylvania Democrat in the House. It declared that as an express and fundamental condition to the acquisition of any territory from Mexico, and to the use of any of the moneys thus appropriated, " neither slavery nor involuntary servitude shall ever exist in any part of said territory, except for crime, whereof the party shall first be duly convicted." The proviso was adopted in the House by a vote of 83 to 64, and the appropriation bill with the proviso passed by a vote of 87 to 64. On August 10, 1846, the appropriation bill was taken up in the Senate and a motion was made to strike out the proviso. As Polk notes, Senator John Davis of Massachusetts began speaking against this motion, and was still speaking when the hour struck for the termination of the session. Davis was attacked for preventing a vote by both the expansionists and the anti-slavery men. Polk was profoundly disappointed by the loss of his two millions, but was unwilling yet to give up the fight to obtain the fund.

leave of me, being about to depart for their home in the West. They had today given their assent to the amendments made by the Senate to the treaty lately concluded with them. They had settled all the difficulties between themselves, and between the nation and the government of the United States. John Ross, the principal chief, addressed me, and said they were all now in harmony and were satisfied. . . This event in my administration I consider an important one. From the commencement of General Jackson's administration down to the present time this tribe (which is probably the most enlightened on the continent) has been torn by factions arrayed in deadly hostility against each other. Ross's party resisted with great stubbornness the wise policy of General Jackson to remove all the Indian tribes residing within the States to the west of the Mississippi. This party constituted the majority of the nation, and since their removal west have pursued and persecuted the Treaty party, so called because they made the treaty of 1835. Many murders have been committed among them, and even this year several of the Treaty party and Old Settlers have been slain by the Ross party. The treaty which I have caused to be made recently has put an end to all these troubles, and I hope they may hereafter be a united and happy people.

Saturday, 15th August, 1846. — The Secretary of War laid before me the finding of the court of inquiry lately convened at Fortress Monroe in the case of General Gaines. The court find General Gaines guilty of violating orders and acting illegally in several instances, in ordering out volunteers in Louisiana and other Southern States and mustering them into service; but the court recommend, in consideration of his long service and the supposed patriotism and purity of his motives, that no further proceedings be had in his case. It is evident from the finding of the court that they have laboured to give a construction to General Gaines's conduct most favourable to him, and if possible to excuse him. General Gaines is now a very old man and although guilty of acts which cannot be justified, and for the commission of which, if brought before a general court-martial, he would without doubt be punished, yet I determined in lenity to him to yield to the recommendation of the court of inquiry and take no further proceedings against him. His late conduct at New Orleans greatly embarrassed the government and will cost the Treasury many hundreds of thousands of dollars. He is now, however, removed from that command and cannot repeat the mischief.

At four o'clock P.M. I took a ride with the Secretary of the Navy in his carriage to the country. We drove to the residence of Francis P. Blair, esq., late editor of the *Globe,* some six miles from Washington. His residence is in Maryland. . . Mr. Blair was alone his family being absent from home. He received me very cordially and was very friendly. During our stay of an hour, he took occasion to remark to me that I had been eminently successful in my administration, and that he approved all my leading measures.

Wednesday, 19th August, 1846. — This morning at nine o'clock I went on board the steamer *Osceola* with Mrs. Polk, her niece, Miss Rucker, and two servants to take an excursion to Fortress Monroe. . . My intention is to take an excursion of only three or four days. It is my first absence from Washington since I have been President, except a single day in the spring of 1845 when I visited Mount Vernon, going and returning on the same day. My long confinement to my office has considerably enfeebled me and rendered some recreation necessary.

Saturday, 22nd August, 1846 [At Fortress Monroe on his excursion]. — After dinner Gov. Tazewell[9] talked freely of public affairs, and among other things took occasion to remark that it had been my fortune to meet more great

---

[9] Littleton W. Tazewell, 1790–1860, had been Governor of Virginia in the thirties. Polk had known him when he was a Senator, had lived in the same boarding-house with him in Washington, and "then thought him, and still do, one of the greatest men I have ever known."

and important questions in the early part of my administration than any of my predecessors had done. He said that my administration had successfully disposed of and settled more important public subjects of great interest in the first eighteen months of my term than any of my predecessors had ever done in eight years. A part of these questions, he said, I had brought forward myself, while others may have come up for action by accident, or without any immediate or direct agency of mine. He enumerated the great questions which had been settled, *viz.*, the annexation of Texas; the settlement of the Oregon question by a definitive treaty, a question which preceding administrations had been endeavoring to settle for more than thirty years; the reduction of the tariff; the establishment of the Constitutional Treasury; and the establishment of the Warehouse system; any one of which he remarked would have been sufficient to mark the success of any one administration if nothing else had been done during its term. He spoke in terms of approbation also of my two vetoes of the Harbour and River bill, and the French Spoliation Bill.

Wednesday, 26th August, 1846. — Twelve months ago this day, a very important conversation took place in the Cabinet between myself and Mr. Buchanan on the Oregon question. This conversation was of so important a character, that I deemed it proper on the same evening to reduce the substance of it to writing for the purpose of retaining it more distinctly in my memory. This I did on separate sheets. It was this circumstance which first suggested to me the idea, if not the necessity, of keeping a journal or diary of events and transactions which might occur during my Presidency. I resolved to do so and accordingly procured a blank book for that purpose on the next day, in which I have every day since noted whatever occurred that I deemed of interest. Sometimes I have found myself so much engaged with my public duties, as to be able to make only a very condensed and imperfect statement of events and incidents which occurred, and to be forced to omit others altogether which I would have been pleased to have noted.

Tuesday, 1st September, 1846. — About two o'clock P.M. Mr. Buchanan . . . informed me that he had just received a note from the secretary of the British legation (Mr. Pakenham being at present absent on a visit to Canada) which he read. On last evening it appears a special messenger arrived in Washington from the City of Mexico bearing despatches to the British Minister here. The substance of the information brought by this messenger, as far as communicated to Mr. Buchanan, is that Commodore Sloat, commanding the United States squadron in the Pacific, took Monterey on the 6th of July last and hoisted the American flag; the same thing had been done by another naval officer at a point south of Monterey. Commodore Sloat had issued a proclamation declaring California to be in the possession of the United States, etc., a copy of which the British Secretary of Legation had submitted to Mr. Buchanan, but to be returned to him. Mr. Buchanan read the proclamation to me. Further intelligence was also communicated that Col. Frémont with his men had been attacked near San Francisco by Castro, the Commandant General of Mexico in California, and that after a short skirmish Castro had retreated.[10] This important intelligence comes

[10] Commodore Sloat, commanding our squadron on the Pacific Coast, had heard of the fighting on the Rio Grande on May 17, 1846; but he had delayed several weeks before acting, with a timidity which later brought upon him the censure of the Navy Department. On July 7 he took possession of Monterey; on July 9 Captain Stockton, acting under his orders, took possession of San Francisco. But meanwhile there had occurred at Sonoma, just north of San Francisco Bay, a revolt of the American settlers in the region, encouraged if not instigated by Capt. John C. Frémont. This young explorer had reached California, with his party of sixty, at the end of 1845, had been ordered out by the authorities, and had clashed with Castro, the Mexican commandant. After moving northward to Klamath Lake, on the Oregon border, he was overtaken by Lieutenant Gillespie, and hastened to return to California. Here he had found the American settlers apprehensive of Mexican attack and ready for a rebellion. The hoisting of the Bear Flag and the seizure of Monterey resulted in the rapid conquest of California by Sloat, Stockton, and Frémont.

to us through no other channel, and we are indebted for it to the courtesy of the British legation.

After dark Mr. Buchanan called again and seemed to be deeply concerned at the removal of a clerk today named King, by Mr. Piper, the acting Commissioner of the Public Lands. . . He then said that he and Col. William R. King of Alabama had boarded with King (the clerk) for seven years, and that his life, when he had a severe attack of illness whilst boarding with King, had been saved by Mrs. King by her kind attention to him in his illness. He said he had just been to King's house and had left his wife and children in tears, while King himself was lying ill of an attack of fever. Mr. Buchanan said he had no relation in office at Washington, that it seemed he had no influence, and could not keep even a poor clerk in office. I then said to Mr. Buchanan that as he seemed to take the matter so much to heart, Mr. King should be restored or appointed to some other place, but upon the express condition that he should hereafter do his duty. He said he desired it very much and I told him it should be done. With this he was satisfied and immediately assumed a cheerful tone in his conversation. Mr. Buchanan is a man of talents and is fully competent to discharge the high duties of Secretary of State, but it is one of his weaknesses (and perhaps all great men have such) that he takes on and magnifies small matters into great and undeserved importance.

Thursday, 3d September, 1846. — Saw no company until twelve o'clock today. A number of persons called at that hour. . . What is very remarkable, not a single office-seeker made his appearance, a thing which I believe has not happened before any day since I have been President when I saw company.

Saturday, 5th September, 1846. — I asked General Jesup's opinion as a military man as to the proper means of transportation for General Taylor's army as they penetrated into Mexico, remarking to him that I had no military experience but that I had a strong conviction that the immense train of baggage wagons which accompanied the army must greatly impede its progress, if indeed it was practicable to take them through such a country. I asked him if in all the wars in Mexico which had preceded the present, the baggage and munitions of war had not been transported on mules. General Jesup gave it as his decided opinion that baggage-wagons should be dispensed with and mules employed, and added that such had been the mode of conducting all the wars which had occurred heretofore in Mexico. I then asked of him and the Secretary of War why a similar means of transportation had not been provided in this instance. General Jesup replied that he had received no communication from General Taylor or the War Department on the subject, and said if he commanded in General Taylor's place he would take mules and not be encumbered with wagons, that he would not take a single tent with him, and that officers and men would cheerfully submit to this if the commanding General set them the example. I invited the special attention of the Secretary of War to the subject, and desired him to see me on the subject again shortly. I find it impossible to give much attention to the details in conducting the war, and still it is necessary that I should give some attention to them. There is entirely too much delay and too much want of energy and promptness in execution on the part of many subordinate officers, which must be corrected. General Taylor, I fear, is not the man for the command of the army. He is brave but he does not seem to have resources or grasp of mind enough to conduct such a campaign.[11] In his communica-

---

[11] Taylor, a hardy frontier soldier, who had never before commanded a real army nor seen a real battle, had fine qualities — courage, self-confidence, resolution, shrewd common-sense — but lacked the higher traits of generalship. He was illiterate, uncouth, and obstinate. He was frequently grossly negligent and lacking in foresight, inclined to exceed his orders, and excessively deliberate in his movements. He was scornful of the West Pointers and of book-strategy. Had not Scott sent him an invaluable aide in the person

tions to the War Department he seems ready to obey orders, but appears to be unwilling to express any opinion or take any responsibility on himself. Though he is in the country with means of knowledge which cannot be possessed at Washington, he makes no suggestion as to the plan of campaign, but simply obeys orders and gives no information to aid the administration in directing his movement. He is, I have no doubt, a good subordinate officer, but from all the evidence before me I think him unfit for the chief command. Though this is so, I know of no one whom I can substitute in his place. After the late battles, which were well fought, the public opinion seems to point to him as entitled to the command.

Tuesday, 8th September, 1846.—The Secretary of the Navy is now, as he has been for a week past, confined to his room by indisposition. . . I walked to Mr. Bancroft's house, which is situated on the President's square, to see how he was. Judge Mason accompanied me. I found Mr. Bancroft walking about his house and much better than he had been for several days. I held a conversation with him in reference to his contemplated mission to England, and it was agreed that I should issue his commission to him as Minister on tomorrow. I informed him that I would commission Mr. Mason at the same time as Secretary of the Navy. I have received no answer from the Hon. Franklin Pierce of New Hampshire, to whom I wrote on the 27th ultimo tendering to him the office of Attorney-General. . .

Hon. Felix G. McConnell, a Representative in Congress

---

of Capt. W. W. S. Bliss, who was his adjutant-general, he would have made more mistakes than he did. Polk felt a certain political jealousy of Taylor, whose Whig views were by no means concealed, but his estimate of the man and his limitations was not greatly unfair or inaccurate. Yet it must be remembered of Taylor that, as Rives says (*The United States and Mexico, 1821–1848*, II, 148), "in a remarkable degree he enjoyed the affection and respect of his army." Taylor and Quartermaster-General T. S. Jesup did not get on well, Taylor complaining of inefficiency in the latter's department.

from Alabama, called. He looked very badly, and as though he had just recovered from a fit of intoxication. He was sober, but was pale, his countenance haggard and his system nervous. He applied to me to borrow $100, and said he would return it to me in ten days. Though I had no idea that he would do so I had a sympathy for him even in his dissipation. I had known him in his youth, and had not the moral courage to refuse. I loaned him $100 in gold and took his note. His hand was so tremulous that he could scarcely write his name to the note legibly. I think it probable that he will never pay me. He informed me he was detained at Washington attending to some business in the Indian office.

Wednesday, 9th September, 1846. — At nine o'clock this morning, accompanied by the Secretary of the Treasury, the Secretary of War, and the Attorney-General, I rode out in my carriage to meet the regents of the Smithsonian Institute on the public grounds lying west of the Capitol and south of the President's House, with a view to locate the site of that institution. I met the regents on the grounds, and spent nearly an hour with them on foot in examining the grounds. Opinions were freely expressed. The most elevated ground, and, as I think, the most eligible site, lies between 12th and 14th Streets containing about 32 acres. If more space be required the ground west of 14th Street may be added, which contains about 45 acres. If this be added the whole area would contain about 77 acres. Most of the regents expressed a preference for this location. Mr. W. W. Seaton, the mayor of Washington, who is *ex officio* one of the regents, earnestly urged that the location should be made west of 12th street and between that street and the Capitol grounds. This is a lower situation than that west of it, and in no sense, as it strikes me, so eligible. I have heard from private sources that the property holders in the vicinity of the Centre Market were exceedingly anxious for their private benefit to have the location at the place insisted on by

Mr. Seaton. I think it is to be regretted that any citizen of Washington was appointed a regent. . .

Today I appointed Mr. Bancroft, the Secretary of the Navy, envoy extraordinary and minister plenipotentiary to England. Upon receiving his commission he sent me his resignation as Secretary of the Navy. Upon receiving it I appointed Mr. Mason, the Attorney-General, to be Secretary of the Navy.

Thursday, 10th September, 1846.—About dark this evening I learned from Mr. Voorhies, who is acting as my private secretary during the absence of J. Knox Walker, hat Hon. Felix G. McConnell, a Representative from the State of Alabama, had committed suicide this afternoon at the St. Charles Hotel where he boarded. On Tuesday last Mr. McConnell called on me and I loaned him $100 (see this diary of that day). I learn that but a short time before the horrid deed was committed he was in the barroom of the St. Charles Hotel, handling gold pieces and stating that he had received them from me, that he had loaned $35 of them to the barkeeper, that shortly afterwards he had attempted to write something, but what I have not learned, but had not written much when he said he would go to his room. In the course of the morning I learn he went into the city and paid a hackman a small amount which he owed him. He had locked his room door, and when found he was stretched on his back with his hands extended weltering in his blood. He had three wounds in his abdomen and his throat was cut. A hawk-bill knife was found near him. A jury of inquest was held and found a verdict that he had destroyed himself. It was a melancholy instance of the effects of intemperance.

Sunday, 13th September, 1846.—I received by today's mail a letter from the Hon. Franklin Pierce of New Hampshire, declining to accept the office of Attorney-General of the United States, which I had tendered to him by my letter of the 27th ultimo.

CHAPTER V

Sept. 15, 1846 — Nov. 19, 1846

MEXICO REFUSES NEGOTIATION — SANTA FÉ CAPTURED —
BATTLE OF MONTEREY — SENATOR BENTON AND THE PLAN
OF CAMPAIGN — SCOTT REAPPOINTED AS CHIEF FIELD
COMMANDER

Tuesday, 15th September, 1846. — The Cabinet held a
regular meeting today. . . The Secretary of War read
despatches which he had received from the army in Mexico.
The manner of prosecuting the war was discussed. Great
embarrassment exists in directing the movements of our
forces, for want of reliable information of the topography
of the country, the character of the roads, the supplies which
can probably be drawn from the country, and the facilities
or obstructions which may exist in prosecuting the campaign
into the interior of the country. General Taylor though
in the country gives but little information on these points.
He seems to act as a regular soldier, whose only duty it is
to obey orders. He does not seem to possess the resources
and grasp of mind suited to the responsibilities of his position. He seems disposed to avoid all responsibility of
making any suggestions or giving any opinions.

Saturday, 19th September, 1846. — About dark this evening the Secretary of the Navy and the Secretary of War
called. Mr. Mason informed me that he had received a
despatch from Commodore Conner off Vera Cruz, transmitting the answer of the Mexican Secretary of Foreign
Affairs to the overture made by the Secretary of State on the

27th of July last, proposing to reopen negotiations with a view to conclude a peace just and honorable to both countries. Mr. Trist, chief clerk of the State Department, and during the temporary absence of Mr. Buchanan the acting Secretary of State, came in to deliver to me some despatches received by the last steamer. The answer from the Mexican government was in the Spanish language. Mr. Trist read it, translating it into English. It is in substance a postponement of any definitive decision until the meeting of a new Congress in Mexico on the 6th of December next, to whom the overture will be submitted for their decision.[1] I directed Mr. Trist to prepare a written translation and furnish it to me tonight or early on tomorrow. I then stated to the Secretary of War and of the Navy that our overture for peace having been in effect declined, my strong impression was that the character of the war which we were waging in Mexico should be in some respects changed. For the purpose of conciliating the Mexican people in the northern and eastern provinces we had heretofore deemed it to be our policy to pay liberally for the supplies drawn from the country for the support of the army. This was rather a helping than an injury to them and my opinion now was, seeing that their government refused to negotiate for peace, to quarter upon the enemy by laying contributions upon them, or seizing the necessary supplies for the army without paying for them, making proper discriminations in favour of such Mexicans as were ascertained to be friendly to the United States. In these opinions they concurred, but as this was an im-

---

[1] A new revolution had occurred in Mexico. Santa Anna landed at Vera Cruz on Aug. 16, 1846, Commodore Conner, who was blockading the Gulf ports, having been ordered by Washington to allow the exile to enter freely. The government in Washington hoped that he would be more willing than Paredes to sue for peace. On the contrary, he showed no desire to end the war, and began labouring effectively to organize resistance to the Americans. On Sept. 17 he had himself appointed commander-in-chief of " The Liberating Army." He exclaimed that " Every day that passes without fighting at the north is a century of disgrace for Mexico," and he labored to concentrate an army of 25,000 at San Luis Potosi. Some heavy fighting was plainly imminent.

portant subject and as but two members of the Cabinet were present, it was adjourned until tomorrow at nine o'clock.

Tuesday, 22d September, 1846. — The Cabinet met at the usual hour, present the Secretaries of State, War, and Navy. . . The responsibility was taken of ordering an expedition to Tampico and eastern Tamaulipas to consist of a column of three or four thousand men, provided such a movement did not interfere with the plan of campaign previously ordered by General Taylor. This column to be under the command of Major-General Patterson, who will be accompanied by Brigadier-Generals Pillow and Shields. . . I sent for General Jesup, the Quartermaster-General, after the Cabinet adjourned and held a conversation with him in relation to the proper provision for transportation, in view of this new movement on the part of the army. Major Eastland, one of the brigade quartermasters of volunteers, was present, and upon consultation with him and General Jesup, I advised the purchase of two additional steamships for the Gulf. I find that I am compelled to give some attention to these details or the movements of the army will be delayed and embarrassed. The Secretary of War is overwhelmed with his labours and responsibilities, and is compelled to rely for the execution of many details of his department on his subordinate officers, some of whom I fear do not feel that they have any responsibility, and others seem to act as though they were indifferent about the success of our military operations. Several of these officers are politically opposed to the administration and there is reason to apprehend that they would be willing to see the government embarrassed. With these apprehensions I shall for the future give more attention than I have done to their conduct. General Scott is no aid to the department, but his presence at Washington is constantly embarrassing to the Secretary of War. I will observe his course, and if necessary will order him to some other post.

Friday, 25th September, 1846. — I was engaged as usual in my office until twelve o'clock today when I opened my doors for the reception of visitors. Several office-seekers called. I soon disposed of them by telling them that I had no vacancies to fill. A female called to beg money. She was no object of charity and I refused to give her any. My kindness to poor McConnell of Alabama has brought upon me a horde of beggars who seem to think it is a fine opportunity to supply their wants.

Saturday, 26th September, 1846. — The Cabinet met at the usual hour; all the members present except the Secretary of the Navy, the Attorney-General's office being vacant. The Secretary of State read a letter which he had prepared in reply to that of the Secretary of Foreign Affairs of the Mexican Government received on the 19th instant (see this diary of that day). . . . The letter in reply prepared by Mr. Buchanan having been read by him, he remarked that he desired the opinion of the Cabinet and then that of the President. I remained silent until the views of the Cabinet were expressed. The Secretary of War objected to that part of the letter which announced that the expenses of the war must be defrayed by Mexico, as impolitic to be announced at this time, because it would be likely to prevent Mexico from entering into negotiations. He was in favour of securing indemnity for the expenses of the war in a treaty of peace, but doubted the policy of announcing that fact in this preliminary stage of the proceedings. The Secretary of the Treasury was in favour of retaining this part of the letter. The Postmaster-General seemed to concur with the Secretary of State and the Secretary of the Treasury that the part of the letter claiming indemnity for the expenses of the war should be retained. The Secretary of War after the discussion had proceeded some time seemed willing to yield his objections. Mr. Buchanan then addressing me said: "And what is the President's opinion?" I remarked to him that I should insist when a treaty was made upon being indemnified for the expenses of the war, and that in arranging a boundary these expenses must be taken into the account, but that I had serious doubts whether this fact should be announced at this time, and that my opinion inclined that it would be time enough to insist upon it after negotiations were opened, and we came to settle the terms of a treaty. I remarked further that whatever indemnity was acquired for the claims of our citizens, for the outrages committed by the Mexicans for a long series of years, as well as for the expenses of the war, must be in the acquisition of territory on our part, because it was well known that Mexico had no money to pay. My opinion was further, that to announce the fact now that Mexico was to pay the expenses of the war would excite that stubborn and impracticable people and prevent them from entering into negotiations. I suggested that this paragraph of the letter should be so modified as to state that the delay on the part of Mexico in acceding to our overture to open negotiations would render a satisfactory adjustment more difficult because of the increased expenses of the war. This suggestion was acceded to, and Mr. Buchanan said he would modify the letter accordingly. . .

Before the Cabinet adjourned, I remarked to them that as the Hon. Franklin Pierce, to whom I had tendered the office of Attorney-General, had declined to accept it, that I must select some other person for that office. I informed them that the Hon. Nathan Clifford of Maine had been recommended to me, but that I had very little knowledge of him and did not know his qualifications as a lawyer, and added that I did not desire to bring anyone into the Cabinet who would be exceptionable to any of its members, as I desired to preserve the harmony which had hitherto prevailed in our councils. All the members present expressed their entire satisfaction with Mr. Clifford, but none of them were able to inform me what his legal attainments were.

Friday, 2d October, 1846. — At ten o'clock this morning the Secretary of War . . . called. . . He had been indisposed for some days past, and, although feeble, was recovering. He had received letters from General Taylor and General Kearny, which I read. General Taylor's letters were under date of Sept. 4, 1846. He was about leaving Camargo for Monterey, and the probability was that a battle would take place at the latter place.[2] General Kearny on the 18th of August had taken possession of Santa Fé without firing a gun or shedding blood, and had proclaimed New Mexico to be a conquered province and a part of the United States. He expected to leave with a part of his command for Upper California early in September, leaving a sufficient force to hold Santa Fé and New Mexico. General Kearny has thus far performed his duty well.

Tuesday, 6th October, 1846. — The Secretary of State presented and read a correspondence between the United States consul and the French consul at Tripoli upon their respective claims to precedence in rank, together with a communication from the French Minister here transmitting a despatch from Mr. Guizot, the French Minister of Foreign Affairs, upon the subject. It was a mere question of etiquette and ceremony between the consuls at Tripoli, and but for the consequence attached to it by Mr. Guizot's despatch would be unworthy of notice. An anecdote is told of Mr. Jefferson to the effect that the French Minister, whom he invited to dinner with the diplomatic corps, had taken offence because he had not been assigned his proper place at the table. Mr. Jefferson had been informed that

[2] The American public and the Polk administration both demanded a vigorous invasion of Mexico, and Taylor determined to occupy Monterey and Saltillo. The first American brigade arrived before Monterey at the end of August, and two others within a fortnight afterward. Taylor's army consisted of some 6,230 troops; the Mexican army was considerably larger, and occupied a strongly fortified position. Both sides prepared for a battle, which began on September 21.

he was dissatisfied and that he intended to call for an explanation. While in his office his porter announced to him that the French Minister was in waiting. Mr. Jefferson was in his shirt sleeves but said promptly, show him in. The French minister entered in state attired in his court dress and found Mr. Jefferson with one foot up in the act of drawing on his boot. Mr. Jefferson turned his head as he entered and said, "Come in, sir; we have no ceremonies here." The Frenchman was astonished, sat a few minutes, and retired without making known his business, and afterwards said it was useless to raise any question of etiquette or ceremony with such a people. The anecdote illustrates the folly of the quarrel between the American and French consuls at Tripoli. I told Mr. Buchanan I was not a man of ceremonies, and that he and Mr. Guizot might settle the dispute between the consuls in any way they pleased.

Saturday, 10th October, 1846. — This was the regular day of the meeting of the Cabinet. . . The manner of prosecuting the Mexican war was the chief subject considered. The expedition to Tampico having been heretofore resolved upon, the question of extending that expedition to Vera Cruz was discussed. From information recently received it appears that an army may land near Sacraficias within three or four miles of Vera Cruz, and invest the town of Vera Cruz in the rear. This was information not heretofore known, and fearing that it might not be correct I requested Mr. Buchanan to write to the late United States consul at Vera Cruz (Mr. Dimond), now in Rhode Island, and request him to come immediately to Washington, believing that from him reliable information could be obtained. It is believed that if an army of a few thousand men can land at the point suggested that they could by besieging the city in the rear cut off all supplies from it, and that by keeping up a strict blockade by sea, the city and fortress of San Juan de Ulloa must in the course of a very few days surrender. If this be practicable, it is of the greatest importance that it be done.

Sunday, 11th October, 1846. — About dark Captain Eaton of the United States Army called in company with the Secretary of War and the Adjutant-General. Captain Eaton was the bearer of despatches from General Taylor, having left Monterey on the evening of the 25th ultimo. These despatches announced that a battle had been fought between the two armies at Monterey commencing on the evening of the 20th ultimo and continuing for between three and four days. The result was a capitulation by which the American army were left in possession of the city, and the Mexican army permitted to retire with their arms, except the larger part of their ordnance and munitions of war which were delivered over to the American forces. An armistice was also agreed upon to continue for eight weeks. In agreeing to this armistice General Taylor violated his express orders and I regret that I cannot approve his course. He had the enemy in his power and should have taken them prisoners, deprived them of their arms, discharged them on their parole of honour, and preserved the advantage which he had obtained by pushing on without delay farther into the country, if the force at his command justified it.[3]

Monday, 12th October, 1846. — General Taylor's despatches from Monterey received last night were read in Cabinet. They were fully considered and discussed. The Cabinet were unanimous in the opinion, judging from all

[3] Taylor had won his three-days' battle at Monterey, and had at first insisted upon unconditional surrender of the city and garrison. But the Mexicans, occupying stone houses and fully supplied with guns and munitions, were still in a strong position. Taylor had not more than 5,000 effective men, most of whom were tired out and a large part of whom were ill-armed. He was short of ammunition and provisions. The attack might have been disastrous, and to retreat through a hostile country with his sick and wounded might be ruinous. He exceeded his authority in granting such generous terms as he did in the armistice, but he and his defenders believed that he had acted wisely. In any event, the Americans had won a resplendent victory, and General Scott was right in speaking of the " three glorious days " at Monterey.

the information which General Taylor had communicated, that he had committed a great error in granting the terms of capitulation to the enemy which he had, and in agreeing to an armistice for the term of eight weeks. But two reasons could have justified the terms granted to the enemy in the capitulation. The first is, if he believed that he could not capture them; and the second is, that General Ampudia may have induced him to believe that in consequence of the recent change of rulers in Mexico that government was disposed to make peace. If the first reason existed General Taylor has not stated it in his despatches, and we have no information to justify the existence of this reason, though it may have existed. If the second reason was the one upon which he acted, then General Ampudia has overreached and deceived him. . . The Cabinet were united in the opinion that if General Taylor had captured the Mexican army, deprived them of their arms, and discharged them upon their parole of honour not to bear arms during the war or until they were regularly exchanged, that it would have probably ended the war with Mexico. As it is, he has permitted them to retire from Monterey, each officer and soldier with his arms, and with six pieces of artillery, not as prisoners of war on parole, but at perfect liberty to reorganize and renew the war at their own time and place, and by granting the armistice has given them eight weeks to effect this object.

It was agreed unanimously that orders should be forthwith sent to General Taylor to terminate the armistice to which he had agreed, and to prosecute the war with energy and vigor. It was agreed that this should be done in terms neither to approve nor condemn his conduct in granting the capitulation and the armistice.

Wednesday, 14th October, 1846. — I was occupied for more than an hour by the Rev. William L. McCalla of the Presbyterian church, and brother of the second auditor of the Treasury. His ostensible object was to be appointed

a chaplain in the army. I found him to be a fanatic, proscriptive in his religious opinions, and most unreasonable. He
read to me a number of letters addressed to me (but which
he did not deliver to me) from persons in Philadelphia, and
among others from Mr. Dallas, Judge Kane, and Mr.
Leiper, giving him a good character and recommending
him for a chaplaincy. He read also a most intemperate
and violent petition which had been written and signed in a
blank book, purporting to be addressed to me, but which
he did not offer to deliver to me. His petition was a violent
and most intolerant attack on the Roman Catholics and a
censure on the administration for employing, as it represented, two or three Roman Catholic priests with the army
in Mexico as chaplains. The prominent idea, aside from
its abuse of Catholics and its fanaticism, was that unless
I appointed the Rev. Mr. McCalla a chaplain, the petition-
ers intended to go before the public and attack the administration upon religious grounds because of the employment
of these Catholic priests. I felt great contempt for Mr.
McCalla and his religion and gave him my mind freely.
I told him that, thank God, under our Constitution there
was no connection between church and state, and in my action as President of the United States I recognized no distinction of creeds in my appointments to office. I told him
that his petition was false, and that before he had written
it and caused it to be signed he ought, as a man of God as he
professed to be, to have ascertained the facts better. He
attempted to explain the petition and denied that it was
intended as an attack on the administration; to which I replied that its plain language was not susceptible of the explanation which he gave. I then stated to him how it happened that two or three Catholic priests had been employed
with the army. I told him that it was known that Mexico
was a Catholic country, that their priests had great influence
over that ignorant people, and that they would probably
deceive them by representing that the United States was

waging war against them to overturn their religion, and that if they succeeded in imposing such a falsehood as this upon the people of Mexico they would infuriate them and induce them to carry on a desperate and more sanguinary war against our army, and that to undeceive the Mexicans two or three Catholic priests who spoke their language, it was thought, would be useful with the army. I told him that these were the reasons and these alone which induced their employment. I told him that Col. Benton and other members of Congress who were well acquainted with the Mexican people had advised their employment for these reasons. I told him that they were not chaplains, that there was no law authorizing the appointment of chaplains for the army, but that they were employees, such as armies often require, who had been sent out for the purposes stated. I told him further that in the Navy, where chaplains were authorized by law, I had appointed several since I came into office, without regard to the sects of religion to which they belonged, and that I had appointed no Catholic priests. He intimated that he wished to have an appointment of chaplain in the Navy. . . I consider him either a knave without vital religion or a fanatic without reason. I have met with no man during my administration, among the numerous office-seekers who have beset me, for whom I have so profound a contempt. To attempt to connect me with religious feuds between sects, either for the purpose of coercing me to give him an office or to give him a pretext to attack me upon affected or pretended religious grounds if I did not, proves him to be a man destitute of both religion and principle.

Thursday, 15th October, 1846. — I received this morning a letter from the Hon. Nathan Clifford of Maine, accepting the office of Attorney-General of the United States in place of Mr. Mason resigned, which I had tendered to him in a letter addressed to him on the 30th ultimo.

Tuesday, 20th October, 1846. — I brought before the Cabinet the subject of the Mexican War and the manner of conducting it, and stated to them that it became necessary to decide the very important question whether General Taylor should advance with the main column of the army further into the interior of Mexico than Monterey where he now is, or whether he should hold and fortify that position and also hold the adjacent northern provinces, and send a part of his force to coöperate with the expedition ordered on the 22d ultimo to invade Tamaulipas and by a combined operation of the navy and the army to take Tampico, and if practicable, Vera Cruz. The subject was fully discussed, and the Cabinet were unanimously of opinion that under existing circumstances General Taylor should not advance beyónd Monterey and the positions necessary to secure that city and the department of New Leon of which it is the capital.

Thursday, 22d October, 1846. — The Secretary of War called with his despatch to General Taylor copied and signed. Mr. McLane was also present. We had a full conversation in relation to the despatch and its objects. The Secretary of War stated that he had communicated its objects and contents to General Scott, who had interposed objections to the contemplated Vera Cruz expedition; that he had expressed a desire to command the expedition himself, but thought twenty-five or thirty thousand men were necessary before it could be undertaken with safety. I told the Secretary that after General Scott's letter in May or June last, I was unwilling to assign him to the command, and that I considered his objections as intended to embarrass the administration.[4]

[4] The Secretary of War, Marcy, believed that Scott was the only fully competent commander in sight for the expedition against Vera Cruz, and was adroitly trying to win others to that view. He convinced Senator Benton and various others of the Cabinet that Scott should have the place. Scott thought that the Mexicans would have 20,000 to 30,000 troops at Vera Cruz, and feared both the strong fortress there and the yellow fever. He was eager to take charge of the expedition. On October 27, 1846, he laid before Secretary Marcy a memorandum on "Vera Cruz and its Castle," in which he urged capturing Vera Cruz early in the year and then proceeding against the City

Friday, 30th October, 1846.—The Secretary of the Treasury called and informed me that he apprehended that he could not raise the amount of money needed upon the issue of Treasury notes bearing an interest of 5.4 per cent. The Secretary of the Navy and Secretary of State happened to come in on other business. The Secretary of the Treasury expressed the opinion that it would be necessary to make a funded loan. In this I concurred, judging from his statement of the condition of the Treasury and the difficulty he had experienced in raising money on Treasury notes. The Secretary of State and Secretary of the Navy concurred in this opinion also. The Secretary of the Treasury then said he would today advertise for a funded loan of four or five millions of dollars, and take the offer of the lowest bidder.

Monday, 2d November, 1846.—Mr. Figaniere, the Portuguese Minister, called. I received him also in the parlour downstairs. He was not in full court dress, but wore a coat with a star and some embroidery on it. He delivered to me a letter from his sovereign announcing the birth of a princess. He talked familiarly, and among other things he said that her Majesty had one every year; that she had now six or seven; and I was much amused at the solemn account which he gave me of one of which she had been delivered some time ago that was still-born. He seemed to regard it as a great misfortune, and went almost as minutely into the Queen's sufferings on the occasion as if he had been the attending physician or the midwife.

Thursday, 5th November, 1846.—After night Mr. Buchanan called and had a long conversation with me on public affairs. He expressed the opinion among other things that it was the tariff of 1846 which had caused the defeat of the Democratic party in Pennsylvania, at the late election. I told him that in my next message I should recommend to

---

of Mexico. A fortnight later he submitted a new memorandum urging a descent on Vera Cruz, and estimating that at least 20,000 men might ultimately be necessary. Marcy was much impressed by Scott's suggestions.

Congress not to modify or change that act until it could
have a fair trial.   The causes of the defeat of the Democratic party in the New York election, which had just taken
place, were spoken of.   I expressed the opinion that it was
attributable to the bad faith of that portion of the Democratic party in New York opposed personally to Gov.
Wright, called Old Hunkers.   I expressed my deep regret
at Gov. Wright's defeat, and my strong condemnation of
that portion of the Democratic party who had suffered their
State factions to control them and had voted against
him.[5] . .   This faction shall hereafter receive no favour at
my hands if I know it.

   Friday, 6th November, 1846. — After night Col. Benton
called. . .   I had a long and interesting conversation with
him on the subject of the Mexican War and the proper
manner of prosecuting it with a view to obtain an honorable
and speedy peace.   He expressed the opinion that a bold
blow should be struck at once.   He thought the city of Vera
Cruz should be taken at once and with it would fall the
castle at that place, and that after this was done there would
be a rapid crushing movement made from Vera Cruz on the
City of Mexico.   He said that commissioners composed of
the first men in the country of both political parties should
accompany the headquarters of the army, who were authorized to offer peace before a battle, during the battle, and
after it was over.   He said this had often been done during
the European wars.   He then said, some months ago you
offered me the first mission in the world.   (I had offered
him the mission to France near the close of the last session
of Congress.)   I declined that, but I am willing to accompany the army as one of these commissioners of peace.   I
told him if it was thought expedient to institute such a commission I would be most happy to avail myself of his ser-

   [5] Governor Silas Wright, of New York, renominated in 1846, was badly
beaten that fall by the Whig candidate, John Young.   The opposition of the
Hunkers, including W. L. Marcy, the anti-rent disturbances, and Wright's
veto of canal appropriations were the chief factors in his overthrow.

vices in that capacity. We had much conversation on the subject of the war and the manner of conducting it. Col. Benton was evidently in a fine humour and said he had returned to Washington to render my administration any aid in his power in conducting the war. He condemned the policy which had been suggested in some quarters of holding the Mexican territory which we had acquired and not prosecuting the war further into the Mexican territory. He said the war would be much protracted by such a policy, and might not be ended for years. He said further the late elections have gone against the administration and that if such a policy of activity was adopted the patriotic spirit of the country would flag and the Democratic party would be overthrown. He said ours were a go-ahead people, and that our only policy either to obtain a peace or save ourselves was to press the war boldly.

Monday, 9th November, 1846. — Col. Benton called and told me he had prepared the letter which he had informed me on Saturday last he would address to me, defending Col. Frémont's conduct in California against the calumnious report of Governor Castro to the Mexican Government against that officer.[6] . .

Just before I started to attend Col. Cross's funeral today, Mr. Robertson, United States consul at Bremen, called and delivered to me a package which he stated contained a small quantity of cotton prepared as a substitute for gun-powder, which he had brought with him from Europe with instructions that it was only to be opened in the presence of the President of the United States. The package was addressed to me with the superscription that it was only to be opened in my presence. The discovery had been made in Germany. I told Mr. Robertson that I was rather an unbeliever in the merits of the discovery, but that as I was about attending the funeral of Col. Cross I had no time then to attend to it.[7]

[6] Some of Frémont's men were accused of pillaging and stealing, a report quite untrue.

[7] C. F. Schönbein of Basel published his discovery of gun-cotton in 1846.

Tuesday, 10th November, 1846. — Before the Cabinet assembled Col. Benton called, as I had requested him to do on Wednesday. The subject of the Mexican War was resumed. Col. Benton repeated the views which he had before expressed, but more in detail and enforced them. I told him if the movement on the City of Mexico was made, it would be necessary to call out a considerable number of additional troops. I had before informed him of the orders which had been issued for the contemplated expedition against Tampico and possibly Vera Cruz, but a movement on the City of Mexico had not been at present contemplated, nor could it unless it was ascertained that peace could not be obtained without it. He said that a small force could, he had no doubt, in coöperation with the navy, starve out or take the town of Vera Cruz, and with it would fall the Castle, but that would not bring peace, unless it was followed with a larger force on the City of Mexico. I told him I apprehended from all I had learned that General Taylor would not willingly spare any considerable portion of the forces with him at Monterey, and that I apprehended he would not heartily coöperate with the government in carrying into effect such an expedition unless he commanded it himself, and that I thought General Taylor a brave officer but not a man of capacity enough for such a command. In this he concurred. I asked who would be the proper officer to command so important an expedition. He did not answer. I spoke of General Scott. He said he had no confidence in him. Some other officers were named by me. He then said there ought to be a Lieutenant-General of the army who should be general-in-chief. He said it required a man of talents and resources as well as a military man for such a command, and that with a view to obtain peace more depended upon the talents and energy of the officer than upon mere bravery. He then said that if such an office was created by Congress, he would be willing to accept the command himself. I remarked generally that I would have confidence in him and would be pleased to see him at the head of the army in such an expedition. He alluded to what was apparent to everyone, that the Whigs were endeavoring to turn this war to party and political advantage. He said, " I have been looking at events as they have transpired this summer, and left Kentucky, where I have spent some weeks, and returned to Washington to render you any aid in my power." He said, " You know what my position has been " (alluding as I inferred to his preference for Mr. Van Buren in the last Presidential election), " but let bygones be bygones. I quarreled and fought with General Jackson; I made friends with him and came to his support, and during the gloomy period of the Bank panic, I have held many consultations with him in this room. Now I will give you any support in this war in my power." I expressed my gratification at hearing these sentiments and said frankly to him that I had never entertained any but the most cordial feelings for him.[8]

After much further conversation in relation to the war he left. Shortly afterwards the Cabinet assembled. The chief topic of conversation today was the Mexican War and Col. Benton's views of the manner of conducting it, which I communicated to the Cabinet, of course in the confidence which belongs to all Cabinet consultations.

No distinct question was presented for a decision but the views of the different gentlemen were freely expressed. The general impression seemed to be that it would be necessary to call out additional troops with a view to the successful

[8] Polk's willingness to appoint Senator Benton to be lieutenant-general was an extraordinary development. He did not wish the Whigs and their two heroes, Scott and Taylor, to win more glory from the war than he could help. He saw that it would be politically wise to conciliate the Van Buren Democrats, to whose ranks Benton belonged. Moreover, he held that the importance of the operations pending in Mexico required a chief of higher grade than a major-general, and he believed that this commander, who might be required to negotiate a peace, should be in full harmony with the President. Benton was in no way qualified, as Scott distinctly was, for so important a military station. Both his headstrong and domineering qualities, and his comparative ignorance of troops and warfare, made him an unsuitable choice. But Polk liked and respected Benton, and was willing to take a chance with him.

prosecution of the campaign against Vera Cruz, and especially if an expedition against the City of Mexico was resolved upon.   No answer had been received from General
Taylor to the despatch of the Secretary of War of the 22d
of September, and it was deemed prudent before any decision was made in regard to the future course of the campaign
to await his answer which must undoubtedly be received
soon.   Mr. Buchanan was in favour of taking Vera Cruz
but disinclined to favour the expedition against the City of
Mexico.   After much conversation on the subject, and in relation to the state of the finances and the probability of obtaining a loan, the Cabinet adjourned. . .

Today at 3 P.M. I went with Mr. Robertson, United States
consul at Bremen, to the War Department, where the package of gun cotton which he delivered to me on yesterday was
opened, and some experiments made by Col. Totten.   Its
explosive qualities surprised me.

Wednesday, 11th November, 1846. —Andrew Jackson,
Jr., of the Hermitage, the adopted son of General Jackson,
called on me today.   Col. Benton called on me tonight at my
request.   I had a still further conversation with him in relation to the Mexican War.   I told him that I did not think it
probable that Congress would create the office of Lieutenant-
General which he had suggested on yesterday.   He said he
thought himself it was doubtful.   After speaking about the
propriety of calling out an increased force, I told him that
in that event I might create an additional Major-General.
He said that if I did so the general appointed would be the
junior officer of his rank, and he would not desire it.   I remarked to him that I had supposed he would not desire it,
and that in addition to this I had come under some commitment to General Houston of Texas, if another Major-
General was to be appointed.   I told him that if the commission to treat for peace, which he had suggested in a
former conversation, should accompany the army, should be
created, it would give me pleasure to place him at the head of

that commission. He said if it was settled that a large force was to march from Vera Cruz on the City of Mexico he would accept, for then it would be important and there would be dignity in it. I told him that the inclination of my mind was to call for eight additional regiments, with a view to the bold movement which he had suggested, and that in the course of tomorrow I would probably decide. I read to him General Taylor's last despatch and also all the orders and communications which had been sent to him relating to the contemplated expeditions against Tampico and Vera Cruz. He agreed with me that General Taylor's answer was unsatisfactory and that he was unfit for command. After much further conversation of a free and friendly character he retired.

Thursday, 12th November, 1846. — The Secretary of War called this morning and informed me that General Scott had informed him that he was preparing, and would deliver to him today, his views of the manner in which the Mexican War should be prosecuted. After night the Secretary sent the communication of General Scott to me, and shortly afterwards called himself. After reading it I returned it to the Secretary, who said he would call on Col. Benton tonight and consult further with him on the subject and communicate to him General Scott's views.

Saturday, 14th November, 1846. — The Cabinet met at the usual hour, all the members present. The chief and almost the only question of conversation today was whether there should be a further call upon the States for an additional force of volunteers, with a view to the vigorous prosecution of the Mexican War. The subject was fully discussed. The Secretary of War expressed his opinion that it was necessary to call out such a force. Mr. Buchanan, the Secretary of State, expressed his opinion in favour of taking Vera Cruz, but strongly against sending any expedition against the City of Mexico. . . It was then unanimously agreed that nine additional regiments to serve during the war should be called for from the States. The Cabinet proceeded to consider of the States from which the call should be made. There was some difficulty in determining this, but finally it was agreed upon. The Cabinet fully discussed the conduct of General Taylor and were agreed that he was unfit for the chief command, that he had not mind enough for the station, that he was a bitter political partisan and had no sympathies with the administration, and that he had been recently controlled, particularly in his expedition to Monterey, by Bailey Peyton, Mr. Kendall, editor of the *Picayune* at New Orleans, and Assistant-Adjutant General Bliss, who are cunning and shrewd men of more talents than himself, and had controlled him for political purposes. I expressed my deep regret that I was compelled from all the information I had received to come to this conclusion. I stated, what all the Cabinet knew, that I had never suffered politics to mingle with the conduct of the war; that I had promoted General Taylor and treated him very kindly and given him my confidence as chief in command of the army, but that I was compelled to believe that he had been weak enough to suffer himself to be controlled by political partisans, who had no command in the army, but had attached themselves to it and had attended his camp for political purposes.[9] All were at a loss to designate who should be the chief in command in the expedition against Vera Cruz. I suggested Major-General Butler of the volunteers, and I think him the best man. Nothing upon this point was decided. . .

Mr. Buchanan proposed in the Cabinet meeting today,

[9] There was a great deal of truth in this view of Taylor's position and attitude. He was deeply distrustful of the administration and had spoken of " Polk, Marcy, and Co." as willing to discredit and ruin him. But he was fundamentally honest and highly conscientious, and for these qualities Polk gives him all too little credit. Scott had now written a third memorandum on the Vera Cruz expedition, showing that with the volunteers just called for there would be 14,000 men available for the attack. Polk's suggestion that Major-General W. O. Butler should be placed in command met no favor from Marcy. All the factors in the situation were so shaping themselves as to make the choice of Scott inevitable. Polk's hesitation over him was perhaps natural, but not wise.

after it had been determined to call out nine additional regiments of volunteers, that one of them should be called from Massachusetts. It did not strike me favourably. My first impression was that we should not extend the call further north than the State of New York. Mr. Clifford doubted the policy on other grounds. He feared that the other New England States might feel that they were overlooked if Federal Massachusetts was the only one among them from which a requisition was made.

Sunday, 15th November, 1846. — The more I had reflected upon the suggestion made by Mr. Buchanan in Cabinet on yesterday, that one of the nine regiments of volunteers to be called out should be taken from Massachusetts, the more favourably I thought of it. . . At three o'clock P.M. Mr. Clifford, the Attorney-General, called and informed me that he had seen Mr. Burke, who entirely approved the suggestion that one of the regiments of volunteers should be called from Massachusetts. If she obeyed the call all would be well. If she refused to obey it and acted as she did in the last war with Great Britain, the country would know it.

Tuesday, 17th November, 1846. — The Cabinet met at the usual hour, all the members present. The Mexican War occupied exclusive attention today. I read to the Cabinet Col. Benton's plan of the campaign as communicated to me last night. The Secretary of War read a written memorandum from General Scott giving a statement of the forces now in Mexico, and of the additional forces and preparations which in his opinion would be necessary to make an attack on the city of Vera Cruz and march to the City of Mexico. The force he proposed was about 14,000 and the whole plan was upon a large scale. Much conversation took place on the subject. . . Great difficulty existed in selecting the commander of the expedition against Vera Cruz. In General Taylor a want of confidence was expressed in his capacity, while it was known that he had suffered his partisan political feelings to render himself hostile to the administration. His constant effort has been to throw the responsibility of any disaster which might happen on the administration. In this he has been most ungrateful for the kindness which he has received at my hands. All agreed that he was unfit, after what had occurred, for the command of the expedition against Vera Cruz. The difficulty was in selecting a proper officer. Major-General Patterson of the volunteers, who had been named for the Tampico expedition, it was feared had not sufficient experience. General Scott it was known was hostile to the administration, and it was apprehended would have no sympathy with it in carrying out its plans. After much discussion Mr. Buchanan, Mr. Walker, Mr. Marcy, and Mr. Mason, although all of them had serious objéctions to him, yet came to the conclusion that as he was the highest officer in command in the army, he should be entrusted with the conduct of this important expedition. Mr. Johnson was opposed to him, and Mr. Clifford was inclined to be so, but expressed no decided opinion. After a long conversation I informed the Cabinet that I would think further on the subject before I decided. I have strong objections to General Scott, and after his very exceptionable letter in May last nothing but stern necessity and a sense of public duty could induce me to place him at the head of so important an expedition. Still I do not well see how it can be avoided. He is General-in-Chief of the army. If I had the power to select a General I would select Col. Benton to conduct the expedition. Without coming to any decision the Cabinet adjourned.

Wednesday, 18*th November,* 1846. — I sent for the Secretary of War this morning, and held a further conversation with him in regard to the officer to be selected to command the expedition to Vera Cruz. He said he had had great anxiety and trouble about it, but upon full reflection, although he would do so reluctantly, he thought we would be compelled to take General Scott. . . I sent my private secretary to invite Col. Benton to see me. Col. Benton called, and upon a full view of the whole subject he advised that General Scott be assigned to the command as the best we could do, although he had no confidence in him. I told Col. Benton I must yield my objections to General Scott, and would see the Secretary and direct that he be ordered to take the command of the expedition to Vera Cruz. I told Col. Benton that if I could induce Congress to create the office of Lieutenant-General I would appoint him to command the whole forces. He said he would take such a command.

I was busily occupied until night in preparing my message. After night upon my invitation the Secretary of the Navy called, and I read to him the part of my message which related to the Mexican War and the tariff. The Secretary of War came in, and I informed him of the result of my interview today with Col. Benton. The Secretary of War said that he had thought over the matter in every possible aspect and he was fully satisfied that we would be compelled to take General Scott for the command against Vera Cruz. The Secretary of the Navy concurred in this opinion. They advised me to send for General Scott and see him myself in the morning. I requested the Secretary of War to ask him to call on tomorrow at nine o'oclock A.M.

Thursday, 19th November, 1846. — General Scott called this morning, having been invited by the Secretary of War, as requested by me on yesterday, to do so. I held a long conversation with him as to the plan of prosecuting the Mexican War. I finally said to him that the capture of Vera Cruz was very important to secure peace. To this he assented. I then told him that it was important that the officer entrusted to command that expedition should have confidence in the government, and that the government should have confidence in him, and that without a cordial coöperation success could scarcely be expected. To this he agreed. I then intimated to him that if I was satisfied that he had the proper confidence in the administration and that he would cordially coöperate with it, that I was disposed to assign him to the command. He appeared to be much affected and said at once that he had the utmost confidence in the administration and in myself, and that he would cordially coöperate with me in carrying out my views in the prosecution of the war. He said that he surrendered his whole confidence to me. I then told him that I had at the commencement of the war given him my confidence and had tendered him the command, but that circumstances had occurred to change my determination. I was willing that bygones should be bygones and that he should take the command. He expressed himself as being deeply grateful to me and said he would show me his gratitude by his conduct when he got to the field. He was so grateful and so much affected that he almost shed tears. He then said he would take with him any of the volunteer generals whom I might indicate, and asked me to suggest such as I wished to accompany him. . . I requested him to prepare a statement of the forces now in Mexico, and inform me what portion of them he would propose to take with him on the Vera Cruz expedition and what corps he would leave under the command of General Taylor. He said he would do so as soon as he could prepare it. He left, apparently the most delighted man I have seen for a long time, and as he retired expressed his deep gratitude to me.[10]

[10] " A new David and a new Jonathan seemed to have discovered each other." The labor of Secretary Marcy to bring Scott to the first command in the field had been crowned with success. Polk still thought Scott pedantic, conceited, and visionary, and distrusted his politics; but he grudgingly admitted his skill and experience, and he may have comforted himself by the thought that he was playing off two Whig leaders, Scott and Taylor, against each other. For his part, Scott at first accepted Polk's friendship with complete trust. He tells us that for a week before he received the appointment, Polk sent for him once or twice daily. " In these interviews every expression of kindness and confidence was lavished upon me. Such was the warmth and emphasis of his professions, that he fully won my confidence. I gave him a cordial reciprocation of my personal sympathy and regard — being again and again assured that the country would be bankrupted and dishonored unless the war could be made plainly to march toward a successful conclusion, and that I only could give to it the necessary impetus and direction. Not to have been deceived by such protestations would have been, in my judgment,

unmanly suspicion and a crime. Accordingly, though oppressed with the labors of military preparation, I made time to write a circular to the leading Whigs in Congress (a few days before their meeting) to say how handsomely I had been treated by the President and Secretary of War — begging that the new regiments might be authorized with the least possible delay, etc., etc."

In all this bestowal of his confidence Scott was unaware that Polk was planning to have Benton appointed lieutenant-general, and that he meant if possible to place the latter over his head. In fact, he did not learn this till he was in the very act of embarking at New Orleans for Vera Cruz. When the news reached him, his indignation was intense. "A grosser abuse of human confidence," he says, "is nowhere recorded." (Scott, *Memoirs Written by Himself*, II, 399, 400.)

CHAPTER VI

Nov. 21, 1846 – Jan. 26, 1847

FRICTION WITH TAYLOR — THE TWO-MILLION APPROPRIA-
TION — THE VERA CRUZ EXPEDITION — PRESTON KING'S
RESOLUTION EXCLUDING SLAVERY — BENTON ATTACKS
SCOTT AND TAYLOR

Saturday, 21st November, 1846. — The Cabinet met at
the usual hour today, all the members present except the
Postmaster-General, who is indisposed as I learn. Despatches were received last night from General Taylor, which
the Secretary of War produced and they were read. They
gave a more detailed account of the battle of Monterey, but
contained no explanation of the reasons which induced him
to agree to the armistice. A separate despatch was in answer to the despatch from the Secretary of War of the 22d
of September last, in relation to the proposed expedition into
the interior of Tamaulipas and against Tampico. It was
written in bad temper, and was wholly unwarranted by the
despatch of the Secretary of War to which it was a reply.
The Secretary had proposed the expedition under the belief,
which was the fact, that a sufficient force was left by General Taylor, who was idle in camp on the Rio Grande, to
constitute the expedition, but still the whole matter had been
left to the discretion of General Taylor. The officers left
with the troops on the Rio Grande were suggested to command the expedition. General Taylor's answer is in very
bad taste and worse temper, in which among other things he
states that he places his protest on file against such inter-

ference with him as chief-in-command of the army in Mexico. I refer to the correspondence itself as containing a more full explanation and statement of the whole matter than I can now give. I was very indignant at General Taylor's letter and directed the Secretary of War to prepare a proper answer. It is perfectly manifest that General Taylor is very hostile to the administration and seeks a cause of quarrel with it. This he shall not have unless he places himself wholly in the wrong, as indeed he has already done. He is evidently a weak man and has been made giddy with the idea of the Presidency. He is most ungrateful, for I have promoted him, as I now think, beyond his deserts, and without reference to his politics. I am now satisfied that he is a narrow-minded, bigoted partisan, without resources and wholly unqualified for the command he holds.

General Scott called in the evening, and referring to General Taylor's despatch which he had read, condemned it and said that he ought to explain it, and that he would cause him to do so. General Scott informed me that he would leave for Mexico to take the command of the army, travelling via New York, where he would take a vessel on Monday next. He was in a good humour and was exceedingly grateful to me for having assigned him to the command. In truth it was the only alternative. I am now satisfied that anybody would do better than Taylor. Taylor is no doubt brave and will fight, but is not fit for a higher command than that of a regiment. I have no prejudice against him, but think he has acted with great weakness and folly.

Tuesday, 1st December, 1846. — Col. Benton called again this morning and resumed the examination of that part of my message which I submitted to him on yesterday in relation to the war with Mexico. I had proposed in my draft to submit to Congress the propriety, at the same time that the war should be vigorously prosecuted, to establish a line of boundary securing to the United States a sufficient territory to afford indemnity for the expenses of the war, and to our citizens who hold pecuniary demands against Mexico. I proposed, also, that a more permanent government should be provided by Congress over the conquered provinces than the temporary governments which had been established by our naval and military commanders according to the laws of war. Col. Benton thought these passages should be omitted, and submitted to me in writing the reasons for this opinion.

Monday, 14th December, 1846. — After night Mr. Boyd of Kentucky, Mr. Cobb of Georgia, Mr. Douglas of Illinois, and Mr. Stanton of Tennessee, all members of the House of Representatives, called. They had been invited by my private secretary at my request to call. I explained to them my embarrassment in conducting the war with the present officers, and consulted them as to the propriety of passing a law authorizing the appointment of a Lieutenant-General to command the army. I explained to them the objections to General Taylor and General Scott, and the impossibility of conducting the war successfully when the General-in-chief of the army did not sympathize with the government, and cooperate with it in the prosecution of the war. This they fully appreciated, but were unanimously of opinion that it would be impossible to pass a law through Congress to authorize the appointment of a Lieutenant-General who should supersede Generals Taylor and Scott.[1] I urged them to pass a law promptly appropriating the two millions of dollars for which I had asked in my message; and also a law as recommended by the Secretary of War to raise 10,000 men to serve during the war with Mexico. To these measures they

---

[1] It was hopeless to try to get the creation of a lieutenant-generalship for Benton through Congress. His irascible, imperious ways had made him unpopular in the Senate, and in both the Cabinet and Congress there were men who strongly disbelieved in his fitness. Moreover, the Calhoun wing of the Democratic party was averse to letting Benton gain prestige, and various aspirants for the Democratic nomination in 1848 regarded him with a jealous eye. Naturally the friends of Taylor and Scott bitterly opposed his elevation. Altogether, it was impossible for Polk to bring about the passage of the desired bill — but he unquestionably made the proposal in good faith.

agreed, and promised to have these measures brought up in Congress without delay. General Cass met me on my walk this afternoon and returned with me to my office. I consulted with him as to the appointment of a Lieutenant-General of the army. He was agreed to it, but thought it could not pass Congress.

Thursday, 17th December, 1846. — I submitted today to the usual trouble and annoyance of members of Congress and others, who called as usual to apply for petty offices for their friends. Many persons called to pay their respects, both ladies and gentlemen, and I was compelled wholly to neglect the business on my table to receive them. . .

At five o'clock P.M. I had invited the diplomatic corps residing in Washington to dine with me. At that hour they commenced assembling. All the foreign ministers now in the city, with their wives and those attached to their respective delegations, attended and dined with me.

Saturday, 19th December, 1846. — I addressed a note to Senator Calhoun of South Carolina this morning requesting him to call on me today. He called about five o'clock P.M. I stated to him my embarrassment in conducting the war with Mexico, when I had to rely upon General Taylor and General Scott, neither of whom had any sympathies with the government, and the former of whom had already thrown obstacles in the way of the prosecution of the plans of the government. I expressed to him my desire to have authority from Congress to appoint a Lieutenant-General to take command of the army, and told him frankly that if I was invested with such authority I would appoint Senator Benton of Missouri to command. He was decidedly opposed to having such an officer and gave his reasons for his opinion at some length. I found that his mind was settled upon the subject and that it was useless to press it. I next introduced the two million appropriation for which I had asked with a view to negotiations with Mexico. Of this he approved, and said he would vote double that sum, or more if necessary.

He said he could not vote for it with the slavery restriction which had been attached to a bill with the same object in the House of Representatives near the close of the last session of Congress, and that if such a restriction were contained in any treaty with Mexico, he would vote against ratifying the treaty. I told him that such a restriction would be most mischievous, and would probably defeat the object in view. I then asked him what boundary I ought to insist upon in a treaty with Mexico, saying to him that I would be pleased to have his opinion upon that point. He mentioned Upper California as being important to us, and intimated that he would be satisfied with the acquisition of that territory. I then told him that the boundary which I proposed to obtain, if practicable, would cede to the United States the provinces of New Mexico, Upper and Lower California. He said that would be entirely satisfactory to him, and added that he attached but little value to Lower California and cared but little about it. I asked what sum I should agree to pay for such a boundary, in addition to the claims due to our own citizens and the expenses of the war. He answered that he would pay a blind sum and would not stand on a few millions of dollars. I told him if such a treaty was made slavery would probably never exist in these provinces. To this he readily assented, and said he did not desire to extend slavery; but that if the slavery restriction was put into a treaty, it would involve a principle, and whatever the other provisions of the treaty were, he would vote against it. My conversation with him was a frank and pleasant one. He was in a good humour, talked in a pleasant tone, and, I inferred, was pleased that I had sent for him.

Hon. Robert Dale Owen of Indiana, one of the Regents of the Smithsonian Institution, called and submitted to me for my approval, and that of the members of the Cabinet named in the act of the last session upon that subject, another selection for a site for the institution, which the Regents proposed. The site now proposed contains about 16 acres, and is the south half of the Mall between 9th and 12th Streets in the city of Washington. He said he had seen Mr. Burke, the Commissioner of Patents, who was willing to give his assent to this selection. When the Cabinet met I submitted the proposed site to them and they all assented.

Monday, 21st December, 1846. — I requested my private secretary to ask Col. Benton to call today. He called about three o'clock P.M. I had a conversation with him in relation to the propriety of creating a Lieutenant-General of the army, and expressed to him my apprehensions, from what I had learned from members of Congress, that such a proposition if made could not pass Congress. Without expressing an opinion upon this point, he urged that I should make the proposition at all events, and if Congress rejected it the responsibility would be theirs, and the country would see that they had refused to grant me the means which I had asked in order to prosecute the war. I found Col. Benton fixed upon this point. If I do not propose it, it is manifest from my interview with him that both he and his friends will be greatly dissatisfied.

Thursday, 24th December, 1846. — I had a dinner party today. Between thirty and forty persons, members of the two houses of Congress and several ladies of their families, dined with me. Among others the Vice-President, his wife and two daughters, and the Speaker of the House of Representatives were of the party. Mr. Calhoun, who was also of the party, remained at my request after dinner until the company had dispersed, when we retired from the parlour to my office. I resumed the conversation which I had with him a few days ago, about the proper manner of conducting the Mexican War. I was particularly desirous to have his concurrence in the proposition to create a Lieutenant-General to command the army during the Mexican War. I found he still had objections to it, which I fear he will not yield. He expressed himself in favour of the policy of establishing a cordon of military posts and holding a sufficient territory to indemnify ourselves, instead of making the crushing movement with a great army upon the City of Mexico. He thought there were almost insuperable difficulties to the latter policy, and that if pursued the war might be of indefinite duration. My conversation with him was of a friendly and pleasant character.

Friday, 25th December, 1846. — Not more than half a dozen persons called today, and they were on business. It being Christmas day, the family attended church. I remained in my office, attended to some of the business on my table, and wrote a rough draft of a message which I have made up my mind to send to Congress recommending the appointment of a Lieutenant-General of the army, who shall be commander in chief during the war with Mexico; and also recommending prompt action upon the recommendations of the Secretary of War in his annual report.

Monday, 28th December, 1846. — An unusual number of visitors called this morning, and among them many members of Congress. With but few exceptions they were all on the business of seeking office for their friends. I closed my office at twelve o'clock and disposed of a part of the business on my table. I saw Senators Benton and Dix and informed them that I would send a message to Congress on tomorrow recommending the increase of the regular army and the appointment of a general officer to take command of the army. Mr. Buchanan called, and suggested some modifications in the message which I had prepared on the subject. After night several members of Congress called.

Tuesday, 29th December, 1846. — The Vice-President, Dallas, called this morning and informed me that he had learned through the telegraph that Senator Barrow of Louisiana died at five o'clock this morning at Baltimore. Mr. Barrow, I learn, left this city four or five days ago, apparently in good health. It is represented to me that the day before he left he was the bearer of a note from Mr. Garret Davis of Kentucky to Mr. Bailey of Virginia relating to a misunderstanding between these two gentlemen which had arisen in debate in the House of Representatives. Mr. Barrow, as I am informed, accompanied Mr. Davis to Baltimore, where the terms of a duel or hostile meeting would be arranged. It was in the prosecution of this unchristian object that Mr. Barrow was suddenly seized with disease and cut off in the prime and vigour of life. I am a firm believer that it was a judgment of heaven upon the immoral, unchristian, and savage practice of duelling.

Friday, 1st January, 1847. — The morning was clear, and unusually mild for this season of the year. According to an invariable custom which has been observed by all my predecessors, the President's mansion is thrown open for the reception of visitors on the first day of every year. Neither House of Congress ever sits on that day, and accordingly both Houses adjourned over on yesterday. Between eleven and twelve o'clock A.M. the company commenced assembling. In the course of an hour an immense throng filled every hall and parlour in the house. The foreign ministers attended in their full court costumes. The Cabinet were of course present; as also the judges of the Supreme Court. Many Senators and Representatives in Congress attended, and among them I observed an unusual number of the Federal members. A large number of strangers as well as citizens, including the subordinate officers of government, were present. I stood on my feet shaking hands with the immense crowd from half past eleven o'clock A.M., till three o'clock P.M. . . About four o'clock the company had all retired. I was very much exhausted by the fatigues of the day.

Saturday, 2d January, 1847. — At eleven o'clock A.M. the Cabinet met, this being the regular day of meeting. The subject of the Mexican War was the subject of a long and free conversation, and especially in regard to our future policy in conducting it. Mr. Buchanan repeated the opinion which upon several occasions before he had intimated, that it was bad policy to think of marching a great army upon the City of Mexico; that if we could do so, and take that city, we would but excite a feeling against us of races and religions and would probably be as far, if not further, from a peace than we now were. His policy as he expressed it was to hold New Mexico and the Californias and defend them. He wished no more territory, but thought we ought to encourage the other northern provinces to revolt from Mexico and form an independent government of their own, and that to effect this we should furnish them aid and assistance. All the other members of the Cabinet seemed to concur in these views. The Secretary of War expressed the opinion that he had no confidence in the success of an expedition on the City of Mexico. Mr. Walker seemed to have changed his former opinions and expressed his concurrence with the Secretaries of State and War. . . I stated that our present object was to take and possess ourselves of Vera Cruz, and that our future operations might be left to be controlled by the circumstances existing after we should have succeeded in capturing Vera Cruz.[2]

Monday, 4th January, 1847. — My private secretary returned from the Capitol and informed me that Mr. Preston King of New York had introduced into the House of Representatives a bill on the subject of slavery which had produced much sensation in the body. He informed me also that Mr. Hamlin, a Representative from the State of Maine, had made a speech against the bill recommended by the Secretary of War for increasing the regular army to serve during the

---

[2] There was much doubt among Americans regarding the plan of campaign in Mexico. Zachary Taylor did not believe in the Vera Cruz expedition, writing that the season of yellow fever was a worse enemy than 100,000 bayonets. Scott believed in it, and thought that 15,000 men could take the city. The instructions which had been given Scott on Nov. 23, 1846, were extremely vague. He was to set on foot a Gulf expedition, but that was all. " It is not proposed to control your operations," Secretary Marcy wrote him, " by definite and positive instructions, but you are left to prosecute them as your judgment, under a full view of all the circumstances, shall dictate." Scott reached Matamoras at the end of December, 1846, and began to make preparations there for the descent on Vera Cruz, drawing away from Taylor part of the latter's army.

war.[3] Mr. Hamlin professes to be a Democrat, but has
given indications during the present session that he is dissatisfied, and is pursuing a mischievous course, not only in
this instance, but on the slavery question, as well as upon
other matters. The slavery question is assuming a fearful
and most important aspect. The movement of Mr. King
today, if persevered in, will be attended with terrible consequences to the country, and cannot fail to destroy the Democratic party, if it does not ultimately threaten the Union
itself. Slavery was one of the questions adjusted in the com-
promises of the Constitution. It has, and can have no legiti-
mate connection with the war with Mexico, or the terms of a
peace which may be concluded with that country. It is a
domestic and not a foreign question, and to connect it with
the appropriations for prosecuting the war, or with the two
million appropriation with a view to obtain peace, can result in no good, but must divide the country by a sectional
line and lead to the worst consequences. Of course the Federalists are delighted to see such a question agitated by
Northern Democrats because it divides and distracts the
Democratic party and increases their prospects of coming
into power. Such an agitation is not only unwise, but wicked.

Tuesday, 5th January, 1847. — The Cabinet met at the
usual hour. The Secretary of War read despatches which
had been received from General Taylor and General Wool.
From them it appears that General Taylor has paid no regard to the views of the Government, but has dispersed the
troops in small bodies at different and distant points from

[3] In his annual message of December, 1846, Polk had again recommended
a special appropriation of two million dollars to facilitate negotiations with
Mexico. On Jan. 3, 1847, Preston King sought to introduce in the House an
appropriation bill for this purpose, with a section excluding slavery from all
subsequent territorial acquisitions of the United States. By a majority of one
the House refused to suspend its rules for the introduction of the bill. However, in February the appropriation and King's exclusion clause were taken
up again, and the House passed both by votes of 115 to 106 and 115 to 105.
Hannibal Hamlin of Maine was a Representative in the 28th and 29th Con-
gresses, and was elected to the Senate in 1848, later becoming Vice-President
under Lincoln.

each other, so that great apprehensions are entertained that they are so exposed that some portions of them may be cut off by the superior numbers of the enemy. It is manifest that General Taylor is wholly incompetent for so large a command. He seems to have no mind or powers of combination. . .

The slavery question has been introduced in the House of Representatives by Mr. Preston King of New York and is a firebrand in the body. . . There is no probability that any territory will ever be acquired from Mexico in which slavery could ever exist. New Mexico and California is all that can ever probably be acquired by treaty, and indeed all that I think it important to acquire. In these provinces slavery ·would probably never exist, and therefore the question would never arise.[4] The dangers of the introduction of the subject were fully considered by the Cabinet. Mr. Buchanan urged the importance and necessity of Congress declaring that we would hold these provinces as indemnity, and establish governments there, subject to the provisions of a treaty of peace. He further expressed his willingness to extend the Missouri Compromise west to the Pacific. All the members of the Cabinet agreed with him in these views. The Postmaster-General was willing to acquire these provinces and agreed that slavery should never exist in them. I suspended any decision on the subject, though it was earnestly urged by Mr. Buchanan and Mr. Walker. Though willing myself to assent to the proposition, I was not ready, until I saw further developments, to recommend it to Congress as the policy of the administration.

Thursday, 7th January, 1847. — Many persons, members of Congress and others, called today; all of them or nearly all on what they may regard as the patriotic, but which I consider the contemptible business of seeking office

---

[4] Slavery did at a later period exist in New Mexico, and might well have flourished there. But Daniel Webster also argued in his Seventh of March speech that slavery was impossible in that territory — Polk's own view.

for themselves or their friends. The passion for office and the number of unworthy persons who seek to live on the public is increasing beyond former example, and I now predict that no President of the United States of either party will ever again be reëlected. The reason is that the patronage of the government will destroy the popularity of any President, however well he may administer the government. The office-seekers have become so numerous that they hold the balance of power between the two great parties of the country. In every appointment which the President makes he disappoints half a dozen applicants and their friends, who, actuated by selfish and sordid motives, will prefer any other candidate in the next election, while the person appointed attributes the appointment to his own superior merit and does not even feel obliged by it. . . Another great difficulty in making appointments which the President encounters is that he cannot tell upon what recommendations to rely. Members of Congress and men of high station in the country sign papers of recommendation, either from interested personal motives or without meaning what they say, and thus the President is often imposed on, and induced to make bad appointments. When he does so the whole responsibility falls on himself, while those who have signed papers of recommendation and misled him, take special care never to avow the agency they have had in the matter, or to assume any part of the responsibility. I have had some remarkable instances of this during my administration. One or two of them I think worthy to be recorded as illustrations of many others. In the recess of Congress shortly after the commencement of my administration I made an appointment upon the letter of recommendation of a Senator. I sent the nomination to the Senate at the last session and it was rejected, and, as I learned, at the instance of the same Senator who had made the recommendation. A few days afterwards the Senator called to recommend another person for the same office. I said to him, well, you rejected the man I nomi-

nated; O yes, he replied, he was without character and
wholly unqualified.   I then asked him if he knew upon whose
recommendation I had appointed him, to which he replied
that he did not.   I then handed to him his own letter and
told him that was the recommendation upon which I had appointed him.   He appeared confused and replied, Well, we
are obliged to recommend our constituents when they apply
to us.   The Senator was Mr. Atchison of Missouri, and the
person appointed and rejected was Mr. Hedges as Surveyor
of the Port of St. Louis.   Other like cases have occurred.

Monday, 11*th January,* 1847. — Immediately after
twelve o'clock the Secretary of War and the Secretary of the
Navy called.   The Secretary of the Navy read to me the
rough draft of a despatch which he had prepared to Commodore Stockton in the Pacific, defining his rights and
powers over the province of the Californias which he had
conquered.   This despatch embodies the laws of nations on
the subject.   I assented to the general principles which it em-
bodied.   The Secretary of War said he would address a
similar communication to General Kearny as applicable to
the province of New Mexico, which he had conquered. . .
I spent the balance of the day in disposing of the business on
my table, and despatched many minor matters which had
been on my hands for some time.   Indeed, I almost cleared
my table.

Thursday, 14*th January,* 1847. — I had a conversation
with Col. Benton about General Taylor's mismanagement of
the war; and about a publication in the New Orleans papers
of the contemplated plans of the campaign.   This could only
have gotten to the public through General Scott, who was
necessarily entrusted with its confidentially before he set out
from Washington for the seat of war.   He has from his in-
ordinate vanity or from some other cause given it out, so
that it has gotten before the public.   The truth is neither
Taylor nor Scott are fit for the command of the army in the
great operations in progress and which are contemplated.

To add to my embarrassment, and it does greatly do so, Congress does not strengthen the executive arm. Nearly half the session has passed and they are engaged in debates about slavery and party politics, and have passed none of the essential measures which I have recommended as indispensable to the vigourous and successful prosecution of the war. With a large nominal majority in both houses, I am practically in a minority. The several cliques and sections of the Democratic party are manifestly more engaged in managing for their respective favourites in the next Presidential election, than they are in supporting the government in prosecuting the war, or in carrying out any of its great measures. The only corrective is in the hands of the people.

Saturday, 16th January, 1847.—I wrote a note to Col. Benton requesting him to call on me this evening. . . I had much conversation with him about the dilatory proceedings of Congress on the measures which I had recommended for the vigorous prosecution of the war. . . Instead of acting upon the great measures of the country, they are spending day after day and week after week in a worse than useless discussion about slavery. This fire-brand was first introduced by Mr. Preston King, of New York, and a fierce and violent discussion has followed. It is a mischievous and wicked agitation, which can result in no good, and must lead to infinite mischief. The pretext for it is to declare in advance that slavery shall never exist in any territory which we may acquire from Mexico. In the Cabinet today this subject was one of conversation. All deprecated the discussion now going on in Congress, but all feared it would be impossible now to arrest it. The Cabinet were unanimous, also, in opinion that if by treaty or otherwise the United States should acquire any territory from Mexico, the line of the Missouri Compromise, viz., 36° 30′, should extend west to the Pacific and apply to such territory. This question was not inconsiderately decided by the Cabinet, but was fully discussed and deliberately considered, and I took the opinion of each member of the Cabinet separately.

Tuesday, 19*th January,* 1847. — This was the regular evening for receiving company, but as tomorrow evening public notice had been given that there would be a drawing room at the President's mansion, not more than half a dozen gentlemen attended. I met them in the parlour. Among them was the Vice-President and Mr. Richard Rush of Philadelphia. Mr. Rush remained for near an hour after the other gentlemen retired. He is an exceedingly intelligent gentleman, and I had a very interesting conversation with him about public affairs.[5] He agreed with me entirely that the dilatory proceedings of Congress were without apology or excuse, and that the spirit of the country in regard to the war was far in advance of that of their Representatives.

Mr. Rush gave me some interesting details which occurred when he was connected with Mr. Madison's administration and when he was a member of Mr. Adams's Cabinet. He said that he was abroad when Mr. Adams was elected President, that he was unexpectedly invited to accept a place in his Cabinet and did so, and remarked that in the election he had been in favour of Mr. Crawford as the nominee in caucus of the Republican party. He gave me a very interesting account of the appointment of a General-in-Chief of the army upon the death of Major-General Brown. He said that Generals Gaines and Scott had both written very exceptionable and violent letters to the President, each claiming the office, the one by virtue of his *lineal* and the other of his *brevet* rank. He said that Mr. Clay was warmly in favour of General Scott; that Messrs. Barbour, Southard, and Wirt also expressed a preference for General Scott. He said that for himself he had been silent during the discussions,

[5] Richard Rush, of Pennsylvania, was Attorney-General and Secretary of State under Monroe, and Secretary of the Treasury under John Quincy Adams; he was Minister to England 1817–1825, and Polk appointed him Minister to France in 1847. A highly cultivated man of the world, he might well strike Polk as an interesting companion.

which had occasionally taken place during a period of more than six weeks, but that finally his opinion was asked in Cabinet by the President and he gave it in favour of General Macomb, upon the ground that he thought neither Gaines nor Scott ought to be appointed after the very exceptionable letters which they had written. The President (Mr. Adams), who had never before expressed an opinion, Mr. Rush said, upon hearing his opinion in favour of General Macomb straightened himself up in his seat, and in his peculiar manner said, " And I think so too." Mr. Rush said this was unexpected and produced great astonishment in the Cabinet, and came very near breaking up the Cabinet. He said as the members of the Cabinet retired, on the walk from the President's mansion Mr. Clay was vehement on the subject, and expressed warmly the opinion that they could not get along under such treatment from the President. He said he interposed to allay the excitement and advised moderation. The President appointed General Macomb and the matter here ended.

Thursday, 21st January, 1847. — After twelve o'clock to-day when I had business with my private secretary, I learned with surprise that without giving me any notice he had gone to Annapolis on a party of pleasure. I was vexed at the occurrence, and think it so thoughtless and inexcusable on his part that I must require an explanation when he returns. In truth he is too fond of spending his time in fashionable and light society, and does not give that close and systematic attention to business which is necessary to give himself reputation and high standing in the estimation of the more solid and better part of the community. This I have observed for some months with great regret.

Saturday, 23d January, 1847. — Saw company this morning until the hour of the meeting of the Cabinet. Among others who called was Senator Crittenden of Kentucky. Mr. Buchanan had previously informed me that he desired to see me, and that he would call this morning. He desired to

converse with me on the subject of the Mexican War, and
the means of prosecuting and bringing it to a close. I told
him I was happy to have a conversation with him on that
subject, and that I would give him my views unreservedly.
Mr. Crittenden, though differing with me in politics, is an
honorable gentleman, and in the confidence that ought to exist
between a Senator and the President I was unreserved in my
conversation.[6] It was in substance what I had said to other
Senators and a few others. I informed him that I was sincerely desirous for peace, but that I believed the most effective
mode of obtaining it was by a bold and vigorous prosecution
of the war; that while this was done I thought it important
that Congress should make the appropriation of the two
millions of dollars for which I had asked at the last and at
the present session of Congress, so that while I presented a
formidable army invading Mexico on the one hand, I might
have the means of inducing her to negotiate for peace on the
other. The two millions I would calculate to pay as a part
consideration for any cession of territory which by a definitive treaty of peace she might make to the United States. I
told him that I did not prosecute the war for conquest, that
I hoped by a treaty of peace to obtain a cession of the Californias and New Mexico, and to pay for them a reasonable
equivalent. That equivalent would probably be the assumption of the debt due by Mexico to our own citizens, to bear
the expenses of the war, and to pay Mexico some millions
of dollars besides. He expressed his concurrence in these
general views and his gratification at hearing them. I told
him I deprecated the agitation of the slavery question in
Congress, and though a southwestern man and from a slaveholding State as well as himself, I did not desire to acquire
a more southern territory than that which I had indicated,
because I did not desire by so doing to give occasion for the

---

[6] John J. Crittenden, who had been Attorney-General under Harrison and
for a brief time under Tyler, resumed his seat in the Senate in 1842, and
sat there throughout Polk's term.

agitation of a question which might sever and endanger the Union itself. I told him the question of slavery would probably never be a practical one if we acquired New Mexico and California, because there would be but a narrow ribbon of territory south of the Missouri Compromise line of 36° 30′, and in it slavery would probably never exist.[7] He expressed himself highly gratified with these views. He expressed an opinion that he would be satisfied with the Rio Grande as a boundary, and with a smaller country including the Bay of San Francisco on the Pacific, than that which I had indicated. I urged him to have speedy action in the Senate upon the war measures which I had recommended. My interview with Mr. Crittenden was a gratifying one. . .

After night several members of Congress called. About ten o'clock at night Senators Benton and Allen called together. They had been dining out. Mr. Benton proceeded immediately to converse in a very animated strain of the developments to the two military committees of Congress, which had been made by the exhibition to them by the Secretary of War today of the correspondence of the Department with General Taylor and General Scott, including the letters of these officers to the Department. He was very strong in his condemnation of both Taylor and Scott, and both he and Mr. Allen concurred in opinion that neither of these officers were fit for the command of the army and that they ought to be superseded. They were both strong and vehement on the subject. Col. Benton among other things said, I was willing to take the command of the army as Lieutenant-General, but the Senate had rejected the proposition to appoint such an officer; but now, Sir! seeing what I

[7] As Polk here indicates, he came to favor a settlement of the troublesome slavery question raised by the Wilmot Proviso and King Proviso by extending the Missouri Compromise line west to the Pacific. This would have given the South much the smaller part of the new acquisitions in the West. For this reason some Southerners, as well as all the Northerners who held to the Wilmot Proviso principle of no extension of slave territory anywhere, opposed it. But Polk thought that for natural reasons slavery would probably never exist in the Southwest, and patriotically wished to quiet the agitation on the subject.

have today, I will go as a Major-General or a Lieutenant-Colonel, or in any other rank, provided I can have the command of the army, and if I can have such command I will close the war before July. They held a conversation with me on the subject of more than an hour. Col. Benton said that every member of the two committees were astonished at the conduct of both Taylor and Scott. At about half past eleven o'clock they retired.

Monday, 25th January, 1847. — Two or three days ago a letter bearing the signature of General Taylor and purporting to have been written near Monterey in Mexico, said to have been addressed to him by a friend in New York, was published in the New York *Express,* and copied into the *Herald.* I read it in the *Herald* on yesterday. It is a highly exceptionable letter, assailing as it does the administration, uttering unfounded complaints, and giving publicity to the world of the plans of campaign contemplated by the government, which it had been desired by the government to keep concealed from the enemy until they were consummated. Several persons have spoken to me of the letter, and expressed doubts whether it was genuine or not. I have myself no doubt it is genuine. Considering the letter not only injurious to the public interests, but unjust to the government and its publication highly unmilitary, I sent for the Secretary of War to consult him as to the steps proper to be taken in reference to it.[8] The Secretary of War called.

[8] Both Scott and Taylor had now by indiscreet publications made it certain that the Mexican army would not be taken by surprise in any of the American operations. Polk elsewhere writes that " I have no doubt the Mexican Government and military commanders are as well apprised of the secret instructions which were given to General Scott when he left Washington as he is himself. His vanity is such that he could not keep the most important secrets of the government which were given him." Polk decided that the best way to vindicate his administration from Taylor's ignorant and biased charges was to publish all the correspondence which had been exchanged by Taylor and the War Department. He therefore had a Democratic Representative, Thompson of Mississippi, introduce a resolution calling for these papers. This resolution was passed and the correspondence was published, with some little effect on public opinion. Private epistles in the volume called *Taylor's*

The Secretary of the Navy was also in my office. I conferred with them fully on the subject. I told the Secretary of War that I thought a letter should be immediately addressed to General Taylor enquiring of him whether he was the author of the letter, and that in the meantime a proper article vindicating the government and exposing General Taylor for writing such a letter should be published in the *Union*. The further consideration of the subject was postponed until tomorrow when the Secretary of War promised to have a suitable article prepared for publication. After the Secretary of War left, a card was brought to me by my porter from General Gaines addressed to the Secretary of War, which I opened and read. It was a letter from General Gaines in which he states that the letter of General Taylor which had been published in the newspapers was addressed to him.

Tuesday, 26th January, 1847. — Saw company this morning until near twelve o'clock. Among the visitors were several members of Congress, to whom I spoke very freely of the inexcusable delay of Congress in acting upon the war measures which I have recommended. . .

The Cabinet met, all the members present except the Secretary of the Treasury, who was understood to be at the Capitol pressing members to push the speedy passage of the loan-bill. The published letter of General Taylor and General Gaines's avowal that it had been addressed to him and had been published by his permission (see yesterday's diary) were considered. The Cabinet were unanimous in condemning Taylor for writing such a letter and Gaines for publishing it, as being not only unmilitary and a violation of their duty as officers, but calculated seriously to embarrass and injure the pending military operations in Mexico. It was agreed that a letter should be written by the Secretary of War to General Taylor condemning his conduct. It was

---

Letters from the Battlefields, 80–88, show that Taylor was deeply suspicious of Polk, Marcy, and Scott, accusing them of intriguing to force him to resign, of jealousy, and so on.

agreed also that as the letter had been published in several public journals, it should be republished in the Washington *Union* with proper comments. The Secretary of War and the Secretary of the Navy stepped into my private secretary's office and prepared an article for the paper. The Secretary of State took their draft and prepared one from it which I thought too mild but assented to in this form. The Secretary of War took it with him when he retired.

CHAPTER VII
Jan. 28, 1847 — April 30, 1847

THE TEN-REGIMENT BILL PASSES — GENERAL SCOTT'S DEFI-
CIENCIES — SENATOR BENTON AND THE LIEUTENANT-GEN-
ERALSHIP — BATTLE OF BUENA VISTA — QUESTION OF
PEACE NEGOTIATIONS — TRIST APPOINTED COMMISSIONER
— THE PEACE TERMS

Thursday, 28th January, 1847. — It is two years ago this day since I left my residence at Columbia, Tennessee, to enter on my duties as President of the United States. Since that time I have performed great labour and incurred vast responsibilities. In truth, though I occupy a very high position, I am the hardest-working man in this country.

Monday, 1st February, 1847. — This morning my office was crowded with visitors. The prospect of the passage of the bill before Congress to raise ten regular regiments for the war against Mexico brought a large number of members of Congress with their constituents and friends seeking commissions in the army. . .

About two o'clock P.M. Mr. Kaufman, one of the Representatives from the State of Texas, called and had a long conversation with me about several matters of business, but chiefly about appointments in Texas. Among other things he informed me that General Houston was dissatisfied with the administration. I told him that I had received an intimation of the kind before, but that he had no cause to be so. The truth is that Senator Houston desires to be a candidate for the Presidency and probably thinks that I do not throw my official influence into the scale to promote his views. He probably thinks, also, that he should have been looked to instead of Col. Benton for Lieutenant-General.

Saturday, 6th February, 1847. — The Cabinet met at the usual hour, all the members present. I stated fully to them the embarrassments to the government, and especially in the prosecution of the war, in consequence of the failure of Congress to act on the war measures which I have recommended. I stated to them that I was seriously considering of the propriety, and indeed the duty, of sending to Congress a message boldly and strongly appealing to Congress, and through them to the country, in favour of speedy action on my war measures. This I thought necessary to vindicate myself before the people and to throw the responsibility for the failure to act upon Congress. All the Cabinet approved the suggestion but Mr. Buchanan, who thought I had better postpone taking such a step until it was ascertained whether the bill to raise ten regiments of regular troops now before the Senate would pass. If that bill failed to pass, Mr. Buchanan was then decidedly in favour of my sending in such a message.

Monday, 8th February, 1847. — Near night Senator Cass called, and informed me that the Senate had rejected the report of the committee of conference of the two houses on the disagreeing votes between them on the bill to raise ten additional regiments. The effect of this vote is the rejection of the bill. I learn it was rejected by the united vote of the Federal party in the Senate, and by the votes of Mr. Calhoun and his peculiar friends in the Senate. I now regard Mr. Calhoun to be in opposition to my administration. He has been dissatisfied ever since I refused to retain him in my Cabinet at the commencement of my administration, and is now, I have reason to believe, as decidedly opposed to my administration in his heart as any member of the Federal party. He is an aspirant for the Presidency, and the truth is that the next Presidential election has divided the Democratic party in Congress into factions, each adhering to their favourites, and the effect is to reduce the administration to a minority in Congress, and to paralyze and defeat all my measures. In the Senate three or four Democrats who may dissent from the body of the party can defeat any measure. The Federal party never fails to unite with such minority and thus constitute the majority. Mr. Calhoun can carry with him that many votes, and I now consider him the most mischievous man in the Senate to my administration. The people must be made to understand this state of things. With a nominal majority in each house, I am in truth in a minority in each.

Tuesday, 9th February, 1847. — I saw a number of members of Congress in my office tonight. The impression now is that the Ten Regiment bill will yet pass.

Wednesday, 10th February, 1847. — The Ten Regiment bill, I learn, passed the two houses of Congress today.

Thursday, 11th February, 1847. — I learn that a motion was made today in the Senate by Senator Yulee of Florida to expel the editor of the *Union* from the privileged seats in the Senate, in consequence of the publication in his paper of a communication signed "Vindicator" censuring the Senate for their rejection of the Ten Regiment bill, and that it had given rise to an animating and exciting debate in the Senate, but was undecided at the adjournment of the Senate today.

Saturday, 13th February, 1847. — About six o'clock P.M. I learned that the Senate had expelled Mr. Ritchie from the privileged seats of that body, in consequence of the publication in the *Union* a few days ago over the signature of "Vindicator." It is a second Duane case, and strikes a blow at the liberty of the press. The foul deed was perpetrated by the votes of the undivided Federal Senators, and Senators Calhoun and Butler of South Carolina and Yulee and Westcott of Florida. These four gentlemen constitute what Senator Turney denominated in debate a few days ago the

Balance of Power party. They have more frequently voted with the Federalists than the Democrats during this session.

After night an unusual number of members of Congress called. They were Democrats and were most excited at the expulsion of Mr. Ritchie from the Senate today. I learn that the public opinion and sympathies are all enlisted in his behalf, and that this act of the Senate is condemned by public opinion, as far as it has been expressed in the city.

Friday, 19th February, 1847. — My office was crowded this morning with visitors, most of them seeking military appointments. For the last week I have been greatly annoyed by this kind of importunity. The city is crowded with young men, many of them loafers without merit, seeking military appointments. Members of Congress tell me that they are compelled to come with their constituents to present their claims, and some of the members apologize for troubling me as much as they do. One thing is certain, and that is that I could soon have an army of officers, such as they would be, if I could appoint all the applicants. . . I am often exceedingly disgusted with the scenes which occur in my office, but keep my temper and endure the painful labour which is imposed upon me with patience. I could bear this labour with more patience if members of Congress and others were more candid, and would not, as they do, constantly deceive me about appointments. I am almost ready at some times to conclude that all men are selfish, and that there is no reliance to be placed in any of the human race.

Saturday, 20th February, 1847. — The official report of General Scott with the correspondence between himself and Col. Harney was read. From these documents it appears that General Scott arbitrarily and without cause ordered Col. Harney, then at the head of seven companies of his regiment on the Rio Grande, to turn over his command to a junior officer and proceed himself to Monterey and take command of the two remaining companies. Col. Harney is known to be one of the most gallant and best officers in the service. He was not under any charges of any kind. He was, however, a Democrat in politics, was one of General Jackson's personal friends, and was appointed by him. I can conceive of no reason but this for the arbitrary and tyrannical conduct of General Scott in doing such gross injustice to this gallant officer. General Taylor had acted with the same proscriptive spirit, not only towards Col. Harney, but other gallant Democratic officers. I have myself been wholly uninfluenced by any reference to the political opinions of the officer of the army in the conduct of the war. It has not been so with the Federal commanders in the field. I have good reason to believe that General Taylor's camp has been converted into a political arena, and that great and palpable injustice has been done to many officers of high merit who happen to be Democrats. General Scott, since he assumed command, has commenced the same proscriptive and tyran-ranical course, and I stated to the Cabinet that I was resolved at any hazard to check it. Mr. Buchanan, though agreeing that great injustice had been done to Col. Harney, expressed the opinion in a zealous and strong manner that as Col. Harney had been put under arrest for disobeying and protesting against General Scott's arbitrary orders, that no order should be issued from here until the result of his trial was known. The Attorney-General, Secretary of War, and Secretary of the Navy advised delay in issuing the proposed order. The Secretary of the Treasury expressed in strong terms his disapproval of General Scott's conduct and seemed, as far as he spoke, to agree with me in opinion, though he was not very distinct. The Postmaster-General expressed no opinion. I told the Cabinet that I had great respect for their opinions, but that in this case I was sure I was right, and would take the whole responsibility. I told the Secretary of War that if he was unwilling to write the letter which I had directed to be written, I would do it myself. He said he would write the letter. I told him to state in it that it was written by my order. I am resolved that Col. Harney shall not be sacrificed to propitiate the personal and political malice of Gen. Scott. . .

The attack on Vera Cruz became the subject of conversasation, when the fact was alluded to that from General Scott's letter of the 12th of January last it would probably be made about this time. The Secretary of the Navy expressed surprise at hearing this, and said the *Ohio* and bombvessels designed to coöperate with the land forces had not gone round, and said he had not heard of General Scott's letter. I expressed equal surprise at hearing him say this, and addressing him and the Secretary of War I remarked that I had taken it for granted that they were constantly in conference with each other, and that each understood the movements and operations of their respective branches of the service. The Postmaster-General remarked that General Scott's letter had been read in Cabinet on last Tuesday week, if his memory served. The Secretary of the Navy replied that he could not have been present. The Secretary of War remarked that he had supposed that the Secretary of the Navy knew all about it. Mr. Mason seemed to be much mortified and left the Cabinet to issue orders today to hasten the movement of the naval forces to the Gulf.

Monday, 22d February, 1847.—About nine o'clock P.M. I was waited upon by a committee consisting of Senators Sevier and Houston and Mr. Kaufman of the House of Representatives, and was conducted by them to the birthnight ball at Carusi's Saloon, where I remained about half an hour, and from thence I was conducted to Jackson Hall, where there was another ball. The assembly at Carusi's was small. That at Jackson Hall was numerously attended. I took supper at the latter, attending Mrs. Dallas to the table. After supper and about twelve o'clock I retired and returned to the President's mansion. It has been customary for the President to attend the birth-night ball, and thus pay his respect to the memory of the father of his country.

Wednesday, 3d March, 1847. — In the course of the evening I tendered the office of Major-General in the army to Senator Houston of Texas, who declined accepting it. I then tendered the same office through Mr. Houston and Mr. Kaufman of the House of Representatives to Senator Rusk of Texas, who also declined accepting it, as Mr. Kaufman reported to me. I saw Senator Benton and had a few minutes' conversation with him. He knew that I had intended to appoint him Lieutenant-General if a law had been passed creating that rank. As no such law had passed, he said to me that if I chose I could nominate him as Major-General. I told him I would do so. I did so accordingly and he was confirmed by the Senate with the other general officers whom I nominated tonight.

Monday, 8th March, 1847. — Tonight I found on my table a letter from General Benton dated on the 6th instant. When it was placed there by my messenger I do not know. There was a large mass of papers and letters on my table to which I have had no time to give any attention, such have been my pressing engagements. This, with many other letters with the seals unbroken, was among the number. On opening it I found that the conditions on which General Benton would accept the appointment of Major-General of the army, which I had conferred upon him by and with the advice of the Senate, were, 1st, that he should have the chief command of the army in Mexico, and 2d, that he should be invested with plenary diplomatic powers to conclude a treaty of peace. Shortly after I opened this letter the Secretary of State called in and I sent for the Secretary of War. I had fully examined my authority under the existing law and was satisfied that I possessed no power to assign the chief command of the army on General Benton, unless it was by recalling four senior Major-Generals, *viz.,* Scott, Taylor, Butler, and Patterson. The two former I should have no hesitation in recalling, but I know of no reason to justify the recall of the two latter. The Secretaries of State and War concurred in this opinion. . . After these gentlemen retired I drew up the draft of a letter to General Benton, expressing the opinion that I was not invested with the power by the existing law to assign him, a junior Major-General, to the chief command, without superseding the senior generals of the same rank. General Benton's letter was in a kind and friendly spirit and the draft of my answer was in the same spirit. The truth is that if Congress at the late session had conferred upon me the power to designate a General-in-Chief, as I asked them to do, I should have selected General Benton for that important command.

Wednesday, 10th March, 1847. — Having seen in the New Orleans papers which arrived last night that Major-General Butler was in New Orleans, and thinking it probable that he had leave of absence from the army in consequence of his wound or from bad health, and that possibly he might not be able to resume his command, it occurred to me, if this was so, that the difficulties which had interposed of placing General Benton in the chief command would be partially removed. I did not still see my way entirely clear to remove three senior Major-Generals who had rank of General Butler, but thought it probable that I might do so in a short time. With a view to such a contingency I requested my private secretary immediately after breakfast to call on General Benton and request him to postpone any final decision as to his acceptance of his commission as Major-General for a few days, and until I could confer with him. My private secretary returned in about an hour and reported to me that General Benton had informed me that he had addressed letters to the Adjutant-General and myself declining to accept the commission. . .

I sent for the Secretary of War, and the Secretary of State happening to come in I read to each the letter which I had received from General Benton and had some conversation with them. After a conference with them I addressed a note to General Benton requesting him to suspend any decision whether he would accept or decline the appointment of Major-General of the army for a few days, and until I could have further developments from the seat of war. I stated to him the fact that General Butler had arrived at New Orleans on leave of absence, in consequence of ill-health produced by his wound, and that he might possibly not be able to return to the army. I told him that I had no power to place him in command but by recalling four Major-Generals, but that if General Butler should not be able to return to the army, there would be less difficulty in placing him in the position he desired. He replied that he could not postpone his decision. . . The result of our conversation was that he declined suspending his decision to decline accepting the office of Major-General. He was in a pleasant humour and his conversation was in a friendly tone. I had a long conversation with him in which he gave his views fully of what he considered to be the proper operations of the army in Mexico under the existing circumstances. He had great apprehensions from the Vomito.[1] He was in favour of raising the blockade at all the ports in our military possession, and levying a tariff of duties, as a condition upon which importation should be allowed. I had, in the first instance, stated to him that such would be my policy and inquired of him if in his opinion I possessed the power under the laws of war to establish such regulations. He said he had no doubt that I possessed the power and ought to exercise it. I inquired of him if he would make any discrimination between the productions of the United States imported into the ports of Mexico in the possession of our arms, and those of foreign countries imported in foreign bottoms. He said that he would not.

Saturday, 13th March, 1847. — I submitted to the Cabinet the propriety of raising the blockade of such of the ports of Mexico as may be in the military possession of our arms, and of levying a tax or tariff of duties on commerce to such ports, to be applied to defray the expenses of the war. . .

---

[1] The yellow fever, which is characterized by vomiting.

The Attorney-General, whom I had requested on yesterday to examine the authorities on the executive power, brought with him the books containing the doctrine on the subject, and gave his opinion that I possessed the undoubted power, and advised that it should be exercised. All the Cabinet concurred with the Attorney-General, and I myself was clear that the power existed, and that it would be wise to exercise it. Some discussion upon the details of the measure took place.

Monday, 15th March, 1847. — Brigadier-General Franklin Pierce of New Hampshire and Col. Caleb Cushing of Massachusetts called on me today and again after night, with both of whom I had much conversation in relation to the war. General Pierce expressed deep regret that General Benton had declined to accept the office of Major-General, and said he had utterly ruined himself with the masses of the people of the country, at least such he thought was the public sentiment at the North. Col. Cushing concurred in this opinion. I think myself that General Benton will have reason to regret his course.

Wednesday, 17th March, 1847. — After night Senator Breese called. He has always an axe to grind. He is perhaps the most troublesome and inveterate seeker for office for his friends in either House of Congress. He has caused me to make some bad appointments. He has no sooner procured an appointment than he sets to work to procure another.

Thursday, 18th March, 1847. — Tonight at eight o'clock I accompanied Mrs. Polk and the other ladies of the family to the residence of General Thomas H. Benton in this city, and witnessed the marriage of his eldest daughter, Miss Eliza Benton, with Mr. Jones of New Orleans. I waited on the bride to the supper table and shortly after supper I retired and returned to the President's mansion, leaving Mrs. Polk and Mr. and Mrs. Walker and Miss Rucker enjoying themselves with the bridal company.

Saturday, 20th March, 1847. — I held a conversation with Col. Stanton in relation to the operations of the Quartermaster's Department. I condemned the purchase and employment of the thousands of wagons for which I learned requisitions had been made by the commander of the army in Mexico. I told him that I would issue no positive order on the subject, but expressed the opinion that long trains of miles of wagons in such a country as Mexico, in which, in all the wars which had ever occurred in that country, they had never been used, could only have the effect of retarding the movements of the army and rendering it inefficient in its operations. I expressed the opinion that pack-mules should be chiefly employed for the transportation of the army, instead of the cumbrous appendage of a long wagon-train, which would require an army for its guard. I learned from Col. Stanton that contracts had been recently made for the purchase of 1,000 horses in Ohio, to be transported to Mexico upon which to mount the 3d Regiment of Dragoons, and that mules were being purchased in the United States for the use of the army. I expressed the opinion strongly that this was great folly, as well as involving the country in a vast expense. I asked them why horses and mules in Mexico, which were to be had in great numbers and which were accustomed to the climate and which could be had at one-fourth the price which must be paid in the United States, were not procured. To this he could give no satisfactory answer, except that he thought the horses and mules in the United States larger and better than those in Mexico. I was much vexed at the extravagance and stupidity of purchasing these animals in the United States and transporting them at vast expense to Mexico. He left with my direction to look into the subject more fully than he had done. The truth is that the old army officers have become so in the habit of enjoying their ease, sitting in parlours and on carpeted floors, that most of them have no energy, and are content to jog on in a regular routine without knowing whether they

are taking care of the public interest or not. I shall find it
to be necessary to give more of my attentiton to these matters of detail than I have heretofore had it in my power
to do.[1a]

The Cabinet met at the usual hour. . . About one o'clock
the Secretary of State came in, and stated that he had been
detained until that hour in consequence of the arrival from
Mexico of Mr. Atocha, who had been sent to Mexico as
bearer of despatches about the 20th of January last. The
answer of the Mexican Government to the renewed overture
of the United States to reopen negotiations, which Mr.
Atocha had borne to them, was presented by Mr. Buchanan.
It was in the Spanish language. . . It was in substance that
the Mexican Government refused to reopen negotiations, except upon the condition that the squadron of the United
States should be withdrawn from the coasts, and the army
from the territories of Mexico which are now in the possession of our arms. I at once declared to the Cabinet that the
preliminary conditions required were wholly inadmissible,
and that no alternative was now left but the most energetic
crushing movement of our arms upon Mexico. Mr. Buchanan expressed the opinion that our army should not attempt to march to the City of Mexico. I replied that I differed with him in opinion, and that I would not only march
to the City of Mexico, but that I would pursue Santa Anna's
army wherever it was, and capture or destroy it. I expressed
the opinion that if I had a proper commander of the army,
who would lay aside the technical rules of war to be found

[1a] Justin H. Smith (*War With Mexico*, I, 227) upholds Polk in this criticism of the field commanders. Speaking of Taylor's wagons, he says that
" A train of pack-mules was the natural supplement. Those animals were
almost universally employed in Mexico; the country abounded in them;
and it was the general's obvious duty to use the facilities within reach." Yet
Taylor, who should have collected at least 3,000 Mexican mules at the beginning of his campaign, gathered barely 1700 of them.
     The victory of Buena Vista was now, however, after a period of agonizing
suspense caused by rumors of Taylor's peril and imminent danger of defeat,
about to burst upon the American people, and cover the old soldier with new
glory.

in books, which required a long train of baggage-wagons; one who would go light and move rapidly, I had no doubt Santa Anna and his whole army could be destroyed or captured in a short time.

Monday, 22d March, 1847. — The Secretary of War called this morning. Upon a full examination of all the newspaper accounts from New Orleans containing all the information from General Taylor's army which had reached that city in the shape of rumours, our conviction was that our forces on the Rio Grande, and especially General Taylor's advanced position, were in a very critical position. If General Taylor's army be in that position it has grown out of his own imprudence in advancing without orders beyond Monterey and too far into the interior. General Scott seems to have assumed the command with the single idea in his head of taking Vera Cruz, and with this view has probably reduced General Taylor's forces to too small a number. We must, however, wait in painful suspense for more reliable and authentic intelligence. It was, upon consultation with the Secretary of War, resolved to hasten with all possible expedition to the seat of war such of the ten regiments as were already recruited, which is estimated to be from 1500 to 2000 men, in companies and fractions of companies. It was resolved also to authorize General Brooke at New Orleans to call upon the governors of Louisiana and Alabama for such numbers of volunteers as he might deem necessary, and as could be speedily moved to the Rio Grande. It was also determined to write to General Scott to afford to General Taylor all the succour in his power. These letters to General Brooke and Scott had been prepared by the Secretary of War and were read to me and approved by me. . . I have great fears for the safety of General Taylor's army, and for the whole line of our military operations in his rear and on the Rio Grande. Surely General Scott upon hearing of their critical situation will rush to their relief. All will be done here that it is in human power to do to reinforce and rescue them from their danger, but I have great apprehensions that any succour from here will arrive too late. This subject engrossed my whole attention today.

Sunday, 28th March, 1847. — Exciting rumours arrived this morning from General Taylor's army. Similar rumours had been received by the southern mails for the last two or three days. If General Taylor is in any danger, as I greatly fear he is, it is in consequence of his having, in violation of his orders, advanced beyond Monterey. The truth is that from the beginning of the war he has been constantly blundering into difficulties, but has fought out of them, but at the cost of many lives. I hope in this instance he may be safe, though I greatly fear he may have had hard fighting and may have lost many of his brave men.

Monday, 29th March, 1847. —General Benton called and read me a letter which he had addressed to the people of Oregon, stating to them that the agitation of the slavery question had caused the rejection of the bill to organize a territorial government over them at the last session of Congress. I disapproved the letter, but knowing his domineering disposition and utter impatience of contradiction or difference of opinion, and knowing that I could not change his opinions, I contented myself with simply stating very briefly my objections to the letter and expressing my doubts of sending such a letter. I feared it might deceive the people of Oregon as to the real state of public opinion in the States in regard to them, and might incline them to set up an independent government of their own. General Benton then asked me to appoint his son-in-law, Mr. Jones, who married his daughter a few days ago, a *chargé d'affaires* abroad. I told him there was no vacancy, and gave him no encouragement. I told him that there was a place of the kind which might be vacant soon, but that there were some commitments in regard to it; and added that I did not see that it would be in my power to gratify his wishes. He said he merely wished to present the application, and leave the disposition of it with me. Mr. Jones had made a similar application in person a few days ago (the day before he was married) and I gave him the same answer. I note this case, out of the thousands of applications which are made to me for office, because I predict if I do not appoint Mr. Jones that it will be the cause of a violent outbreak of opposition to me by General Benton. Mr. Jones has no claims upon me for this or any other office. He was but a short time ago the editor of a Federal paper in New Orleans.

Thursday, 1st April, 1847. — By the Southern mail of this evening official despatches were received from General Taylor giving a detailed account of the battle of the 22d and 23d ultimo. It was a severe battle. Many valuable officers and men fell, and among them my old esteemed friend, Col. Archibald Yell of the Arkansas Mounted Regiment. I deeply deplore his loss. He was a brave and good man, and among the best friends I had on earth, and had been so for twenty-five years. His eldest, and perhaps his only son, is now at college at Georgetown, and as my impression is that Col. Yell died poor, I will in that event educate the boy, and shall take great interest in him.

A despatch from Commodore Conner was received to-night, communicating the information that General Scott's forces had landed near Vera Cruz on the 7th instant without serious resistance.

Had General Taylor obeyed his orders, and occupied Monterey and the passes beyond it, the severe loss of our army, including many valuable officers, would have been avoided. It was great rashness to take the position he did in advance of Saltillo. Having done so, he is indebted not to his own good generalship, but to the indomitable and intrepid bravery of the officers and men under his command for his success. He exposed them to an opposing army of three or four times their number. The Mexican army were suffering from want of food, and took up their retreat shortly after the battle. General Taylor is a hard fighter, but has none of the other qualities of a great general. From the beginning of the existing war with Mexico he has been constantly blundering into difficulties, but has fought out of them, but with very severe loss. His first blunder was in separating his army from his supplies, which caused the battle of Palo Alto and Resaca de la Palma. His second was in moving upon Monterey with an inadequate force, leaving more than two thirds of his whole army behind him with the batteries and trains, and this caused the hard battle and some loss at Monterey; and the last is in taking his position so far in advance of Monterey, which caused the late sanguinary battle. I rejoice that our brave army have been successful in this battle, but deeply lament the severe loss they have sustained.[2]

Tuesday, 6th April, 1847. — Mr. Mason, the Secretary of the Navy, mentioned to me that he had been informed by the Hon. John S. Barbour of Virginia that he had recently received a letter from Senator Calhoun of South Carolina, the object of which was to obtain his signature to an address to the people of the United States on the subject of slavery, thus making and endeavouring to make the question a test in the next Presidential election. Mr. Barbour informed Mr. Ma-

---

[2] Taylor had, as Polk states, deliberately disobeyed his instructions. The government had informed him that its wish was he should hold no territory beyond Monterey, and Scott had bade him to concentrate his army at that city. With Santa Anna advancing with a large and well-drilled army, it was the course of prudence for him not to lengthen his line of communications. But Taylor chafed under his orders, believing that both the Polk administration and Scott wished him relegated to obscurity, and meant to efface him in the future operations of the war. He defied them and the rules of caution by moving at the end of January, 1847, to Saltillo, and soon afterward pushing still farther toward the enemy. " He showed himself, in fact, both unwise and insubordinate." (Smith, *War With Mexico,* I, 369.)

Despite his imprudence, he scored a brilliant victory at Buena Vista. Santa Anna's army, advancing with more than 20,000 men, encountered Taylor a few miles south of Saltillo, with only about 5,000 men, on Feb. 23, 1847. Had the Mexicans charged *en masse* at the first opportunity, the Americans would have been overwhelmed. As it was, for a few hours the issue of the day seemed indecisive. But the Americans beat back all attacks, and Santa Anna retreated with heavy losses. The Americans lost 673 officers and men killed or wounded.

son, as Mr. Mason told me, that he had refused to sign the address; but that he learned that Mr. Calhoun desired that it should be signed by leading men in all the Southern States, and the Hon. Mr. Seddon among others was named by Mr. Barbour as one of those who was expected to sign it. I remarked to Mr. Mason that Mr. Calhoun had become perfectly desperate in his aspirations to the Presidency, and had seized upon this sectional question as the only means of sustaining himself in his present fallen condition, and that such an agitation of the slavery question was not only unpatriotic and mischievous, but wicked. I told him further, that I had learned from a reliable source that the New York politicians who were favourable to the election of Gov. Wright to the Presidency would be rejoiced at the opportunity to take issue with Mr. Calhoun on such a question. I did not tell Mr. Mason my authority for this opinion, but I think it proper to record the fact. I derived this information from General Benton in a conversation with him a few days ago . . . in which I had protested against his addressing a letter to the people of Oregon informing them that the bill to establish a territorial government over them had been rejected at the last session of Congress on account of the attempt made by Mr. Calhoun to leave the question of the existence of slavery in that territory an open one. In the course of the conversation General Benton dropped the idea distinctly that the New York gentlemen had gone home from Congress with a full record of all the facts and intended to make an issue on that question. I find I omitted to state this in Tuesday's diary. The truth is there is no patriotism in either faction of the party. Both desire to mount slavery as a hobby, and hope to secure the election of their favourite upon it. They will both fail and ought to fail. The people of the United States, I hope, will cast off all such intriguers, and make their own selection for the Presidency, and this if they are wise they will do. I now entertain a worse opinion of Mr. Calhoun than I have ever done before. He is wholly selfish, and I am satisfied has no patriotism. A few years ago he was the author of Nullification and threatened to dissolve the Union on account of the tariff. During my administration the reduction of duties which he desired has been obtained, and he can no longer complain. No sooner is this done than he selects slavery upon which to agitate the country, and blindly mounts that topic as a hobby. Gov. Wright's friends in Congress as unpatriotically have shown by their course that they desire to mount the same hobby in the North and hope to be successful by their opposition to slavery. They both forget that the Constitution settles these questions which were the subjects to mutual concessions between the North and the South. I am utterly disgusted at such intriguing of men in high place, and hope they will be rebuked by the people.

Saturday, 10*th April,* 1847.— I received a telegraphic despatch from the office of the Baltimore *Sun* stating that by a special express who had come from Pensacola, beating the mail one day, information had been received that the city of Vera Cruz and the castle of San Juan de Ulloa had surrendered on the 27th *ultimo* to the combined operation of our land and naval forces, with the loss of only 36 men on our part. This was joyful news. In about two hours afterwards a more detailed account of the capitulation was received, published in the *Sun* and taken from a Pensacola paper. . .

The Cabinet assembled at the usual hour. . . The subject of consideration today was the Mexican War. I had several times mentioned to Mr. Buchanan the importance of having a commissioner vested with plenipotentiary powers, who should attend the headquarters of the army ready to take advantage of circumstances as they might arise to negotiate for peace. I stated to the Cabinet today that such was my opinion, and that I thought it the more important since the news of the recent victories, and especially since the information receiving this morning of the fall of Vera Cruz and the castle of San Juan de Ulloa. All the members of the

Cabinet present concurred in this opinion. The embarrassment in carrying it out consisted in the selection of a suitable commission or commissioners who would be satisfactory to the country. This was a great difficulty. Such is the jealousy of the different factions of the Democratic party in reference to the next Presidential election towards each other that it is impossible to appoint any prominent man or men without giving extensive dissatisfaction to others, and thus jeopardizing the ratification of any treaty they might make. In this also the Cabinet were agreed. I stated that I preferred that the Secretary of State should be the sole commissioner to negotiate the treaty, and that I would have no hesitation in deputing him on that special service if the Mexican authorities had agreed to appoint commissioners on their part, but as they had refused to do this he could not attend the headquarters of the army for an indefinite period of time and with no assurance whether the Mexican authorities would agree to negotiate. Mr. Buchanan expressed his entire concurrence in this view. He said he would be willing to go in person if there was any assurance that negotiations would be speedily opened, but under existing circumstances and with our present information he could not, of course, think of going. Mr. Buchanan then suggested that Mr. N. P. Trist, the chief clerk of the Department of State, might be deputed secretly with plenipotentiary powers to the headquarters of the army, and that it might be made known that such a person was with the army ready to negotiate. Mr. Trist, he said, was an able man, perfectly familiar with the Spanish character and language, and might go with special and well-defined instructions.[3] The suggestions struck

[3] Nicholas P. Trist was a man of no mean qualifications for this important post. He had studied law with Jefferson, and was connected with his family by marriage; he had been Jackson's private secretary; he had attended West Point; and he had been consul at Havana for some years. Not only did he know the Spanish language, but he was well acquainted with the Latin-American character. He was a man of dignified appearance, agreeable presence, superior intelligence, and great industry. Several times he had served as acting Secretary of State, and Buchanan and Polk trusted him. But he was

me favourably. After much conversation on the subject it
was unanimously agreed by the Cabinet that it would be
proper to send Mr. Trist, and that he should take with him
a treaty drawn up by the Secretary of State and approved by
the Cabinet, which he should be authorized to tender to the
Mexican Government, and to conclude a treaty with them if
they would accept it; but that if they would not accept it, but
would agree to appoint commissioners to negotiate, Mr.
Trist should in that event report the fact to his government,
when Mr. Buchanan could go out as the commissioner. This
being agreed upon by the members of the Cabinet present,
and it being desirable, as it was a very important matter, that
every member should be consulted, I sent for the Secretary
of the Treasury, who had retired. He came, and I laid the
whole matter fully before him. He fully concurred in
opinion with the other members of the Cabinet.

After the consideration of some other matters all the
members of the Cabinet retired except Mr. Buchanan, whom
I requested to remain. I sent to the Department of State
for Mr. Trist, and in the presence of Mr. Buchanan I opened
the matter fully to him. He gave his assent to go on the
mission. I then charged him to keep the matter a profound
secret. I requested Mr. Buchanan to go to work immediately and with the least practicable delay to prepare the project of a treaty and the necessary instructions, and in order
that it might be kept a profound secret. I impressed it upon
him that no clerk or other person in his Department should
have any knowledge of it. Both Mr. Buchanan and Mr.
Trist said that Mr. Derrick, one of the clerks in the Department of State, could render important aid in preparing

---

inclined to a visionary kind of self-conceit, and was at times lacking in sober
perspective and common sense. Polk was destined to find him an insecure
support.

Scott had begun his operations against Vera Cruz with an army of 13,600
men. The total Mexican force in the City consisted of only 3,360 men. A
brief land-and-sea siege ended in the capitulation of the city and castle on
March 29 without an assault.

and copying the necessary papers. After some hesitation I agreed that he might be so employed, but that he should be placed under the strictest injunctions of secrecy.

Monday, 12th April, 1847. — I took a ride with Judge Mason in his buggy this evening. He told me that he had understood that Mr. Calhoun had come out for Mr. Taylor for President. I had heard the same rumour this morning but could not believe it. If it be true, I have no hesitation in saying that Mr. Calhoun is wholly destitute of political principle. General Taylor is a Whig alias Federalist of the most decided character. He is a Kentuckian and a devotee of Mr. Clay, and holds no one of the strict construction opinions which Mr. Calhoun has heretofore professed. If the rumours be true then all Mr. Calhoun's loud professions in favour of a strict construction of the Constitution and of State Rights are false. It was but a few years ago that Mr. Calhoun was ready to nullify and dissolve the Union about the tariff. Now that the tariff has been reduced under my administration and all has been effected on that subject which he desired, he is obliged to mount some other political hobby to keep himself before the public, and for that purpose some weeks ago selected the slavery question. . . I cannot express the contempt I feel for Mr. Calhoun for such profligate political inconsistency. If I had retained him in my Cabinet and consented to yield myself up to his control, I might have secured his support, but not by the support of principle.[4]

Tuesday, 13th April, 1847. — At the request of Mr. Buchanan I summoned the Cabinet to meet at ten o'clock this morning. All the members attended shortly after that hour. Mr. Buchanan submitted for consideration the project of a treaty with Mexico, which he had prepared in pursuance of the decision of the Cabinet on Saturday last, to be borne by

---

[4] It was of course untrue that Calhoun supported Taylor for the Presidency, and in 1848 he gave cordial assistance to the Democratic nominee, Lewis Cass.

Mr. Trist to the headquarters of the army in Mexico and to be concluded and signed by him if the Mexican government acceded to it. The boundary proposed in the project was the Rio Grande from its mouth to the point where it intersects the southern boundary of New Mexico, the whole of the provinces of New Mexico and Upper and Lower California to be ceded to the United States. There was a stipulation in a separate article securing to the United States the right of passage and transit from the Gulf of Mexico and the Pacific Ocean across the isthmus of Tehuantepec. The consideration which Mr. Buchanan is his draft of a treaty proposed to pay, in addition to the assumption of the claims of our citizens against Mexico, was $15,000,000, in instalments of $3,000,000 per annum. I expressed the hope that this boundary and concession might be obtained for this or even a less sum, but that I was willing to pay a larger sum for it if it could not be had for that sum, and that I thought Mr. Trist should be authorized to give more, if he found that to be the only obstacle in concluding a treaty. I was willing to make the consideration double that sum ($30,000,000) if the cession could not be obtained for a less sum, rather than fail to make a treaty. Mr. Buchanan earnestly resisted this and was in favour of restricting the offer to the $15,000,000. This point gave rise to much conversation and discussion. I stated my reasons at some length for being willing to enlarge the sum to $30,000,000, if the treaty could not be had for that sum. Among these reasons were, first, that the continuance of the war for less than twelve months would cost more than that sum; and secondly, that the country ceded to the United States would be worth, in the public lands acquired and commercial advantages, more than fourfold the $30,-000,000. The members of the Cabinet expressed their opinions freely. Mr. Walker attached greater importance to the free passage across the Isthmus of Tehuantepec than to the cession of New Mexico and the Californias, and if that object could be obtained he was willing to pay $30,000,000, but without it he was not. Mr. Buchanan still opposed the enlargement of the consideration. Finally all the Cabinet except Mr. Buchanan yielded to my views, and it was agreed that Mr. Trist should be furnished with confidential instructions authorizing him in his discretion, if the treaty could not be obtained for a less sum, to stipulate to pay $30,000,000. It was further agreed that if the passage across the Isthmus of Tehuantepec could not be obtained, the maximum sum to be paid for the other cessions of the proposed treaty should not exceed $25,000,000. It was agreed, also, that if Lower California could not be obtained, that then the maximum sum to be paid for the Rio Grande as a boundary and the cession of New Mexico and Upper California should not exceed $20,000,000. To these several propositions all the Cabinet except Mr. Buchanan agreed, and he being overruled yielded and said he would modify the project of the treaty and prepare the instructions accordingly. I stated, and it was understood by all, that the several sums mentioned were maximums to which Mr. Trist might go in the last resort, but that he would procure the treaty for as much less sum as possible. In the course of the discussion Mr. Walker insisted that the free passage across the Isthmus of Tehuantepec should be a *sine qua non* to the making of any treaty. To this I objected and stated that it constituted no part of the object for which we had engaged in the war. The balance of the Cabinet, though agreeing that it was important, yet concurred with me in opinion that it should not be a *sine qua non* in the making of a treaty. . .

About two o'clock P.M. it was announced to me that General Tom Thumb, a dwarf, who is being exhibited in this city and who has become quite celebrated by having been exhibited at all the principal courts of Europe, was in the parlour below stairs and desired to see me. I invited the Cabinet to take a short recess and to walk down with me, and they did so. We found a number of ladies and gentlemen in the parlour. Tom Thumb is a most remarkable person. After spending twenty or thirty minutes in the parlour I returned with the Cabinet to my office.[5]

Wednesday, 14th April, 1847. — After night Mr. Buchanan called and read me a letter which he had received this evening from Moses Beach of the New York *Sun,* written in the city of Mexico and dated on the 17th of March last. In his letter Mr. Beach describes the revolutionary condition of Mexico, but expresses the opinion that a treaty may be made which would be satisfactory to the United States, and leaves the inference that he make such a treaty. Mr. Beach was in Washington in November last and had several interviews with Mr. Buchanan and one with me. He was then on the eve of leaving for Mexico on private business, but from his intimacy with General Almonte expressed the opinion that he could exert a favorable influence on him and other leading men in Mexico, with a view to the restoration of peace. He induced Mr. Buchanan and myself to believe that he could do so. Mr. Buchanan informed him confidentially of the terms on which we would treat, and it was deemed advisable to constitute him a secret agent to Mexico. He was so constituted accordingly, but was not clothed with any diplomatic powers. The object of constituting him a secret agent was that he might collect and furnish useful information to his government. He may misconstrue his authority and it may be possible that he may induce the Mexican rulers, if they are reduced to great straits by the pressure of the war, upon the production to them of the letter of the Secretary of State making him an agent of the government, to make a treaty with him. It is clearly to be inferred from his letter that he will make a treaty with them if he can. Should he do so, and it is a good one, I will waive his authority to make it, and submit it to the Senate for ratification. It

[5] Tom Thumb was first engaged by P. T. Barnum at the close of 1842, and became famous during 1843 as one of the chief attractions of Barnum's American Museum. He was taken to England in 1844, and presented to Queen Victoria and Prince Albert among others. Barnum mentions this visit to the White House in his autobiography.

will be a good joke if he will assume the authority and take the whole country by surprise and make a treaty. Mr. Buchanan's strong impression is that he may do so.[6]

Friday, 16th April, 1847.— Mr. Trist set out on his mission to the headquarters of the army this morning, with full powers to treat with the authorities of Mexico for peace. His mission has, as far as I have learned, been kept a profound secret, and is known only to the Cabinet. I deemed it important that it should be so. Had his mission and the object of it been proclaimed in advance at Washington I have no doubt there are persons in Washington, and among them the editors of the *National Intelligencer,* who would have been ready and willing to have despatched a courier to Mexico to discourage the government of that weak and distracted country from entering upon negotiations for peace. This they would do rather than suffer my administration to have the credit of concluding a just and honourable peace. The articles in the *National Intelligencer* and other Federal papers against their own government and in favour of the enemy, have done more to prevent a peace than all the armies of the enemy. The Mexican papers republish these treasonable papers and make the ignorant population of Mexico believe that the Democratic party will shortly be expelled from power in the United States, and that their friends (the Federal alias Whig party) will come into power. If the war is protracted it is to be attributed to the treasonable course of the Federal editors and leading men.

Tuesday, 20th April, 1847.— On yesterday official despatches were received from Col. Price, commanding at Santa Fé, announcing that a battle had been fought and a signal victory won by the troops under his command over the enemy. The number of troops engaged was comparatively small, but I consider this victory one of the most

[6] Beach, the proprietor and editor of the *Sun,* visited Mexico with large financial enterprises in mind, bearing a British passport. His intrigues came to nothing, and he had to flee to Tampico.

signal which has been gained during the war. Accounts through the newspapers were received on yesterday, containing the Mexican account of a victory obtained by Col. Doniphan, commanding the Missouri Volunteers, over the enemy, and that he had taken the city of Chihuahua.[7] The truth is our troops, regulars and volunteers, will obtain victories wherever they meet the enemy. This they would do if they were without officers to command them higher in rank than lieutenants. It is injustice, therefore, to award to the generals all the credit.

Wednesday, 21st April, 1847. — My attention was called this morning to two letters purporting to have been written at this city and published in the New York *Herald,* in which the writer discloses with remarkable accuracy and particularity the fact of the departure of Mr. N. P. Trist, chief clerk in the Department of State, on a mission to Mexico. The statement is so accurate and minute that the writer must have obtained information on the subject from someone who was entrusted with the secret. It was a profound Cabinet secret, and was so expressly declared by me to be, and was communicated to no one but to Mr. Trist himself and to Mr. Derrick, a clerk in the Department of State. For a full statement of the importance of keeping it a secret, see this diary of the 10th instant. In disclosing the fact of the mission of Mr. Trist and its objects, contrary to my solemn injunction, there has been treachery somewhere. I cannot believe that any of my Cabinet have betrayed my confidence, and conclude, in the absence of further information on the subject, that the disclosure must have been made by Mr. Derrick, the clerk in the State Department recommended by Mr. Buchanan as worthy of all confidence, and who was employed in preparing the writing. I have not been more vexed or excited since I have been President than at this occur-

[7] After his capture of Santa Fé, Kearny pressed on to California with part of his troops, while Col. A. W. Doniphan marched south with others; Sterling Price remained in Santa Fé.

rence. The success of Mr. Trist's mission I knew in the beginning must depend mainly on keeping it a secret from that portion of the Federal press and leading men in the country who, since the commencement of the war with Mexico, have been giving "aid and comfort" to the enemy by their course. I do not doubt that there are men among them who would incur the expense of sending a courier to Mexico, and incur any other expense, to discourage Mexico from making a peace, for the purpose of having the war continued, in the hope that the Democratic administration might be brought into disrepute by continuing it to a protracted length, and that they might gain some political advantage in the next Presidential election by it. I do not doubt that Mexico has been and will be discouraged from making peace, in the hope that their friends in the United States will come into power at the next Presidential election. That this has been the effect of the unpatriotic and anti-American course of the *National Intelligencer* and other Federal papers, all know.

Wednesday, 28th April, 1847. — At an early hour today the Secretary of War accompanied by the Adjutant-General of the army called. They had done so at my request. After much consultation with them I directed the organization into brigades and divisions of the ten regiments of troops authorized by Congress to be raised to serve during the war. I also directed the organization into brigades and divisions of the volunteer forces called out in November last and during the present month, which had not heretofore been done. I directed also the apportionment of these forces to the two columns commanded by Generals Scott and Taylor. According to this apportionment, General Scott will have with him something over 20,000 men, and General Taylor will have with him something over 12,000 men. The Santa Fé column will be about 2,500 strong.

Friday, April 30, 1847. — I received a telegraphic despatch from Baltimore before breakfast this morning, brought to that city by an overland express, announcing several days later news from Vera Cruz. The Baltimore *Sun* which arrived about eleven o'clock contained the detailed information as late as the 14th instant inclusive. It is probable that a general battle may have taken place between the two armies two or three days after that time. Santa Anna was reported to be in front of the American army with 15,000 troops to resist their passage from Vera Cruz to Jalapa. I shall await the result with much anxiety, but have no fears of it. Our forces are the best troops in the world, and would gain victories over superior forces of the enemy, if there was not an officer among them. This proves the injustice of giving all the credit of our victories to the commanding general and none to his inferior officers and men. I sent for the Secretary of War and had a consultation with him. He read to me a despatch which he had prepared to General Scott. He brought with him despatches which had been received at the War Department from Brigadier-General Kearny in California. They are duplicates of despatches transmitted by Lieut. Emory, who has not yet arrived at Washington. An unfortunate collision has occurred in California between General Kearny and Commodore Stockton, in regard to precedence in rank. I think General Kearny was right. It appears that Lieut.-Col. Frémont refused to obey General Kearny and obeyed Commodore Stockton and in this he was wrong.[8] I saw Mr. Buchanan and several other officers today on official business.

This was reception evening. A number of persons, ladies and gentlemen, called. Among them was Miss Adams, the granddaughter of Mr. John Quincy Adams, and daughter of his son and private secretary during his Presidency, John

---

[8] The collision between Stockton and Kearny was due to the vagueness of the instructions sent them from Washington, each believing himself authorized to erect a civil government in California. Frémont, obeying Stockton, was appointed civil governor of California by the latter. His defiance of Kearny led to a famous court-martial trial in Washington, which was fated to cost Polk much labor and anxiety.

Adams, Jr. I note the call of this young lady because it is the first that has been made by any of the family of Mr. John Quincy Adams during my Presidency except, as I understand, a card left by the female members of the family some months ago. Mr. John Quincy Adams has a house in this city, and resides here during many months of the year. He with his family are now residing in this city. I met the company in the parlour this evening and treated Miss Adams with marked respect, as it was her first visit.

CHAPTER VIII
May 1, 1847 – July 9, 1847

THE SMITHSONIAN INSTITUTION — THE FRÉMONT-KEARNY
DISPUTE — VERA CRUZ AND CERRO GORDO — VISIT TO THE
UNIVERSITY OF NORTH CAROLINA — KIT CARSON — TOUR
TO THE NORTH — QUARREL OF SCOTT AND TRIST

Saturday, 1st May, 1847. — This being the day appointed
for laying the cornerstone of the building for the Smithsonian Institution, no business was transacted in the Cabinet.
About twelve o'clock a large procession, consisting of the
military, Masons, the order of Odd Fellows, and citizens
appeared before my door. Accompanied by the members
of my Cabinet who were present, I took the place which
had been assigned me in the procession, and moved with it
to the site of the building of the Smithsonian Institution
on the public mall, south of Pennsylvania Avenue.[1] The
Vice-President, the Secretary of War, and my private secretary took seats in my carriage. Delegations of the Masonic lodges of Pennsylvania and Maryland were present,
as also a large number of the Masonic fraternity and the
Odd Fellows of the District of Columbia. The occasion on
the ground opened and closed with prayer. The ceremonies

---

[1] Polk on August 10, 1846, had signed the act establishing the Smithsonian
Institution, for which James Smithson of England had bequeathed a total
of more than $500,000. The regents first met in September, 1846, and in
December they elected Joseph Henry, then professor of natural philosophy at
Princeton, to be the first secretary and director of the Institution. Polk
took a warm interest in the growth of the establishment. But it was due
to the efforts of J. Q. Adams that the income of the fund only was used, and
the principal invested, so that its permanence was assured.

of laying the cornerstone of the building were performed chiefly by B. B. French, esquire, grand master of the Masonic fraternity of the District of Columbia. The Vice-President, after this ceremony was over, delivered an address to the multitude assembled on the occasion. A large crowd of ladies and gentlemen were present. About half past two o'clock P.M. the ceremonies were concluded and I returned to the Presidential mansion. The Vice-President took a family dinner with me today. . .

I received today a short letter from Charles J. Ingersoll of Philadelphia in answer to mine of the 28th ult. (See letter-book.) In his letter Mr. Ingersoll denies that he sought the French mission from me.[2] In this he states what he knows to be untrue. I affirm that he did solicit the mission in private interviews with me, and that he was importunate on the subject. He sought it also through Vice-President Dallas. There was no witness present and Mr. Ingersoll has now the baseness to deny it. It is also false, as stated by him, that I got him to give up the Russian mission and suggested the French mission in its stead.

Sunday, 2d May, 1847. — I was much indisposed this morning from the effects of cold, and much fatigued by the labours of the past week, and remained quietly at home. It was, moreover, a damp uncomfortable day and unusually chilly for this season. Mrs. Polk and her niece, Miss Rucker, attended church. The quiet rest of the Sabbath day is always desirable to me, but has seldom been more acceptable than on this day. When Mrs. Polk returned from church she complained of being very cold, and it was

[2] Charles J. Ingersoll of Pennsylvania, who was a Representative in Congress 1813–1815, and 1841–1847, had been nominated by Polk to be Minister to France, and owing to the warm opposition of Daniel Webster and others, was immediately rejected by the Senate. Polk then nominated Richard Rush, who was confirmed. Ingersoll was so angry at his rejection that he prepared a challenge to Webster to fight a duel, which friends induced him to withhold; and he vented his spleen also upon Polk, who elsewhere in his *Diary* says that "after all that has transpired, I am compelled to regard him as a base and unprincipled man."

manifest she had a chill. In a short time afterwards a reaction took place and she had a fever. She had slight symptoms of a chill on Friday last, which had not attracted much attention as she casually mentioned it, but had not complained of much indisposition in consequence of it.

Tuesday, 4th May, 1847. — I rose this morning as usual about six o'clock, and while I was shaving in my chamber (for I am my own barber) Mrs. Polk, who had not arisen, asked me if it was not a cool morning, and complained of being very cold. I answered her that I thought it was more chilly than usual. I soon discovered that she had a chill, and threw more covering on the bed. Her chill continued for more than three hours. I have never seen her suffer or complain more than she did for several hours after the chill subsided and her fever rose. My family physician (Dr. Miller) I learned was absent from the city, and I sent for Dr. Hall, who is one of the most eminent physicians of the city. He prescribed for her. She spent a restless and uncomfortable afternoon and night though her medicine had its desired effect.[3]

The Cabinet met at the usual hour, all the members present except the Secretary of the Treasury, who was detained by indisposition. I have observed that he has been sinking for several weeks past under the immense labours of his department. He has not been able to speak above a whisper for the last month, and there is danger that he may lose his voice entirely and that his general health may be destroyed and his life endangered, if he continues to apply himself as

---

[3] Washington, with its swampy flats along the Potomac, the hunting-ground of innumerable crows, was a city subject to malaria or " chills and fever." At high tide the flats attracted a great deal of garbage and rubbish, which festered in the hot sun at low tide; while in spring they hatched myriad swarms of mosquitoes. In Lincoln's day his young secretary, Nicolay, wrote a comrade that " I am alone in the White pest-house. The ghosts of twenty thousand drowned cats come in at night through the south windows." During the Mexican War it was said that the crows and buzzards which fed on the flats had flown all the way from the battlefields, where they had been gorging on the bodies of the slain.

he has heretofore done to the very laborious duties of his office.

The Secretary of War presented and read in Cabinet the official despatches from Col. Doniphan of the Missouri volunteers, giving an account of the battles he and his brave forces had fought at the Passo and at Sacramento, in which, in the latter especially, he had obtained decisive victories over vastly superior forces of the enemy. The battle of Sacramento I consider to be one of the most decisive and brilliant achievements of the war. The despatches of General Kearny and Commodore Stockton giving an account of events which had occurred in California were considered. The despatches of Commodore Stockton had been brought to the Navy Department by Lieut. Gray of the Navy some days ago, and those of General Kearny to the War Department by Lieutenant (now Major) Emory, a day or two ago. It appears that an unfortunate collision had occurred between Commodore Stockton and General Kearny. Upon a full examination of the correspondence of both, I was fully satisfied that General Kearny was right, and that Commodore Stockton's course was wrong. Indeed both he and Lieut.-Col. Frémont, in refusing to recognize the authority of General Kearny, acted insubordinately and in a manner that is censurable.[4] A reference to the official documents will show

[4] Kearny claimed that his orders from Washington gave him the right to govern California; Stockton and Frémont insisted that it was they who had conquered California, that Stockton's orders gave him the right to set up a civil government, and that Kearny's orders were conditional upon his effecting a conquest which had been already made when he arrived. In reality the fault for the clash lay with Polk and his Cabinet, who had sent conflicting instructions to the naval and military officers on the Pacific Coast. Stockton soon left the coast, leaving Frémont to carry on the quarrel with Kearny. Orders sent to the latter resulted in his establishing his complete authority, whereupon he treated Frémont in a way that was, as Justin H. Smith says, " grasping, jealous, domineering, and harsh," arrested him, and carried him back east for court-martial. The dispute became a *cause célèbre* which attracted the attention of the nation.

Polk had good reason for speaking highly of the campaign by Colonel A. W. Doniphan. This energetic and capable officer had been detached by Kearny from his army in New Mexico, with a separate force of about 850 men, and had been ordered to march south to reinforce General Wool's ex-this. I expressed a decided opinion on the subject to the Cabinet. All the Cabinet agreed that Commodore Stockton and Lieutenant-Colonel Frémont had been in the wrong, but all agreed as I did that they were both gallant and meritorious officers, and all regretted the occurrence. None of the Cabinet censured General Kearny. The two former have subjected themselves to arrest and trial by a court-martial, but as all collision has probably been since that time avoided, I am disposed not to pursue so rigorous a course. The Secretary of War thought in answering General Kearny's despatches he ought to express the approbation of the Government of his course. The Secretary of the Navy thought this inadvisable, because this would be to pass a censure on Commodore Stockton; and he desired that no opinion should be expressed and that the matter should be passed over as lightly as possible. Such seemed to be the inclination of the Cabinet, and was my own, as far as it could be done with propriety. The subject was postponed for further consideration.

Wednesday, 5th May, 1847. — I opened my office at one o'clock P.M. today. A number of persons called and among others Mr. Jones (General Benton's son-in-law) who informed me that it was rumoured in the New Orleans papers, that the postmaster of that City was to be removed, and that he was to be appointed. He said he did not ask for the removal of the postmaster at New Orleans, but if he was to be removed the place would be agreeable to him. I promptly replied that there was no foundation for the rumour and

pedition against Chihuahua. Wool unfortunately failed to reach his objective, and his command was withdrawn eastward and used to strengthen Taylor's army. But Doniphan, setting forth on December 14, 1846, marched southward through El Paso, won gallant victories over the Mexicans at Sacramento and Brazito on his way, and on March 1, 1847, triumphantly occupied Chihuahua. His two months' occupation of this city was marked by the Capuan excesses of his men, who behaved so badly that he indignantly reported that they were " wholly unfit to garrison a town or city." At the end of April, 1847, Doniphan abandoned Chihuahua and marched his little army to join Taylor's, which was now at Saltillo.

that I had no intention to remove the postmaster at New Orleans, that he was a faithful officer and I knew of no reason to disturb him in his office. He then repeated the request which he had previously made to me, to be appointed *chargé d'affaires* abroad, and wished to know if I could give him any encouragement. I told him, as I had previously done, that I could not. I note the case of Mr. Jones particularly among the numerous office-seekers who annoy me daily, because I predict that he will violently oppose my administration because of his disappointment. Some weeks ago General Benton applied to me in person for the appointment of *chargé* for Mr. Jones, then just married to his daughter. I gave him no encouragement, and I predict that he too wlll be excited at my refusal.

Friday, 7th May, 1847. — Several persons called, and while they were in my office I received a telegraphic despatch from Fredericksburg, Va., in advance of the Southern mail, announcing a victory achieved by our army in Mexico under the immediate command of Major-General Scott. The battle was fought at the mountain pass called Cerro Gordo, between Vera Cruz and Jalapa, on the 17th and 18th of April, and resulted in the triumph of our arms and the total rout of the enemy.[5] I communicated to the persons who were present the information I had received. The Southern mail in the evening confirmed the news, but brought no despatches from the army.

Saturday, 8th May, 1847. — The Cabinet adjourned

[5] General Scott had landed 10,000 men near Vera Cruz, where they invested the city, brought up artillery from the fleet, began a bombardment, and captured the place with a loss of fewer than twenty men killed (March 26, 1847). He shortly afterward set out on the march inland to Jalapa. At Cerro Gordo on April 18 he encountered the Mexican troops thrown across his path, Santa Anna and some 12,000 men holding what they regarded as an impregnable position. The result was a signal American victory. The Mexican casualties were estimated at 1,000 to 1,200, and some 3,000 Mexican prisoners were released on parole, while the Americans lost 417 men killed and wounded. The way to Jalapa was thrown open, and Scott exuberantly announced, " Mexico has no longer an army."

about two o'clock P.M. I requested Judge Mason to walk
with me to the House of Mr. Walker, the Secretary of the
Treasury, as I was becoming concerned for the state of his
health from what I learned of his condition. We walked to
Mr. Walker's house. I found him in appearance enjoying
usual health except that his throat was bandaged and he had
almost entirely lost his voice. He conversed with me by
writing on a slate. In a very low and indistinct whisper he
attempted to converse with me, but was compelled to give it
up. I told him that he required rest and recreation, and advised him to leave his office and travel for a few weeks, saying to him that his department could be conducted in his absence by Mr. Young, his chief clerk. He replied in writing
on his slate, that he thought he would do so. My opinion
is that he will live but a short time, unless he relaxes his labours in his office.

On our return Judge Mason and myself called at the office of Gov. Marcy, the Secretary of War.

This evening had been designated by the citizens of Washington for the illumination of the city, in honour of the triumph of our arms by land and sea in the pending war with
Mexico. I learned that some of the officers of some of the
public departments were preparing to illuminate. Some of
these buildings, and especially those of the War, Navy, and
State Departments, are not fireproof, are very combustible,
and contain the most valuable public records of the Government. I thought there was danger from fire to have them
illuminated, and after consultation with the Secretary of the
Treasury, when I visited him, and afterwards with the Secretaries of War and the Navy, who concurred with me that it
might be unsafe, I gave directions that none of the public offices should be illuminated. I illuminated the Presidential
Mansion, and each of the Heads of Departments illuminated
their respective residences. Many houses in the City were
also illuminated. Official despatches giving an account of
the battle of Cerro Gordo were received from General Scott

tonight.   Mrs. Polk fortunately missed her chill this morning and was better today.

Tuesday, 11th May, 1847. — I brought to the notice of the Cabinet and particularly of the Secretary of War, the importance of re-inforcing the column of the army under the immediate command of General Scott, now on the march from Vera Cruz to the City of Mexico.   I had brought the same matter to the notice of the Secretary of War some days ago; and also to the Adjutant-General of the army, and on the 8th instant handed to the latter a written memorandum, the object of which was to ascertain from the records of the War Department the precise amount of force in General Scott's column, and also in General Taylor's column.   As General Scott's is the advancing column and must be constantly diminished as it advances into the enemy's country from casualties and in order to keep his rear open, and as General Taylor in one of his late despatches gives it as his opinion that he cannot advance with his column beyond his present position without at least 2,000 veteran troops of the regular army, which amount of force cannot be spared to him by General Scott, I informed the Cabinet that I was of opinion that all our available force should be ordered without delay to join General Scott's column, leaving with General Taylor all his present force, and such additions as would render his present position secure.   The Cabinet concurred with me in these views. . .   Mr. Moses Y. Beach, editor of the New York *Sun,* called and had a long converation with me on Mexican affairs.   He had recently returned from the City of Mexico, where he had gone several months ago in the character of a secret agent from the State Department.   He gave me valuable information.

Friday, 14th May, 1847. — I transacted business today with several of the heads of departments and officers of government, but spent more time with the Secretary of War than with any other.   The conduct of the war with Mexico devolves upon him and myself a vast amount of labour.   The subordinate officers at the head of the different bureaus in the War Department are generally Federalists, and many of them are indifferent and seem to think they perform their duty if they are in their offices the usual number of hours each day. They take no sort of responsibility on themselves, and this renders it necessary that the Secretary of War and myself should look after them, even in the performance of the ordinary routine of details in their offices.

Saturday, 15th May, 1847. — Col. Bankhead[6] of the army arrived in Washington from Vera Cruz on yesterday, bringing with him several flags of the enemy which were captured at the surrender of Vera Cruz. They were exhibited today in front of the War Office, for the gratification of the public. Col. Bankhead called and paid his respects to me on his arrival in the city on yesterday. He was in the siege at Vera Cruz. I disposed of several matters of business of minor importance on my table today.

Monday, 17th May, 1847. — I was engaged this forenoon in disposing of the business on my table. I saw the Secretaries of War and the Navy on business connected with their respective departments. I have desired very much to gratify the wishes of General Robert Armstrong, now United States consul at Liverpool, to enter the military service of the United States. General Armstrong was a gallant young officer in the War of 1812, was under the immediate command of General Jackson, and was severely wounded (see my letters to General Armstrong of the 28th and 29th *ultimo* and the 13th *instant*). General Jackson shortly before his death presented to General Armstrong the sword which he had worn during the war, as an evidence of his high esteem of him as a military man. General Armstrong is my personal friend, and it would give me sincere pleasure to have appointed him as a brigadier-general if I could have done so with propriety. When I wrote to him on the 28th

---

[6] James Bankhead, of Virginia, colonel of the 2d Artillery, was brevetted brigadier-general for his gallant behavior at the siege of Vera Cruz.

ultimo, I thought I could have done so. Since that time, however, I have become satisfied that the public opinion of the country is so strong in favour of Col. Jefferson Davis of Mississippi,[7] who behaved most gallantly in the battles of Monterey and Buena Vista and was severely wounded in the latter battle, that to appoint any other, and especially one who had not been heretofore engaged in the war, however competent and worthy he might be, would give great dissatisfaction. Today I appointed Col. Davis a brigadier-general in place of Gideon J. Pillow, promoted to be a major-general.

Tuesday, 18th May, 1847. — Official despatches from General Scott received last night, giving a detailed account of the battle of Cerro Gordo and the movements of the army since that time, were read. They were very interesting in the minute details which they gave.

Wednesday, 19th May, 1847. — The Secretary of War called in pursuance of a previous appointment about ten o'clock this morning, and remained until near one o'clock P.M. I was considering in consultation with him many matters, chiefly of detail relating to the military service in Mexico. Among these was the arrangement of the staff officers of the volunteer forces, upon the expiration of the term of the twelve-months men. A decision was necessary as to the members of the staff, who should be discharged and who should be retained at that time. Several vacancies of officers of the army which had occurred, it was necessary to fill. I had repeatedly for several days past called on the Secretary of War for a list of these vacancies. He informed me

[7] Jefferson Davis, the future President of the Confederacy, was a son-in-law of Zachary Taylor, a West Pointer, and in command of the Mississippi " Rifles," which were armed with a more efficient piece than the muskets used by most of the American troops. He won fame by an impetuous charge at Monterey, where he stormed the enemy's works and advanced through the streets almost to the Grand Plaza, and by spectacularly breaking up a Mexican cavalry charge at Buena Vista. He was regarded by many as a soldier-genius — but his work was actually far less important than that of Winfield Scott's chief engineer, Robert E. Lee.

that he had several times called on the Adjutant-General for the list, but that it had not been furnished. When a vacancy occurs in the regular army, it is filled usually by regular promotion, down to the grade of second lieutenancies, and these are usually filled by the appointment of brevet second lieutenancies who are graduates of West Point, though there is no law requiring this to be done. I had determined to appoint a few private soldiers, who had greatly distinguished themselves in battle. To this the Adjutant-General and the officers of the army are generally opposed, and this I suspected was the reason that the Adjutant-General had failed to report a list of vacancies as he had been requested to do. With the assent of the Secretary of War I sent for him and requested him to furnish me the list. He was disposed to debate the matter with me, and to urge the claims of the graduates at West Point. He promised, however, to furnish the list. He retired and returned in about an hour, but did not bring the list. He resumed his argument in favour of the graduates at West Point. I became vexed at his hesitancy in furnishing me with the information which I had required. His presumption in withholding the information which I had requested from me, and in attempting to control my action, vexed me, and finally I spoke shortly to him. Among other things I remarked that as I was constituted by the Constitution commander-in-chief of the army, I chose to *order* him to furnish the list of vacancies from the records of his office which I had desired. I repeated to him that he must regard what I said as a military order and that I would expect it to be promptly obeyed.

Thursday, 20th May, 1847. — Having some weeks ago yielded to the request of the Dialectic Society of the University of North Carolina to sit for my portrait, which they wished to obtain for their debating hall, Mr. Sully,[8] the cele-

---

[8] Thomas Sully, 1783–1872, was one of the most famous American artists of the day; he resided in Philadelphia from 1809 till his death. His works include "Washington Crossing the Delaware," and a painting of the corona-

brated artist of Philadelphia, whom the Society had engaged to paint it, called this morning, and commenced the portrait. I gave him a sitting of one and a half hours. Judge Mason, the Secretary of the Navy, also gave him a sitting for his portrait which he was taking for the Philanthropic Society of the University of North Carolina. We both sit in the red parlour above stairs in the President's House. Judge Mason was a member of the Philanthropic, and I was a member of the Dialectic Society when we were at College.

Tuesday, 25th May, 1847.—I brought before the Cabinet the propriety of issuing an order to General Scott to send to the United States as prisoners of war all Mexican officers who may be hereafter taken, instead of liberating them on their parole of honour. All agreed that this would be proper, and especially so as we learned that Major Borland, Major Gaines,[9] and other prisoners of our army are confined in prison in the City of Mexico, notwithstanding several hundred Mexican officers and several thousand private soldiers who have been taken prisoners have been set at large on their parole of honour. The Secretary of War was directed to write a despatch to this effect to General Scott. I brought also before the Cabinet the importance of running an express from Mobile to Montgomery, in Alabama, so as to gain a day upon regular mail time, and thereby receive at Washington despatches from the army as early as the express of the Baltimore *Sun* newspaper obtains the latest news from the seat of war. After some discussion and some difference of views on the subject, I directed the necessary steps to be taken to have such an express run.

Friday, 28th May, 1847.— At half past eight o'clock this morning I left Washington on my visit to the University of

tion of Queen Victoria. His portrait is reproduced as the frontispiece of this volume.

[9] Solon Borland, a major in Col. Yell's Arkansas Regiment, served in the United States Senate 1848–1853, and became a Confederate brigadier-general. John P. Gaines was a Representative from Kentucky 1847–1849, and Governor of Oregon Territory 1850–1853.

North Carolina.[10]   I was accompanied by Mrs. Polk and
her niece Miss Rucker, and Col. Walker, my private secretary, of my own family; by Judge Mason (the Secretary of
the Navy) and his son, John Y. Mason, Jr., and his daughter Betty, and Lieutenant Maury of the United States
Navy. . . About five o'clock P.M. I arrived at Richmond.
I was met at the railroad depot at that city by the mayor
and a committee of citizens without distinction of political
party, who gave me a cordial welcome to their city.   The
military companies were on parade, and a very large number of people were present.   I was placed in an open carriage
and conducted by the mayor and committee to the Capitol,
where many thousand persons, ladies and gentlemen, were
assembled.   I exchanged salutations and shook hands with
many hundreds of them.   The artillery company fired a
salute.   Mrs. Polk was received by the ladies of the city at
the executive chamber in the Capitol, that being the place
arranged by the committee of reception for that purpose.
After remaining one and a half hours I was conducted in an
open carriage to the Southern railroad depot, preceded by
the military companies and a large concourse of citizens.
The demonstration of respect at Richmond was without distinction of party and was highly gratifying to me.   From
Richmond I proceeded on the railroad to Petersburg, where
we arrived shortly after dark.   I was met by a committee of
that town at the railroad depot.   I was conducted to a hotel,
which was brilliantly lighted up.   I found there a very large
crowd of people, ladies and gentlemen.

   Saturday, 29th May, 1847. — Proceeding on my journey
from Petersburg, Va., in the railroad cars, I arrived at Gaston, North Carolina, at about four o'clock this morning.   I
retired to a room in the hotel, shaved, and dressed.   About

   [10] Polk entered the University of North Carolina in 1815 and was graduated from it in 1818.   He was a serious-minded and hard-working student,
who impaired his health by close application, and won first honors in both
mathematics and the classics.

sunrise, on entering the parlour below stairs, I was received by a committee of citizens of North Carolina, and was addressed by Col. John D. Hawkins, their chairman, who welcomed me to my native State. I made a brief reply to this address. The committee was composed of leading gentlemen of both political parties. Gov. Branch also joined me at this point, though he was not of the committee, and accompanied me on my journey. After taking breakfast I proceeded on my journey. At intervals of every few miles, and especially at all the railroad depots, many persons, male and female, were assembled to see me. At most of these places I descended from the cars and shook hands with as many of them as my time would permit. Near Warrenton and near the residence of Mr. Nathaniel Macon,[11] who was greatly beloved in that section of the country up to the hour of his death, I met a very large crowd of ladies and gentlemen. I observed many carriages, probably forty or fifty in number, in which the ladies present had come to greet me. At Henderson, where I dined, several thousand persons, ladies and gentlemen, old persons, middle aged persons, young persons, and children of both sexes were assembled. At this place I remained about one and a half hours and was constantly engaged in being introduced to the people and shaking hands with them. At Franklinton, twenty miles before reaching Raleigh, a very large crowd of ladies and gentlemen were also assembled. I regretted that I could remain with them but a few minutes. I was met by a committee of citizens of the place and its vicinity, who made a short address to me, to which I briefly responded. I was met at this place also by a committee of citizens of Raleigh, who welcomed me on my approach to the capital of the State. I responded to them also. The Chairman was Mr. McCrea, accompanied by the Hon. John H. Bryan and about a dozen

[11] Nathaniel Macon, 1757–1837, was a Representative from North Carolina 1791–1815, becoming famous as one of the "war-hawks"; and a United States Senator from 1815 to 1828.

others. This committee took charge of me at this point. I reached Raleigh at about half past five o'clock P.M. I was met at the railroad depot by the intendant or mayor of the city (Mr. William Dallas Haywood) the military on parade, and a large concourse of citizens. I was welcomed to the City and returned my thanks in a brief reply. . . At the appointed hour, eight o'clock, I was conducted to the Capitol by the Mayor, the committees of the city of Raleigh, and of the University. Judge Mason accompanied me. I spent one and a half hours at the Senate chamber, which was crowded with ladies and gentlemen, many of whom were introduced to the Secretary of the Navy and myself. From the Senate chamber we were conducted to the front of the Capitol, where a very dense crowd of persons, ladies and gentlemen, were assembled. The street between the Capitol and the Governor's House was brilliantly illuminated, and there was a most imposing display of fire works. About eleven o'clock I retired to my lodgings, much fatigued. From Gaston to Raleigh was a continued triumphal procession. Salutes were fired at several places. My reception could not have been more gratifying than it has been. I observed not the slightest party feeling, but on the contrary I was received in the most distinguished manner by both political parties as the guest of the State.

Monday, 31st May, 1847. — At nine o'clock this morning I set out with my family and suite for Chapel Hill. I was accompanied by Professor Green and the committee of students from the University. I was accompanied also by Gov. Branch, Col. Hawkins, and several others, ladies and gentlemen, making quite a long train of carriages. We stopped half an hour at Mrs. Jones's, ten miles on the way, where we were overtaken by Ex.-Gov. Moorehead, Gov. Graham and others. I stopped at Moring's, eight miles from Chapel Hill, and took dinner. Gov. Graham, Gov. Moorehead, and some others did not stop for dinner, but proceeded on to Chapel Hill in advance of me. At about 6 o'clock P.M. I reached the village of Chapel Hill. On approaching the hotel at which quarters had been provided for me, I was received by a procession comprised of the faculty and students of the college and citizens. I was conducted into the hotel by Professor Green and the committee of students who had met me at Raleigh, and after remaining there a few minutes was conducted on foot to the college chapel, where a large assembly of ladies and gentlemen were collected. I was addressed by the Hon. D. Y. Swain, the President of the College, tendering to me a cordial welcome on my return to the classic shades of the University. I briefly responded to his address. President Swain also addressed Judge Mason, who made a short reply. I was then introduced to the Trustees who were present, to the faculty and many of the students, as well as to many others, ladies and gentlemen. Of all the Professors I had left at the University twenty-nine years ago, Professor Mitchell [12] alone remained. He met me most cordially, and I was much gratified to see him. These ceremonies being over, I returned to the hotel, where I had the pleasure to meet many old college friends whom I had not seen since I graduated in June, 1818. Our meeting was delightful. Some of the incidents of our college life were at once recited. After supper I attended the chapel and heard a sermon preached by Bishop Ives of the Episcopal Church to the students.

Tuesday, 1st June, 1847. — As soon as I rose this morning I found a large crowd at the hotel desiring to see me. After breakfast I visited the college buildings. They have been greatly enlarged and improved since my day at college. I attended the examination of the senior class on international and constitutional law. They were examined by

[12] David L. Swain was Governor of North Carolina 1832–1835, and President of the University of North Carolina 1835–1868, his courage and constancy in facing the discouragements of the Civil War and Reconstruction being especially notable. Elisha Mitchell was noted for his scientific talents, and Mount Mitchell was named after him. He did much for the geological and botanical exploration of all western North Carolina.

President Swain. I visited the Dialectic and Philanthropic Library rooms. I visited also the room which I occupied when I was in college. The old chapel I found had been converted into recitation rooms, and for the use of the trustees when they attended the University. After dinner I took a walk with some of my old college friends to Vauxhall Spring, and through a portion of the village. Many objects were perfectly familiar to me, and brought up fresh to recollection many of the scenes of my youth. I was constantly surrounded by crowds of people, and was introduced to hundreds, male and female. The weather was warm, and I had no rest. After night I attended the Chapel and heard several members of the sophomore and freshman classes recite speeches which they had committed to memory. I retired to the hotel when these exercises were over, and was kept from retiring to rest until a late hour receiving company and being introduced to them, and in conversation with my college friends.

Wednesday, 2nd June, 1847. — The crowd in attendance was much increased today. I was constantly on my feet, receiving and being introduced to them. All seemed desirous to see the President and shake him by the hand. At eleven o'clock A.M. I attended the chapel and heard Mr. Osborne of Charlotte deliver a literary address to the two societies of the college. When his speech was over I attended a meeting of the alumni of the college. Many of them were present, some of whom graduated as early as 1801. At two o'clock P.M. accompanied by Mrs. Polk, Judge Mason, and our families who accompanied us, I dined with President Swain.

Thursday, 3rd June, 1847. — This was the commencement day of the college. It was to me a most interesting occasion. The number of persons in attendance was greatly increased. Hundreds from the adjoining country had come in. As soon as I left my room in the morning I was surrounded by them, and, except while at breakfast, continued to receive them and to shake hands with them until the hour at which the commencement exercises commenced. These exercises commenced between ten and eleven o'clock. About one o'clock the President announced there would be a recess of one and a half hours. I returned to the hotel and took dinner. The crowd in waiting to see me was so great that it was impossible that they could all see me if I remained in the house. Several of my friends who thought the people present, many of whom had come a considerable distance, ought to be gratified, insisted that I should go out to the grove, and I did so. I was soon surrounded by hundreds of persons, and for an hour or more was constantly engaged in shaking hands with them. At the appointed hour the commencement exercises were again commenced. I attended. They were concluded and the degree of bachelor of arts conferred on thirty-seven young gentlemen, and the whole ceremony closed about half past five o'clock P.M.

Saturday, 5th June, 1847. — We arrived at Petersburg shortly after day light this morning, and after being detained a short time at the hotel proceeded to Richmond, where we took breakfast. Proceeding on our journey we arrived at Washington about five o'clock P.M. and thus ended my excursion to the University of North Carolina. It was an exceedingly agreeable one. No incident of an unpleasant character occurred. My reception at the University, and the attentions paid me on the route going and returning, was all that I could have desired it to be. My visit was wholly unconnected with politics, and all parties greeted and welcomed me in the most cordial manner.

Monday, 7th June, 1847. — At one o'clock P.M., I opened my office for company. Many persons called but none of them had any business of importance with me. The most important business of most of them was that they wished to obtain offices, either for themselves or for their friends. There were no vacancies to fill and I soon disposed of their applications. Among others who called was Mrs. Frémont, the wife of Lieut.-Col. Frémont of the United States army, and the daughter of General T. H. Benton. She introduced me to Kit Carson,[13] who had been with her husband, Col. Frémont, and had recently returned from California. She informed me that Mr. Carson had been waiting several days to see me, for the purpose of conversing with me, and tendering his services to bear despatches to California, if any were to be sent. Mr. Carson delivered to me a long letter from Col. Frémont which had been addressed to General Benton. It related in part to the recent unfortunate collision between General Kearny and Commodore Stockton, and between the former and Col. Frémont in California. Mrs. Frémont seemed anxious to elicit from me some expression of approbation of her husband's conduct, but I evaded making any. In truth I consider that Col. Frémont was greatly in the wrong when he refused to obey the orders issued to him by General Kearny. I think General Kearny was right also in his controversy with Commodore Stockton. It was unnecessary, however, that I should say so to Col. Frémont's wife, and I evaded giving her an answer. My desire is, that the error being corrected, the matter shall pass over quietly without the necessity of having an investigation by a court-martial. I saw Kit Carson again after night, and had a full conversation with him concerning the state of affairs in California, and especially in relation to the collision between our land and naval commanders in that distant region.

[13] Kit Carson, the famous trapper, scout, and guide, had accompanied Frémont on his second and third exploring expeditions and had proved invaluable to him. He had fought with Frémont in California, had been with Kearny at the battle of San Pascual, and had rejoined Frémont, to whom he was always loyal, when the latter was made civil governor of California. Late in February, 1847, he was sent by Frémont with despatches for Benton at St. Louis, for Polk and the departments in Washington, and for the Frémont family. It was his first visit to the East. In Washington he was given the hospitality of Senator Benton's home, and was appointed by Polk to be second lieutenant in the United States Mounted Riflemen. An object of much curiosity to easterners, he had valuable information to give Polk and Benton. Naturally Jessie Benton Frémont was eager to have him use his influence upon the President for favorable treatment to Frémont.

Tuesday, 8th June, 1847. — The Cabinet met today, all the members present except the Secretary of the Navy, who is absent in Virginia on a visit to his father. . .

Various matters connected with the operations of our army and navy in Mexico and the prosecution of the war were considered. Among other things it was determined to send Kit Carson with despatches to General Kearny in California, and to the commander of our Squadron in the Pacific. All the Cabinet agreed that in the unfortunate collision which had taken place between Commodore Stockton and General Kearny, respecting the right to command the land forces in California, General Kearny was in the right, and that Commodore Stockton and Lieut.-Col. Frémont were in the wrong. One object of sending the despatches by Carson was to put an end to this most unfortunate controversy.

Saturday, 12th June, 1847. — Despatches received from General Scott, dated on the 20th ultimo, were read. They were of a highly exceptional character. It appears that General Scott has taken offence because Mr. Trist was sent to his headquarters as a commissioner invested with diplomatic powers and full authority to conclude a treaty of peace.[14]

[14] Once more the administration was largely to blame for a conflict between its agents. Trist had been equipped with a commission, credentials, letters, a draft or project of a peace treaty, and other papers, and was expected to open negotiations if and when the Mexicans seemed disposed to meet our terms. He reached Vera Cruz on May 6, 1847, and fell ill there; meanwhile sending to General Scott a letter from Marcy and a despatch from Buchanan, together with a letter — doubtless egotistical and tactless — of his own. Scott was now highly suspicious of the administration, which had tried to have a civilian, Benton, placed in command over his head. He read in Secretary Marcy's letter the statement: "Mr. Trist is clothed with such diplomatic powers as will authorize him to enter into arrangements with the government of Mexico for the suspension of hostilities." This seemed mysterious, and might be interpreted as another move to supersede and humiliate him. He felt that he was being fettered in the management of the campaign, and that the government was trying to subordinate him, in important respects, before the view of his army and the two nations, to a mere clerk from a government department. The result was an explosion. He wrote a defiant letter to Trist, and the high-strung and somewhat conceited Trist replied in an equally injudicious and irritating epistle. When

He desired to be invested with this power himself, and although Mr. Trist had been in his camp for six days at the date of his despatch, he states he had not seen him. It is clear from this despatch, as well as one of the previous date enclosing a letter from General Scott to Mr. Trist, that he would not coöperate with Mr. Trist in accomplishing the object of his mission, the conclusion of an honourable peace. His last two despatches are not only insubordinate, but insulting to Mr. Trist and the Government. I gave my views on the subject, in which the Cabinet unanimously concurred. In accordance with them I directed the Secretary of War to prepare a despatch to General Scott rebuking him for his insubordinate course, and repeating the order in a peremptory manner to him to carry the despatch borne to him by Mr. Trist addressed to the Mexican Government to that Government, and requiring an immediate answer, to be returned by the bearer of the despatch, whether he had obeyed or intended to obey the former order of the Secretary of War. He deserves for his conduct in this matter to be removed from the command. I concluded, however, to delay action on his conduct until his answer to the communications which I have this day ordered to be addressed to him shall be received. The Secretary of the Navy also read a despatch from Commodore Perry, commanding the squadron in the gulf, enclosing a correspondence between General Scott and Lieut. Sims of the Navy, of a highly insubordinate and exceptionable character. Lieut. Sims had been sent to General Scott's headquarters under orders from the Secretary of the Navy, with a view to ask General Scott's coöperation in pro-

---

Trist reached Scott's headquarters on May 14, Scott would not see or talk with him. Marcy, who knew them both, wrote in dismay that he feared both Trist and Scott had got to writing letters; if so, all was over. But in time all ended well. Trist bethought him to explain his mission in full to Scott, and to send more official documents, and when Scott realized that he was not to be unhorsed, he responded with cordiality. The two became trustful and generous friends. Meanwhile, Polk was insisting on his " rebuke " and talking of removing Scott forthwith!

curing the release of passed midshipman Rogers, now a prisoner in Mexico. General Scott arrogates to himself the right to be the only proper channel through whom the United States Government can properly communicate with the Government of Mexico on any subject; which is an assumption wholly unwarrantable and which I will not tolerate. The truth is that I have been compelled from the beginning to conduct the war against Mexico through the agency of two generals highest in rank who have not only no sympathies with the government, but are hostile to my administration. Both of them have assumed to control the government. To this I will not submit and will as certainly remove General Scott from the chief command, as he shall refuse or delay to obey the order borne to him by Mr. Trist. My doubt is whether I shall delay to remove him until I can hear further from him.

The Secretaries of War and the Navy read despatches which they had respectively prepared to our commanders of our land and naval forces in California and on the Pacific. The object of these despatches was to remove the collision which had arisen between the two arms of the service in regard to the rank of their officers.

Monday, 14th June, 1847. — Among others who called today was Mrs. Frémont, the wife of Lieut.-Col. Frémont. Lieut. Kit Carson was with her. She expressed a desire that her husband should be retained in California. I informed her that the despatches which Lieut. Carson would bear to General Kearny in California, who was the military officer highest in command in that country, left it to the option of Lieut.-Col. Frémont to remain in the service in California or to return to the United States and join his regiment (the Mounted Rifles) now serving in Mexico.

Tuesday, 15th June, 1847. — Mr. Buchanan read to the Cabinet the draft of a despatch to Mr. Trist, having made the modifications which I suggested to him on yesterday. After some conversation they were agreed to by the Cabinet unanimously. Mr. Buchanan thought it better to delay his despatch to Mr. Trist until he heard from him again. In this I differed from him in opinion. On the contrary, I thought time was important, and that the two despatches to Mr. Trist and General Scott should be borne to them with all practicable speed by the same messenger. I expressed in strong terms my disapprobation of General Scott's conduct, in failing or refusing to communicate to the Mexican Government, as he had been ordered to do by the Secretary of War, the despatch addressed to the Minister of Foreign Affairs of Mexico by the Secretary of State, which had been borne to him by Mr. Trist, and expressed my determination, if he persisted in disobeying the order, to have him arrested and tried by a court martial.

Saturday, 19th June, 1847. — I informed the Cabinet that I contemplated leaving on Tuesday next, the 22d *instant,* on a short tour to the North, that I would (if the state of the public business did not require my return sooner) be absent about two weeks. I have received many invitations to go north, and among others, two from the legislatures of New Hampshire and Maine, now in session, to visit the capitals of these States. I desire to make the tour at some time during my administration, and unless I do so now I probably cannot do so during my administration. The Attorney-General (Mr. Clifford) will accompany me, and the Secretary of State (Mr. Buchanan) may, if the state of the public business will permit it, join me at New York. . . I shall at no time be at more than two days' travel from Washington.

Monday, 21st June, 1847. — It had become generally known that I contemplated leaving Washington on tomorrow on a short tour to the North, and an unusual number of office-seekers pressed in upon me. When I opened my office at one o'clock it was filled with them. Applications were made to me for all grades of office, from a mission abroad to a messenger's place in one of the public offices. The herd of loafers who thus annoyed me seemed to act as though they had concluded that the Government was about to come to an end because of my expected absence, and because in consequence of it they would lose their chance for that time to get an office. I gave none of them offices, but treated them almost harshly.

Tuesday, 22nd June, to Wednesday, 7th July, 1847.—At twelve o'clock noon on Tuesday, the 22nd of June, 1847, I left Washington on a tour through the northern and eastern States and returned to Washington on the evening of Wednesday, the 7th of July, 1847. Mrs. Polk and her niece, Miss Rucker, accompanied me as far as Baltimore, where they separated from me on the morning of Wednesday, the 23rd of June. At seven o'clock on the morning of that day they set out for Tennessee, accompanied by Mr. Russman, and I set out for Philadelphia. I was accompanied by Mr. Clifford, the Attorney General of the United States, Mr. Burke, Commissioner of Patents, and Mr. Appleton, the chief clerk of the Navy Department, the latter acting as my private secretary. At Philadelphia Commodore Stewart of the United States Navy joined me, upon my invitation, as one of my suite, and accompanied me throughout my tour until my return to Philadelphia on the evening of the 6th of July, 1847. On Sunday afternoon, the 27th of June, 1847, Mr. Buchanan, the Secretary of State, joined me, and accompanied me throughout the balance of the tour until my return to Philadelphia, where he remained a day and arrived at Washington one day after I did. Mr. Appleton left me on my return journey at Portland in Maine, on the morning of Monday, the 5th of July, and Mr. Burke left me at Boston on the evening of the same day.

Wednesday, 7th July, 1847.—My whole tour was an exceedingly gratifying one. My reception everywhere was respectful and cordial. Not an unpleasant incident occurred to mar its pleasure. I saw many hundreds of thousands of my fellow citizens, of all ages and sexes; I saw a section of my country in New England which I had never before visited. I am much delighted with my tour and do not doubt but that I shall be profited by it.

I do not undertake to record the history of the tour. It would require a volume to do so. . . One incident only will I record, *viz.*: At New York, as I proceeded north, Mr. Benjamin F. Butler delivered me a verbal invitation from ex-President Van Buren, inviting me to visit him. I declined it, stating that my arrangements, previously made, did not contemplate a visit to that part of the State. I thought also (though I did not say so to Mr. Butler) that if Mr. Van Buren really desired me to visit him he would have written to me inviting me to do so, and that he would not have postponed this verbal message, delivered through Mr. Butler, to so late a period. I considered it a mere act of formal courtesy, which Mr. Van Buren, probably, thought public opinion constrained him to extend to me.

The truth is Mr. Van Buren became offended with me at the beginning of my administration, because I chose to exercise my own judgment in the selection of my own Cabinet, and would not be controlled by him and suffer him to select it for me. I have preserved his most extraordinary letter addressed to me on that subject. I made no reply to that letter, and since that time have had no direct correspondence with him further than to send him under my frank my two annual messages, and to receive two notes from him acknowledging their receipt.

Friday, 9th July, 1847. — I convened the Cabinet this morning at half past nine o'clock, all the members present. The subject which I submitted for consideration was the conduct of General Scott and Mr. Trist, and the angry personal controversy into which these two functionaries had allowed themselves to be engaged. Despatches from General Scott to the Secretary of War, and from Mr. Trist to the Secretary of State, were read. They exhibited a wretched state of things. So far from harmony prevailing between these two officers, they are engaged in a violent personal

correspondence. It does not as yet appear that they have
had any personal interview, although Mr. Trist had been in
General Scott's camp for many days. For a statement of the
cause of their difference, see statements contained in this
diary, and particularly of the 12th and 15th of June. From
the last despatches received it appears that the breach between them had been widened instead of being healed. General Scott, it appears, had returned to Mr. Trist the letter
from the Secretary of State addressed to the Minister of
Foreign Affairs of Mexico which had been borne to him by
Mr. Trist, and which he was ordered by the Secretary of
War, in a despatch which accompanied it, to convey to the
Mexican Government. Mr. Trist committed a great error
in receiving it from his aide-de-camp. General Scott has
written very foolish and bitter letters to Mr. Trist and Mr.
Trist has written as foolish a letter to him. Between them
the orders of the Secretary of War, and the Secretary of
State have been disregarded; and the danger has become
imminent that because of the personal controversy between
these self-important personages, the golden moment for concluding a peace with Mexico may have passed. General
Scott's last despatch to the Secretary of War is full of passion and vanity and is highly insubordinate.

CHAPTER IX
July 12, 1847 — Nov. 20, 1847

GEN. SCOTT'S ERRORS — BUCHANAN'S WAGER — BENTON AND THE FRÉMONT COURT-MARTIAL — CONTRERAS AND CHERUBUSCO — SCOTT AGREES TO AN ARMISTICE — DISSATISFACTION WITH TRIST — CAPTURE OF MEXICO CITY

Monday, 12th July, 1847. — The Secretary of War laid before me despatches which he had received from General Taylor at Monterey, of as late date as the 16th of June. In one of these despatches General Taylor repeats the opinion which he had previously expressed that he could not march with his present force on San Luis Potosi, and advises that he shall not attempt it, but occupy a defensive line. He states further that he will encamp the forces not required to maintain his present position at the town of Muir, and intimates that a part of his forces may be spared to reinforce General Scott's column. I informed the Secretary of War that I approved this suggestion, and that I thought an order should be given to General Taylor to send all the forces which he did not require to maintain his present position to General Scott's column.

Tuesday, 13th July, 1847. — The Cabinet met at the usual hour today, all the members present. . . Matters connected with Mexico and the prosecution of the war were considered. General Scott has undoubtedly committed a great military error by breaking up the post at Jalapa and leaving his whole rear exposed to the enemy. Our latest reports are that General Cadwallader was marching with a

249

reinforcement of some 1,500 or 1,800 men, and that General Pillow was marching some days in General Cadwallader's rear with a force of 1,800 or 2,000 men, both from Vera Cruz, to General Scott at Puebla, and that both had been several times attacked by large guerrilla parties and were fighting their way through them. The guerrillas were undoubtedly encouraged to make these attacks by the fact, which was known to them, that General Scott had left his rear unprotected.

Thursday, 15th July, 1847. — I was engaged this morning in transacting various matters of business which were on my table, and with several of my Secretaries and other officers of government. At twelve o'clock noon I received Mr. Bodisco, the Russian Minister, who called on an official visit, in the parlour below stairs. He delivered to me an official letter from the Emperor, his sovereign, announcing the important event of the birth of *a grandchild. This ceremony, which has been often repeated since I have been President by the representatives of foreign governments, is to a plain American citizen a most ridiculous one. I said to Mr. Bodisco jocosely that I was sorry I could not reciprocate the civility by making a similar announcement on my part. When Mr. Pakenham, the British Minister, announced to me some months ago that Victoria, his sovereign, had given birth to another child, I congratulated him upon the fact that there was no likelihood of a failure in the direct line of a successor to the throne. He replied humorously, "O, no, sir! I have made a similar announcement to this government every year since Her Majesty has been married." I have of course to sign a stereotyped answer to all such communications. Had I not found such to be the settled practise, I never would have signed or sent such answers.

Friday, 16th July, 1847. — I sent Mr. Buchanan for the despatch which he had informed me last evening he had received from Mr. Trist. It conveyed very important information. General Scott and himself up to its date (13th of June) had held no personal intercourse. Mr. Trist had written to the British Minister in Mexico, informing him that he was with the headquarters of the army and that he was invested with full diplomatic powers to negotiate for peace, and inquiring of that minister if he would be the medium of delivering the despatch from Mr. Buchanan addressed to the Minister of Foreign Affairs of Mexico, if it was forwarded to him. The British minister without the least delay sent Mr. Thornton, his secretary of legation, to Puebla, where Mr. Trist was, who took the despatch and returned with it to Mexico. This was the same despatch which General Scott was ordered by the Secretary of War to convey to the Mexican Government, but who after having retained it for several days after it had been conveyed to him with the Secretary's order by Mr. Trist, had failed to do so and returned it to Mr. Trist. Mr. Trist learned from Mr. Thornton that had it been delivered at the time General Scott first received it, which was shortly after the battle of Cerro Gordo, there was but little doubt that peace would have been made. The protraction of the war may properly be attributed to the folly and ridiculous vanity of General Scott.

Saturday, 17th July, 1847. — The Cabinet met at the usual hour this morning, all the members present. An hour or more was taken up in considering measures relating to the war, and to the orders which had been issued within the last three days for withdrawing a part of General Taylor's forces and strengthening Scott's column. I am devoting all my time and energies to these matters, and am examining all the details of everything that is done, so far as it is possible for me to do so. The Secretary of War is almost overwhelmed with his labours, seems to be care-worn, and is almost broken down with his great labours.

Thursday, 22nd July, 1847. — Nothing of interest transpired today. I attended as usual to various matters of business with some of my secretaries and other public officers.

Despatches were received by last evening's mail from General Kearny in California and from Commodore Shubrick and Commodore Biddle in the Pacific, from which it appears that the unfortunate collision between the officers of the army and navy in that distant region, in regard to their respective rank, had been adjusted, and that they were acting a harmony.[1] I opened my office at one o'clock P.M., when a number of persons called.

Saturday, 24th July, 1847. — One incident occurred in the Cabinet which I will note. It was this. — I called Mr. Buchanan's attention to a letter which had been prepared at the Department of State and sent to me for my signature, addressed to the Emperor of Brazil, in answer to the Emperor's letter notifying me of the recall of Mr. Lisboa as Envoy Extraordinary and Minister Plenipotentiary to the United States (see this diary of the 22nd instant). To one part of it I took exceptions and remarked that I thought it was unusual in similar cases and improper. It was that part of the letter which informed the Emperor that he might place full credence in whatever Mr. Lisboa might say to him in my behalf. I told Mr. Buchanan that this was usual in a letter of credence given to our own Ministers who went abroad, but that I was not aware that it had ever been done with a Foreign Minister on his return to his own country. . . He insisted that he was right. I then jocosely said to him, I will stand you a basket of champagne that this letter is not in the usual form as you insist, and that the precedents in the State Department will not sustain it. He promptly said, Done, I take you up, and rising in a fine humour, said, now I will go over to the Department and bring the precedents. I replied, very well. He left my office and after some time returned with a bound letter-book, remarking as he entered the office, I think I have got you. He said, now I will read

---

[1] The adjustment consisted in a complete triumph of General Kearny, and the humiliation of Frémont; Kearny having been sustained by later orders sent out from Washington.

you a letter from General Jackson to the King of the French.
When the letter was read it did not sustain Mr. Buchanan,
and had no such paragraph in it. Mr. Buchanan admitted
that they were not similar. He searched the letter-book
for some time and could find no such precedent. He seemed
to be confounded and disappointed and said, Well, if I don't
find such a precedent today, I will send you the basket of
champagne. I smiled and told him I would not accept it, and
that I had been jesting when I proposed it, and had done so
only to express in an earnest manner my conviction that I
was right. But, he said, if I had won it I would have made
you pay it, and I will pay it to you. I repeated that I would
not accept it. I record this incident for the purpose of showing how necessary it is for me to give my vigilant attention
even to the forms and details of my subordinates' duties.

Friday, 30th July, 1847. — A telegraphic despatch was
received about eight o'clock this morning from Richmond,
Va., communicating later intelligence from the army, which
if true is of great importance. It is to the effect that General
Pierce had had an engagement with the enemy in considerable force at the National Bridge and had routed them; and
that General Pillow had had an engagement with the enemy
at a pass in the mountains beyond Jalapa, and had routed
them, and had overtaken and joined General Cadwallader's
command at Perote, and that the Mexican Government had
appointed three commissioners to meet and treat with Mr.
Trist at a place eight leagues beyond Puebla. . .

The mail of tonight brings despatches from Vera Cruz of
no later date than the 13th *instant*. They in part confirm
the telegraphic news. Other portions of this news were
brought by the vessel which left Vera Cruz two or three
days later. The news may be, and probably is, substantially
true, but it rests mainly on the unauthenticated rumours
which had reached Vera Cruz. All communication between
Vera Cruz and General Scott's army had been cut off, except
by strong bodies of troops.

Sunday, 1st August, 1847. — I was somewhat indisposed today and did not attend church as is my usual habit. I rested and remained quiet through the day, seeing no company. I had taken some cold and was, moreover, wearied by my unceasing labours and responsible duties in my office.

Saturday, 7th August, 1847. — The question of calling out 5,000 more volunteers was discussed, and it was finally concluded to postpone making such a call until further information should be received from General Scott, which we are expecting daily.

Wednesday, 11th August, 1847. — This morning I sent my nephew, Marshall T. Polk, to a school on the heights of Georgetown of which the Reverend Messrs. Whittingham and Spencer are Principals. I have had him at Georgetown College for the last two years. He is idle and inattentive to his studies. It is now vacation at the college, and I conclude to give him another trial at the school to which I now send him. If I find that he does no better than he has done, I must send him home to his mother.

Monday, 16th August, 1847. — The information for several days past has indicated the probable defeat of Gov. A. V. Brown [2] and of the Democratic party in the Tennessee election.

Tuesday, 17th August, 1847. — Before the hour for the meeting of the Cabinet today Senator Benton called. He returned to Washington from the West, he informed me, two or three days ago. After some general conversation, of a pleasant character he introduced the subject of the difficulty between Col. Frémont (his son-in-law) and General Kearny in California. He remarked that he had some time ago addressed a letter to the Adjutant-General demanding that Col. Frémont should be recalled and a court of inquiry organized in his case, as due to the Colonel's honour and military character. I replied that I had read his communication,

---

[2] Aaron Venable Brown, 1795–1859, was Governor of Tennessee 1845–1847; later he was Postmaster-General under President Buchanan.

but that it had not been deemed necessary to take any action
upon it. I told him that there had been some difficulty between the officers in California, which I much regretted, and
that I hoped it might not be necessary to institute any trial
by a court martial. I also made a general remark to the effect that I had not deemed it necessary to do so. General
Benton to this remarked in substance, I am glad to hear
from you, Sir, as President of the United States, that there
has been nothing in Col. Frémont's conduct which requires a
court martial in his case.[3] I instantly said to him that he
must not understand me as expressing any opinion in reference to the difficulty which had arisen between Col. Frémont,
General Kearny, and Commodore Stockton in California;
but that what I meant to say was that I hoped that the difficulty upon the arrival of the instructions of the 5th of November last had been settled, that they would act in harmony
in carrying out the views of the government, and that it
might not be necessary to institute proceedings by a court-
martial in reference to the matter, and that I desired to
avoid doing so if it could be done. To this General Benton
said there was of course no commitment on my part. I hold
him certainly not, that if proceedings by court-martial did
take place I would, in a certain contingency, have to act officially, and ought not and could not with propriety decide or
express an opinion in advance in reference to the matter.
He said he did not desire me to have anything to do with it,
unless it should come regularly before me for my official action; that he had addressed his communication demanding a

[3] Kearny had assumed the office of Governor of California at Monterey
on March 1, 1847. After placing the government in operation, and turning
it over to Col. Richard B. Mason on May 31, he set out to return to the
East. He ordered Frémont to accompany him under separate escort, though
the Polk administration had plainly indicated that Frémont was to be allowed
to proceed to Mexico to join his regiment there. At Fort Leavenworth
Frémont was placed under arrest, and ordered to report to the Adjutant-
General in Washington. Both were to arrive in Washington in a few weeks
to lay their grievances before the government. Senator Benton was determined to do everything in his power to injure Kearny and obtain a vindica-
tion of Frémont.

court martial to the Adjutant-General, and not to the Secretary of War or the President, that he had done so purposely that the case might take the usual course, according to military usage and law. He then remarked that he was a Senator and I was President, and that each would act officially in his place, without reference to any former friendships between us; and added he should introduce a resolution into the Senate instituting a full recommendation into this whole California business. I answered him with some spirit that so far as the administration was concerned I had nothing to fear from the most searching investigation, and indeed that I would court such an investigation as he proposed to institute. He remarked that he did not propose it in reference to the conduct of the administration, but that investigations before courts-martial were technical and limited, but in the Senate they could be broad and full and embrace transactions and matters which a court martial could not take cognizance of. I repeated that I could have no objection to the fullest and broadest investigation which might be instituted. He said such investigations were usual in the British Parliament, where all matters could be spread before the public. I then said to General Benton that he could, if he wished, have access to all the official correspondence between the War and Navy Departments with Commodore Stockton and General Kearny, and to all the records of the action of those Departments in relation to difficulty which had occurred between our officers in California. I told him that I thought he ought to see them before he took action in relation to the court of inquiry, and that I desired that he should do so if he desired it. I told him that every facility would be afforded him at the War and Navy Departments for that purpose, if he desired to do so. He thanked me. He was evidently much excited, but suppressed his feelings and talked in a calm tone.

Monday, 23d August, 1847.—The Attorney-General called this morning on official business, and after disposing of it we entered into a conversation about the Mexican War. He expressed the opinion strongly that I should immediately call an additional volunteer force into the field; and also that if the war was not closed before the meeting of Congress, it should be prosecuted with the whole strength of the nation if necessary. He was utterly opposed to withdrawing our forces, as destructive of national character and interests, as well as destructive of the Democratic party and of the administration. He thought there was but one course to pursue and that was to fight boldly through, holding all the places we have conquered until there is an honourable peace. In this respect he differed from the views of Mr. Buchanan as several times expressed by him in Cabinet. Judge Mason, the acting Secretary of War, called and held a further conference with me in relation to the contemplated call on the States for an additional volunteer force of five regiments of men.

I sent for General Jesup and General Gibson, and conferred further with them in relation to the adequacy of the funds in their respective departments to defray the expenses until after the meeting of Congress. They both assured me that I could safely call forth the additional force proposed, and that the money on hand unexpended would be sufficient to defray the additional expense. I am greatly vexed by the looseness with which General Jesup has kept an account in his office of the funds for the quartermaster's department, and am resolved that there shall be a reform in this respect. I disposed of much business on my table today.

Tuesday, 24th August, 1847. — General Benton called at three o'clock P.M. and informed me that he would leave this afternoon for the West. I gave him a statement of the unfortunate collision between General Scott and Mr. Trist in Mexico and said that in consequence of it the golden moment to conclude a peace with Mexico had probably been suffered to pass, and expressed the opinion that the duration of the war might be indefinite. I informed him of the amount of force in the field, and of the present condition of things, and that I had resolved to call out an additional force. He fully approved it, and advised that the additional force should be called out.

Wednesday, 25th August, 1847. — Mr. Buchanan . . . informed me that he had prepared the rough draft of a letter, in answer to an invitation which he had received to attend the Harvest Home celebration in Berks County, Pennsylvania, on Saturday next, which he wished to read to me. It was in favour of the election of the Democratic candidate for governor (Gov. Shunk) and in favour of extending the Missouri Compromise line on the subject of slavery west to the Pacific Ocean, over any territory that the United States might acquire from Mexico. The trend of the letter was to satisfy northern Democrats that that compromise line would be adhered to. I made some suggestions to him with a view to make it more acceptable to the South. They were not, however, very material, but such as to prevent his views from being misunderstood or misconstrued.

Sunday, 29th August, 1847. — Intelligence reached the City today of the sudden death by apoplexy of the Hon. Silas Wright, late Governor of New York. He was a great and a good man. At the commencement of my administration I tendered to him the office of Secretary of the Treasury, which he declined to accept. I was intimate with him when he was in Congress. He was my personal and political friend, and I deeply regret his death.[4]

Tuesday, 31st August, 1847. — I . . . submitted to the Cabinet the propriety of issuing positive orders to General Scott to exact military contributions from the Mexicans, and especially if he should take and occupy the City of Mexico. I stated that such instructions had been heretofore given to

---

[4] Silas Wright, who after his defeat for reëlection as Governor had retired to his farm at Canton, N. Y., died Aug. 27, 1847. Many men had thought of him as a possible Presidential candidate in 1848, and his death caused a more profound sensation in New York than any similar event since the end of De Witt Clinton's career.

both General Taylor and General Scott, but leaving to them
a discretion on the subject, and, as the Cabinet knew, neither
of them had made such exactions. I thought that the orders
to General Scott should now be more peremptory and
stringent, and that nothing should prevent him from levying
such contributions upon the wealthy inhabitants of Mexico
to defray the expenses of his army, unless he should find that
by adopting such a policy, his army could not be subsisted.
The subject was discussed. Mr. Buchanan expressed some
doubts, upon the ground that the wealthy inhabitants were
understood to be favourable to peace and that such a policy
might make them change their policy. I thought if they
were made to feel the burthens of the war they would be
more likely to be sincere in their desire to bring about a
peace. The other members of the Cabinet concurred in the
policy of levying such contributions, or, in other words, in
favour of quartering upon the enemy.

My brother, William H. Polk, was commissioned as
Major of the 3rd Dragoons today and immediately received
orders to proceed and join his regiment, under the command of General Scott in Mexico.

Saturday, 4th September, 1847.—The Cabinet met at
the usual hour today; all the members present except the
Secretary of War and the Secretary of the Navy, who are
both absent from the City. . . I brought before the Cabinet
the importance of uniting the forces of General Taylor with
those of General Scott, except a sufficient number to hold
Monterey and the line of the Rio Grande. This had been
in effect ordered by the Secretary of War. . .

I remarked to the Cabinet that it was time we were considering what was to be done and what distinct policy I
should recommend to Congress, if the war should continue
until the meeting of that body. I remarked that we should
deliberately settle upon our plans and policy and be prepared
to maintain them, before Congress met. I remarked that
I called the attention of the Cabinet to this **most important**

subject to-day, not for the purpose of asking a decision upon it at this time, but to draw the attention of the Cabinet to it with a view to have the aid of their matured advice when it did come up for decision, which must be before long. I then went on to state my present impressions, which were in brief that we should unite the two columns of the army, except a sufficient force to hold Monterey and the line of the Rio Grande, and press the war upon the capital and vital parts of Mexico by all the means which the nation could command, until a peace was obtained. I expressed the opinion further that as our expenses had been greatly enlarged by the obstinacy of Mexico in refusing to negotiate, since Mr. Trist's instructions were prepared in April last, if a treaty had not been made when we next heard from Mexico that his instructions should be modified. I remarked that if we were compelled to continue the war at so great expense I would be unwilling to pay the sum which Mr. Trist had been authorized to pay, in the settlement of a boundary by which it was contemplated the United States would acquire New Mexico and the Californias; and that if Mexico continued obstinately to refuse to treat, I was decidedly in favour of insisting on the acquisition of more territory than the provinces named. I repeated that these were my present impressions, and that they were thrown out now that the Cabinet might reflect upon them by the time it would be necessary to decide upon them. No formal expression of opinion was made by the Cabinet but there seemed to be an acquiescence in these views.

After the Cabinet adjourned I transacted business on my table. When I retired at night I was much fatigued, having passed a week of great labour and responsibility, and of great solicitude and anxiety. With me it is emphatically true that the Presidency is "no bed of roses."

Tuesday, 7th September, 1847. — I submitted for consideration to the Cabinet, whether, as the Mexican Government had continued stubbornly to refuse to enter upon negotiations for peace for several months after they had been notified that Mr. Trist was with the headquarters of the army clothed with full diplomatic powers, and as the United States had been subjected to great expense since Mr. Trist's instructions were given to him in April last: whether under the changed circumstances since that time the instructions to Mr. Trist should not be modified. The distinct questions submitted were, whether the amount which Mr. Trist had been authorized to pay for the possession of New Mexico and the Californias and right of passage through the Isthmus of Tehuantepec should not be reduced, and whether we should not now demand more territory than we now did. All seemed to agree that the maximum sum to be paid for the cessions above described should be reduced. Mr. Buchanan suggested that this sum should be reduced from thirty to fifteen millions, and that the cession of the right of passage through the Isthmus and Lower as well as Upper California and New Mexico should be made a *sine qua non*. He suggested also that the line should run on the parallel of 31° or 31° 30″ of north latitude from the Rio Grande to the Gulf of California, instead of on the parallel of 32° which Mr. Trist had been authorized to accept. Upon the question of acquiring more territory than this there was some difference of opinion. The Secretary of the Treasury and the Attorney General were in favor of acquiring in addition the Department or State of Tamaulipas, which includes the port of Tampico. The Secretary of State was opposed to this. The Postmaster General and the Secretary of the Navy concurred with him. I expressed myself as being entirely agreed to reduce the sum to be paid from thirty to fifteen millions, and to modify the line as suggested by Mr. Buchanan. I declared myself also as being in favour of acquiring the cession of the Department of Tamaulipas, if it should be found practicable to do so. The subject was fully discussed and at full length. . . In the course of the discussion the Attorney General expressed the opinion that if an army took possession of the City of Mexico, and the Mexicans still refused to make peace, that Mr. Trist should be re-

called, and that Mexico and the world should be informed
that we had no further propositions of peace to make, and
that we should prosecute the War with the whole energy of
the nation and over-run and subdue the whole country, until
Mexico herself sued for peace. The Secretary of the Treasury expressed his concurrence in these opinions. I dissented
from the opinion that Mr. Trist should be recalled, but concurred with the Attorney General in his views in all other
respects. I thought we should still keep our minister with
the headquarters of the army ready to receive any propositions of overtures of peace which Mexico might have to
make.

   Saturday, 11th September, 1847. — No subject of general importance was considered today. Several matters of
minor importance were disposed of. While the Cabinet
were in session, Brigadier General Kearny of the United
States army called. General Kearny returned recently from
California. I received him in my office and introduced him
to my Cabinet. He stated that he had arrived in Washington this morning, and had called to pay his respects and to
report himself to me. I received him kindly, for I consider
him a good officer. He has performed valuable and important services in his late expedition to New Mexico and California. He remained but a few minutes. I invited him to
call again.

   Tuesday, 14th September, 1847. — The Southern mail of
this evening brought intelligence (which had been conveyed
a part of the way from New Orleans by a government express) of two battles between forces under the command of
General Scott and the Mexican army, before the City of
Mexico. They were fought on the 19th and 20th of August,
and resulted in decisive victories of the American arms,
though with heavy losses on both sides.[5] An armistice was

[5] These were the battles of Contreras and Cherubusco. The former was
the less important, though the Mexicans lost 1,700 men as against 100 lost
by the Americans. In the second battle Santa Anna sustained a crushing
defeat, and his troops were chased almost to the gates of Mexico City. He

entered into between the two armies after the battles, which
had been followed by the appointment of commissioners by
Mexico to meet and negotiate for peace with Mr. Trist. A
despatch was received from Mr. Trist, dated on the 29th
August, stating that he had had two meetings with the Mexican commissioners and was to meet them again on the next
day, the 30th of August.

This being reception evening, the company, ladies and
gentlemen, had assembled in the parlour for some time before I met them. I had been detained in my office examining the despatches from Mr. Trist and the unofficial information received from officers of the army in letters addressed
to persons in Washington. Official letters were also received from Vera Cruz, but none from General Scott.
When I met the company in the parlour I communicated
to them the substance of the information which had been
received.

Wednesday, 15th September, 1847. — Further details of
the battle of the City of Mexico were received today through
the New Orleans papers, but no official report has come to
hand. I fear General Scott has agreed to an armistice for
too long a time. Judging at this distance, I would think he
should have improved his victories by pressing the Mexican
Government to an immediate decision upon the terms of
peace which Mr. Trist was authorized to offer to them, and
if they refused these terms I think he should have taken immediate possession of the city, and levied contribution upon
it for the support of his army. I fear the armistice was
agreed to by the Mexican commander only to gain time to

---

lost more than 4,000 in killed and wounded, and the Americans reported more
than 2,600 prisoners. It was now plain that the war was practically over,
and that the Americans could enter the capital whenever they liked. But
Scott unselfishly gave up the personal glory of at once occupying Mexico
City because he felt that such action might delay a favorable peace. He
agreed upon an armistice with the express purpose of permitting negotiations
for a treaty; and the next two weeks were wasted in talk with Santa Anna.

reorganize his defeated army for further resistance.[6] The battles were fought on the 19th and 20th of August, and it appears that on the 29th, from Mr. Trist's despatch of that date, that no decision had been made upon the terms of peace which had been proposed by him.[7] I shall wait very anxiously for further information from the army.

Thursday, 16th September, 1847. — Brigadier General Kearny of the United States army called today, and I had a conversation of more than an hour with him, in relation to his late expedition to California and to affairs in that country. He is a good officer and an intelligent gentleman. He gave me much valuable information in relation to affairs in California and the military operations in that country. No conversation took place in relation to his recent difficulty with Commodore Stockton and Lieut.-Col. Frémont. Col. Frémont is under arrest, charges having been preferred against him by General Kearny, and I preferred not to converse with him on that subject. I did not introduce the subject, and I was glad that he did not. My conversation with him was a pleasant and interesting one.

Friday, 17th September, 1847. — I saw and transacted business today with the Attorney General, the Secretary of the Navy, and some other public officers. Being engaged in

[6] Polk's complaints about the armistice later seemed sustained by the facts. Yet Americans and neutrals who resided in Mexico City assured Scott that by capturing the capital, breaking up the government, and scattering to the winds the substantial propertied men who desired peace, he would only delay the termination of hostilities. He felt that the presence of a victorious American army at the gates of the city, arousing fears of bloodshed and pillage, would be influential for negotiation.

[7] Santa Anna was prevented by political considerations and factional manœuvrings from accepting the terms offered by Trist. He was willing to consent to a cession of Texas and Upper California, but he wished the region between the Nueces River and the Rio Grande to be made neutral, perhaps under a European guarantee. Trist proposed to consult Washington upon the exclusion of American sovereignty and settlers from the region between the two rivers, but Santa Anna refused to consent to an extension of the armistice. The breakdown of the negotiations caused great disappointment in the United States.

my office, I directed no one to be admitted until two o'clock
P.M. At that hour, I opened my door, and quite a number
of persons called. Most of them were on patriotic business
of serving themselves by seeking office. I had no offices to
bestow and dealt with them in a very summary manner.
Some beggars for money were also among the number. To
one poor woman I gave something. I also made a donation
towards the building of the Washington Monument. No
news was received from the army today. Mr. Barnett, who
married my niece, Jane Walker, left for his residence in
Tennessee today. This was reception evening. A number
of persons, ladies and gentlemen, called.

   Saturday, 18th September, 1847. — I learned last evening that Lieut.-Col. Frémont had arrived in this City.
Brigadier General Kearny had arrested him and ordered him
to report to the Adjutant-General at Washington. General
Kearny filed charges against him with the Adjutant-General
some days ago. I was informed in the parlour last night by
Mr. Jones, the brother-in-law of Col. Frémont, that it was
the Colonel's desire to be absent for a few days to visit his
sick mother in Charleston, S. C., but that he had desired him
to say to me that he wished to have his trial speedily and
that he would be ready in thirty days. I also received a letter from Senator Benton on the subject this morning. Col.
Frémont's case was the subject of conversation in the Cabinet. The Secretary of War sent over to his Department
for the charges which were exhibited against Col. Frémont
by General Kearny. They were brought over and were read
in Cabinet. I requested the Secretary of War to examine
the charges and report to me as soon as practicable, whether
in his opinion the charges preferred by General Kearny were
of such a character as to make it proper to order a court
martial for the trial of Col. Frémont, or whether he would
deem it better to order a court of inquiry in the first instance.
No other business of importance was considered in the
Cabinet.

Saturday, 25th September, 1847.—I am waiting with great anxiety for the next arrival from Mexico. Shortly before the meeting of the Cabinet this morning Lieut.-Col. Frémont called. Col. Frémont is under arrest but had made no allusion to that fact or to his case while in conversation with me.

Sunday, 26th September, 1847.—General Robert Armstrong called about twelve o'clock and spent the balance of the day with me. I rested on a sofa in my office. General Armstrong in the course of our long familiar conversation upon various subjects inquired of me how Mr. Charles J. Ingersoll of Philadelphia stood affected towards my administration. I told him that Mr. Ingersoll had become very hostile to me, and had written to me a very exceptionable letter, complaining of me because after he was rejected by the Senate as minister to France I had not renominated him, or kept the office vacant from the end of the last to the beginning of the next session of Congress, so as to give him another chance to be confirmed. I told him that I had answered his letter, and that I thought Mr. Ingersoll would never venture to publish the correspondence. General Armstrong then told me that Mrs. Maury (an Englishwoman who visited the United States a year or two ago and after her return to England had published a book on her travels and observations in the United States) had shown him a letter addressed to her by Mr. Ingersoll, complaining of me because I had not appointed his (Mr. Ingersoll's) son to an office in the army of the United States, that he had applied to me to do so, and that I had refused. I note this fact because it shows the want of discretion and principle on the part of Mr. Ingersoll, an American representative, when he can so far forget the proprieties of his position and his own self-respect as to be making known his complaints of his own government, and his personal griefs and disappointments, to a gossiping woman of a foreign kingdom. Doubtless he calculated to have the sympathies and condolence of this

Englishwoman and her English friends with him in his sore troubles and griefs.

Monday, 4th October, 1847. — I resolved today to recall Mr. Trist as commissioner to Mexico, and requested Mr. Buchanan to prepare the letter of recall.

I directed the Secretary of War to prepare another letter to General Scott, directing him more stringently than had been done to levy contributions upon the enemy, and make them as far as practicable defray the expenses of the war.

Tuesday, 5th October, 1847. — The unofficial information received shows that Mexico has refused to treat for peace upon terms which the United States can accept; and it is now manifest that the war must be prosecuted with increased forces and increased energy. We must levy contributions and quarter on the enemy. This is part of the object of the letter to General Scott. Mr. Trist is recalled because his remaining longer with the army could not, probably, accomplish the objects of his mission, and because his remaining longer might, and probably would, impress, the Mexican Government with the belief that the United States were so anxious for peace that they would ultimately conclude one upon the Mexican terms. Mexico must now first sue for peace, and when she does we will hear her propositions.

The Cabinet remained upwards of three hours, and when they adjourned I found myself much exhausted and fatigued.

Sunday, 10th October, 1847. — I spent this day in my chamber until about four o'clock, when I took a short ride in my carriage for exercise. I drove to the house of the Postmaster-General, who joined me in the ride. I am still very weak from my late attack, and felt fatigued on my return from my ride. Mrs. Polk was no better today. She had another chill and suffered much and rested badly through the day and night. The physician (Dr. Miller) called several times in the course of the day and after night, and prescribed for her. She is very nervous and restless, had fever in the latter part of the day, and I thought her very ill.

Tuesday, 12th October, 1847. — I met the Cabinet today in my office, all the members present. No business of general importance was considered definitely acted on. I communicated to the Cabinet my views in regard to the future prosecution of the War in Mexico. I cannot undertake to state these views in detail. They were in substance that the war should be prosecuted with increased energy, that I was opposed to withdrawing the army altogether, or retiring to a defensive line, but that I was in favour of holding all the ports, towns, cities, and provinces which we had conquered, of pressing forward our military operations, and of levying contributions upon the enemy for the support of our army. I was in favour, also, of establishing more stable governments than those established over the cities or provinces which we have conquered, by the right of conquest. I was in favour, also, of avowing in my message to Congress in December next that the provinces of New Mexico and the Californias should be retained by the United States as indemnity, and should never be restored to Mexico, and that in these provinces permanent territorial governments should be established. The Cabinet were unanimous in concurring with me in these views. I then told them that I would prepare shortly a rough draft of my message to Congress upon the subject, embodying these views, and would submit it to them for consideration.

Thursday, 14th October, 1847. — The Secretary of State called and sent me a message that he had come with the Hon. Henry A. Wise, late United States Minister to Brazil, who desired to pay his respects. I went to my office, and a few minutes afterwards the Secretary of State and Mr. Wise came in. Mr. Wise appeared at first to be somewhat embarrassed. I received him courteously, and he was soon apparently at his ease. He very soon returned to me his thanks, and expressed his gratitude to me for my kind treatment to (of) him while in Brazil. He said he desired to express to me his personal gratitude as well as that of a public functionary. I entered into a free conversation with him in regard to affairs in Brazil. No allusion was had to his former hostility to me, and his unprovoked and unjustifiable assaults upon me when I was Speaker of the House of Representatives in 1836 and 1827. He and Baylie Peyton were then acting a part for John Bell, who used them for his own malignant purposes. I can never justify Mr. Wise's course at that time, but it has long since passed and I forgive it.[8] He is now very grateful to me for not having recalled him from Brazil, and for having approved his conduct in the recent difficulties in which he was involved with the Government of that country. I learn that he returns to the United States my friend, and his expressions of gratitude to me today were as strong and decided as human language could make them, so that I have lived to conquer the hostility of at least one of my political opponents and persecutors. This I have done by performing my duty in a magnanimous and liberal manner.

Saturday, 16th October, 1847. — I attended the meeting of the Cabinet in my office today, all the members present except the Secretary of the Treasury, who was absent from the city, and the Secretary of State, who was detained in his office.

I read to the members of the Cabinet who were present the draft which I had prepared within the last few days of a message to Congress upon our relations with Mexico, and our future policy in the conduct of the war. They all expressed their approbation of it.

Wednesday, 20th October, 1847. — At an early hour this morning information was received by telegraph from Peters-

---

[8] Henry A. Wise and Baylie Peyton had for a short time been law-partners in Tennessee. John Bell of Tennessee was a Representative in Congress from 1827 to 1841. He became a Whig in 1833, and in 1834 was elected Speaker of the House over Polk. Thereafter he was a bitter opponent of Polk's in Tennessee politics.

burg that the steamer *Fashion* had arrived at New Orleans from Vera Cruz, bringing despatches from the City of Mexico bearing date as late as the 18th of September. This intelligence is that our army was in peaceable possession of the City of Mexico; that Santa Anna had resigned the Presidency; and that Pena y Pena, who had succeeded him, had convened the Mexican Congress to meet at Queretaro on the 5th instant.[9] A state of great confusion prevailed in Mexico. The names of many officers who were killed and wounded in the late engagements before the City of Mexico are given, some of them, indeed I may say all of them, very valuable officers. Among the wounded are Major-General Pillow severely, and Brigadier General Shields. I waited with much anxiety for the arrival of the Southern mail in the afternoon, and was much disappointed that no official despatches were received from General Scott. Letters were received from the army and navy at Vera Cruz.

Thursday, 21st October, 1847. — I was occupied in my office as usual today; saw several public officers on business, and saw company at two o'clock P.M. Nothing of much interest occurred. By the Southern mail this evening despatches were received from Mr. Trist from Mexico, of as late date as the 28th of September, giving an account of his negotiations with the Mexican commissioners, which had resulted in a failure to come to any agreement with them. Mr. Trist had exceeded his instructions and had suggested terms to the Mexican commissioners which I could not have approved if they had agreed to them. I can never approve a treaty or submit one to the Senate, which would dismember the State of Texas, and Mr. Trist's suggestion, if agreed to, would have done this by depriving that State of the country between the Nueces and the Rio Grande. Mr. Trist in

[9] After the battle of Molino del Rey (Sept. 8, 1847) and the capture of the fortress of Chapultepec (Sept. 13), Scott's troops marched into the City of Mexico. Santa Anna fled, and Pena y Pena, as president of the supreme court, took charge of the executive department of the government, holding this position until the Mexican Congress elected a provisional President.

other respects had in his conferences departed from his instructions and the simple duty with which he was charged,
which was to submit and enforce the ultimatum of his government. He had no right to depart from his instructions,
and I disapprove his conduct in doing so. He proposed, it
is true, if they agreed to his suggestions, to submit it to his
government before he would enter into a treaty, but in this
he has committed himself and embarrassed future negotiations. His course is much to be regretted.

Friday, 22nd October, 1847. — I was in my office at the
usual hour this morning. I had many calls by public officers
through the day. Many other persons also called, and
among them was Senator Benton, who returned to the city
from the West last evening. I had a long and pleasant
conversation with him about the war and upon other topics.
He finally introduced the case of Lieut.-Col. Frémont, who
is under arrest at the instance of General Kearny. Mr.
Benton made a long statement of events which had occurred
in California in which he thought Col. Frémont had been
badly treated by his superior officers. He said that he had
written me a letter some time ago, stating that events had
occurred in California which the government ought to know,
and he insisted that in his approaching trial before a court
martial, all the events and facts to which he had alluded
should be investigated and exposed. This, he said, could not
be done under the present charges against Col. Frémont, and
that Col. Frémont would on Monday next apply in writing
to the Secretary of War, asking that other charges, some of
them having been published at the instance of officers of the
army, should be preferred against him, so as to make the
investigation a full and complete one. He said if this was
not done there would be four other court-martial, in order
to bring out the whole of the facts; one against General
Kearny, one against Capt. Emory, one against Capt. Turner,
and one against Capt. Cooke. He said if a full investigation
could not be had on his (Col. Frémont's) trial, he would file

charges against these officers, but that he did not wish to do so if the facts could come out incidentally on his own trial. Mr. Benton became excited and exhibited much deep feeling on the subject. He spoke of the bad treatment of Col. Frémont in this matter. I was careful to say as little as possible, but listened attentively to all Mr. Benton said. I finally said to him that I would act justly in the matter; that I regretted the whole affair but had no agency in producing the difficulty. He said he knew I would act justly. He left in a good humour towards me, as far as he expressed himself in relation to any action of mine in the matter.

Saturday, 23rd October, 1847. — The official despatches which had been received at the Department of State from Mr. Trist as late as the 28th ult., giving an account of his negotiations with the Mexican commissioners, were read by Mr. Buchanan. Mr. Trist has managed the negotiation very bunglingly and with no ability. He has done more. He has departed from his instructions so far as to invite proposals from the Mexican commissioners to be submitted to his government for its decision upon them, which can never be accepted by the United States. These proposals, if made and accepted, would require the United States to surrender to Mexico the country between the Nueces and the Rio Grande, now a part of the State of Texas, which he had ought to have known could never be acceded to. He departed from his instructions also in intimating to the Mexican commissioners that the United States might not insist upon the whole of California as indemnity, but might surrender its demands for a part of it. I expressed in strong and decided terms my disapprobation of his conduct. The Cabinet concurred with me in my opinions. I directed Mr. Buchanan to prepare a despatch expressing in strong terms my disapprobation, and to repeat his order of the 6th instant for his immediate recall.

Monday, 25th October, 1847. — At two o'clock P.M. I opened my office for the reception of company. Five or six persons came in as soon as the door was opened, and among them was John Randolph Benton, the son of Senator Benton. I received him pleasantly and kindly. In a manner somewhat excited he said to me that he wanted an appointment of lieutenant in the army, and asked me if he could get it. I told him in a mild tone that I could not promise to appoint him, that there were embarrassments in the way, which I commenced explaining to him. He interrupted me and in a manner still more excited than at first, he said he wished to know distinctly whether he was to be appointed or not. I told him that in the first place I knew of no vacancies, and that if there were, as a general rule I gave the preference to privates who were in the ranks in Mexico (some of whom had been wounded, and otherwise distinguished themselves, and all of whom had suffered great privation) when they were equally well qualified, over citizens who had remained at home, and had never been in the service. I told him that I observed this a general rule, but that there might be cases of exception to the rule. He rose to his feet, and was impertinent and still excited. As he was young, and on his father's account, I still spoke in a mild and kind tone, and told him to be patient, and that I would talk to his father and the Secretary of War on the subject. He said that his father would not urge his appointment, and that the Secretary of War had told him this morning that his application would be rejected. I told him I had seen the Secretary today, and that he had mentioned his case to me, but had not told me that he had so informed him. He left my office in quite a passion, and very rudely, swearing profanely as he went out of the door. In a loud and boisterous tone he used the exclamation as he passed out of the door, " By God! " he would do something, but I lost the remaining words which he uttered. As soon as he was gone one of the gentlemen, Mr. Cable of Massachusetts, asked me in his astonishment, if such occurrences were common in my office. I told him it was the first of the kind, I believed, which had occurred since I had been President. I enquired of those present, some of whom sat nearer the door than I did, what his last exclamation was, as I had not heard the latter part of it distinctly. Mr. Cable said he thought it was, " By God, I will have vengeance," or something to that effect. Mr. Arthur [10] of Baltimore, who was present, said he smelt liquor on his breath and thought he was drunk. All present expressed their amazement at his conduct. Col. Walker was present when he first came in, but left the office before he used the violent expression as he went out of the office. He thought he was drunk also. He gave evidence of his ill manners and impertinence, and I have no doubt is in all respects worthless.

I note this incident, 1st, because of its marked character, and 2nd, because I may hereafter incur the hostility of his family because his wishes have not been gratified. His brother-in-law, Jones, is also an applicant to me for office. I promoted Lieut. Col. Frémont, another brother-in-law. He is now under arrest, and today Col. Benton has addressed a letter to the Secretary of War making requests or demands in reference to his trial, some of which cannot be granted. I have always been upon good terms with Col. Benton, but he is a man of violent passions and I should not be surprised if he became my enemy because all his wishes in reference to his family and their appointments to offices are not gratified, and especially if I do not grant his wishes in reference to Col. Frémont's trial. I am resolved that Col. Frémont shall be tried as all other officers are tried, against whom charges are preferred. I will grant him no favours or privileges which I would not grant to any other officer, even though I should incur his displeasure and that of his friends by refusing to do so.

Tuesday, 26th October, 1847. — The Cabinet met at the usual hour today, all the members present. The principal

[10] T. S. Arthur, the future author of " Ten Nights in a Bar-Room," would naturally smell liquor on the breath of Senator Benton's impetuous son.

matter considered today was a letter addressed by Senator
Benton and his son-in-law, Mr. Jones, in which, as counsel for
Col. Frémont, they request that additional charges based
upon anonymous newspaper publications, may be preferred
against that officer, and that the place of trial may be
changed from Fortress Monroe to Washington. They state
also that his arrest was a surprise, as some of his witnesses
are in the army and navy in California. After full consideration an answer was agreed upon and the Secretary of
War was directed to prepare it. As the questions involved
in the application are some of them important, and as Senator Benton manifests much excitement on the subject, it was
resolved that the Cabinet would meet tomorrow to consider
the answer to be prepared by the Secretary of War. I know
of no reason why this case should produce more interest
or excitement than the trial of any other officer charged with
a military offense, and yet it is manifest that Senator Benton
is resolved to make it do so. I think he is pursuing a mistaken policy so far as Col. Frémont is concerned, but that is
an affair of which he must judge.[11] I will do my duty in the
case without favour or affection. In doing so I am sensible
that it will be very difficult to avoid giving offense to Senator Benton. Should such be the result, I shall have the con-
sciousness of having done my duty to the public and justice
to Col. Frémont, and more than this I cannot do to secure
the friendship of Col. Benton, or his support of my administration, or that of any one else.

Wednesday, 27th October, 1847. — A special meeting of
the Cabinet was held at eleven o'clock this morning, all the
members present, to consider the reply of the Secretary of
War to the letter of Senator Benton and his son-in-law, Mr.
Jones, in relation to Lieut.-Col. Frémont's case (see this
diary of yesterday). The Secretary of War read the letter

[11] Benton was very much mistaken indeed. If the charge against Frémont
had been confined to mutiny, he would have escaped any penalty. By
insisting that other charges be included, Benton laid the basis for a severe
reprimand to Frémont, and for his resignation from the service.

which he had prepared. It was carefully considered, and after undergoing some modifications was agreed to unanimously. No other subject was considered by the Cabinet.

Monday, 1st November, 1847. — After night Mr. Buchanan called, and complained that persons employed in the customs house at Philadelphia were personally abusive of him, and that if it was not checked his friends would apply to me, and that he would do so, to remove Col. Page, the collector. He stated that he did not object that they should be the friends of Mr. Dallas, but he thought that I should not permit a member of my Cabinet to be personally abused by persons holding office under my administration. I told him that I had never heard of it before, and it was certainly wrong. . . He alluded, in speaking of Mr. Dallas, to the rivalry between Mr. Dallas and himself for the next Presidency. I told Mr. Buchanan, in reference to that matter I must stand still and take no part between Democratic friends who might be aspirants for the Presidency, at least at present. Mr. Buchanan has of late had his mind very much fixed upon being a candidate for the Presidency, which, I fear, may embarrass my administration. . . When the Democratic national convention shall nominate a candidate for the Presidency, I will support the nominee, whoever he may be. Until that time I shall take no part between the Democratic aspirants.

Tuesday, 2nd November, 1847. — I am fifty-two years old today, this being my birthday. I have now passed through two-thirds of my Presidential term, and most heartily wish that the remaining third was over, for I am sincerely desirous to have the enjoyment of retirement in private life.

Thursday, 4th November, 1847. — After night Senator Douglas of Illinois called. I had a long conversation with him upon public affairs. He agreed with me in my full policy, except in relation to river and harbour improvements. He said, however, that he felt no great interest on the subject, and should oppose my views on that subject only by a silent vote.

Monday, 8th November, 1847. — I was in my office at the usual hour this morning. I transacted some of the current business which had accumulated on my table, and saw several public officers on business. In the course of the day Senator Dix of New York called. He informed me that he had brought his family to the city that he might select quarters and be settled before the meeting of Congress. I had a conversation with him about the Mexican war and other topics of public interest. He did not introduce the subject of the divisions and defeat of the Democracy of New York at the late election. If he had done so, I would have given him my opinion plainly, that Mr. John Van Buren, Cambreleng, Preston King, Rathbun, and those who acted with them in bolting from the regular nominations of the party and who attempted to agitate the slavery question, were wholly inexcusable, and were responsible for the defeat of the party. Senator Dix belongs to the same section of the party that the disorganizers referred to do. As he did not introduce the subject, I did not.

Tuesday, 9th November, 1847. — Mr. Buchanan spoke today in an unsettled tone, and said I must take one of two courses in my next message, *viz.,* to designate the part of the Mexican territory which we intended to hold as indemnity, or to occupy all Mexico by a largely increased force and subdue the country and promise protection to the inhabitants. He said he would express no opinion between these two plans, but after the despatches which were expected from the army were received, he would do so. I remarked that I thought our policy had been settled upon some time since, but, as the subject was not brought up as one that was still open, I would read what I had written on the subject, and I did so. My views as thus reduced to writing were in substance that we would continue the prosecution of the war with an increased force, hold all the country we had conquered or might conquer, and levy contributions upon the enemy to support the war, until a just peace was obtained; that we must have indemnity in territory, and that as a part indemnity the Californias and New Mexico should under no circumstances be restored to Mexico, but that they should henceforward be considered a part of the United States, and permanent territorial governments be established over them; and that if Mexico protracted the war, additional territory must be required as further indemnity. Mr. Buchanan seems to have changed his views upon the subject. Until recently he had expressed his opinion against acquiring any other territory than the Californias and New Mexico. He did not positively express a distinct opinion today; but it was pretty clearly to be inferred from what he did say that he was now for more territory; and that he would favour the policy of acquiring, in addition to the Californias and New Mexico, the Province of Tamaulipas and the country east of the Sierra Madre Mountains, and withdrawing our troops to that line. The Secretary of War expressed his dissent to this policy and approved the views I had reduced to writing and read. I did not propound a distinct question to the Cabinet on the subject. The Secretary of the Treasury said that it would prostrate the administration and be condemned by the country if we withdrew the army from the City of Mexico and the heart of the country which we now occupied, without making a satisfactory peace. The subject was discussed at considerable length. My opinions were unchanged. Mr. Buchanan's opinions have evidently undergone a change in the course of a few weeks, or rather he seems to be now in an unsettled state of mind. Since he has considered himself as a candidate for the Presidency it is probable he looks at the subject with different considerations in view from those which he entertained before that time.

Thursday, 11th November, 1847. — I transacted business in my office as usual today. At two o'clock P.M. I saw company. Several persons called. After night the Secretary of the Treasury, who had been invited by me to do so, called. I submitted to him the full draft of my message on the subject of the Mexican War, a part of which I had read to the Cabinet on the 9th instant (see this diary of that day). He agreed to it, suggesting some modifications, not important, which were made.

Saturday, 13th November, 1847. — At an early hour this morning I learned that official despatches from the army in Mexico had been received at the War Department by last evening's mail. Before breakfast I addressed a note to the Secretary of War, enquiring if such despatches had been received and expressing my surprise, if the fact was so, that they had not been communicated to me last night. Immediately after breakfast he called and brought voluminous despatches with him. He had not received my note. I expressed my surprise that they had not been sent to me last night as he knew I had been long anxiously waiting to receive them. He said he had not himself seen them until nine o'clock P.M. last night, having been prevented from doing so by company. They were the official accounts of the battles near Mexico. They were very voluminous, but in the course of the day I read them.

Monday, 15th November, 1847. — In pursuance of my summons of Saturday, the 13th *instant* (see this diary of that day) a special meeting of the Cabinet was held at eleven o'clock this day; all the members present. The subject for consideration was the proposition to impose an export duty on gold and silver exported from Mexico through the ports in our military occupation. Mr. Buchanan gave his opinion against levying such a duty, and gave his opinion at some length against it. Mr. Walker was in favour of levying the duty and assigned his reasons for his opinion. I then took the opinion separately of Messrs. Marcy, Mason, Johnson, and Clifford, each of whom was in favour of levying a duty, and each assigned his reasons for his opinion. I then decided that an order should be issued to our military and naval commanders directing the export duty to be levied. I directed also that an order should be issued directing all the internal revenues, as well as the import and export duties collected under the Mexican laws, to be also seized and appropriated to the use of our own army and navy; and directed the Secretary of the Treasury to prepare an order for my signature accordingly.

Saturday, 20th November, 1847. — The Cabinet met at the usual hour today; all the members present. I read to them the draft of my message to Congress which I had prepared, and invited any suggestion of any modification of it which any member of the Cabinet might think proper to make. One or two immaterial modifications were suggested and made. The paragraph in relation to the Mexican war which I had requested Mr. Buchanan to prepare on the 18th instant, and on receiving his draft on yesterday I had prepared a paragraph of my own, constituted the principal topics of discussion. The Cabinet all agreed that there should be a paragraph to the effect that the citizens of Mexico in favour of peace should be protected by our army in establishing a government able and willing to make a just peace, but, if we failed to obtain a peace by this means, the question was what I should state would be our policy. In Mr. Buchanan's draft he stated in that event that "we must fulfil that destiny which Providence may have in store for both countries." I thought this would be too indefinite and that it would be avoiding my constitutional responsibility. I preferred to state in substance that we should, in that event, take the measure of our indemnity into our own hands, and dictate our own terms to Mexico. Both my draft and Mr. Buchanan's draft were read and discussed at considerable length. Mr. Walker preferred Mr. Buchanan's draft. Mr. Clifford was not entirely satisfied with it or with mine. The other members of the Cabinet expressed no distinct opinion, but my impression was that they were inclined to favor Mr. Buchanan's draft. No final

decision was made. After the Cabinet retired I prepared
a third draft of the paragraph, and after night sent for Mr.
Clifford and consulted with him on the subject. I made
some further modifications, which Mr. Clifford approved.
This paragraph constituted a small but important part of
my message.

CHAPTER X

Nov. 22, 1847 — May 16, 1848

BUCHANAN AND THE PRESIDENTIAL NOMINATION — QUARRELS OF SCOTT, PILLOW, AND WORTH — TRIST'S NEGOTIATIONS WITH MEXICO — THE FRÉMONT COURT-MARTIAL — TERMS OF PEACE — DEATH OF J. Q. ADAMS — RATIFICATION OF THE TREATY OF GUADELOUPE-HIDALGO

Monday, 22nd November, 1847. — I received a letter marked Private, late this evening, from Senator Benton, stating that he would decline to serve as chairman of the committee on military affairs at the next session of the Senate, because of his opinion of the conduct of Gov. Marcy, the Secretary of War, in relation to the trial of Lieut-Col. Frémont, now pending in this city. He stated that he gave me this information to avoid misapprehension as to the motive of his course. It is a singular communication, and I will preserve it.[1] I think it probable that Col. Benton intends to break with the administration, and will make a quarrel with the Secretary of War the ostensible ground for doing so. I am satisfied that he has no just cause of complaint against the Secretary of War on account of his conduct in the Frémont trial.

Sunday, 28th November, 1847. — In the evening Daniel Graham, esquire, called and brought with him William

---

[1] Benton charges in his *Thirty Years' View* (II, 715–719) that Marcy had altered the original charges against Frémont, inserting new and outrageous charges; and for this reason Benton refused to have anything more to do with Marcy.

Bass, the son of John M. Bass, esquire, of Nashville, and the grandson of the late Felix Grundy.[2] The boy stated that in consequence of a difficulty in which he had become involved at the Catholic college at Emmetsburg, in Maryland, where his father had sent him a few weeks ago, he had left the institution, and having no other friends near he had come to Washington. His story was a reasonable one, and knowing all his family, I invited him to remain with me until it was determined what it was best for him to do. He agreed to do so. He had nothing with him except the clothes on his person. I felt a sympathy for him, and knowing his father and mother and all his family, I will take care of him until his father can be written to. Mr. Graham promised to write to him.

Thursday, 2d December, 1847. — After night I submitted confidentially to Senator Douglas of Illinois that part of my message relating to the Mexican War. He read some other passages also. He approved the message.

Friday, 3rd December, 1847. — Many members of Congress called today, and I was much occupied in my office. The two clerks, Mr. Williams and Mr. Whitthorne, were engaged in making two fair copies of my message, to be transmitted to the two Houses of Congress. After night I submitted to the inspection of Senator Turney of Tennessee, and to Mr. Ritchie, editor of the *Union,* that part of my message relating to Mexico and the Mexican war. It was the first time Mr. Ritchie had seen any part of it, or knew what it would contain. The truth is that the old gentleman's passion to put everything he learns into his newspaper is so great that I did not think it prudent to entrust its contents to him at an earlier period.

Saturday, 4th December, 1847. — All the members of the Cabinet were present at the usual hour. I submitted to them some modifications of my message, which I had made since it was read to them on a former day, the most

[2] Polk had studied law in the office of Judge Felix Grundy.

material of which consisted in a modification of a paragraph
in relation to Mexico. As I had originally prepared it I had
declared that if Mexico continued to protract the war and
involved us in largely increased expenditures, that in addition to New Mexico and the Californias, it would become
a grave question whether territorial governments should
not be established over other of the Mexican provinces in
addition to these. The modification of this paragraph
which I suggested was that if Mexico continued the contest,
etc., then what further provision it would become necessary
to make and what final disposition it would be proper to
make of them, must depend on the future progress of the
war and the course which Mexico may think proper hereafter to pursue. My object in suggesting the modification
was that I might not be embarrassed in the future negotiations with Mexico. The Secretaries of State and the Treasury preferred the paragraph as it originally stood. The
other four members of the Cabinet preferred the modification proposed, and it was made.

Thursday, 9th December, 1847.—About four o'clock
P.M. I learned that Mr. Walker, the Secretary of the Treasury, had been taken suddenly ill and had fallen down in the
Treasury building. He was attended by his physician to
his own house. I appointed McClintock Young, his chief
clerk, to perform the duties of Secretary of the Treasury *ad
interim.*

Saturday, 11*th December,* 1847.—Several members of
Congress called this morning. The Cabinet met at the
usual hour, all the members present except the Secretary
of the Treasury, who is confined at his house by severe
indisposition, brought on undoubtedly by severe labour and
mental exertion. The subject of the Mexican war and our
future action in reference to it were considered, but no
action was taken. I informed the Cabinet that I had received information that General Scott and Mr. Trist had,
before the City of Mexico was taken, entered into an agree-

ment to pay to Santa Anna a million of dollars as secret money if he would agree to make a treaty of peace. I expressed in the strongest terms my condemnation of such conduct. Mr. Mason and Mr. Marcy said they had seen a statement to the same effect in a New Orleans paper. Mr. Buchanan expressed his indignation at such conduct in strong terms, and said if it was true he would advise that General Scott should be immediately recalled. I fully concurred with him in opinion. It was suggested that General Shields and General Quitman were expected here in a few days, and that it would be prudent to delay action until we could obtain authentic information from them.

Tuesday, 21st December, 1847.— Several members of Congress called this morning. The Cabinet met at the usual hour, all the members present except the Secretary of the Treasury. Mr. Buchanan read to the Cabinet a copy of the letter which he had addressed to Mr. Trist condemning in strong terms the reported negotiations or correspondence between General Scott and Mr. Trist on the one part and General Santa Anna on the other. He read also the copy of a private letter to Mr. Trist on the same subject, which he said he had addressed to him. The subject of the Mexican War and the policy proper to be pursued in its further prosecution was considered, but nothing definitely decided.

Thursday, 23rd December, 1847.— I received company as usual this morning. Several members of Congress and many other persons called. I disposed of business on my table. After the company had retired I sent for Mr. Buchanan. He called, and I informed him that I learned that an anonymous letter purporting to have been written in this city had appeared in the New York *Herald,*[3] but which I had not read, to the effect that by my agency the Tennessee State convention, which is to meet at Nashville on the 8th of January next, would nominate General Cass for the

[3] This letter, signed " Tony Lumpkin," appeared in the New York *Herald* of December 21, 1847.

Presidency, and that my object was to produce confusion among the Democratic aspirants, with a view ultimately to obtain the nomination myself. I told him that the whole story was false, that I had written to no one in Tennessee on the subject, and that I thought it proper to say to him that the story was false. He asked me if I had written to General Cass in the last recess of Congress, requesting him to be chairman of the military committee of the Senate. I promptly replied that I had not written to him on that or any other subject. He said he had read the letter in the *Herald,* and such was the statement made by the writer. I told him it was false. He then said that it was generally understood among the members of Congress that I was favourable to General Cass's nomination, at which he could not complain. I replied with some emphasis that I had never given the slightest indication for any one of the Democratic party as my successor, and repeated two or three times that he gave me the first intimation to that effect that I had ever heard. I told him frankly that I had not taken and should not take any part in the selection by the Democratic party of a candidate to succeed me; that when the Democratic national convention should make a nomination, I would be for the nominee, be he whom he might. . . Mr. Buchanan no doubt considers himself a candidate for the nomination, and is nervous and exhibits a degree of weakness on the subject that is almost incredible. My object in holding the conversation with him today was, first, to tell him that the letter published in the *Herald* was false, and secondly, that I should act a neutral part and have no agency in selecting the candidate of the Democracy to succeed me. He seemed to be in a gloomy mood, and, judging from his manner, left me dissatisfied. If this be so, I shall regret it, but shall not change my determination. While I am President I cannot become the partisan of Mr. Buchanan or anyone else.

Tuesday, 28th December, 1847. — Shortly after the

Cabinet met Brigadier-General Shields of the army called. I invited him into my office where the Cabinet were. He remained an hour or more, and conversed freely about our military operations in Mexico, and our future policy in conducting the war. Some minor subjects were considered and disposed of by the Cabinet, but nothing worthy of special notice occurred. After the Cabinet retired I found General Shields in my private secretary's office in conversation with him. Among other things General Shields voluntarily spoke of General Pillow, and accorded to him high merit as an officer. . . He spoke of the story in the newspapers of the alleged council of war held at Puebla, and the proposition to bribe Santa Anna. He said that he had not seen the newspaper publication. I repeated to him, as well as I could, its substance. He said it was not true that any consultation had been held about a proposition to bribe. He said there was a confidential conference at General Scott's headquarters, not about bribing, but whether it would be proper, if it was ascertained that a satisfactory treaty could be obtained, to pay a part of the consideration for a cession of territory in advance of the ratification of such a treaty. He repeated that the idea of bribery was not suggested or considered, but the question was that stated by him, and whether, if deemed proper, there was any legal authority to apply any part of the public money in that way. He did not mention the names of the officers present at this council, but said Mr. Trist was not present. . . I expressed to him my disapprobation of Mr. Trist's conduct in intimating to the Mexican commissioners that if they would submit a proposition to make the Nueces the boundary, he would transmit it to his government for consideration. I did not proceed to detail to him the many other objections which I had to his [Mr. Trist's] conduct since he has been in Mexico. They are numerous. I informed him that he had been recalled.

Thursday, 30th December, 1847. — I received company

as usual this morning.   At twelve o'clock I closed my office.
Mr. Buchanan sent over to me despatches which he had
received by last night's mail from Mr. Trist.   He had re-
ceived his letter of recall, and is manifestly displeased at it.
The Secretary of War called and handed to me despatches
which he had received by last night's mail from General Scott.   Among them were charges preferred by General
Scott against Major General Pillow, Brevet Major General
Worth, and Brevet Col. Duncan of the United States army.
He left the despatches with me and I read them carefully.
I deplore the unfortunate collisions which have arisen between the general officers in Mexico, as they must prove
highly prejudicial to the public service.   They have been
produced, as I have every reason to believe, more by the
vanity and tyrannical temper of General Scott, and his want
of prudence and common sense, than from any other cause.[4]
I read his despatches with sincere regret.   The officers
whom he arraigns upon charges, and for whose trial he demands a court-martial, have each of them been presented in
General Scott's own official reports as having acted a gallant
and praiseworthy part in all the late battles in Mexico.   The
whole difficulty has grown out of letters written from the
army and published in the newspapers of the United States,

[4] Polk is again unjust to Scott. G. J. Pillow, now second in command in
the army, was a political general, devoid of real military ability, but keenly
ambitious for the first place and cherishing dreams even of the Presidency.
W. J. Worth was an abler man, but jealous of Scott. Pillow and Scott
indulged in a systematic campaign of detraction. The reports of the battles
of Contreras and Chapultepec written by Pillow represented Scott as incompetent and negligible, and Worth supported the same view, referring to
Scott in terms of contempt. Pillow wrote or inspired a letter signed by
"Leonidas," which he had inserted in the New Orleans *Delta* of Sept. 10,
1847, and which praised himself to the skies and belittled Scott. Another
newspaper letter appeared in the United States attempting to show that Worth
had saved Scott from gross blunders in the approach to the capital. Scott
rightly resented these improper letters, and in general orders of Nov. 12
he dealt with them in such a way as to prevent a repetition of the offence.
Col. James Duncan and Worth then assumed a frankly defiant attitude
toward Scott, and the commander-in-chief brought formal charges against
them and Pillow. The two generals retaliated by charges against Scott
and appealed to Washington, where Polk was ready to give ear to them.

in which General Scott is not made the exclusive hero of the war.

Friday, 31st December, 1847. — Mr. Davis read me a short passage from a letter which he had received on yesterday from General Twiggs of the army in Mexico, expressing the opinion that if a commissioner with power to treat was now in Mexico a treaty might be concluded. This led to a conversation of some length in relation to the state of affairs in Mexico. Both Mr. Davis and General Cass deplored the collisions which had arisen between the general officers of our army in Mexico, both condemned in strong terms the published general order of General Scott, which was the immediate precursor, if not the cause, of the arrest of Generals Pillow and Worth and Col. Duncan; and both expressed the opinion in strong and decided terms that General Scott should be immediately recalled from the command of the army in Mexico. . . A most embarrassing state of things exists in the army, all produced by General Scott's bad temper, dictatorial spirit, and extreme jealousy lest any other general officer should acquire more fame in the army than himself. The arrests which have taken place have grown out of no official misconduct of the officers arrested, in the line of their duty, but out of letters written in the army and published in the newspapers of the United States, in which General Scott was not made the sole hero of the battles which have been fought.

This was reception evening, but a wet night, and very dark and but few persons attended.

Saturday, 1st January, 1848. — The Secretary of War called this morning and held a further conversation with me in relation to the difficulties which have grown up among the general officers of the army in Mexico. He said he had reflected on the subject since his conversation with me on yesterday. He now thought that we would be obliged to supersede General Scott in the command, and devolve the command on General Butler. He thought that if Pillow,

Worth, and Duncan were ordered to the United States for trial, we might have to order almost half the other officers of the army home with them as witnesses. His opinion, therefore, was that the trials must take place in Mexico. I told him that among the papers left with me by him on yesterday was one from General Worth, preferring grave charges against General Scott, and appealing to the President to take the proper orders in the case, and I asked him what was to be done with it. Before we concluded the conversation, I was notified by a servant that company had begun to assemble in the parlour below stairs. . .

After night the Postmaster-General and the Attorney-General called, having been requested to do so by me. I consulted them freely upon the subject of the difficulties of the army in Mexico, stated the substance of the despatches which had been received; the arrest of Generals Pillow and Worth and Col. Duncan; and the charges preferred by General Worth against General Scott. I stated, also, the consultations I had held with the Secretary of War and with Senators Davis of Mississippi and Cass of Michigan (see this diary of yesterday) and after full consideration of the whole subject, they were of opinion that it was indispensable for the good of the service that General Scott should be superseded in the command of the army and that General Butler should be placed in command.

Sunday, 2nd January, 1848.—. . . At seven o'clock P.M. Mr. Buchanan called. I had a full conversation with him on the subject [of General Scott]. He agreed that General Scott should be recalled, that General Butler should be placed in command, and that the military trials should take place at Vera Cruz, as had been suggested.[5] He was not de-

---

[5] The administration would have done well to treat Scott with generosity. Though he had often clashed with it, he had performed great services to the country; and in his controversy with Pillow and Worth he was essentially right. But there was nothing generous about the administration. Justin H. Smith narrates succinctly the action taken by Polk's government. " The confines of mediocrity hemmed it in. Pillow and Duncan were therefore by its

cided as to the propriety of investing General Butler with
power to conclude a treaty. I conversed with him as to the
terms to which we should agree. He at first declared that
we should secure Tamaulipas and all the country east of the
Sierra Mountains. I expressed a doubt as to the policy or
practicability of obtaining a country containing so large
a number of the Mexican population; and reminded Mr.
Buchanan that his original opinion had been against acquiring any territory south of New Mexico. This he admitted
and added that he had been opposed to the campaign
of our army to Vera Cruz and the City of Mexico. I told
him that campaign was my own measure and that I remembered his opposition to it. He said, however, that this campaign had been carried out against his opinion, that we had
spent much money and shed much blood since Mr. Trist's
instructions were given to him in April last, and that he
would not now be willing to agree to the terms then proposed. I replied that I would not be willing to agree to
those terms after all that had occurred since that time.
I suggested that we might accede to a cession of New Mexico, the two Californias, and the passage across the Isthmus
of Tehuantepec, paying for them a much less sum than Mr.
Trist had been authorized to offer, and that we should in
addition secure the port of Tampico. I told him I would
be glad to acquire all the country he suggested, but that I
apprehended that would not be practicable after the terms
which Mr. Trist had already offered.

Monday, 3rd January, 1848. — Saw company until

---

orders relieved of arrest; Worth was not only relieved, but assigned to duty
according to his highest brevet rank; and 'in view of the present state of
things in the army,' chiefly or entirely caused by Polk's agent and Marcy's
friend, Scott was deposed. He had performed his task, said Robert E. Lee,
and now was 'turned out as an old horse to die.' April 22, 1848, amidst the
lamentations, cheers, and blessings of the army as a whole — trembling himself with emotion — he took his leave, and Major-General Butler, who was
a Democrat and looked well on a horse, bore sway at headquarters." This
was Gen. W. O. Butler, who had fought well at Monterey and had taken
reinforcements to Scott.

twelve o'clock today.   Many persons, members of Congress and others, called.   I convened a special meeting of the Cabinet at one o'clock P.M. today; all the members attended except the Secretary of the Navy, who is absent from the city on a visit to Virginia.   The subject submitted for consideration was the unfortunate collision among the general offices of the army in Mexico, and the steps proper to be taken.   These difficulties have been already stated (see this diary for the last three or four days) from which it appears that General Scott has arrested Generals Pillow and Worth and Col. Duncan, and that General Worth has preferred charges against General Scott.   After a full discussion the Cabinet were unanimous that General Scott should be superseded in the command of the army.   Upon the question whether the command should devolve upon Major General Butler, who is next in rank now with the army; or whether General Taylor, who is now in the United States on leave of absence for six months, shall have the option of proceeding to the City of Mexico and taking command, there was division of opinion and some discussion.   Mr. Buchanan, Mr. Walker, Mr. Marcy, and Mr. Johnson, though each of them expressed themselves with some hesitancy and doubt, were in favour of sending General Taylor to take command, if he was willing to go.   Mr. Clifford expressed his opinion strongly against it, and was in favour of placing General Butler in command.   My opinion was that General Butler should take command, and I so expressed myself, but remarked that I would postpone a final decision until to-morrow.   After full discussion it was decided that the charges preferred by General Scott against General Worth were not such as to require a court-martial for his trial, and it was unanimously decided that General Worth should be released from arrest and that a court of inquiry should be instituted to examine and report upon the cases of General Scott's charges against General Worth and General Worth's charges against General Scott.   It was also finally agreed that a court-martial must be appointed to try the charges preferred against General Pillow and Col. Duncan. Under the law, it is my duty to appoint these courts. In consideration of the fact that almost every officer in Mexico has taken sides, or had his feelings excited, in the quarrel between the general officers, it was decided, first, that it would be difficult to procure an unbiased court composed of the officers of the army in Mexico, and therefore it was determined that the court should be composed of officers now in the United States, who had not been involved in the feuds or quarrels in the camp, and from General Taylor's column of the army.

Tuesday, 4th January, 1848. —. . . The Secretary of War read a letter which he had received, dated at Vera Cruz on the 16th *ult.,* stating that the British courier had just arrived at that place from the City of Mexico without bringing down any letters, a most unusual thing; and that the writer (Col. Wilson) had learned confidentially from the courier that negotiations had been renewed by Mr. Trist with the Mexican commissioners recently appointed. This information is most surprising. Mr. Trist has acknowledged the receipt of his letter of recall, and he possesses no diplomatic powers. He is acting, no doubt, upon General Scott's advice. He has become the perfect tool of Scott. He is, in this measure, defying the authority of his Government. His conduct in the former negotiations has been disapproved. He is, no doubt, offended because it has been disapproved, and because of his recall. He seems to have entered into all Scott's hatred of the administration, and to be lending himself to all Scott's evil purposes. He may, I fear, greatly embarrass the Government.[6]

[6] Polk, who was misinformed by Pillow, and who knew almost nothing of the true state of affairs in Mexico, had on Oct. 4, 1847, ordered the recall of Trist as peace commissioner. When he heard that Trist had been willing to consider the possibility of giving up the territory between the Nueces and Rio Grande, he followed the recall with a reprimand and a repetition of his orders. Trist received both despatches on the same day, Nov. 16. He at once

Wednesday, 5th January, 1848. — Saw company as usual
this morning.   Many persons called.   The Secretary of
War called, and we agreed upon the court-martial to be
ordered for the trial of the charges preferred by General
Scott against General Pillow and Col. Duncan; and upon
the court of inquiry to be organized to examine and report
upon the charges preferred by General Worth against General Scott; and that the same court should inquire into
General Scott's complaint against General Worth.   It was
agreed also that the castle at Perote should be the place
of these trials.   The Secretary of State called and informed
me confidentially that he had been shown a letter from Mr.
Trist to his wife, which contained a post-script in cipher
which he had requested her to show to Mr. Buchanan in
confidence, the substance of which was, that on the day
he wrote (4th December) at twelve o'clock, he would open
negotiations with the Mexican commissioners, and would
offer to agree to a treaty with them upon the ultimatum which
he was authorized to propose in April last, taking the
parallel of 32° from the Rio Grande as the boundary, and
that he would offer to pay them $15,000,000 in addition

---

prepared to pack up and leave for the United States, hoping he could give the
President some of the information which he obviously lacked.   But there
was no escort available till Dec. 4, and meanwhile the Mexican government
appointed peace commissioners and pressed for the drafting of a treaty.
If Trist broke off his contacts with Pena and went home, the peace party
in Mexico would be overthrown, and the war renewed.   Under the circumstances, Trist was in a painful dilemma.   He was a private citizen, who had
not merely been discharged from his special mission but placed under reprimand.   Yet he knew from Buchanan's despatches that the United States
wanted peace, and that Polk totally misapprehended the situation.   The head
of the Mexican government, Pena, appealed eloquently to him to act.   The
British *chargé*, Edward Thornton, supported these appeals.   Gen. Scott favored
negotiations and probably told Trist that if he made a treaty, it would be
accepted by the United States.   Yet Trist knew that if he made a treaty and the
government repudiated it, he might be called a traitor and at the very least
dealt with harshly under the Logan Act.   It is to his credit that he made
the right decision — a noble decision.   Accepting all the grave risks of his
act, he proceeded to continue the negotiations and to draft a treaty which
would end the war between the two nations.   In the end Polk had to admit,
tacitly if not explicitly, that he had acted aright.

to the $3,000,000 appropriated by Congress at the last session for this cession of territory. His conduct astonishes both the Secretary of State and myself. He has acknowledged the receipt of his letter of recall and has no power to treat. I fear he may greatly embarrass the Government.

Sunday, 9th January, 1848. — Before church hour this morning the Secretary of War called. . . He acquiesced in the propriety of having a court of inquiry instead of a court-martial in the cases of General Pillow, General Scott, and Lieut.-Col. Duncan, and agreed, also, that while the investigation by the court of inquiry was going on, General Pillow and Col. Duncan should be released from arrest. I directed him to prepare, at his earliest convenience, the necessary orders and despatches to carry out this decision and the decision made on other points on yesterday.

Wednesday, 12th January, 1848. — After night Senator Rusk of Texas called and held a long conversation with me about the Mexican War, and gave me many facts within his knowledge of the Mexican character and feelings, and his views of our future policy. He seemed to have two objects in view, 1st, that I should not commit myself, further than I have done in my messages, against acquiring the whole of Mexico; and 2d, to induce me to consent to be a candidate for reëlection, expressing the opinion that I was the strongest man in my party and that they could not unite on any other.

Thursday, 13th January, 1848. — I transacted business with public officers and disposed of much business on my table. Mr. Conrad F. Jackson of Pennsylvania, a bearer of despatches to the army in Mexico, left Washington tonight. He bore the despatches superseding General Scott and placing General Butler in command of the army; and also the order directing the court of inquiry in the cases of Generals Scott, Pillow, and Col. Duncan. I learn that my message sent to the House of Representatives on yesterday, in answer to their resolution of the 4th instant, in which

message I declined to communicate the instructions to Mr.
Slidell as Minister to Mexico, which the House had requested, gave rise to excited discussion, the Federal members denying my right to withhold the information called
for.

Saturday, 15th January, 1848.— I saw several persons
who called this morning. The Cabinet met at the usual
hour; all the members present except the Secretary of the
Treasury, who is still confined to his house by indisposition.
I brought before the Cabinet the future operations of the
army in Mexico, and the terms of peace to which we ought
now to accede. I had stated that from present indications
Congress would probably either refuse to increase the army,
as I had recommended, or postpone it to a late period of the
session, and that we ought to decide upon our future operations with a view to the forces now in the field; when the
messenger from the State Department brought to Buchanan
his mail containing a very long despatch from Mr. Trist.
It was dated on the 6th of December last, and is the most
extraordinary document I have ever heard from a diplomatic representative. Though he had in a previous despatch acknowledged the receipt of his letter of recall from
the Secretary of State, he announced that he had re-opened
negotiations with the Mexican authorities and had resolved
to conclude a treaty with them. His despatch is arrogant,
impudent, and very insulting to his government, and even
personally offensive to the President. He admits he is acting without authority and in violation of the positive order
recalling him. It is manifest to me that he has become the
tool of General Scott and his menial instrument, and that
the paper was written at Scott's instance and dictation. I
have never in my life felt so indignant, and the whole Cabinet expressed themselves as I felt. I told Mr. Buchanan
that the paper was so insulting and contemptibly base, that
it required no lengthy answer, but that it did require a short,
but stern and decided rebuke, and directed him to prepare

such a reply. I directed the Secretary of War to write at once to Major-General Butler, directing him, if Mr. Trist was still with the Headquarters of the army, to order him off, and to inform the authorities of Mexico that he had no authority to treat. If there was any legal provision for his punishment he ought to be severely handled. He has acted worse than any man in the public employ whom I have ever known. His despatch proves that he is destitute of honour or principle, and that he has proved himself to be a very base man. I was deceived in him. I had but little personal knowledge of him, but could not have believed it possible that any man would have acted so basely as he has done.

Wednesday, 19th January, 1848. — The board of managers of the American Colonization Society, accompanied by the Hon. Mr. Kaufman of Texas, called and paid their respects tonight. There were about twenty persons who called. Mrs. Polk and myself, having been previously notified that they would call, received them in the parlour. In the general conversation which occurred it was suggested that the United States should recognize the independence of the government of Liberia, and my opinion was asked. I gave the proposition no countenance, but avoided engaging in a discussion on the subject.

Sunday, 23rd January, 1848. — Mrs. Polk and myself attended the first Presbyterian church today. After night Senators Cass and Sevier called at my request. . . I informed them of Mr. Trist's most reprehensible conduct in Mexico, and of his refusal to return after his recall. They advised that I should at once give an order to General Butler, now commanding the army in Mexico, to send him out of Mexico, and to inform the Mexican Government that he had been recalled. They concurred with me that his conduct was not only insubordinate but infamous, and that if there was any law to punish him he should be punished. They agreed also that if after his recall he went on to negotiate a treaty within his instructions given to him in April

last, that it would present a question of great responsibility
and embarrassment whether I should send it to the Senate
for ratification or not.   I inferred from what Mr. Sevier
said that he thought I would be bound to do so.   Mr. Cass
said it would be time enough to decide that question, if such
a treaty was made, when it was presented to me for my consideration.   I told them that after the blood which had been
shed and the money which had been expended since the date
of Trist's instructions in April last, that if it was now an
open question I would not now approve the terms of the
treaty which I then authorized.

Saturday, 29th January, 1848. — After night Senators
Bagby of Alabama and Turney of Tennessee called.   They
said they came to urge me not to commit myself irrevo-
cably against serving a second term in the Presidential
office if the party should find it to be necessary to renominate me, as they believed they would, for a second term.   I
told them that my decision had been long since made, and
had been often declared, that I would voluntarily retire
at the close of my present term, and that this decision I
could not change.   I assured them that I had no desire
to continue beyond the present term, and that I looked
forward to the period of my retirement with sincere pleasure.   They said they had no doubt of that, but that the
condition of the country was such, and the divisions among
the Democratic party, as between the present aspirants
for the nomination, that it might become indispensible
to renominate me as the only means of restoring harmony, and of preserving harmony in the next election,
and that it might become my duty to yield.   They said all
they wished me to do was to cease making the declaration,
as I was in the habit of doing to all who conversed with me
on the subject, that I would under no circumstances consent
to be a candidate for reëlection.   They urged that when the
Democratic National Convention met at Baltimore they
might be compelled to renominate me without consulting my

wishes, and in that case it would be my solemn duty to yield
to their wishes. They urged also the condition of the country being engaged in a foreign war, and their conviction that
I would be the strongest man of the party. I still adhered
to my often expressed determination to retire at the close
of my present term. A few days ago Senator Rusk of Texas
called and held a similar conversation with me. Many
members of Congress have done the same thing during the
present session. To all of them I have given the same answer, and repeated my sincere desire to retire and my fixed
purpose to do so.

Friday, 4th February, 1848. — I closed my doors at
twelve o'clock. Shortly afterwards, I was informed by my
porter that the Hon. Henry Clay of Kentucky, who was the
opposing candidate for the Presidency when I was chosen,
had called to see me, and that he was in the parlour below
stairs. I proceeded at once to the parlour and received him
with all the politeness and courtesy of which I was master. I
had a pleasant conversation with him. He apologized for
not having called on me earlier. He had been in the city several weeks, but had been very much occupied by his friends.
He said he entertained no feelings towards me of an unkind
character. I at once replied that I entertained none such
towards him, and that I was glad to see him, and added that
there was no citizen of the United States whom I would be
more gratified to see in my parlour than himself. Mrs.
Polk, for whom he had also enquired, came into the parlour. Mr. Clay continued and intimated that differences in
political opinion had separated us, and although he had no
feelings which would have prevented him from calling, he
was not certain how I might feel, until he saw a common personal friend (Judge Catron) on yesterday, and after conversing with him he had determined to call very soon. I
repeated that I was gratified that he had done so. He continued the pleasant conversation with Mrs. Polk and myself, and after remaining near half an hour he left. As he

was leaving he remarked to Mrs. Polk in a very pleasant manner that he would visit her drawing-room soon, that he had heard a general approbation expressed of her administration, but that he believed there was some difference of opinion about her husband's administration. She replied pleasantly that she was happy to hear from him that her administration was approved and added, if a political opponent of my husband is to succeed him I have always said I prefer you, Mr. Clay, and in that event I shall be most happy to surrender the White House to you. There was a hearty laugh, and he left in an excellent humour.

Saturday, 5th February, 1848. — The Cabinet met at the usual hour, all the members present except the Secretary of the Treasury. . . Mr. Buchanan inquired what the finding and sentence of the general court-martial in the case of Lieut.-Col. J. C. Frémont was. I turned to the record and read the finding and the sentence. The court find him guilty of all the charges and specifications preferred against him, and sentence him to be dismissed the service. A majority of the court, including the President of the court, recommended him to the executive clemency. I informed the Cabinet that I would desire to have their advice as to my action on the case, but would not ask that it should be formally given to-day; but, if any of them were prepared with any suggestions or opinions, that I would be pleased to hear them. Mr. Buchanan remarked that though he did not doubt the correctness of the finding of the court, he would dislike to see him dismissed the service altogether, under all the circumstances of the case, as far as he could understand them without having read the testimony. The other members of the Cabinet, except the Secretary of War, expressed similar opinions. The Secretary thought it would not do to disapprove the finding and sentence, but intimated that I might approve both, and then, if I thought it right, I might pardon him. A legal question arose and was discussed, whether I had the power to mitigate the sentence of dismissal from the service, and the punishment of suspension from rank and command for a specified term of time. The point was discussed, and was considered a doubtful question.

Monday, 7th February, 1848. — I received letters from the City of Mexico last night dated as late as the 10th *ult.,* but they contained no information in relation to the rumoured negotiations between Mr. Trist and the Mexican Government. . . It is most strange that neither General Scott nor Trist has written a line to the government by the train that left Mexico on the 13th of January, and which brought these private letters. That they did not write was undoubtedly from design. Mr. Trist after the receipt of his recall is acting in violation of his orders and in open defiance of the government. That there is a conspiracy between Scott and himself to put the government at defiance and make a treaty of some sort, I have but little doubt. A few days more will, I trust, develop what they have been doing.

Saturday, 12th February, 1848. — The Cabinet met at the usual hour; all the members present except the Secretary of the Treasury, who is confined at his house by indisposition. The case of Lieut.-Col. Frémont, who has been recently tried by a court-martial and sentenced "to be dismissed the service," was the subject of consideration today. A part of the proceedings were read. The Cabinet all advised that he should not be dismissed, but there was much difficulty in arriving at a satisfactory conclusion whether, in remitting the sentence of the court, I should approve or disapprove the finding of the court. He had been found guilty of, 1st, mutiny, 2nd, disobedience of orders, and 3rd, of conduct prejudicial to the public service. I had doubts, and so had the Cabinet, whether the facts as proved amounted to the legal definition of mutiny. That he had been guilty of disobedience of orders all agreed. After much discussion a decision of the case was postponed, but as it was absolutely necessary to decide it soon, I requested the Cabinet to meet at my office at eight o'clock tomorrow night.

Sunday, 13th February, 1848. — In pursuance of the understanding on yesterday, a special meeting of the Cabinet took place at eight o'clock this evening; all the members present except the Secretary of the Treasury, who is confined to his house by indisposition. The case of Lieut.-Col. Frémont was resumed. The Attorney-General read from many authorities which he had collected to show what acts constituted mutiny. The Secretary of War also read some authorities on the same subject. The Secretary of the (?) returned to his office and brought an authority which he had examined. Mr. Buchanan and Mr. Clifford were clear that the facts proved in this case were not mutiny. The Secretary of War doubted whether some of the specifications upon which Lieut.-Col. Frémont had been convicted amounted to "mutiny." Mr. Johnson and Mr. Mason inclined to the opinion that they did not amount to mutiny. All agreed that he had been guilty of disobedience of orders; and conduct to the prejudice of good order and military discipline. There were, however, mitigating circumstances in the case. Mr. Buchanan and Mr. Clifford advised that I should disapprove the sentence of dismissal from the service upon the ground that it was too severe. Mr. Marcy, Mr. Mason, and Mr. Johnson advised that I should approve the sentence and remit the penalty. Some sharp remarks were made, in the course of the discussion, between Mr. Buchanan and Mr. Marcy. In speaking of General Kearny, who preferred the charges, Mr. Buchanan used the word pusillanimity as applied to him; if he believed he had the authority, he yielded it to Commodore Stockton and did not enforce it. To this Mr. Marcy took exception and said that General Kearny had no forces to command obedience to his orders and had acted with great forbearance and propriety. After hearing the discussion I gave my opinion. It was that I was not satisfied that the proof in the case constituted "mutiny," that I thought the proof established disobedience of orders and conduct to the prejudice of good order and military discipline; and that I ought to approve the sentence, but that under all the circumstances of the case and in consideration of the recommendation of a majority of the court, I ought to remit the penalty and restore Lieut.-Col. Frémont to duty.

Wednesday, 16th February, 1848. — I copied my decision in the blank pages attached to the record of proceedings of the court-martial in the case of Lieut.-Col. Frémont, and the Secretary of War being confined to his house by indisposition, I sent for the Secretary of the Navy and Lieut.-Col. Cooper, Assistant Adjutant-General, and read it to them. I then sent for Mr. Campbell, the chief clerk of the War Department, and delivered it to him with directions to deliver it to the Adjutant-General to have my decision carried into effect. The decision in this case has been a painful and a responsible duty. I have performed it with the best lights before me, and am satisfied with what I have done. My decision is appended to the record of proceedings of the court-martial and it will speak for itself.[7]

Thursday, 17th February, 1848. — About twelve o'clock Madame Iturbide, the widow of the former Emperor of Mexico of that name, called. I saw her in the parlour. She was accompanied by Miss White, the niece of the late Mrs. General Van Ness of this city. Madame Iturbide did not speak English, and Miss White interpreted for her. Her business was to see me on the subject of her pension from the Mexican Government, which had been granted to her on the death of her husband, and of which, in consequence of the existing war, she had been deprived. Her object was to have it reserved and paid to her out of the military contributions levied by our forces in Mexico.[8]

[7] Polk acted in the Frémont case with the same narrow legal rectitude and the same lack of any large generosity with which he acted toward Scott and Trist. The real blame for Frémont's "insubordination" rested upon the government in Washington, which had sent conflicting orders to the coast. Frémont indignantly resigned from the service, and went west; when next he appeared in Washington it was as one of the two first Senators from the new State of California.

[8] The widow of Augustin de Iturbide, who made himself Emperor of Mexico in 1822 and was shot in 1824, established herself in Philadelphia, and died there in 1861.

Friday, 18th February, 1848. — About two o'clock P.M. Mr. Buchanan called and brought with him a telegraphic despatch which he had just received, dated at Charleston, S. C., today. It was in cipher. The figures had been confused in the transmission and there was great difficulty in deciphering it. As well as it could be made out it was from Mr. Trist, though his name was not signed to it, announcing that he had arrived at Charleston from Mexico, with a treaty which had been signed and ratified.

Saturday, 19th February, 1848. — The Cabinet met at the usual hour; all present except the Secretary of the Treasury and Secretary of War, who are indisposed. Nothing of much importance was considered today. . . After night a messenger arrived from Mexico bearing despatches from the army, and a treaty of peace entered into on the 2nd inst. by Mr. Trist with Mexican plenipotentiaries appointed for that purpose. This messenger was Mr. Freanor, who has been with the army for some time in the capacity of a correspondent for the New Orleans *Delta,* over the signature of Mustang. About nine o'clock Mr. Buchanan called with the treaty. He read it. Mr. Trist was recalled in October last, but chose to remain in Mexico and continue the negotiation. The terms of the treaty are within his instructions which he took out in April last, upon the important question of boundary and limits. There are many provisions in it which will require more careful examination than a single reading will afford. Mr. Trist has acted very badly, as I have heretofore noted in this diary, but notwithstanding this, if on further examination the treaty is one that can be accepted, it should not be rejected on account of his bad conduct. Mr. Buchanan left the treaty with me. The same messenger (Mr. Freanor) who brought the treaty was the bearer of despatches from General Scott. They are not important, except on one point. One of his despatches is in answer to the letter of enquiry addressed to him in December, in relation to an alleged meeting of general officers at

Puebla in July last, which had been published in certain
newspapers in the United States and which purported to give
an account of an arrangement to pay money to Santa Anna
to induce him to make a Treaty.   General Scott's answer
is evasive, and leaves the irresistible inference that such a
transaction took place and that it will not bear the light.
Whatever it was it was wholly unauthorized, and probably
led to the fatal armistice in August, which enabled the enemy
to reinforce himself, and cost so many valuable lives in taking the City of Mexico.   It must be further investigated.[9]

Sunday, 20th February, 1848. — The treaty with Mexico
received last night was of so much importance that I deemed
it a public duty to give it a critical examination today, and I
did so.   Mr. Buchanan also examined it and made notes of
its several articles.   Mr. Mason, Mr. Johnson, and Mr.
Clifford also read it, or rather it was read by one of them
in the presence of the others.   Much conversation was had
on the subject.   I deemed prompt action upon it so indispensable that I called a special meeting of the Cabinet for
tonight at seven o'clock, and sent my private secretary, Col.
Walker, to see Mr. Walker and Mr. Marcy, to invite them,
if they were able to attend.   At the appointed hour (seven
o'clock) all the members of the Cabinet were present.   The
treaty was again read, and the question to be decided was
stated, *viz.,* whether the treaty should be rejected by me or

[9] Trist had brought home the treaty of Guadeloupe-Hidalgo, signed on
Feb. 2, 1848.   This fixed much our present boundary with Mexico, modified
later by the Gadsden Purchase; and agreed that the United States was to
satisfy the claims of its citizens upon the Mexican government, and to pay
an additional sum of $15,000,000.   Polk could not do less than accept the
treaty, however grudgingly.   In his December message to Congress he had
said that the American government might find it necessary to take " the
full measure of indemnity into its hands," a phrase which was generally
interpreted as meaning the annexation of the whole of Mexico.   The Cabinet, including Buchanan, but with Attorney-General Clifford dissenting,
leaned toward such annexation.   In the country at large there was more
and more popular support for the " all of Mexico " policy.   But Trist
had made a good treaty, which met Polk's original views, and he decided
to present it to Congress.

sent to the Senate for ratification. A free discussion ensued. I took the advice of the Cabinet separately and individually. Mr. Buchanan and Mr. Walker advised that I should reject it. Mr. Mason, Mr. Marcy, Mr. Johnson, and Mr. Clifford advised that I should accept it and send it for ratification to the Senate. All agreed that if it was sent to the Senate it should be with a recommendation that the 10th article, which related to grants of land in Texas, and in the territories proposed to be ceded to the United States, should be rejected. I reserved my opinion and requested the Cabinet to meet again at twelve o'clock on tomorrow. All condemned Mr. Trist's disregard of the orders of his government, to return to the United States when he was recalled.

Monday, 21st February, 1848.—At twelve o'clock the Cabinet met; all the members present. I made known my decision upon the Mexican Treaty, which was that under all the circumstances of the case, I would submit it to the Senate for ratification, with a recommendation to strike out the 10th article. I assigned my reasons for my decision. They were, briefly, that the treaty conformed on the main question of limits and boundary to the instructions given to Mr. Trist in April last; and that though, if the treaty was now to be made, I should demand more territory, perhaps to make the Sierra Madre the line, yet it was doubtful whether this could ever be obtained by the consent of Mexico. I looked, too, to the consequences of its rejection. A majority of one branch of Congress is opposed to my administration; they have falsely charged that the war was brought on and is continued by me with a view to the conquest of Mexico; and if I were now to reject a treaty made upon my own terms, as authorized in April last, with the unanimous approbation of the Cabinet, the probability is that Congress would not grant either men or money to prosecute the war. Should this be the result, the army now in Mexico would be constantly wasting and diminishing in numbers, and I might at last be compelled to withdraw them, and thus lose the two Provinces of New Mexico and Upper California, which were ceded to the United States by this treaty. Should the opponents of my administration succeed in carrying the next Presidential election, the great probability is that the country would lose all the advantages secured by this treaty. I adverted to the immense value of Upper California; and concluded by saying that if I were now to reject my own terms, as offered in April last, I did not see how it was possible for my administration to be sustained. Mr. Buchanan repeated his objections to the treaty. He wanted more territory, and would not be content with less than the line of the Sierra Madre, in addition to the provinces secured in this Treaty. He admitted the fact that Mr. Trist had been recalled before he signed the treaty ought to have no influence upon the decision to be made. I deemed it to be my duty to remind Mr. Buchanan of his total change of opinion and position on the subject. I told him that I remembered well that at a Cabinet meeting which took place on the night of the day on which war was declared (13th of May, 1846) or about that time, he had been opposed to acquiring any Mexican territory. I told him that at that meeting he had prepared and read in Cabinet a circular which he proposed to address, as Secretary of State, to our ministers and consuls abroad, authorizing them to inform the governments at which they were accredited, that we did not desire or intend to acquire any Mexican territory. . . I told him I repeated these facts because it was proper that we should understand our relative positions on the subject, formerly and now. The rest of the Cabinet were silent. Mr. Buchanan replied that I might have gone further and added that he had been opposed to the military expedition to the City of Mexico (as I remember he was) but that he was overruled, that since April we had spent much money and lost much blood, and that he was not now satisfied with this treaty. He added that he gave his advice as a member of the Cabinet that the treaty should be rejected, because that was now his opinion. I cannot help laboring under the conviction that the true reason of Mr. Buchanan's present course is that he is now a candidate for the Presidency, and he does not wish to incur the displeasure of those who are in favour of the conquest of all Mexico. That he earnestly wishes me to send the treaty to the Senate, against his advice, I am fully convinced; not from anything he has said, but from circumstances and his general bearing, I do not doubt. No candidate for the presidency ought ever to remain in the Cabinet. He is an unsafe adviser.

Wednesday, 23rd February, 1848. — My private secretary took my message to the Senate with the Mexican Treaty today. He delivered it to the Senate, and informed me that the Senate went immediately into executive session to consider it. By this treaty it is provided that upon its ratification by Mexico three millions of dollars are to be paid, and as the 10th article had been inserted without instructions, and could not be ratified by this Government, I determined that it was proper to transmit a despatch to Major General William O. Butler, who is now in command of the army in Mexico, instructing him to prevent the payment of the money until the treaty as it might be ratified by the Senate of the United States should be transmitted to Mexico and ratified by that Government. . .

I learned from my porter tonight that the Hon. John Quincy Adams died in the Speaker's Room in the Capitol a few past seven o'clock this evening. Mr. Adams was struck down with a paralytic affection while in his seat in the House of Representatives on Monday, the 21st instant. He was borne to the Speaker's room, where he remained speechless and in a state of insensibility until his death this evening. The House of Representatives has met and adjourned each day since he was taken ill, without transacting any business.

Thursday, 24th February, 1848. — In testimony of respect for the memory of the Hon. John Quincy Adams, who

died at the Capitol last evening, I issued an order this morning directing all the executive offices at Washington to be
placed in mourning, and all business to be suspended during
this day and tomorrow.   Under this order the President's
Mansion was placed in mourning by putting black crape over
the front door.   Orders were also given through the Secretaries of War and the Navy to cause the melancholy event
to be observed with appropriate solemnity by the army and
navy.   Mr. Adams died in the 81st year of his age.   He had
been more than half a century in the public service, had
filled many high stations, and among them that of President
of the United States.   He was the sixth President under the
Constitution.   The first seven Presidents are all now dead.
The ninth President is also dead.   Mr. Van Buren, who
was the eighth President, and Mr. Tyler, who succeeded to
the Presidency upon the death of President Harrison, are
the only two of my predecessors who now survive.   I am the
tenth President elected by the people. . .

Mr. Buchanan handed me two despatches from Mr.
Trist, one dated December 29, 1847, and the other January
12, 1848, which he stated Mr. Freanor, the bearer of the
treaty from Mexico, had not delivered to him until this
morning.   Mr. Freanor's apology for the delay in delivering them was that they were placed in a different part of his
baggage from that in which he carried the treaty, and had
been overlooked by him until this morning.   After the members of the Cabinet retired I read these despatches, and
found them to be arrogant, highly exceptionable, and even
of an insulting character.   I immediately sent for the Secretary of War, and informed him that I wished him to add a
paragraph to his despatch to General Butler, directing him,
if Trist should attempt to exercise any official authority in
Mexico, to prevent it, and to require him to leave the headquarters of the army as soon as a safe escort could be furnished to conduct him to Vera Cruz.   Trist has proved
himself to be an impudent and unqualified scoundrel.   The

Secretary of War hesitated about inserting the paragraph, and said if, after thinking of it tonight I still thought it proper, it could go in a separate despatch tomorrow and could undertake the bearer of despatches at New Orleans. To this I assented with some reluctance.[10]

Friday, 25th February, 1848. — I sent for Senator Douglas tonight and had a conversation with him about the Mexican Treaty. Mr. Johnson, the Postmaster-General, came in while we were conversing on the subject. After Mr. Douglas left Mr. Johnson expressed the opinion that the treaty was in great danger, from what he had learned, of being rejected. He stated, among other things, that it was believed in the city that Mr. Buchanan and Mr. Walker were exerting their influence to have it rejected. He mentioned another astounding fact to me, *viz.,* that it was reported and believed that Mr. Walker, the Secretary of the Treasury, had joined in a letter to General Taylor on the subject of the tariff and the Constitutional Treasury, and that Mr. Walker was in favour of General Taylor for the Presidency. If this be so, it presents the singular spectacle of a member of my Cabinet supporting a Whig and an op-

[10] Polk actually sent this despatch the following day to General Butler, ordering Trist to be sent back from headquarters under escort. Indeed, the President says in his diary that its language " was made stronger than that I had suggested on yesterday." The successful negotiator of a treaty which Polk had now accepted as satisfactory was to be returned to the United States in something like disgrace. It is to Marcy's credit that he opposed this ungracious treatment of the government's agent, and to Buchanan's discredit that he did not interpose in behalf of his former lieutenant in the State Department. But Buchanan was thinking only of himself and of his chances for the Presidency, and he and Polk were again on bad terms. The Washington correspondent of the New York *Herald*, signing himself Galvienses but named Nugent, had published some letters abusive of Polk. The President thought that they had been inspired by Buchanan, who admitted talking with Nugent. He wrote that " If I obtain any reliable proof that Mr. Buchanan has given countenance to Galvienses he shall not remain in the Cabinet." For his part, Buchanan intimated to Attorney-General Clifford that he was thinking of resigning. The administration was for the moment in a state of dissension, which fortunately did not last long. Buchanan vigorously denied to Polk that he had countenanced Nugent's attacks on the President, though he admitted his frequent contacts with Nugent.

ponent of my administration as my successor. If I ascertain this to be the fact it will be inconsistent with the success of my measures for Mr. Walker to remain in my Cabinet. I will require strong proof, however, before I can believe it to be true. The truth is that the scheming and intriguing about the Presidential election, and especially by Mr. Buchanan, is seriously embarrassing my administration.

Saturday, 26th February, 1848. — This being the day appointed by two Houses of Congress for performing the funeral ceremonies of the late John Quincy Adams, the Cabinet assembled at the President's Mansion at half past eleven o'clock A.M. and proceeded with me to the Capitol. On reaching the hall of the House of Representatives I was conducted to a seat provided for me on the right of the Speaker, the Cabinet occupying seats on the floor of the House. On similar occasions heretofore the President has been seated on the floor with the Cabinet. I of course conformed to the order of the arrangements which had been made by the Speaker, and took my seat on his right. The Vice-President of the United States was seated on the left of the Speaker. An immense crowd attended at the Capitol, many more than could gain admittance to the hall of the House. Every seat was occupied. In addition to the members of both Houses of Congress, the Judges of the Supreme Court of the United States, the officers of the army and navy in uniform, foreign ministers, most of them in their court dresses, and a vast multitude of citizens and strangers were present. The galleries as well as the floor were crowded with ladies and gentlemen. Mrs. Polk, Mrs. Madison, Mrs. Dallas, and many other ladies occupied the ladies' gallery. The family of the deceased were on the floor. The corpse was brought into the hall. Divine service was performed by the Rev. Mr. Gurley, the chaplain of the House of Representatives. The service being over, a long procession of carriages, persons on horseback and on foot, of military, the order of Odd Fellows, the fire companies, and citizens moved with the corpse to the Congressional Burying-ground, where further religious ceremonies were performed and the body deposited in a vault, where, I understand, it will remain a few days, when it will be removed to the late residence of the deceased in Massachusetts. It was the most numerous funeral procession I ever witnessed. The whole ceremonies were conducted with order and solemnity. It was a splendid pageant. I returned to the President's mansion about four o'clock P.M. I transacted no business in my office of any importance today.

Monday, 28th February, 1848. — Near twelve o'clock Senator Sevier called and informed me that the Committee of Foreign Affairs of the Senate, of which he is chairman, and to which the Mexican Treaty had been referred, had held a meeting this morning and had resolved to recommend the rejection of the treaty by the Senate, and to advise the Executive to appoint an imposing commission to be composed of three or five persons belonging to both political parties, to proceed to Mexico to negotiate a treaty. Mr. Sevier informed me that he stood alone in the committee opposed to this course. The other members of the Committee are Senators Webster, Benton, Mangum, and Hannegan. . . I consider the course of the committee of the Senate weak, if not factious, and cannot doubt that the object of Mr. Webster is to defeat any treaty, clamorous as the Whig party profess to be for peace, until after the next Presidential election. Indeed, Mr. Sevier informed me that Mr. Webster said he wanted *no* territory beyond the Rio Grande, and that he said also that if he voted for this treaty and Mexico should not ratify it, he would be bound to vote for men and money to carry on the War, a position which he did not wish to occupy. I do not wonder at his course, but I am surprised at that of Mr. Hannegan and Mr. Benton. Extremes sometimes meet and act effectively for negative purposes, but never for affirmative purposes. They have done so in this instance. Mr. Webster is for *no* territory and

Mr. Hannegan is for *all* Mexico, and for opposite reasons both will oppose the Treaty. It is difficult upon any rational principle, to assign a satisfactory reason for anything Col. Benton may do, especially in this present temper of mind, wholly engrossed as he seems to have been for some months past with the case of his son-in-law, Col. Frémont. The truth is the approaching Presidential election absorbs every other consideration, and Senators act as if there was no country and no public interests to take care of. The factions are all at work, and votes are controlled, even upon a vital question of peace or war, by the supposed effect upon the public mind. If the treaty in its present form is ratified, there will be added to the United States an immense empire, the value of which twenty years hence it would be difficult to calculate, and yet Democratic and Whig Senators disregard this, and act solely with the view to the elevation of themselves or their favourites to the Presidential office.

Tuesday, 29th February, 1848.—In the afternoon I learned that the Mexican Treaty had been under discussion in executive session in the Senate, and that its fate was doubtful. From what I learn, about a dozen Democratic Senators will oppose it, most of them because they wish to acquire more territory than the line of the Rio Grande and the provinces of New Mexico and Upper California will secure. What Mr. Benton's reason for opposing it may be no one can tell. He has heretofore maintained that the true boundary of Texas was the Nueces instead of the Rio Grande, and he is apt to think that nothing is done properly that he is not previously consulted about. Mr. Webster's reason for opposing it is that it acquires too much territory. The result is extremely doubtful. If eight or ten Whig Senators vote with Mr. Webster against it, it will be rejected. Nineteen Senators will constitute one third of that body, and will reject it.

Thursday, 2nd March, 1848.—The Mexican Treaty is still under consideration in the Senate. I saw Senator

Turney this morning, and am inclined to think he will vote for the ratification of the treaty. The prospect now is that it may be ratified, but by a very close vote.

Friday, 3d March, 1848. — I saw company as usual this morning. Among others several Senators called. The probabilities now are that the Mexican treaty will be ratified, though the vote will probably be close. Nineteen Senators constitute one third of the body and can prevent its ratification. Mr. Benton and Mr. Webster are the leading opponents of the treaty. Eight or ten, perhaps twelve Democratic Senators, it is said, will act with Mr. Benton; and six or eight Whig Senators with Mr. Webster. Most of the Democratic Senators who will vote against the ratification will do so because they desire to secure more territory than the treaty acquires; and most of the Whig Senators, perhaps all of them, who will vote against ratification, will do so because they are opposed to acquiring any territory. My suspicion is that if the Whig party in the Senate shall ascertain that a sufficient number of Democratic Senators will vote against the treaty to constitute a majority of the nineteen required to reject, Whig Senators enough will join them, and then attempt to cast the responsibility of the rejection upon the Democratic party. The Whig Senators who have been so long denouncing the war and clamouring for peace would, notwithstanding this, like to see the treaty rejected, provided they can throw the responsibility upon the Democratic party.

Wednesday, 8th March, 1848. — About two o'clock P.M. I received two resolutions passed by the Senate in executive session, calling for additional information of the subject of the Mexican Treaty. I promptly answered them and sent messages to the Senate in reply.

Friday, 10th March, 1848.— About ten o'clock P.M. Mr. Dickens, the Secretary of the Senate, brought me official notice that the Mexican Treaty had just been ratified by the Senate by a vote of 38 ayes to 14 nays, four Senators not voting.[11] I immediately retired from the parlour to my office and sent for the Secretary of War, with a view to have a messenger despatched to General Butler in Mexico, to carry intelligence to him that the treaty with Mexico had been ratified by the Senate of the United States, with certain amendments, and that it would be sent out by a commissioner invested with plenipotentiary powers in the course of four or five days.

Wednesday, 15th March, 1848.— I learned with much surprise last evening that a motion had been made in Executive Session of the Senate to remove the injunction of secrecy from the proceedings of that body on the ratification of the Mexican Treaty. Believing that if the motion prevailed it would endanger, if not defeat, the ratification by Mexico, I spoke to several Senators, who called last night and this morning, and requested them to prevent it. There is no precedent for removing the injunction of secrecy from the proceedings of the Senate on treaties, until after both parties have ratified the treaty, and the ratifications have been exchanged. In this case, it would be peculiarly unfortunate to do so, because it would expose to Mexico, whilst the ratification of the treaty on her part was still pending, the divisions in the Senate, as shown by the recorded votes on various propositions of amendment and on the final ratification, and would excite their hopes that by refusing to ratify they might hereafter obtain better terms.

Thursday, 23rd March, 1848. — I was much astonished at having the fact called to my attention this morning by my private secretary that the New York *Herald* of yesterday contained my confidential message to the Senate transmitting the Mexican Treaty to the Senate for their ratification. After learning the fact I mentioned it to two or three Sena-

---

[11] Part of the opposition to the treaty came from those, including Secretaries Buchanan and Walker, who desired the annexation of much more Mexican territory, if not the whole of Mexico. Part of it came from Northern Whigs who objected to the addition to the Union of so much territory which might be thrown open to slavery.

tors who called, and expressed my indignation at the breach of confidence which had been committed by someone, by which it had been communicated to the press. I learned also, but did not see the paper, that a portion of the confidential correspondence which accompanied my message with the treaty to the Senate, had also been published in some other paper in New York. All communications relating to treaties are made to the Senate in confidence, and in executive session. The Senate are in the habit of ordering such executive communications to be printed in confidence of their own use; and some Senator has probably furnished a printed copy for publication, either to the editors or to some of the unprincipled letter-writers who are stationed at Washington to collect news for them.

Saturday, 25th March, 1848. — . . . The subject of the investigation now going on in the Senate in relation to the publication in the New York papers of the Mexican Treaty and the confidential documents accompanying it . . . took place between Mr. Marcy, Mr. Mason, Mr. Johnson, and myself. After they retired I felt it to be proper to send for Mr. Buchanan and hold a conversation with him on the subject, and I did so. It was the first conversation I had had with him on the subject. He had not mentioned it to me, and I had felt a delicacy and reluctance to mention it sooner. He said he had had no agency in causing the publication to be made; that he had heard all that had occurred before the committee of the Senate who were investigating it; and that he was able to account for all the printed copies of the treaty and correspondence which had been furnished to the State Department. He said that a conspiracy had been formed by certain Senators to fix the publication on him, or rather that Nugent, the correspondent of the New York *Herald,* had obtained the copy of the treaty and correspondence from him, or from the State Department. He said that he had written a letter to Senator Cameron denying it, but had not sent it, as, on reflection, he thought his position as

Secretary of State and his character should protect him from such an imputation. He spoke very harshly of Senator Westcott, and said he was capable of selling the copy to which he was entitled as Senator for two dollars. He asked me if I thought he had furnished the copy to Nugent. I told him I did not. Of course I could not say otherwise after his positive denial that he had. I expressed my contempt for Nugent and all the other hired letter-writers at Washington, regarding them, as I did, as employees wholly destitute of principle, and my regret that he had had any connection or intercourse with them.

Tuesday, 28th March, 1848. — Several members of Congress called before the hour of meeting of the Cabinet this morning. The Cabinet assembled at the usual hour this morning, all the members present. . . Despatches were presented and read by the Secretary of War from General Scott and General Butler, dated at the City of Mexico on the 2nd inst. The despatches of General Butler related exclusively to military operations, and gave no information of the prospects of the assembling of the Mexican Congress, or the ratification by Mexico of the treaty of peace. The despatch from General Scott was filled with complaints at being superseded in the command, and contained an uncourteous and even violent attack upon the Secretary of War, and through him on the government. The despatch is weak and malignant, and requires an answer, which can be very easily given, placing General Scott wholly in the wrong. After the transaction of some other business of no general importance the Cabinet adjourned. I learn tonight that the Senate in executive session were again occupied a part of the day in relation to the investigation into the publication of the Mexican treaty and confidential correspondence accompanying it in the New York papers, and had come to no conclusion. This Nugent still persists in refusing to disclose how or from whom he obtained the copy which he admits he sent to the New York *Herald*.

Thursday, 30th March, 1848. — Mr. Buchanan brought to me the foreign mail, brought by the steamer *Caledonia* and received this morning. There was a private letter from Mr. Rush to Mr. Buchanan, stating that he had forwarded an official despatch on the day preceding its date. Unfortunately the despatch was not received. Despatches were received from Mr. Donelson, United States Minister to Prussia, and from several of the United States consuls in Germany and the Two Sicilies. A great sensation had been produced by the Revolution in France, and the people of the German States and of Italy were making large demands of their sovereigns and the latter were making large concessions to their subjects. It is impossible to anticipate what the effect of the French Revolution may be upon the other Powers of Europe. One of two things will probably happen; either there will be a general war, or more liberal institutions must be granted by every European sovereign to their subjects than they have heretofore enjoyed.

Thursday, 6th April, 1848. — My office was crowded up to the hour of twelve o'clock with visitors, and I was greatly annoyed by the importunities of office-seekers. It is most disgusting to be compelled to spend hour after hour almost every day in hearing the applications for office made by loafers who congregate in Washington, and by members of Congress in their behalf, and yet I am compelled to submit to it or offend or insult the applicants and their friends. The people of the United States have no idea of the extent to which the President's time, which ought to be devoted to more important matters, is occupied by the voracious and often unprincipled persons who seek office. If a kind Providence permits me length of days and health, I will, after I retire from the Presidential office, write the secret and hitherto unknown history of the workings of the government in this respect. It requires great patience and self-command to repress the loathing I feel towards a hungry crowd of unworthy office-hunters who often crowd my office.

Sunday, 9th April, 1848. — Mr. Cave Johnson called after night and I had a full and confidential conversation with him in relation to the Presidential election. We both occupied the same position in one respect. We neither of us took any part between the aspirants for the nomination at the Democratic national convention at Baltimore in May next. Mr. Johnson remarked that many leading Democrats looked to my nomination as the means of harmonizing the party, and expressed the opinion that I would be stronger than any other candidate who could be run by the Democratic party. The same thing has been repeatedly said to me by leading Democrats of late. I told Mr. Johnson, as I have all others who have mentioned the subject to me, that I was not a candidate for the nomination and did not desire it.

Monday, 10th April, 1848. — In the midst of the annoyances of the herd of lazy, worthless people who come to Washington for office instead of going to work and by some honest calling making a livelihood, I am sometimes amused at their applications. A case of this kind occurred on Saturday last. One of these offices-seekers placed his papers of recommendation in the hands of Judge Mason to present to me. No particular office was specified in the papers; and the Judge reported to me that he enquired of him what office he wanted, to which he answered that he thought he would be a good hand at making treaties, and that as he understood there were some to be made soon he would like to be a minister abroad. This is about as reasonable as many other applications which are made to me.

Thursday, 20th April, 1848. — Shortly after 12 o'clock Mr. Elisha Whittlesey, formerly a member of Congress from Ohio, accompanied by Mr. Cave Johnson, the Postmaster-General, called. Mr. Whittlesey represented to me that great excitement existed in the city, and that there was danger that a portion of the people would engage in a riot tonight, tear down and destroy the printing office of the

New Era,[12] an abolition paper printed in this city, and requested me to exert my authority to prevent it. The cause of the excitement is as follows. On Saturday or Sunday last a schooner, called the *Pearl*, left Georgetown and after night took on board at Greenleaf's Point a number of slaves and sailed with them on board. On the afternoon of Sunday the schooner was pursued by a steamboat and about thirty citizens of Washington and Georgetown on board. The schooner was overhauled by the steamboat near the mouth of the Potomac. Three white men and seventy-seven slaves were captured and brought back to Washington and put in jail on Tuesday last. The outrage committed by stealing or seducing the slaves from their owners, and the attempt of abolitionists to defend the white men who had perpetrated it, had produced the excitement and the threatened violence on the abolition press. I told Mr. Whittlesey that I would coöperate with the city authorities, if necessary, in any proper steps to preserve the public peace and to cause the laws to be respected.

Saturday, 29th April, 1848. — Senator Ashley of Arkansas died at his lodgings in this city about 2 o'clock today. His attack was sudden and very violent. I observed him at church with his family on the last Sabbath in his usual health. He attended the Senate on Monday, was taken ill the same evening, and today he died. "What shadows we are and what shadows we pursue." One week ago no member of either House of Congress had a better prospect of long life than Mr. Ashley.

Tuesday, 2d May, 1848. — I note an incident which occurred in the Senate Chamber today. Immediately after the sermon of the Rev. Mr. Slicer (at Senator Ashley's funeral) and when the Senators were leaving the chamber

---

[12] Polk means the *National Era*. These disturbances are described in its issues for April 20 and 27, 1848. Elisha Whittlesey, 1783–1863, who had been a Representative from Ohio 1823–1838, was now director and general agent of the Washington Monument Association. Senator Chester Ashley, whose death is noted below, sat in the upper house for Arkansas 1844–1848.

to join in the funeral procession, Senator Benton, in passing near where I was seated, bowed to me and saluted me, a civility which I, of course, returned. It is the first time he has done so since the commencement of the trial of his son-in-law (Col. Frémont) in the beginning of November last, before a court-martial. I approved and remitted the sentence of dismissal from the service of Col. Frémont, but this does not seem to have satisfied Col. Benton. I meet Col. Benton almost every Sabbath at church, but he never speaks to me as he was in the habit of doing before the trial of Col. Frémont.

Wednesday, 10th May, 1848. — I closed my doors at twelve o'clock. Shortly after that hour Senator Douglas of Illinois called with John O'Sullivan, Esq., of New York. Their business with me was to urge that I take early measures with a view to the purchase of the island of Cuba from Spain. I heard their views but deemed it prudent to express no opinion on the subject. Mr. O'Sullivan read to me and left with me a paper embodying his views in favour of the measure. Though I expressed no opinion to them I am decidedly in favour of purchasing Cuba and making it one of the States of the Union.

Saturday, 13th May, 1848. — Mr. Cave Johnson remained after the other members of the Cabinet retired. I read to him the draft of a letter which I had prepared to be addressed to some member of the Democratic national convention to assemble at Baltimore on the 22d inst., to be by him presented to the convention if, as has been suggested to me it might be, my name should be brought before the convention for nomination. I will probably address the letter to Dr. J. G. M. Ramsay, a delegate to the convention from Tennessee. In this letter I reiterated and declared my desire to retire at the end of my present term and not to be a candidate for reëlection.

Tuesday, 16th May, 1848. — A large number of strangers, chiefly Delegates to the Democratic National

Convention to be assembled at Baltimore, on the 22nd instant, called this morning. Several members of Congress called with them to introduce them. The Cabinet met at the usual hour; all the members present. Despatches received from General Price were read. They give a detailed account of the battle of Santa Cruz, and the capture of Chihuahua by the forces under his command. In this instance as well as in all others during the Mexican War, our arms were successful.[13]

[13] Even after Taylor's Buena Vista campaign, northern Mexico remained in a state of great unrest. Gen. Sterling Price, who now commanded in New Mexico, was alarmed by reports of dangerous enemy movements. He therefore launched a brisk little campaign which resulted in the recapture of Chihuahua in March, 1848.

CHAPTER XI
May 17, 1848 – Sept. 30, 1848

DEMOCRATIC NATIONAL CONVENTION — NOMINATION OF
LEWIS CASS — BARNBURNERS VS. THE HUNKERS — VISIT TO
PENNSYLVANIA SPRINGS — THE "BUFFALO HUNTERS" —
BENTON AND CALIFORNIA

Wednesday, 17th May, 1848. — Many persons called
this morning and among them several of the delegates to the
Democratic National Convention to be assembled at Baltimore on the 22nd instant. My old acquaintance and associ-
ate in Congress, Col. Abraham McClellan of Tennessee,
and Col. Bowers of North Carolina, called. Whilst they
were with me Mr. Stanton of the House of Representatives
from Tennessee came in. In the course of conversation he
said in the presence of the other two gentlemen that he
wished to ask me a question, which I could answer or not, as
I chose. His question was: are you a candidate before the
Democratic convention at Baltimore for the nomination of
President? I answered him promptly that I was not. He
knew that I was not a candidate, and it struck me as very
strange that he should propound such a question.[1]

Friday, 19th May, 1848. — A large number of delegates
to the Democratic National Convention, and others, called
on me today. In the morning my office was crowded, and

---

[1] The Democratic National Convention met at Baltimore on May 22, 1848.
It found on its hands an ugly feud between the Barnburner and Hunker
factions in New York State, with two rival sets of delegates. It tried to
compromise by admitting both delegations, and giving each half the votes
of the State; but both refused to take part.

throughout the day I had calls. Several of them expressed their desire to run me for a second term. I replied to them as I did to others on the same subject on yesterday (see this diary of yesterday). I have been informed by many delegates that among the large body of them now assembled in this city there is general expression of approbation of the measures of my administration, and a general expression of regret that I ever made the pledge not to be a candidate for reëlection. Several of them have expressed to me the opinion that a large majority of the delegates desire to see me reelected. These expressions of approbation are, of course, gratifying to me, but I have firmly maintained the ground I have heretofore occupied of not being again a candidate, and have repeated to many of them my fixed purpose of retiring to private life at the close of my present term. I sent for the Hon. George S. Houston of Alabama this afternoon, and read to him the letter which I had prepared to the convention at Baltimore.

Monday, 22nd May, 1848. — A few persons only called. Among them were Mr. Rhett of South Carolina, Mr. Johnson of Arkansas and Mr. Venable of North Carolina, all of the House of Representatives. I read to each of them a copy of my letter to the Baltimore Convention. They all approved it and expressed their gratification that I had placed myself on high ground by writing such a letter. They all expressed a strong and decided preference for me over all others, if I had permitted my name to be used as a candidate. Mr. Rhett said that the people of South Carolina approved my administration and would have supported my reëlection with unanimity, notwithstanding Mr. Calhoun's course. He declared that he could not support General Cass if he should be the nominee, and that South Carolina could not and would not support him. He spoke enthusiastically in approbation of the principles and measures of my administration. Mr. Venable expressed similar opinions, and declared that if I had been a candidate North Carolina could have been carried for me, but that she could not be for either of the candidates spoken of.

Tuesday, 23d May, 1848. — This was a remarkably quiet day. Not half a dozen persons called. Congress having adjourned over until Thursday, almost all the members, I learn, have gone to Baltimore to attend the Democratic national convention, now sitting in that city. . . Information was received by telegraph from the proceedings of the convention at Baltimore at two or three periods in the course of the day. The convention had not fully organized at the last date, half past three o'clock P.M. After the Cabinet dispersed today, I took a walk around the President's square, and meeting Mr. Dallas, the Vice-President of the United States, he walked with me. I informed him of the letter I had written to be read to the Baltimore convention, and of its purpose. He approved it.

Thursday, 25th May, 1848. — Congress having adjourned over from Monday last until today, at the hour of meeting scarcely a quorum attended in either House. No business was transacted and the Senate adjourned over until Monday next. The members are still absent at Baltimore. Several persons called today and I transacted business in my office as usual. About two o'clock P.M. a telegraphic despatch was received announcing that Lewis Cass of Michigan had, on the fourth ballot, been nominated by the Democratic convention at Baltimore as the candidate of the Democratic party for President of the United States.[2] About five o'clock General Cass called (I having sent for him) and I congratulated him on his nomination. He was in a fine humour, and I had a pleasant conversation with him. About eight o'clock P.M. I was informed that the convention had nominated General William O. Butler of Kentucky as the Democratic candi-

[2] Cass was far in the lead at the Convention from the beginning, and obtained the requisite two-thirds majority on the fourth ballot. The only other candidates who developed any significant strength were Buchanan and Woodbury. Though belonging to the conservative wing of his party, Cass was an excellent nominee.

date for Vice-President of the United States, and that the convention had adjourned to meet again on tomorrow. . .

My letter addressed to Dr. Ramsay, I learn, was read to the convention at Baltimore before any balloting was had. In this letter I declared that I was not a candidate for the nomination, and that it was my intention to retire to private life at the close of my present term. General Cass informed me in my interview with him that in his letter accepting his nomination he would declare his intention, if elected, to serve but a single term.

Tuesday, 30th May, 1848. — I informed the Cabinet to-day that I desired to invite their attention, not for the purpose of immediate decision, but for consideration, to the important question whether a proposition should not be made to Spain to purchase the island of Cuba. The subject was freely discussed. The great importance of the island to the United States, and the danger, if we did not acquire it, that it might fall into the hands of Great Britain, were considered. Mr. Walker, the Secretary of the Treasury, was earnestly in favor of making the attempt to purchase it, and was willing to pay one hundred millions of dollars for it. Mr. Mason, the Secretary of the Navy, concurred in opinion with Mr. Walker. Mr. Johnson, the Postmaster-General, had objections to incorporating the Spanish population of Cuba into our Union, and did not seem to favour the idea of purchasing it. Mr. Buchanan, the Secretary of State, expressed a general wish to acquire Cuba, but thought there were objections to making the attempt at this time. He feared if it became known that such a step was contemplated, that it might act prejudicially to the Democratic party in the next Presidential election. He said he would reflect on the subject and be prepared to give me his advice upon the subject hereafter. I intimated my strong conviction that the effort should be made without delay to purchase the island.

Friday, 9th June, 1848. — A telegraphic despatch from

the South reached this city last night to the effect that the
treaty with Mexico had been ratified by the Mexican Senate.
The treaty had previously received the ratification of the
House of Delegates of the Mexican Congress. Half a
dozen members of Congress, all of the Democratic party,
called early in the day to congratulate me on the news of
peace. I sent for the Secretary of War and consulted with
him in regard to the orders necessary to be given, in addition
to those which had heretofore been given, in relation to the
disbanding all the forces engaged to serve during the Mexican War.

Saturday, 17th June, 1848. — The Cabinet met at the
usual hour; all the members present. Mr. Buchanan read
the despatch to Mr. Saunders, United States Minister to
Spain, on the subject of the purchase of Cuba, which he had
prepared in pursuance of the decision made at a previous
Cabinet meeting (see this diary of the 9th June, 1848). It
was an able and well-written despatch. It authorized Mr.
Saunders to inform the Spanish Minister of Foreign Affairs
of the Secretary of State's despatch to the United States consul at Havana for the purpose of satisfying him of the good
faith of the United States towards Spain. He was authorized to inform him in conversation that the United States
could never permit Cuba to pass into the hands of any European Power and that whilst the Island remained a possession
of Spain the United States would in no way interfere with
it. He was authorized, after having done this, to signify
to him in a detailed manner that the United States would be
willing to purchase the Island if it would be agreeable to
Spain to cede it for a pecuniary consideration to the United
States. In his confidential instructions he was authorized
to stipulate to pay one hundred millions of dollars in convenient installments for the island. He was furnished with
full powers to make a treaty to this effect. The whole
matter was profoundly confidential, and the knowledge of it
was to be confined to the Cabinet alone. I will not even

make known the result of the Cabinet deliberation on the subject to Mr. J. L. O'Sullivan of New York, who first suggested to me the idea of purchasing Cuba, and who takes much interest in the subject.

Saturday, 24th June, 1848.— After the Cabinet adjourned I requested my private secretary to invite Senators Breese of Illinois and Bradbury of Maine to call this afternoon. They did call at different hours, and I held with each a conversation in which I presented to them the urgent considerations which made it proper to adopt the Missouri Compromise line of 36° 30', as applied to the territories of Oregon, California, and New Mexico, and thus quiet the agitation of the slavery question in and out of Congress. Mr. Breese expressed his readiness to take the Missouri Compromise line. . . The necessity for settling the question is the greater since the convention of Barnburners, held at Utica, N. Y., on the 22d instant, have bolted from the regular Democratic nominations made by the Baltimore convention in May last, and have nominated Martin Van Buren for President and Henry Dodge for Vice-President distinctly upon the ground of the Wilmot Proviso. This is a most dangerous attempt to organize geographical parties upon the slave question. It is more threatening to the Union than anything which has occurred since the meeting of the Hartford Convention in 1814. Mr. Van Buren's course is selfish, unpatriotic, and wholly inexcusable. The effect of this movement of the seceding and discontented Democrats of New York will be effectually counteracted if the slave question can be settled by adopting the Missouri Compromise line as applied to Oregon, New Mexico, and Upper California at the present session of Congress. If the question can be thus settled harmony will be restored to the Union and the danger of forming geographical parties be avoided. For these reasons I am using my influence with members of Congress to have it effected.

Tuesday, 4th July, 1848. — This being the day appointed

for laying the cornerstone of the Washington monument in
Washington, and having been invited by the committee of
arrangements to attend the ceremonies of the occasion, and
having determined, though in feeble health, to do so, I had
invited my Cabinet to meet and accompany me at ten o'clock
this morning. . . At ten o'clock, the Cabinet assembled; all
the members present. Accompanied by the Cabinet and escorted by General Walton, the United States marshall of
the District of Columbia, and his deputies, and by a troop
of horse commanded by Col. May of the United States
Army, we were conducted in carriages to the City Hall,
where the procession was formed and moved to the site of
the Washington Monument on the banks of the Potomac and
south of the President's Mansion. I witnessed the ceremony of laying the cornerstone, and heard an address delivered by Mr. Speaker Winthrop of the House of Representatives. I returned to the President's House and in
about an hour, at the request of General Quitman, I received
the military on horseback. They were drawn up to receive
me in Pennsylvania Avenue. This afternoon Dr. Rayburn
arrived, bearing despatches and the ratified treaty with
Mexico.

   Saturday, 8th July, 1848. — I saw several persons before
the meeting of the Cabinet this morning. The Cabinet met
at the usual hour; all the members present. After transacting several matters of business I informed the Cabinet of the
conversation which Mr. Birdsall of New York held with
me last evening, urging the removal of Benj. F. Butler and
other office-holders in New York. I also read to them a letter of this date from Senator Dickinson of New York, urging their removal. I asked the Cabinet for their opinion
on the subject. They all agreed that the Barnburners who
had bolted from the regular Democratic nominations in
New York and held office under the Federal Government
deserved to be removed, but Mr. Buchanan and Mr. Toucey
advised against it at this time for fear of its bad effect on

the pending Presidential election. Mr. Buchanan said he would remove them the moment the election was over. Mr. Mason, Mr. Walker, and Mr. Marcy were in favour of their removal. Mr. Johnson expressed no opinion. I told the Cabinet that I had sent for Senator Felch and Mr. McClelland of the House of Representatives, who are understood to be the confidential friends of General Cass, for the purpose of consulting them on the subject. The Cabinet all concurred in the propriety of this step. At six o'clock Mr. Felch and Mr. McClelland called, and I had a full conversation with them on the subject. They both thought that the removals would operate prejudicially to General Cass's election. They informed me that they had within a day or two consulted with Democratic members of Congress in both Houses from the free States other than New York, and that the opinion was general that though the Barnburners who held office in New York deserved to be removed, it would be highly inexpedient to make the removals at this time.

Wednesday, 12th July, 1848. — I learn that after much discussion today, the Senate agreed to a resolution referring the Oregon Bill and my message in relation to the organization of territorial government in California and New Mexico to a select committee of eight members, four from the North and four from the South, and an equal number of each political party. The object was to see if a proposition of compromise upon the subject of slavery in these territories could be agreed upon.[3]

Friday, 14th July, 1848. — I saw company as usual this morning. The number of the office-seekers continues to be quite as great as at any former period of my term. I have

[3] President Polk was in favor of statehood for California and a territorial government for New Mexico. The feeling aroused by the slavery issue was now plainly becoming dangerous. As a result, as Polk here notes, a special committee of eight, two Northern and two Southern men from each of the great parties, was appointed under the chairmanship of Senator J. M. Clayton of Delaware to deal with the questions before Congress relating to the possible extension of slavery; and to attempt to settle them by recommending a single compromise measure, acceptable both to the North and the South.

no offices to confer, and I am greatly annoyed by them.   Col.
Franklin H. Elmore of Charleston, S. C., called this morning and I expressed to him freely my anxiety that in the organization of Territorial Governments in Oregon and in the
recently acquired territories of New Mexico and Upper
California, the slavery question might be settled upon the
principles of the Missouri or Texas compromise on that subject.   He agreed with me in opinion.   I discussed the subject
fully with him, and then remarked that as Mr. Calhoun had
agreed to serve on the select committee of the Senate which
had been raised on the subject, I hoped he would not be
disposed to adhere to extreme views, but to compromise.

Sunday, 16th July, 1848. — About sunset Senator Calhoun and Mr. Franklin H. Elmore of South Carolina called.
They took tea with my family, after which I invited them
to my office.   Mr. Calhoun desired to converse with me
upon the difficulties attending the organization of territorial governments in Oregon, California, and New Mexico
on account of the slavery question. . .   He informed me
that the select committee of eight in the Senate, which had
been raised on that subject, had held two or three meetings,
one of them of several hours duration today, and that they
had been unable to agree either upon the Missouri or Texas
compromise.   He stated that a proposition of non-interference with the subject in California and New Mexico had
been suggested by Senator Dickinson of New York, which
might be agreed upon by the committee.   He said that after
much discussion in that committee the proposition had assumed a form substantially as follows, *viz.,* that in Oregon
the existing land laws, which prohibited slavery, should be
left in force until altered, changed, or amended by the territorial legislature; and that in California and New Mexico
the legislative power should be vested in the governor, secretary, and three judges each, and that they should be restrained by Congress from legislating on the subject of
slavery, leaving that question, if it should arise, to be de-

cïded by the judiciary. He said he would support this proposition, and I told him I approved it, though I would prefer the Missouri or Texas compromise. He said that much would depend on me, in the appointments to be made of governor, secretary, and judges; that they might be Northern men in Oregon, but that they ought to be Southern men in California and New Mexico, who would maintain the Southern views on the subject of slavery. The tone of his conversation on this point seemed to be designed to elicit a pledge from me to this effect. I at once felt the delicacy of my situation and promptly replied that that was a subject on which I could not speak, that if the laws passed in the form suggested I would do my duty, and jocosely added that my friends, as General Harrison's Cincinnati committee in 1840 said for him, must have a " generous confidence " that I would do so.

Thursday, 27th July, 1848. — At breakfast this morning I learned from Col. Walker, my private secretary, that he had just returned from the Senate chamber where he had been all night. He informed me that the Senate had remained in session until eight o'clock this morning, when the vote was taken on the compromise bill to establish territorial governments in Oregon, California, and New Mexico, and that the bill had passed by ayes 33 to noes 22.

Friday, 28th July, 1848. — I learned in the afternoon that the House of Representatives had, by a majority of 15 votes, laid on the table the bill, passed by the Senate on yesterday morning, to compromise the slavery question as it relates to the organization of territorial governments in Oregon, California, and New Mexico.[4] I regard this vote of

4 The Clayton Committee reported out a single bill for the organization of territorial governments in Oregon, New Mexico, and California, which passed the Senate on July 27, 1848, after a heated debate which lasted all night. The bill assented to the anti-slavery laws of Oregon, provisional in nature, but forbade the territorial legislature of New Mexico and California to pass any law relating to slavery. It provided that the status of slavery in these territories might be finally decided by appeals from the territorial courts to the Federal Supreme Court. This was the so-called Clayton Compromise.

the House as most unfortunate. The majority, I learn, was
made up of every Northern Whig, of about half the Northern Democrats, and of eight Southern Whigs. Those of
the Democratic party whose sympathies are with the Barnburners of New York, or who are timid and afraid to risk
their popularity at home, united with the Whigs to defeat
the bill. The result of leaving the slavery question an open
one, to be agitated by ambitious political aspirants and gam-
blers and their friends, will be to produce an organization
of parties upon geographical lines, which must prove dangerous to the harmony if not the existence of the Union itself. The political factions in Congress are all at work,
and they seem to be governed by no patriotic motives, but by
the effect which they suppose may be produced upon the
public mind in the pending Presidential election. A heavy
responsibility rests upon these, and especially the eight
Southern Whigs, who have united to defeat this measure
of compromise of this most delicate and vexatious question.
If no Presidential election had been pending, I cannot doubt
the compromise bill would have passed the House. If it had
done so the agitation would have ceased and the question
would have been at rest. It is difficult to foresee what the
effect of the defeat of this bill may be. The political agitation is very great, and the result of the next Presidential
election is becoming every day more and more doubtful.
The probabilities are that a Northern candidate will be more
distinctly on anti-slavery ground, that the electoral colleges
may fail to make a choice, and that the election may devolve
on the House of Representatives.

Monday, 31st July, 1848. — My private secretary called
my attention on yesterday to the New York *Evening Post*

After it passed the Senate it was at once tabled in the House, which passed
a bill of its own for the organization of the Territory of Oregon alone.
The Senate amended this bill by extending the Missouri Compromise line
to the Pacific. President Polk had hoped that the whole agitation over
slavery would be given its quietus by acceptance of the Clayton Compromise.
He also wished the entrance of California to the Union expedited.

of the 28th instant, containing two letters over the signature of Benjamin Tappan, formerly a United States Senator from Ohio, and Francis P. Blair, formerly editor of the Globe. They purport to give a statement of facts of the manner in which the resolutions for the annexation of Texas were passed by Congress, on the 1st of March, 1845, and profess to give conversations held with me by different persons on the subject. . . I cannot, whilst President of the United States, descend to enter into a newspaper controversy with them. The time may come when I may deem it proper to notice their errors and to correct their misrepresentations of me. I deem it proper at present to record in this diary a brief statement of facts, so that they may not be unknown if I shall be called hence before the proper occasion arises to make the statement over my own signature. I arrived in Washington on the evening of the 13th of February, 1845. I stopped at Coleman's Hotel and had much company every day from that time until the day of my inauguration as President. The question of the annexation of Texas to the United States was pending before Congress. I had been elected as the known advocate of the annexation of Texas and was very anxious that some measure with that object should pass Congress. I expressed myself to this effect to many persons with whom I conversed. I believed that if no measure proposing annexation was passed at that session that Texas would be lost to the Union. I had no time or opportunity to examine minutely, or indeed at all, the particular provisions of any of the propositions on the subject which were before Congress or had been suggested. I repeatedly expressed the opinion that any measure was better than none, and that Congress ought not to adjourn without passing a measure in some form on the subject. I had no opportunity to compare the different plans which had been proposed or suggested with each other, or to decide between them. My great anxiety was to secure the annexation in **any** form before it was too late. I remember that Senator

Haywood had several conversations with me on the subject, and to him as well as to others I expressed my opinion without reserve. I remember to have understood from him and others near the close of the session, that the form in which the resolutions had passed the House was not acceptable to a few of the Democratic Senators, who preferred another form. I remember to have said that if the measure cannot pass in one form, it was better to pass it in any form than not at all. The proposition to appoint commissioners to negotiate, as one of the forms which some preferred, was mentioned in these conversations, and I may have said, and probably did, that if this form was adopted I would endeavour to effect annexation under it, and that for that purpose the first men of the country should be appointed on the commission. But I certainly never understood myself as pledged to select that mode, if the Resolutions passed in the alternative form. I never authorized Mr. Haywood or anyone else to make such pledges to Senators, and if any such pledges were made it was in a total misconception of what I had said or meant. I could not have made such a pledge understandingly, for I had never compared the two propositions with each other, or given them such examination as would enable me to form a judgment between them. I may have said, and doubtless did, that if the plan of appointing commissioners was adopted, I would appoint able men and men of experience. My great object was to secure annexation, and I was more anxious that that should be effected than I was as to the particular manner in which it should be accomplished. The resolutions passed in the alternative form and were approved by President Tyler on the 1st of March, 1845.

Monday, 7th August, 1848. — After night Senator Hannegan called and informed me that the Senate adjourned for the day at eight o'clock P.M. and that the House of Representatives were still in session. He informed me that the Senate had been, during the whole day, in executive session, lis-

tening to a most impassioned and violent speech of Senator
Benton against confirming the nomination of Brigadier-
General Kearny, United States Army, as a brevet Major-
General, for gallant and meritorious services in New Mexico
and California.[5] Mr. Hannegan informed me that Senator
Benton was violent beyond what is usual even for him, and
that he had avowed his intention to speak out the balance
of the Session, and defeat all the public measures before
Congress, rather than suffer the vote on General Kearny's
nomination to be taken. I appointed General Kearny a
Brigadier-General mainly upon Senator Benton's recommendation, and his hostility to him now arises from the fact
that he preferred charges against Lieut.-Col. Frémont, his
(Senator Benton's) son-in-law, upon which he was convicted
by a court-martial. The House of Representatives, I learn,
have been engaged during the whole day in making violent
party speeches on the Presidential election and the merits and
demerits of the Presidential candidates. They seem wholly
to have forgotten that they have any public business to transact, and have converted the House of Representatives into an
arena for making violent party speeches. This is a great outrage and they should be held to a strict account by their constituents for their wanton waste of the public time and disregard
of the public interest. The remainder of the session of
Congress is probably to give rise to scenes of unusual violence and party excitement.

Tuesday, 8th August, 1848. — Many persons called this
morning, most of them seeking office as usual. The Cabinet
met at the usual hour, all the members present. . . I informed them that from present appearances in Congress
no bills would be passed establishing territorial governments
in New Mexico and Upper California, but that it was probable that a bill would be passed establishing a territorial

---

[5] Senator Benton indulged in a violent thirteen-day philippic against
Kearny, incidentally defending Frémont at great length; but the confirmation
of Kearny's nomination to a higher rank by brevet nevertheless finally passed.

government in Oregon, with a restriction in it against the existence of slavery in that territory, and I asked the advice of the Cabinet whether I should approve and sign such a bill. I took their opinions severally and separately, and they were unanimously of opinion that as the whole territory of Oregon lay north of 36° 30', that being the Missouri Compromise line, I ought to sign it.

Thursday, 10th August, 1848. — The Senate tonight passed the Oregon Territorial Bill, with the Missouri Compromise provision in it, by a majority of eleven votes. I hope it may receive the sanction of the House but fear it will not. Congress is in great excitement and confusion on the subject and the importance of settling the question at this session becomes every day more important.

I learn tonight that Mr. Van Buren has been nominated for the Presidency by the Buffalo Convention composed of Whigs, Abolitionists, and Barnburners.

I retired tonight exceedingly fatigued and exhausted, caused from my great labours and anxiety concerning public affairs, and especially the uncertain action of Congress upon any subject whatever. The members are so much engaged in President-making that they attend to little else. It is a Congress as reckless of the public interests as any I have ever known. They are enlarging the appropriations to an enormous and unnecessary amount, and if all their internal improvement schemes could prevail, a further loan would be indispensable.

Friday, 11th August, 1848. — I learn that the House of Representatives rejected the Missouri Compromise amendment of the Senate to the Oregon Territorial Bill. This I deeply deplore. I fear that nothing will be done at this session and that the slavery agitation will be kept up in the country.

I learned tonight that the Buffalo Convention of Whigs, Abolitionists, and Barnburners have nominated Charles F. Adams, the son of the late John Quincy Adams, who is an avowed Abolitionist, for the Vice-Presidency on Mr. Van Buren's ticket, the latter having been nominated for the Presidency. Mr. Van Buren is the most fallen man I have ever known.[6]

Saturday, 12th August, 1848. — The Cabinet met at the usual hour this morning; all the members present except the Secretary of the Treasury, who, I learn, is confined to his house by indisposition. Several matters of business were disposed of. The subject of the propriety of sending a message to Congress, if the Oregon Bill should pass with the restriction as respects slavery, was further discussed (see this diary of Tuesday, the 8th instant). The draft which Mr. Buchanan prepared at my request was read by him. I expressed the opinion, in which the Cabinet all concurred, that if the Oregon Territorial Bill with the slavery restriction in it passed and was presented to me for my approval and signature, I ought not to withhold it from my signature, and that I could not do so without arraying the country into geographical parties on the slavery question, and greatly increasing the excitement, already great, which existed in and out of Congress upon that question.

Sunday, 13th August, 1848. — At breakfast this morning I learned that the flag was flying over the Senate chamber,

---

[6] As already noted in this diary, the Barnburner faction of the New York Democracy — disgusted with the nomination of Lewis Cass at Baltimore — held a convention at Utica on June 22, and nominated Martin Van Buren for President and Henry Dodge of Wisconsin for Vice-President. Steps were then taken by some Whigs who objected to Zachary Taylor, and by some abolitionists, to convoke a national convention of all who opposed the extension of slavery. This body was brought together at Buffalo on August 9, and consisted of 465 delegates from eighteen States. The two leading names proposed for the Presidential nomination were Van Buren, and John P. Hale of New Hampshire; and on the first ballot Van Buren obtained 244 votes to Hale's 181. Since the Barnburners' nominee for the Vice-Presidency, Dodge, had declined, it was necessary to choose another in his stead; the convention nominated by acclamation Charles Francis Adams of Massachusetts. A platform was adopted declaring that the policy of the Free Soil party was to "limit, localize, and discourage" slavery, and the convention proclaimed as the party motto, "Free soil, free speech, free labor, and free men." Polk naturally thought Van Buren "fallen"; but the vote he was destined to poll in the autumn election gave Lewis Cass a still heavier fall.

which indicated that the Senate was still in session. The
Senate continued in session all night and until near ten
o'clock this morning, when they passed the Oregon Territorial Bill with the restriction of slavery in it, and adjourned
to meet at nine o'clock tomorrow morning. . . About sunset Senator Calhoun and Mr. Burt of South Carolina called.
Mr. Calhoun expressed the opinion strongly that I should
veto the bill. I told him I had made up my mind to sign it,
though I would do so reluctantly, and that I proposed to
send a message to the House stating the considerations
which had induced me to do so. He still insisted that I ought
to veto it on constitutional grounds. I told him that if the
question of imposing the restriction was an original one aris-
ing for the first time, I would have serious doubts of its con-
stitutionality. I remarked that there might be questions
arise affecting the very existence of the Union, upon which
we ought to yield inidvidual opinions, in deference to what
our predecessors had done, and I considered this one of
them. I reminded him that I had in conversation with him
some days ago, when he had called to see me on the subject
(pending the deliberations of the committee of eight of the
Senate), told him that I was willing to accept the Missouri
Compromise line. I told him that I was willing to accept the
compromise reported by that committee. Both having now
failed, I did not see that I could veto the naked Oregon Bill,
inasmuch as all the territory of Oregon lay north of the Missouri Compromise line.[7]

[7] The passage of this Oregon bill ended a very complicated bit of Congressional manoeuvring and bickering. The Clayton Compromise bill for organizing California, New Mexico, and Oregon, which has already been described, passed the Senate but was tabled in the House. The House then
brought forward a new bill for the organization of Oregon alone, excluding
slavery from that territory by applying the " restrictions and prohibitions "
of the Northwest Ordinance to it. As we have already seen, the Senate amended
it by extending the Misssouri Compromise line to the Pacific. The House
rejected this amendment, 121 to 82, and the Senate after an all-night session
gave way. The Oregon bill thus passed, as Polk says, " with the restriction
of slavery in it." This having been done, the great question was whether the
President should sign it. As this diary-entry indicates, he had made up his

Monday, 14th August, 1848. — I am heartily rejoiced that the session of Congress is over. My long confinement and great labour has exceedingly exhausted me, and I feel the absolute necessity of having some rest. I have not been three miles from the President's mansion since my return from my tour through the Eastern States in June and July, 1847, a period of more than thirteen months. Judge Mason left with his wife tonight to visit a sick child in Virginia.

Tuesday, 15th August, 1848. — I informed the Cabinet that I was so much fatigued and worn down that I proposed to leave on Friday next on a visit to the Bedford Springs in Pennsylvania for the benefit of my health, and that I desired the members of the Cabinet to remain in Washington during my absence.

Friday, 18th August, 1848. — This morning I set out from Washington on a visit to the Bedford Springs in Pennsylvania. I took the morning train of cars and proceeded to Cumberland, Maryland, where I arrived at six o'clock P.M. I was accompanied by my nephew, Samuel P. Walker, of Tennessee, and by Dr. Foltz, a surgeon in the Navy. It had been known a day or two before that I intended to make the visit, though no public notice of it had been announced. My object was to have some repose and relaxation after my long and severe confinement and labour. Since my return early in July, 1847, from my Northern tour, I have not been more than two or three miles from my office, and during that whole period (thirteen months) my labours, responsibilities, and anxieties have been very great. Indeed I was exceedingly wearied and almost prostrated by fatigue. I regret that Mrs. Polk could not accompany me. Some friends

---

mind to do so. Calhoun earnestly pleaded with him to veto it on constitutional grounds, but he wisely refused. The Cabinet unanimously supported him in this position. Polk insisted, however, against Buchanan's advice, on sending Congress a message in which he explained that he signed the bill only because Oregon lay wholly north of the Missouri Compromise line — a characteristic act.

who were on a visit to us made it proper, in her opinion, that she should remain.

Saturday, 19th August, 1848. — After breakfast this morning I left Cumberland, Md., for the Bedford Springs, Penn., in a special coach furnished for my accommodation by Mr. Johnson, the very obliging stage contractor on the line. . . We proceeded on our way to the Springs, where we arrived about one o'clock P.M. It was known at the Springs that I was expected today, but I was not looked for until about four o'clock, the usual hour for the arrival of the stage. It was not known that I would come over in a special coach and, arriving two or three hours earlier than the usual hour for the arrival of the stage, the proprietor and company at the Springs were taken by surprise. I was informed that the citizens of the village of Bedford, situated about two miles from the Springs, and the company at the Springs had made arrangements to give me a formal reception, and had provided a band of music for the purpose. I prefer to have arrived quietly as I did than to have had a public reception. I found about fifty visitors at the springs, and among them was my old friend, the Hon. John Laporte, with whom I served in Congress many years ago. Col. Black, lately commanding the United States volunteers in Mexico, and his wife, Mr. Magraw of Pittsburg, Mr. McKinley, editor of the leading Democratic paper at Harrisburg, were also of the number. In the course of the evening General Bowman and a number of other citizens of the village of Bedford came out to see me. In the evening I was requested to walk into the ballroom, where there was music and a number of young people dancing. I remained but a short time and then retired for the night. I find the buildings large and the accommodations good. The Springs are situated in a valley between two mountains. The valley is not more than two hundred yards wide. One of the head streams of the Juniata runs between the mountains, and the springs flow out of the sides of the mountain. The spring

of greatest medicinal virtue and chiefly used is a bold, strong
fountain. I have not been furnished with an analysis of its
properties. The water, however, contains portions of mag-
nesia and iron; and when used operates chiefly on the kidneys
and bowels. There are also a white sulphur spring; a slate
spring; a very large limestone spring, and three or four
other springs, all within a circumference of less than three
hundred yards in diameter. The walks and grounds are neat
and well shaded, and everything about the establishment has
the appearance of comfort. I used but little of the water
this evening. There is a great difference between the hot
and sultry atmosphere of Washington and this place. I
slept under a blanket tonight and would have been uncomfortable without it.

Sunday, 20th August, 1848. — I rose early this morning
and walked to the main spring, drank some of the water, and
then ascended the mountain by a winding path to its summit,
where a summer-house or shed had been erected. The fog
rose and presented the view over the valley below, which
is said to be very fine. I returned and drank more of the
water before breakfast. This being the Sabbath was a quiet
day, and I remained chiefly in my chamber. I wrote letters
to Mrs. Polk and to J. Knox Walker. In the afternoon I ascended to the top of the mountain again and had a fine view
of the valley below and of the surrounding country. At dinner and in the afternoon I shook hands with a number of
people from the village and the neighbourhood, who from
curiosity had come to see the President of the United States.
The day became cloudy and the atmosphere cold, so much
so that about two o'clock I had a fire made in my room.
Towards sunset a cold rain commenced falling. At eight
o'clock P.M. the company assembled in one of the large parlours and an excellent sermon was preached by the Rev. Mr.
Purviance of the Presbyterian church.

Tuesday, 22nd August, 1848. — This morning was cool
and fires were comfortable. It is almost too late in the sea-

son to visit this watering place. In the hot weather it must be a delightful spot. I rode two miles and visited Major Watson at his house this morning. Major Watson had invited me to do so. I was accompanied by a party of gentlemen. When we arrived we met Judge Black, who is a candidate for the Democratic nomination for Governor of Pennsylvania. There was a cold collation and other refreshments. I returned to the Springs and after dinner rode to the village of Bedford at the invitation of several of the citizens. A party of gentlemen accompanied me. We stopped at a hotel where many citizens of the village called and were introduced to me. We took supper and returned to the Springs. I spend my time very comfortably.

Friday, 25th August, 1848. — After breakfast this morning I set out in the stage for Cumberland, Md., on my return to Washington.

Washington, Tuesday, 29th August, 1848. — The Secretary of State brought to my notice the numerous statements and rumours in public newspapers of a contemplated movement or expedition of citizens of the United States, of hostile character towards Mexico, the object of which was said to be to revolutionize the northern provinces of Mexico and to establish the Republic of Sierra Madre. If such a movement is on foot, or such an expedition contemplated, my attempt to execute it would be a clear violation of our international obligations under the late treaty with Mexico, and a violation of our neutrality laws as applied to all nations with which the United States are at peace, and it would be an imperative duty of the President of the United States to take all legal measures in his power to arrest and prevent it. The persons supposed to be engaged in the contemplated expedition against Mexico are called in the newspapers Buffalo Hunters, meaning that they are to organize and invade Mexico, under the pretense that they are engaging simply in a Buffalo Hunt. After discussing the subject it was the unanimous opinion of the members of the Cabinet present

and myself that precautionary measures should be adopted
to repress and prevent any such contemplated expedition.
With that view it was agreed that the Secretary of State
should immediately address instructions to the Attorneys of
the United States in Louisiana, Texas, and other Western
States to be vigilant in ascertaining if such a design was on
foot, and if so and he could obtain the requisite proof, to
institute prosecutions against all persons concerned in it. It
was agreed also that the Secretary of War should address
without delay instructions to General Taylor, commanding
the Western Division of the army, including Texas and the
Rio Grande frontier, to use military force if necessary to
check and repress such a movement, if one were attempted.

Wednesday, 30th August, 1848. — I was surprised to
learn, as soon as I rose this morning, from the servants that
an old servant named Smith, a colored man whom I have
hired and had in my employment as firemaker during my
whole term, died in his room in the President's House about
one o'clock this morning. He has been confined to his room
by a chronic disease for some weeks past, but his immediate
dissolution was not anticipated. He was a free man and a
faithful old servant. During his illness he was waited on
and all his wants supplied by the other servants. I directed
my steward to procure a coffin and see that he was decently
and properly interred. He was interred late in the evening.
The expenses, as the steward reported, were twenty dollars,
which I directed him to pay and he did so.

Friday, 1st September, 1848. — Today I appointed
Charles McVean of New York to be attorney of the United
States, vice Benjamin F. Butler removed. Shortly after I
became President I removed a Whig from this office and
appointed Mr. Butler. I did so upon the general principle
that the important subordinate general offices should be
filled by persons who agreed in opinion with the President
as to the policy to be pursued by the government, and who
would coöperate in carrying out that policy. Mr. Butler at

the time he was appointed was a Democrat. He has since abandoned the Democratic party; has bolted from and does not support the regularly nominated candidates of the Democratic party for President and Vice-President; has united himself with Federalists and abolitionists; and is endeavoring to divide the country into geographical parties.

Sunday, 10th September, 1848. — I attended the First Presbyterian church today. Mrs. Polk, Miss Rucker, and Miss Hays accompanied me. The Rev. Dr. McGuffey, a professor at the University of Virginia, preached.[8]

Saturday, 23d September, 1848. — The Hon. James Buchanan, Secretary of State, who has been absent from Washington on an excursion to the North for the last three weeks, returned this afternoon, and about nine o'clock P.M. called to see me. Mr. Walker and Mr. Marcy are still absent, but I hope will return next week. I have not had my full Cabinet together in council since the adjournment of Congress on the 14th of August last. I have conducted the government without their aid. Indeed, I have become so familiar with the duties and workings of the government, not only upon general principles, but in most of its minute details, that I find but little difficulty in doing this. I have made myself acquainted with the duties of the subordinate officers, and have probably given more attention to details than any of my predecessors. It is only occasionally that a great measure or a new question arises, upon which I desire the aid and advice of my Cabinet. At each meeting of the Cabinet I learn from each member what is being done in his particular Department, and especially if any question of doubt or difficulty has arisen. I have never called for any written opinions from my Cabinet, preferring to take their opinions, after discussion, in Cabinet and in the presence of each other. In this way harmony of opinion is more likely to exist.

[8] Dr. William Holmes McGuffey, compiler of the famous series of readers of which more than one hundred million copies have been sold, is now buried at the University of Virginia.

Thursday, 28th September, 1848. — It having become known two days ago that Dr. J. L. Martin, the United States *chargé d'affaires* to Rome, was dead, the applications for the place begin to pour in upon me. I received several letters upon the subject this morning. Lewis Cass, Jr., of Michigan called and was exceednigly importunate that I should appoint him. I told him frankly that whilst his father was a candidate for the Presidency, if I were to gratify his wishes it would do his father great injury in his election, because it would dissatisfy every other applicant. They would be apt to think that the son of a candidate for the Presidency whom they were supporting should have given way to them. He then insisted that I should promise him the office as soon as the election was over. This I declined to do. Mr. Cass manifested great anxiety and was scarcely rational on the subject. There is nothing that is more unpleasant or that I dislike more than these personal importunities for office. My interview with Mr. Cass was a painful one.

Saturday, 30th September, 1848. — . . . I brought to the notice of the Cabinet an extraordinary letter from Mr. Thomas H. Benton, Senator from Missouri, addressed "To the people of California," and closing as follows, *viz.,* "written at Washington City, this 27th day of August, 1848, and sent by Col. Frémont." This letter is published in the New York *Herald* of the 26th inst. I am told it first appeared in a western paper. It assumes to speak as from one in authority, and is in an arrogant tone and calculated to do much mischief. Among other things it advises the people "to meet in convention" and form an independent government of their own until Congress shall act, and instructs them what kind of government they should form. It is sent by Col. Frémont, the son-in-law of the writer, and the inference is plain enough that he means they shall make Col. Frémont the Governor of the independent government they shall form. Indeed I think it pretty clear that this was the main object. The arrogance and whole tone of the letter are offensive and must do harm, unless the people of California have assurances from the government that they will be taken care of by the government. I expressed the opinion that the Secretary of State should address a letter to them, similar to the one he addressed by my direction to the people of Oregon on the 29th of March, 1847, when Congress had failed to establish a territorial government and the extension of our laws over them. This would probably satisfy them until Congress can act, and prevent any revolutionary movement among them.[9]

[9] Benton's letter was intended for the advice of both California and New Mexico. He suggested that the people meet in convention, frame a " cheap and simple government," and look after themselves until Congress should make proper provision for them. Polk's Cabinet agreed, as it is here indicated, to combat this advice. They instructed the Federal postal agent who was about to set out for California to tell the people that they had no legal right to take any such step, and that they should continue to give their allegiance to the *de facto* government already existing. But the great gold rush began in January, 1848, and under the new conditions the Californians preferred Benton's advice to Polk's. They held a convention in September, 1849, drew up a constitution prohibiting slavery, and set up a State government which they expected Congress to recognize. Polk's fears of a " revolutionary movement " were fatuous.

CHAPTER XII

Oct. 4, 1848 – Feb. 14, 1849

THE AMERICAN SYSTEM — GOLD IN CALIFORNIA — THE
WILMOT PROVISO — THE POSTAL TREATY WITH GREAT
BRITAIN — CALHOUN AND SLAVERY — A GOVERNMENT FOR
CALIFORNIA

Wednesday, 4th October, 1848. — I disposed of business
on my table as usual, and devoted a considerable portion of
the day in preparing an exposé of the "American System"
as it was falsely called by its authors. This I designed to in-
sert either in my next annual message or reserve it for the
next veto message I may have to send to Congress on the
subject of internal improvements. I consider it almost certain that at the next session of Congress I may have occasion
to send such a message. With this view I occasionally devote a leisure hour to the examination of the subject, and
in reducing to writing such views as may occur to me.

Friday, 13th October, 1848. — I was closely engaged in
my office today. I disposed of the current business on my
table. I devoted the greater part of the day in preparing an
elaborate draft of my views on the subject of internal improvements, and especially harbour and river improvements,
by the Federal government. Denying, as I do, the power of
the general government to make such improvements, and
deeming it probable, if not certain, that such a bill will be
presented to me for my approval at the next session of Congress, I desire to be prepared to meet it with a veto. Should
another veto become necessary, I desire to make it a strong

348

paper, so that if I should be over-ruled, as I may be, by a united Whig vote and a part of the Democratic members, making a vote of two-thirds, I may leave my full views on record to be judged of by my countrymen and by posterity. I can add to the strength of my veto message on the same subject of the 15th of December last. If I should not have occasion to use it, it will be left among my papers at my death. I am thoroughly convinced that I am right upon the subject, and therefore I have bestowed much labour in preparing a paper which may contribute to convince others that I am so.

Wednesday, 18th October, 1848. — It happens to occur to me and I therefore record it, that thirty years ago this day I arrived at my father's house in Tennessee on my return from the University of North Carolina, where I had graduated in the month of June preceding. I closed my education at a later period of life than is usual, in consequence of having been very much afflicted and enjoyed very bad health in my youth. I did not commence the Latin Grammer until the 13th of July, 1813. My instructor was the Rev. Dr. Robert Henderson of the Presbyterian church, who taught an academy two or three miles south of Columbia, Tennessee.

Thursday, 19th October, 1848. — I transacted business on my table and at two o'clock opened my office for the reception of company. Quite a number of persons came in, several of whom were begging money and others who from their appearance were too lazy to work, were asking for office. The office of President is generally esteemed a very high and dignified position, but really I think the public would not so regard it if they could look in occasionally and observe the kind of people by whom I am often annoyed. I cannot seclude myself but must be accessible to my fellow-citizens, and this gives an opportunity to all classes and descriptions of people who obtrude themselves upon me about matters in which the public has not the slightest interest. There is no class of our population by whom I am annoyed so much, or for whom I entertain a more sovereign contempt, than for the professed office-seekers who have beseiged me ever since I have been in the Presidential office.

Tuesday, 24th October, 1848. — Col. John A. Thomas of New York called about three o'clock. I held a conversation with him about the prospects and probable result of the Presidential election. He agreed with me that if General Cass carried Pennsylvania he would be elected. He agreed with me also that the vote of that State would probably depend upon the course of Mr. Wilmot and the Free Soil faction. He suggested the importance of seeing Mr. McClelland, a member of Congress from Michigan, who was understood to have influence upon Wilmot and might induce him to abandon the Free Soil ticket and vote for General Cass.

Thursday, 26th October, 1848. — Judge Mason, the Secretary of the Navy, called this morning at my request. I read to him a paper of some length which I had prepared on the subject of the system which was called by its authors and advocates the "American System." The object of this paper was to show that the "American System" consisted of several branches, *viz.,* a Bank, protective tariff, distribution of the land fund, and internal improvements; that it had been overthrown in all its branches except the internal improvement branch, and that if this was revived the others would necessarily be revived also.

Thursday, 2nd November, 1848. — This is my birthday . . . fifty-three years old. It will be twenty-one years on tomorrow since my father died. My mother is still living. Upon each recurrence of my birthday I am solemnly impressed with the vanity and emptiness of worldly honours and worldly enjoyments, and of the wisdom of preparing for a future estate. In four months I shall retire from public life forever. I have lived three-fourths of the period ordinarily allotted to man on earth. I have been highly honoured by my fellow-men and have filled the highest station on earth, but I will soon go the way of all earth. I pray God to prepare me to meet the great event.

I was busily occupied in my office during the whole day. A part of the day I spent in preparing my annual message.

Tuesday, 7th November, 1848. — This is the day appointed by law for the election of President and Vice-President of the United States. Heretofore the people of the several States have by State laws fixed the period of holding the election in each State. Since the last Presidential election Congress for the first time exercised the power vested in them by the Constitution, and fixed the same day for holding the election in all the States. There will probably be not less than three millions of votes polled in this election.

The Cabinet met at the usual hour, all the members present. There being no other pressing business, I read to the Cabinet the portions of my next annual message which I had prepared, and invited the freest suggestions or criticism which any members of the Cabinet might think proper to make. The subjects mainly treated of in the paper which I read, were the veto power, a review of the system established shortly after the close of the war with Great Britain in 1815, called the "American System," the physical strength of our country in war, the vast territorial acquisitions we had made, their great importance and value, and the urgent necessity of establishing territorial governments over them. In connection with the latter subject the slavery question was considered, and concession and compromise recommended. Mr. Buchanan expressed his approbation of the paper. He said in that part of the paper which treated of the "American System" he did not go as far as I did in relation to internal improvements. He thought the government had power to make improvements for purely military or naval purposes, and if in making such as were strictly of this character incidental advantages accrued to commerce, it was well. He avowed himself opposed to a system of internal improvements as such. As to that part of the paper which treated of the protective tariff as a branch of the American system he said he approved the doctrines of my inaugural address. He was opposed to the tariff of 1842, and thought there should be increased protection by specific duties on coal and iron, and that the tariff of 1846 should be modified in this respect. With the expression of these general views he approved that part of the paper as I had written it, and thought it should go into the message.

Wednesday, 8th November, 1848. — Information received by the telegraph and published in the morning papers of this city and Baltimore indicate the election of General Taylor as President of the United States. Should this be so, it is deeply to be regretted.[1] Without political information and without experience in civil life, he is wholly unqualified for the station, and being elected by the Federal party and by the various factions of dissatisfied persons who have from time to time broken off from the Democratic party, he must be in their hands and be under their absolute control. Having no opinions or judgment of his own upon any one public subject, foreign or domestic, he will be compelled to rely upon the designing men of the Federal party who will cluster around him, and will be made to reverse, so far as the Executive can reverse, the whole policy of my administration, and to substitute the Federal policy in its stead. The country will be the loser by his election, and on this account it is an event which I should deeply regret.

Thursday, 9th November, 1848. — At six o'clock this morning Mrs. Polk left in the Eastern cars for New York. She was accompanied by my private secretary (Col. Walker) and our two nieces (Miss Rucker and Miss Hays),

---

[1] Taylor had a majority over Cass of nearly 150,000 in the popular vote, and of thirty-six in the electoral college. If either New York or Pennsylvania had voted for Cass, Cass would have become President. But the Walker Tariff was still resented in Pennsylvania, while in New York the antagonism between the Barnburners and Hunkers was disastrous to the Democratic Party. Taylor carried eight slave and seven free States, while Cass carried seven slave and eight free States.

a man-servant (Bowman) and a maid servant (Teresa). Her object in visiting New York was first to afford the young ladies an opportunity of seeing that city, but mainly to select some articles of furniture for our house, which is building at Nashville, Tennessee, and to have them shipped home *via* New Orleans. She will probably be absent ten days, as she contemplates visiting my nephew, Cadet Marshall T. Polk, at West Point.

Wednesday, 22nd November, 1848. — I was occupied in my office as usual today. I devoted a part of the day to my annual message, endeavoring to condense it. It will be very long in spite of any condensation which I can make. Mr. Marcy and Mr. Toucey called at my request and spent three or four hours in the private room adjoining my office, in examining my message with a view chiefly to suggest any parts of it which might be omitted, so as to reduce its length without impairing its strength. They called again after night and spent some time on the same business. They found this a difficult work. The subjects embraced in the paper are very important, requiring not a casual notice but a full examination. To make it as full as I desire the danger is that it will be so long that it will not be read by the mass of people, and by none but the politicians.

Thursday, 23rd November, 1848. — This morning I had made a material change in that part of the message which relates to the slave-question, as connected with the establishment of territorial governments in California and New Mexico. I read the modification to Mr. Walker and Mr. Mason, who highly approved it and thought it a valuable change of my original draft. The substance of the modified draft was, 1st, non-interference by Congress, which I thought the true course; 2nd, the Missouri Compromise line, to which I was willing to accede as a compromise; and 3rd, to leave the subject to the decision of the judiciary.

Sunday, 26th November, 1848. — After night Senator Dix of New York and his son called. Senator Dix has been in the city some days, but had not before called. He was the candidate of the Barnburners for Governor of New York and was defeated at the late election. He was the Free Soil candidate, and ran on the same ticket with the abolitionist, Seth M. Gales, who was a candidate for Lieutenant-Governor. He had contributed with Mr. Van Buren, therefore, to defeat the Democratic candidate for President at the late election. I received him courteously but no allusion was made during his visit to the late election or to any party political subject.

Wednesday, 29th November, 1848. — The *Union* of this morning contains an article undertaking to state what my message will contain. I was much vexed when I saw it. It is an infirmity of Mr. Ritchie that he cannot keep a secret. I had read to him some days ago a considerable portion of my message, but I informed him expressly that it was communicated to him confidentially. Without meaning to do wrong, such is his propensity to give news to the public, and to appear to the public to be the Executive organ, that in this morning's paper he shadows forth what I may say in it. Mr. Ames, the assistant-editor of the *Union,* called, and I expressed my dissatisfaction at Mr. Ritchie's course in strong terms.

Thursday, 30th November, 1848. — Mr. Ritchie called this morning and appeared to be very much mortified at the indiscreet publication of the article in his paper on yesterday. He meant no harm, I am satisfied. It is a constitutional infirmity with him, I believe, that he cannot keep a secret: all he knows, though given him in confidence, he is almost certain to put into his newspaper. My sympathies were excited at seeing his mortification, and I relieved him by telling him to let it all pass (see this diary of yesterday).

Tuesday, 5th December, 1848. — This was the regular evening for receiving company. A large number of persons, ladies and gentlemen, called. Among those present were the Vice-President of the United States, the Speaker of the

House of Representatives, and a number of Senators and Representatives. The French Minister and several other members of the diplomatic corps were also present. Many persons expressed to me their approval of my message. I learn that it is generally received well by the Democratic party in Congress.

Thursday, 7th December, 1848. — The Secretary of War called and exhibited to me specimens of California gold, which had been sent him by Col. Mason commanding the United States troops in California.[2] A portion of these specimens he will retain in the War Department, and the balance he will send to the mint of the United States at Philadelphia to be coined.

Sunday, 10th December, 1848. — After night Judge Mason called. . . In the course of conversation he asked me if I had ever written any letter to Col. Benton which could do me any injury if published. I told him I had not. I told him I had held no corresponrence with Col. Benton, unless it might be to address him a note during the earlier period of my administration, when he professed to support it and be my friend; that any such notes, if published, could do me no harm. I stated to him that Col. Benton had occasionally addressed notes to me during the same period. Judge Mason then said that his reason for asking the question was that he had learned from a lady, whose name he did not give, that she had learned from the Blair family that Col. Benton would probably publish some letter of mine which would do me an injury. I told Judge Mason that he had no such letter. I do not know what this means. I am, however, at the defiance of both Blair and Benton. The former has proved himself to be unprincipled and the latter, I fear, is no better. From the day I approved the sentence of the court-martial in Col. Frémont's case, Col. Benton, for no other

---

[2] Gold was discovered in the lower Sacramento Valley on Jan. 14, 1848, and when the news reached the outside world a mad rush for California began.

cause than that I dared to do my duty, has been exceedingly hostile to me. He has not called on me, nor have I spoken to him for more than twelve months.

Monday, 11*th December,* 1848. — After night . . . Senator Douglas of Illinois called and held a long conversation with me on the subject of a bill which he had introduced into the Senate to admit California and New Mexico into the Union as a State, instead of establishing territorial governments in the first instance over them.

Tuesday, 12*th December,* 1848. — The Cabinet met at the usual hour. . . Several matters of detail were considered and disposed of, none of them of much importance. I then stated to the Cabinet that I feared no action would be had at the present session of Congress for the government of California and New Mexico; that I feared this would be the case from the want of concert of action or any common views among the members of Congress with whom I had conversed. I stated further that I apprehended if these territories were left without a government for another year, and especially California, they might be lost to the Union. I gave my views at some length for this apprehension. They were, in substance, that in the course of the next year a large population would be attracted to California by its mineral wealth and other advantages, that among the emigrants would be men of enterprise and adventure, men of talents and capital; and that finding themselves without a government or the protection of law, they would probably organize an independent government, calling it the California or Pacific Republic, and might endeavor to introduce Oregon to join them. I stated that if this state of things existed when Congress came together twelve months hence, that the leading Federalists (alias Whigs) would be glad to avail themselves of the opportunity to give up the country for the purpose of relieving General Taylor of his embarrassments upon the Wilmot Proviso. I added that the Federal party had from the commencement of our history been opposed to the extension of our limits; that they opposed the acquisition of Louisiana as they had recently done that of our new possessions. To guard against the loss of California I deemed it very important that the question of its government should be settled at the present session of Congress. I then stated that I thought it indispensable that we should agree upon a plan of settlement (for Congress seemed to have no plan) and exercise what influence we might possess to carry it through at the present session. All present agreed that this would be proper and, indeed, our duty. It is a question rising above ordinary party considerations.

Wednesday, 13th December, 1848. — I learn from my private secretary this afternoon that a vote was taken in the House of Representatives today approving the Wilmot Proviso by a considerable majority. Some of the Northern Democrats are giving way and reversing their votes of the last session, and I am the more satisfied that unless Senator Douglas's bill is accepted, no adjustment of the territorial questions can be effected at the present session.

Friday, 15th December, 1848. — After night Senators Atchison of Missouri and Cameron of Pennsylvania called and enquired of me if I had nominated Lewis Cass, Jr., to the Senate as *chargé d'affaires* to Rome (his nomination is now before the Senate) at the request of his father (General Cass). I replied that it was a question of some delicacy, but, as they were both the friends of General Cass, I would say to them confidentially that it was done at the request of General Cass, who was anxious he should receive the appointment and thought him well qualified for it. I told them I knew very little of the young man personally, and had nominated him from the belief that he was qualified and from the great respect I had for his father. They expressed deep regret at it, and expressed the opinion that he had no claims and that he would be rejected by the Senate. Mr. Atchison declared his intention to vote against his nomination. They desired to know if I would withdraw his nomination. I told them I could not unless his father voluntarily requested it.

Tuesday, 19th December, 1848. — This was the regular weekly evening for receiving company. An unusually large number of persons, ladies and gentlemen, members of Congress and of the Judiciary, Foreign Ministers, strangers, and citizens called. The circular parlour, and one or two of the adjoining parlours were filled. Among others who were present I noticed Mr. John Van Buren. Though he had been several times in Washington and had called on me this was the first time he had called on Mrs. Polk. Upon two or three occasions I had decided that he should be invited to dinner, and in each case Mrs. Polk had countermanded the order. This she did upon the ground that if he so far neglected the courtesies of life as not to call and pay his respects to her that he should not be honoured with an invitation to dinner by the President. Upon one of these occasions I was amused when she told me she had burned John Van Buren's dinner ticket, which I requested my private secretary to send to him. During the past year he has been traversing the country making violent political speeches against my administration, and advocating the " free-soil " doctrine and his father's claims to the Presidency. I, of course, treated him courteously in our parlour.

Friday, 22nd December, 1848. — About two o'clock the Hon. Mr. Inge of Alabama called to see me about the appointment of a land officer at Tuscaloosa, Ala., to fill a vacancy which had occurred in consequence of the death of the former incumbent. After conversing on that subject Mr. Inge informed me that considerable excitement existed in the House of Representatives today in consequence of the resolution passed on yesterday directing the Committee on the District of Columbia to bring in a bill to abolish the slave-trade in the said District.[3] He informed me that

[3] The agitation over slavery and the slave-trade in the District of Columbia had now reached an acute point. On December 13, 1848, John G. Palfrey of

before he left the House a paper was being handed round
for the Southern members to sign calling a meeting of all
the Senators and Representatives from the slave-holding
states, to take place this evening. He said that the movement had been set on foot by Southern Senators, and that
Senator Foote of Mississippi had been in the hall of the
House and was active in promoting it. He informed me
that the Southern Whig members disapproved the vote of
yesterday and were as much excited at it as Southern Democrats, but that some of them had declined to sign the paper,
and among these he named Mr. Stephens of Georgia. This
was the first intimation I had that such a movement was
contemplated. I felt the delicacy as well as the responsibility of my station and gave no expression of opinion further
than my disapproval of the resolution passed on yesterday
and my hope that the Northern members would not press
so mischievous a proposition. . .

The agitation of the slavery question is mischievous and
wicked, and proceeds from no patriotic motive by its
authors. It is a mere political question on which dema-
gogues and ambitious politicians hope to promote their own
prospects for political promotion. And this they seem
willing to do even at the hazard of disturbing the harmony
if not dissolving the Union itself. Such agitation with such
objects deserves the reprobation of all the lovers of the
Union and of their country. I disposed of much business
on my table today.

Massachusetts, the historian and preacher, asked leave to introduce a bill to
repeal all legislation maintaining slavery or the slave-trade in the District.
This was refused, 69 to 82; but the struggle had only begun. On December
18, Giddings of Ohio introduced a bill for a referendum in the District on the
continuance of slavery, which was tabled. Then on December 21 Gott of
New York offered a resolution instructing the committee for the District of
Columbia to frame a bill prohibiting the slave trade. This resolution passed,
98 to 88, but on January 10, 1849, was reconsidered. As Polk notes, the Gott
resolution caused a Southern outburst. Many Southern members were at once
up in arms, and Calhoun, taking charge of the movement, artfully fed their
indignation and made the most of their resentment.

Saturday, 23d December, 1848. — Between sunset and dark, Senator Foote of Mississippi called and enquired of me if I had heard what had occurred at the meeting of the Southern members of Congress held at the Senate chamber last night on the subject of the slavery question. . . He informed me that about seventy members of both political parties from the Southern States were present, and that Mr. Bayley of Virginia had offered resolutions, which on motion of Mr. Stephens of Georgia had been referred to a committee of one from each of the slaveholding States, who were to report to an adjourned meeting on or before the 15th of January next. He informed me that this was done by the unanimous voice of those present. He said there was no violence, but a calm and firm purpose on the part of those present to assert and maintain the constitutional rights of the Southern States if the majority in Congress should attempt to carry out the purpose indicated by the late votes in the House of Representatives on the subject of slavery in this District. He said that the committee appointed would prepare an address to the State governments of the slaveholding States on the subject, if the measures threatened in Congress assailing the constitutional rights of the South were pressed. I said but little in reply, but said generally that my position as President of the United States made it my duty to represent all the States and to preserve the harmony of the Union as far as I possessed the power to do so. I expressed the hope to him that the threatened interference from the North with the delicate subject of slavery would not be pressed to extremities.

Friday, 29th December, 1848. — Many matters of minor importance and of detail remain on my table to be attended to. The public have no idea of the constant accumulation of business requiring the President's attention. No President who performs his duty faithfully and conscientiously can have any leisure. If he entrusts the details and smaller matters to subordinates constant errors will occur. I prefer to supervise the whole operations of the government rather than entrust the public business to subordinates, and this makes my duties very great.

Monday, 1st January, 1849. — This being the first day of a new year the President's mansion was thrown open for the reception of visitors. Between eleven and twelve o'clock company commenced arriving. A very large crowd called, larger than is usual on such occasions. Every parlour, the East Room, and outer hall were crowded. All the foreign ministers and the persons attached to their respective legations appeared in their court dresses. Many officers of the army and navy were present in their full uniform. The Cabinet and their families, Judges of the Supreme and District Courts, Senators and Representatives in Congress, citizens and strangers, were of the immense crowd. I received the crowd in the circular parlour and for three hours shook hands with a dense column of human beings of all ages and sexes. The Marshal of the District of Columbia and his deputies and the Commissioner of Public Buildings stood near me and preserved order and caused the crowd, after shaking hands, to pass on into the other parlours and the East Room. So dense was the crowd and so great the jam that many persons, I learn, left early. During the period of reception the fine Marine Band of music played in the outer hall. I must have shook hands with several thousand persons. Toward the close of the day some gentlemen asked me if my arm was not sore, and if I would not suffer from the day's labour. I answered them that judging from my experience on similar occasions I thought not. I told them that I had found that there was great art in shaking hands, and that I could shake hands during the whole day without suffering any bad effects from it. They were curious to know what this art was. I told them that if a man surrendered his arm to be shaken, by some horizontally, by others perpendicularly, and by others again with a strong grip, he could not fail to suffer severely from it, but that if he would shake and not be shaken, grip and not be gripped, taking care always to squeeze the hand of his adversary as hard as he squeezed him, that he suffered no inconvenience from it. I told them also that I could generally anticipate when I was to have a strong grip, and that when I observed a strong man approaching I generally took advantage of him by being a little quicker than he was and seizing him by the tip of his fingers, giving him a hearty shake, and thus preventing him from getting a full grip upon me. They were much amused at my account of the operation, which I gave to them playfully, but admitted that there was much philosophy in it. But though I gave my account of the operation playfully, it is all true. About three o'clock the company dispersed. . .

Among the visitors whom I observed in the crowd today was Hon. Andrew Johnson of the House of Representatives. Though he represents a Democratic District in Tennessee (my own State) this is the first time I have seen him during the present session of Congress. Professing to be a Democrat, he has been politically if not personally hostile to me during my whole term. He is very vindictive and perverse in his temper and conduct. If he had the manliness or independence to manifest his opposition openly, he knows he could not be again elected by his constituents. I am not aware that I have ever given him cause of offense.

Tuesday, 2nd January, 1849. — Nothing of much importance was before the Cabinet today. The Secretary of War handed me a letter to his Department from General Taylor tendering his resignation as major-general of the army of the United States to take effect on the 31st of January, 1849. He seems resolved to hold on to the office as long as possible, and therefore fixes the period when his resignation is to take effect about the period when he will probably leave his residence in Louisiana to enter on his duties as President of the United States.

Saturday, 6th January, 1849. — A number of members of

Congress called this morning. The Cabinet met at the usual hour; all the members present except the Secretary of the Navy, who is detained at his house, as I learn, by indisposition. Several matters of no general importance were considered and disposed of, and the Cabinet dispersed about two o'clock P.M. I signed the ratification of the Postal Treaty with Great Britain this afternoon. This is an important treaty, and Mr. Bancroft deserves high credit for the zealous ability with which he conducted the negotiation. It places our own steamers and packets upon an equal footing with the British and relieves our merchants, naturalized citizens, and others from a heavy discriminating charge of postage on letters and other mailable matter conveyed in American ships. This change has been effected by the policy of the administration. Had it occurred under other circumstances and when so many other great events had not been crowded into a single Presidential term it would have attracted more public attention and been regarded as an important achievement. After the Cabinet adjourned today I disposed of much business on my table.

Tuesday, 9th January, 1849.—... After my doors were closed and I had directed no one to be admitted a man who had evaded the vigilance of my porter opened my office and stepped in. He wished, he said, to sell me wine to take home with me, and to get an office for a friend. I was at the moment very much engaged writing at my table and was vexed at his unceremonious intrusion. As I wanted no wine and had no offices to confer, and was, moreover, much engaged in my official duties, I made short work of it with him. His name was Lawrence. It is not the first time that the same person has annoyed me about matters in which neither the public nor myself could have any interest. A telegraphic despatch was received in the city today to the effect that Paymaster Dix of the United States Army had died of cholera. The rumour thus brought requires confirmation. In less than an hour I had application for his place as paymaster. In the course of the evening several other applications were made for it.

Saturday, 13th January, 1849.——. . . The members of the Cabinet entered into a general conversation among themselves whether it would be proper for them to resign to me on the 3rd of March, or to General Taylor after he was qualified. They agreed that their resignations should be made to me, but there was some diversity of opinion whether they should take effect immediately, or when a successor was appointed. If they resigned to me on the 3rd of March there would be no Cabinet on Sunday, the 4th, and Monday the 5th of March, and on the latter day there might be official business to transact requiring their signatures. Mr. Walker objected to resigning to take effect when a successor was appointed, because he was unwilling to serve under General Taylor. Mr. Buchanan was willing to continue a few days if General Taylor should request it, until his successor could be appointed. Finally, upon the suggestion of Mr. Toucey, they agreed to resign to me on the 3rd of March, and suggested that I should accept them and enclose them to General Taylor on the 3rd, so as to enable him to appoint persons *ad interim* to take charge of the several departments and conduct the business until permanent appointments could be made.

Sunday, 14th January, 1849.——. . . After night the Hon. Mr. Houston of Alabama and the Hon. Messrs. Cobb and Lumpkin of Georgia called to consult me about an adjourned meeting of the Southern members of Congress on the subject of slavery which was to take place on tomorrow night. I have heretofore carefully avoided having anything to do with this movement. It was gotten up originally without consulting me. I have feared from the time I first heard of the first meeting of the Southern members of Congress on the slavery question that there might be a design on the part of one or two leading men to agitate the slavery question for selfish purposes and that it might end in no good. These gentlemen informed me tonight that Mr. Calhoun had drawn up an address to the Southern States to be signed by all the Senators and Representatives from the slave-holding states, and that from what they had heard of its import they could not sign it. They informed me further that from what they had heard, the Whig Senators and Representatives from the South would decline in a body to sign it. They asked my opinion on the subject. I replied that if there was anything in the proceedings or the address that looked like or might tend to disunion I was opposed to it. . . I think the movement of the Southern members was originally ill-advised. The Whigs, I learn, at first went zealously into it, but upon consultation have concluded to leave the consummation of the proceedings exclusively to the Democratic members, alleging that they have confidence in General Taylor, who is a large slave-holder, that he will protect the rights of the South. If they take this course it will produce a division in the South upon the slave question and encourage, rather than discourage, the aggression of the Northern Abolitionists and Whigs upon the rights of the South. Should this be the result great mischief will be produced by the proceedings of the portion of the Southern members who may attend the meeting and send forth an address. My advice to the gentlemen who called this evening was to attend the meeting tomorrow night and endeavour to prevent anything from being done; but not themselves to sign any address.

Tuesday, 16th January, 1849.—. . . Between ten and eleven o'clock Senator Calhoun of South Carolina called. He has not been to see me since his arrival in Washington shortly after the meeting of Congress, when he called to pay his respects. I anticipated his business the moment he entered my office, and I was not mistaken. He very soon introduced the subject of the slavery question and the meeting of the Southern members of Congress at the Capitol last night. He was very earnest in the expression of his opinion that the South should no longer delay resisting the aggressions of the North upon their rights. As soon as I had an opportunity I expressed my strong attachment to the Union of the States, the great importance of preserving it, and my hope that governments might be provided for California and New Mexico, and especially the former, by admitting into the Union as a State without having the bill for that purpose embarrassed by the Wilmot Proviso. I found he was opposed to an adjustment in this mode. I urged the importance of the measure, and expressed the opinion that the admission of California into the Union as a State was the only practical mode of settling the slave question. In this form the question of slavery would be left to the people of the new States when they came to form a State constitution for themselves. I told him that I deemed it of the greatest importance that the agitation of the delicate and dangerous question of slavery should be arrested, as I thought it would be by the organization of governments for the territories acquired by the treaty with Mexico. I told him that Senator Douglas of Illinois had suggested to me that the question as to New Mexico might be settled with the assent of the State of Texas, by making the Northern boundary of that State the parallel of 36° 30″ North Latitude and extending that parallel west of the Rio Grande, leaving all of New Mexico on both sides of that River and south of that parallel to be a part of the State of Texas, and that that State should cede to the United States all the territory within her limits lying north of that line. I told him that the area acquired by Texas by such an arrangement would be about equal to the area which would be ceded by Texas to the United States. I told him also, that all the inhabited portion of New Mexico lay south of 36° 30″, and would fall under the government of the State of Texas, while the country north of that line to be ceded by Texas to the United States was a wilderness country. I told him that the proposition struck me favourably, that

I presumed it would be satisfactory to the members of Congress from Texas and to that State, and that coming as it did from a Northern Senator there was a fair prospect, if the South, as I thought it should do, supported a bill of this kind, that it would pass. I told him this would provide a government for all the inhabited portion of New Mexico; and that if California, bounded by the California mountains, was admitted as a State, the whole difficulty would be settled, and that the Free-Soil agitators or Abolitionists of the North would be prostrate and powerless, that the country would be quieted, and the Union preserved. He was opposed to all this; spoke in excited terms of the Texas members and said that they had betrayed the South; that he had heard of this proposition about New Mexico ten days ago, and that it was a bid for the Texas men. I told him I had never heard of it until last Saturday night, when it was suggested by Senator Douglas of Illinois in the presence of Senator Downs of Louisiana. He was opposed to the admission of California as a State, because slaveholders had been prevented from emigrating with their property to it and it would be a free State. I replied that whether admitted now or hereafter the people inhabiting the country would have a right when they came to form a State constitution to regulate their own domestic institutions, and that Congress could not prevent this. He proposed no plan of adjusting the difficulty but insisted that the aggressions of the North upon the South should be resisted and that the time had come for action. I became perfectly satisfied that he did not desire that Congress should settle the question at the present session, and that he desired to influence the South upon the subject, whether from personal or patriotic views it is not difficult to determine. I was firm and decided in my conversation with him, intending to let him understand distinctly that I gave no countenance to any movement which tended to violence or the disunion of the States. The conversation was interrupted by the arrival of a member of the Cabinet, this being the regular day for the meeting of the Cabinet.

Thursday, 18th January, 1849. — I conversed with several members of Congress of both Houses who called to-day, and urged upon them the great importance of passing a law to admit California into the Union as a State as proposed by bills introduced into the Senate by Senators Downs and Douglas, and providing a government for New Mexico (see this diary of the 16th and 17th instant). All with whom I conversed listened favourably to the plan suggested, except Mr. Robertson of the House of Representatives, from Indiana. He wished to throw the responsibility of settling the slavery question on General Taylor's administration, and thought that nothing should be done at the present session. I told him we had a country to save as well as a party to obey, and that it was the solemn duty of the present Congress to settle the question.

Friday, 19th January, 1849. — Among others who called this morning was rather an elderly woman who said she lived in Alexandria. She wanted money to pay her rents and for other purposes. She brought no letters. I did not learn her name. She said she had lived in Alexandria many years. She had a genteel appearance. I endeavored to waive her application by treating her civilly and telling her she should apply to her neighbours and friends, who knew her. She became more and more importunate and I was forced at last to give her a positive denial. This did not satisfy her, and she named a sum which would satisfy her. I declined to give it to her and was compelled at last to tell her plainly that I did not know her or that she was worthy. I informed her that I contributed to objects of real charity, as far as my means permitted, and asked her again why she had not applied for aid to her neighbours in Alexandria, to which she replied that she did not wish to expose her necessities. I note this case to show some of the annoyances to which a President of the United States is subjected.

Saturday, 20th January, 1849.—. . . The Cabinet met
at the usual hour; all the members present. The Secretary
of the Navy read a despatch received last night from Commodore Jones, commander of the Pacific squadron; the Secretary of War read a letter to the Paymaster-General from
Paymaster Rich serving in California; and the Secretary
of State read a letter from Mr. Larkin, formerly United
States consul at Monterey in California. These several
communications represent the increased richness of the gold
region recently discovered in California, the rage of which
prevails among all classes to go in pursuit of it. Commodore Jones and Paymaster Rich represent the desertions
from the squadron and the army to go in pursuit of gold
to be such as to destroy all efficient service in both arms
of the service. They represent also the state of anarchy
and confusion existing in California, where, without any
regularly organized government, there is no security for
life, liberty, or property, and they represent the urgent
necessity for the establishment of the authority of the
United States by the organization of a government of some
kind in that Territory. It occurred to me at once that it
would be proper for me to transmit these communications
to Congress with a message urging the establishment of civil
Government for the inhabitants of California at the present
session, and I submitted two questions to the Cabinet, 1st,
whether these communications should be sent to Congress,
and if so what the recommendations of my message should
be. The views of all the members of the Cabinet were
freely given. Mr. Marcy and Mr. Walker advised that
the communications be sent to Congress with a message.
Mr. Buchanan, Mr. Mason, Mr. Johnson, and Mr. Toucey
advised against it. The latter gentlemen thought they
should be published without delay in the *Union* newspaper,
and that if called for by Congress, as they probably would
be, they should then be transmitted. They assigned their
reasons for this opinion. Among other reasons they said

that I had already in my annual message said all that could be said to induce Congress to act, and that exception might be taken by the Whig members, and perhaps some Democrats, if I repeated my views. After their views were expressed Mr. Marcy expressed his willingness to acquiesce in them, though he rather preferred that the papers should be sent to Congress with a message. Finding that Mr. Walker alone concurred fully with me in my first impressions, I stated that I would for the present yield to the views of the majority of the Cabinet. I then directed that copies of the communications, or of the material parts of them, should be furnished to the editor of the *Union* for publication. I then stated to the Cabinet that I had become perfectly satisfied that no bill to establish a territorial government could be passed through the House of Representatives without having the Wilmot Proviso attached to it as a condition, that with this provision the bill would probably be rejected by the Senate, and that if it was not, and the provision was made to apply to territory South of 36° 30" I must veto it, and in either event the people of California would be left without a government. I expressed to them the opinion that the only hope of providing a government for California at the present session was to admit her as one of the States of the Union, as had been proposed in the Senate by Senators Downs of Louisiana and Douglas of Illinois. In this opinion all the members of the Cabinet concurred, and expressed their desire that such a proposition might pass. I expressed my fears that the extremes of the South headed by Mr. Calhoun and the extremes of the North headed by Hale and Giddings might unite to prevent such a measure from passing and thus keep the subject of slavery open for political agitation. I expressed my strong desire that California might be admitted as a State, because I believed if this was not done at the present session the danger was imminent that the inhabitants of this fine country would, before the next session of Congress, set

up an independent government for themselves, and that the
Whig party, who would then be in power, would suffer the
country to be lost to the Union. I gave my reasons at some
length for this opinion. I expressed my disapprobation of
any further proceedings of the Southern members of Congress on the slave question in caucus.[4]

After night I sent for Senator Douglas and held a long
conversation with him in relation to his bill to admit California into the Union as a State, and the prospect of passing it. I told him confidentially that I and every member of
my Cabinet were in favour of his bill, as the only thing that
could probably be done at the present session so as to
provide a government for California, and thus secure
that valuable country to the Union and put an end to the
slavery excitement. He expressed himself as much
gratified, and thought there was a fair prospect for passing
the bill.

Monday, 29th January, 1849.— . . . The Secretaries
of State, War, and Navy called in the course of the day on
business. I disposed of business on my table as usual. I
learned tonight that the select committee of the Senate reported a bill today providing for the admission of California
and New Mexico into the Union as two States. Senator
Douglas called and informed me that five out of the seven
members of the committee, two from the non-slaveholding
and three from the slaveholding States, concurred in the bill.
Mr. Douglas said it was favourably received by the Senate,

---

[4] Polk, vigorously supported by Alexander H. Stephens of Georgia, tried
to prevent action by the caucus of Southern members led by Calhoun. He
failed. The caucus issued an address to the Southern people. This dwelt upon
the growing antagonism between North and South, attacked the North for its
failure to render up fugitive slaves and for its lack of respect for the Missouri
Compromise, declared that the North was trying to refuse the South its due
share of the Mexican cession, and lamented the attacks by Northern Congress-
men upon slavery. It called for unified action by the South to meet these
affronts and aggressions. This Congressional address to the South found
loud echoes in the resolutions drawn up by various Southern legislatures and
mass meetings. Polk's administration was closing amid a rising storm of sectional dissension and distrust.

and has strong hope that it may pass. I am myself anxious, from what I learn of its provisions, that it may pass.

Tuesday, 30th January, 1849. — The Secretary of War read a letter which he had received from General Persifor F. Smith, United States Army, dated at Panama on the 7th instant. General Smith was waiting at that point for a passage to California and Oregon to assume the command of the army in those territories. Among other things he gives a description of the bad condition of the road across the Isthmus and the difficulty of obtaining transportation. Some of the Cabinet engaged in a conversation, in which Mr. Buchanan led, about the practicability of making a road across the Isthmus or at some other point, and seemed to treat the subject as though it was within the constitutional competency of the government of the United States to apply the public money in the form of a contract with a company to make the road. I listened to the conversation for some time, when I arrested it by expressing a decided opinion that no such power existed. And in relation to the bill now before Congress, which proposed to pay to Aspinwall, Stephens, and others $250,000 per annum for twenty years, to enable them to construct a road and for transporting the mails and public property across the Isthmus, I informed the Cabinet that if it passed I should veto it. I consider that the government possesses no constitutional power to apply the public money either within or without the United States for any such purpose. I stated that I considered the proposition of that bill as but little better than a proposition to plunder the Treasury, and that it should never pass with my approval. I then stated that this bill was but one of many measures proposing expenditure of public money, which I understood was pressed on Congress by a lobby influence, consisting of leading men out of Congress whose special business it was to induce members of Congress to vote for and support them. It is said that there are persons now in Washington, ex-members of Congress and others, who make this their special business. Some member of the Cabinet intimated, indeed expressed, the conviction that some members of Congress were feed attorneys to get some of these large claims through Congress. It is hoped for the honour of the country that this may be so. Such a thing as an organized lobby influence, such as there is every reason to believe now exists, was wholly unknown while I was in Congress.

Thursday, 1st February, 1849. — Among others I saw the Hon. Mr. Venable of North Carolina, and after he retired Senator Johnson of Georgia, to each of whom I assigned my reasons for desiring to see the bill introduced into the Senate to admit California and New Mexico as two States into the Union. This bill I consider the only practical means of providing governments for these territories at the present session of Congress, and of thereby allaying the geographical excitement on the subject of slavery. I had invited these two gentlemen to call because I had been informed they were among the most impracticable of the Democratic members of Congress from the South. I have ascertained that a number of Northern Democrats will vote against attaching the Wilmot Proviso to a bill to provide for admitting them as States, who would feel constrained by the public sentiment among their constituents to vote for it as a condition on any Bill to establish a territorial government.

Wednesday, 7th February, 1849. — General notice had been given in the city papers that the President's Mansion would be open for the reception of visitors this evening. All the parlours including the East Room were lighted up. The Marine Band of musicians occupied the outer hall. Many hundreds of persons, ladies and gentlemen, attended. It was what would be called in the society of Washington a very fashionable levée. Foreign Ministers, their families and suites, judges, members of both Houses of Congress, and many citizens and strangers were of the company present. I stood and shook hands with them for over three hours.

Towards the close of the evening I passed through the crowded rooms with the venerable Mrs. Madison on my arm. It was near twelve o'clock when the company retired. I was much fatigued with my labours in my office during the day, and in the parlour during the evening.

Tuesday, 13th February, 1849. — It is four years ago this day since I arrived in Washington, preparatory to entering on my duties as President of the United States on the 4th of March following. They have been four years of incessant labour and anxiety and of great responsibility. I am heartily rejoiced that my term is so near its close. I will soon cease to be a servant and will become a sovereign. As a private citizen I will have no one but myself to serve, and will exercise a part of the sovereign power of my country. I am sure I will be happier in this condition than in the exalted station I now hold.

Wednesday, 14th February, 1849. — The number of persons, male and female, who called this morning was unusually great, and the importunate applications for office were exceedingly annoying. The impression has obtained that General Taylor may possibly not be proscriptive, and the herd of persons who are without political principle, and who are willing to profess to belong to either party to obtain or hold office, are anxious to get in before I retire, in the hope that they will not be turned out after I retire. I have great contempt for such persons, and dispose of their applications very summarily. They take up much of my time every day. I yielded to the request of an artist named Brady,[5] of New York, by sitting for my daguerreotype likeness today. I sat in the large dining-room.

---

[5] This is Mathew B. Brady, the pioneer photographer, who in 1842 or 1843 established a portrait studio on Broadway in New York, and whose Civil War photographs have made his name well-known.

CHAPTER XIII

Feb. 17, 1849 — March 5, 1849

VISIT OF PRESIDENT-ELECT TAYLOR — LAST RECEPTION —
THE APPROPRIATION BILL AND WILMOT PROVISO — END OF
CONGRESS — INAUGURATION OF PRESIDENT TAYLOR

Saturday, 17th February, 1849. — Mr. Mason and Mr.
Johnson remained a few minutes after the other members of
the Cabinet retired. Mr. Mason said he felt it to be his
duty to inform me of a matter of some delicacy which had
come to his knowledge, which I ought to know, but not desiring to stand in the attitude of an informer, he desired that I
would not use his name. He then informed me that he had
learned from Mr. Collins, the First Auditor, that Mr.
Fletcher Webster, who was chief clerk in the State Department during the period when his father (Hon. Daniel Webster) was Secretary of State, had presented an account for
eighteen or nineteen hundred dollars for salary as acting
Secretary of State during his father's temporary absence
from the seat of Government. He informed me that Mr.
Collins, the auditor, had refused to allow the account, and
that Mr. Collins informed him that he had been overruled by
Mr. McCulloch, the First Comptroller. Mr. Mason expressed the apprehension that Mr. McCulloch was making
this and similar payments very loosely, if not illegally. I
immediately sent for the Secretary of the Treasury and gave
him the information, but without giving the source from
which I had obtained it. I expressed to him my astonish-

375

ment. He expressed the opinion that such payments were legal and that similar payments had been made. I replied this could not be, for Congress had appropriated but one salary for a Secretary of State, and that having been drawn by Daniel Webster, it could not be again legally paid to his son. I told him I must have the opinion of the Attorney-General on the legal question, as I was strongly impressed that such payments were illegal, and was very sure that they were improper. Mr. Walker said he would take the opinion of the Attorney-General and enquire further into the matter.

Sunday, 18th February, 1849. — Mr. Buchanan called in after night and informed me that he had been informed at a party last evening that Mr. Stephens of Georgia and Mr. Wilmot of Pennsylvania had made a violent assault upon me in the House of Representatives the day before, in which the effort was made to prove that I had at one time been in favour of the Wilmot Proviso. Such an allegation is false, come from what quarter it may.

Tuesday, 20th February, 1849. — The Cabinet met at the usual hour; the members all present except the Secretary of War and the Attorney-General. . . A conversation took place on the subject of the attack made on me in the House of Representatives on Saturday last by Stephens and Wilmot (see this diary of yesterday). The members present were indignant at the charge and remembered distinctly my repeated expressions of hostility to the Wilmot Proviso, and my determination to veto it if it extended beyond the Missouri compromise. Mr. Walker stated a conversation he had held with Wilmot, which may hereafter become important, in which he had argued with Wilmot to prove that without the Proviso slavery could never exist in California, and that Wilmot had declared to him that if the views he presented had occurred to him before he offered the Proviso he never would have offered it.

Friday, 23rd February, 1849. — I fear that after all my efforts to induce Congress to provide some government for

California and New Mexico they will adjourn without doing so. Should this be the result theirs and not mine will be the responsibility of doing so.

Saturday, 24th February, 1849. — Mr. Buchanan and Mr. Marcy engaged in conversation between themselves while the other members of the Cabinet conversed with me. One of them enquired of me at what time it would be proper for them to call and pay their respects to General Taylor, the President-elect. I answered to that that it was a matter for their own decision, but that it occurred to me that until the President-elect had called on the President in office, as it was his duty to do under the established etiquette (if he desired to have any intercourse with him) a proper self-respect should prevent the Cabinet of the latter from calling on him. As soon as this suggestion was made they assented to its correctness. Mr. Buchanan and Mr. Marcy being still engaged in their conversation and not attending to the conversation with me, I requested Mr. Toucey to mention it to them, and he replied he would do so. Before he had time to do so, my porter came in and informed Mr. Buchanan that his messenger from the State Department had brought a message to him that General Shields was waiting for him at the Department to meet him on an appointment he had made with him. Mr. Buchanan on receiving this message immediately enquired if the members of the Cabinet should not call on the President-elect in a body, addressing himself to me. I then informed him of the conversation which I had just had while he and Mr. Marcy were engaged, and which they had not heard, and added that if my Cabinet called on General Taylor before he called on me, I should feel that I had been deserted by my own political family. . . My private secretary informed me tonight that he had received a note from Senator Davis of Mississippi, informing him that General Taylor was too much indisposed to call today, but that it was his intention, if his health permitted, to call on me on Monday next. Senator Davis married a daughter of General Taylor. His wife is dead and he is married a second time.[1]

Monday, 26th February, 1849. — Many persons called this morning and among them several Whig members of Congress with whom I had served. They are doubtless congregating at Washington to importune General Taylor for offices. Several Democratic members of Congress and others called, and it was gratifying to receive from them expressions of their warm approbation of my public conduct and of the policy of my administration. I received today a letter from the Mayor of Charleston, S. C., inviting me on behalf of the City Council to visit Charleston on my way home as the " guest of the city." I answered the letter and accepted the invitation (see my letter-book). I had previously received similar invitations from Augusta, Georgia, and Wilmington, N. C. The former I declined and the latter I accepted (see my letter-book). Between twelve and one o'clock my messenger announced to me that General Taylor, the President-elect of the United States, had called to pay his respects, and that he was in the parlour below. I immediately repaired to the parlour and was introduced to him, for I had never before seen him. He was accompanied by a number of friends, among whom were Senator Clayton of Delaware, who, it is understood, is to be his Secretary of State, Senator Davis of Mississippi, Mr. Hall of New York, and Mr. Barrow of Tennessee of the House of Representatives, Cols. Bliss and Garnett of the United States Army. Shortly after I entered the parlour, Mrs. Polk, my two nieces, Miss Davis of Baltimore and Mrs. Judge Catron, came into the parlour. I received General Taylor with courtesy and cordiality. He remained some twenty or thirty minutes. I invited him to dine with me on Thursday next. He replied that he would do so if his health would permit

---

[1] Jefferson Davis married Sarah Knox Taylor, daughter of Zachary Taylor, in 1835; she died within three months, and in 1845 he married Varina Howell of Natchez, Miss.

it. After he retired I requested my Private Secretary to issue tickets of invitation to my Cabinet, Vice-President Dallas, and others to meet him at dinner on Thursday next. During his visit Mr. Ward of Boston and Mr. W. W. Corcoran (the banker of Washington) came into the parlour.

Tuesday, 27th February, 1849.— I had learned this morning that Mr. Buchanan had taken exception to my remark on Saturday last (see this diary of that day) that I should feel that I was deserted by my political family if the members of my Cabinet should call on the President-elect before he called on me. The remark was made because it might have happened that if my Cabinet called on General Taylor he might not afterwards have chosen to call on me at all. As General Taylor belongs to a different political party from myself, and as it was his duty to call on me, if he desired to exchange civilities, I thought it was due to their own self-respect as well as to me that my Cabinet should wait until General Taylor paid his respects to me before they paid their respects to him. In this view all the members of the Cabinet expressed their concurrence on Saturday, except Mr. Buchanan. I learned this morning that Mr. Buchanan had said to a member of the Cabinet that notwithstanding my remark on Saturday he had left the Cabinet-room resolved to call on General Taylor on that day, as General Shields by appointment had called at the State Department to accompany him. He did not, however, do so; but called on General Taylor on yesterday, immediately after General Taylor had called on me. Mr. Buchanan is an able man, but is in small matters without judgment and sometimes acts like an old maid.

Wednesday, 28th February, 1849. — This evening [2] in

[2] In a brief statement prefaced to the entry for this day, Polk adverts to the harassing stream of calls " made upon me by the crowd of persons who had congregated at Washington to witness the inauguration of my successor." He adds that he has " found it impossible to record in this diary the daily events as they occurred." Repeatedly in the next few days he mentions this pressure of duties. It was from an exhausting final week in the White House that he plunged into his exhausting trip home.

pursuance of previous notice the parlours of the President's Mansion were thrown open and the last drawing-room or *levée* of my administration was held. It was the most brilliant and crowded room of my term. The house was brilliantly lighted up and the fine Marine Band of music was stationed in the entrance hall. About eight o'clock P.M. the company commenced assembling. Among those who attended early in the evening, were many officers of the army and navy, who called in a body in full uniform. The foreign Ministers and their families and legations resident at Washington were present in their court dresses. The members of my Cabinet and their families, members of Congress, citizens, and a vast number of strangers made up the large number of visitors. I received them in the circular parlour, standing with my back against the marble centre table and Mrs. Polk standing a few feet to my right. The marble centre table proved to be an important protection to me. All the parlours and outer halls soon became crowded with human beings, ladies and gentlemen, so that it became very difficult for them to make their way to the place where Mrs. Polk and myself stood. I remained stationary and shook hands with several thousand persons of both sexes. I learned afterwards that many persons came to the door and the jam was so great that they could not make their way to me, and retired without entering. The line of carriages approaching the President's House, I was afterwards informed, extended several hundred yards. About twelve o'clock at night the last of the company retired. I remained on my feet continuously for several hours and was exceedingly fatigued.

Thursday, 1st March, 1849. — General Taylor, the President of the United States elect, having called and paid his respects to me on the 26th *ultimo,* I have invited him to dine with me today. I invited a large party of both political parties to meet him at dinner. He attended the dinner accordingly. Among others who composed the dinner party

were General Cass, who was the Democratic candidate for
the Presidency at the last election, Mr. Fillmore, the Vice-
President-elect. . . Senator Davis of Mississippi. . .
Senator Bell of Tennessee. . . Mr. Seaton, the mayor of
Washington, and his wife, and Mr. Ritchie, editor of the
Union. All the members of my Cabinet and the wives of
Secretaries Walker, Marcy, and Toucey attended the dinner. . . General Taylor, the President-elect, waited on
Mrs. Polk to the table. He sat on one side of Mrs. Polk
and General Cass on the other. I waited on Mrs. Dallas to
the table. The dinner was finely gotten up in Julian's
(the French cook's) best style. It passed off well. Not the
slightest allusion was made to any political subject. The
whole company seemed to enjoy themselves. After dinner
and between nine and ten o'clock P.M. the company dispersed.

Friday, 2nd March, 1849. — (See commencement of this
diary of the 28th *ultimo*.) This was a very busy day with
me. Many members of Congress and an unusual number
of strangers called. The city was much crowded with
strangers, chiefly of the Whig party, who have come to witness the inauguration of General Taylor. A large number of
them have called on me during the last week, and today a
greater number than on any one day previously.

Saturday, 3rd March, 1849. — (See this diary of the 28th
ultimo.) I was in my office at an earlier hour than usual
this morning, and was constantly and incessantly occupied
throughout the day. A large number of persons, members
of Congress and strangers, called in the course of the forenoon. This was the regular day for the meeting of the
Cabinet, but no formal meeting was held. All the members
of the Cabinet tendered to me their respective resignations,
which I accepted. The resignations of the Secretary of the
Treasury and the Postmaster-General were to take effect
from and after this day. The resignations of the other
members of the Cabinet were to take effect from and after

the 6th or 7th instant. They were made to take effect
at that time at the special request of General Taylor, made
through Mr. Clayton, whom he had designated as his Secretary of State. He made this request in order to avoid any
public inconvenience until the new Cabinet could be appointed. I am not certain whether the resignation of the
Attorney-General was to take effect from and after this
day, or whether he held on until the 6th or 7th instant. The
Cabinet dispersed and I disposed of all the business on my
table down to the minutest detail and at the close of the day
left a clean table for my successor. I signed my name to the
several hundred commissions for military, naval, and civil
officers, and to other official papers. The Senate had within
the last few days confirmed numerous nominations which I
had made in the course of the session of Congress, commissions for whom I signed. Many of these nominations were
for brevet promotions of officers of the army. Others were
for regular promotions in the army and navy. I resolved to
leave nothing undone, and therefore spent several hours in
signing them. I saw in the course of the day many public
officers and transacted business with them. About sunset,
having cleared my table of all the business upon it, I left the
President's Mansion with my family, and went to the quarters previously engaged for me at Willard's Hotel. We were
accompanied by the members of my Cabinet. My private
secretary had gone with his family to Willard's and taken
lodgings on yesterday evening. I left Mrs. Polk and our
two nieces, Miss Rucker and Miss Hays, with our servants
at the hotel, and proceeded, accompanied by my Cabinet, to
the Capitol, as is usual on the last night of the session of
Congress so that the President may be convenient to Congress to receive such bills as may be passed and presented
to him for his signature. I reached the Capitol about dark
and occupied the Vice-President's room. . . The Civil and
Diplomatic Appropriation Bill had been amended in the
Senate, on motion of Senator Walker of Wisconsin, by insert-

ing in it a provision for the temporary government of California and New Mexico. This amendment was pending in the House of Representatives, and it was threatened that the Wilmot Proviso would be attached to it by that House, and it was uncertain whether a majority of the Senate might not give way and yield to the Proviso. In that event the alternative would be presented to me of defeating the whole appropriation bill by a veto, or of yielding my assent to the Wilmot Proviso. I did not hesitate for a moment in my course. I was prepared to veto the bill though the consequence would have been to convoke an extra session of Congress. My Cabinet concurred with me in my determination. At a late hour of the night I learned that the House of Representatives had by a vote adopted an amendment to Walker's provision for the government of California and New Mexico, the substance of which was to declare all the laws of Mexico in force in these territories before their acquisition by the United States to continue in force until altered or changed by Congress. I did not see the amendment, but this was its substance as reported to me. Many of the Southern members of Congress of both Houses came into my room in great excitement about it. The effect of the amendment was to sanction the law of Mexico abolishing slavery in that Republic and to sanction other very obnoxious laws. I caused my room to be cleared of all but my Cabinet that I might consult them. Messrs. Buchanan, Walker, Marcy, and Toucey advised me to sign the bill if it came in this form. They drew a distinction, which I did not perceive, between the amendment in this form and the Wilmot Proviso. Mr. Mason advised me to veto it. Mr. Johnson thought I ought not to sign it, because, among other reasons, it was now past twelve o'clock at night, and he was of opinion that my Presidential term had expired. I opened the doors without announcing to my Cabinet what I would do. As soon as the doors were opened many members came in and urged me to veto the Bill if it came to me. Among others General Bayley of Virginia and General George S. Houston of Alabama, Lynn Boyd of Kentucky, and Cobb of Georgia came in and earnestly urged me to veto the bill. My mind was made up, but I did not communicate my decision to them. Some minutes after they retired, Mr. Houston returned and informed me that the excitement among the Southern men of the House of Representatives was intense, and that they were signing a paper addressed to me requesting me to veto the bill. I at once told him to return to the House and stop the signatures to the paper, for the President could not perform a high constitutional duty of this kind upon a petition. I then told him he might rest easy, that I was prepared with a veto message in my pocket, and that I should veto the bill if it came to me. He was greatly rejoiced, immediately left my room, and I heard nothing more of the petition. I informed the members of my Cabinet of my determination. It was fixed and settled, although four members of the Cabinet had advised against it. I sat down at my table and wrote a paragraph modifying the introductory part of the prepared message on the Wilmot Proviso which I had in my pocket, so as to meet the new form in which the amendment of the House had presented the question. Mr. Stanton of Tennessee was present when I wrote this paragraph, though I did not inform him what I was writing. It was a moment of high responsibility, perhaps the highest of my official term. I felt its weight most sensibly, but resolved to pursue the dictates of my own best judgment and to do my duty. I had gone to the Capitol this evening under the impression that, without a critical examination of the subject, my official term as President of the United States would expire at midnight on the night of this, the third day of March. The correctness of this impression was shaken by the view presented by some members of my Cabinet and by many members of Congress, Whigs and Democrats, who called on me as the hour of twelve o'clock at night approached and insisted that as by the Constitution the President shall hold his office for the term of four years, and as I had not taken the oath of office until between the hours of twelve and one o'clock on the 4th of March, 1845, my term of office would not expire until the same hour on the 4th of March, 1849. It was certain, too, that if my term as President had expired that of the House of Representatives and of one third of the Senators had also expired. The two Houses of Congress were still in session, and the General Appropriation Bill without which the Government could not get on remained to be passed. On the other hand several Senators and Representatives, and among them Senators Cass, Allen, and others, I learned, were of opinion that the term of the Congress and of the President had expired, and declined to vote. In the state of doubt upon the question which had been produced in my mind by the conflicting views which were presented I had remained at the Capitol until between one and two o'clock by the timepiece in the Vice-President's room. Great confusion, I learned, prevailed in the two Houses, as well as great excitement upon the slave-question. After two o'clock I proposed to retire from the Capitol to my lodgings. This was strongly opposed by Messrs. Buchanan, Walker, Marcy, and Toucey. Mr. Mason and Mr. Johnson thought I ought to retire. Mr. Charles A. Wickliffe of Kentucky, formerly Postmaster-General, came into the room and I asked his opinion confidentially, and he advised me not to retire. I remained until between three and four o'clock A.M. of the 4th of March, when I informed the Cabinet of my determination to retire to my lodgings. Messrs. Buchanan, Walker, Marcy and Toucey still opposed it. I informed them that I would retire to my quarters at Willard's Hotel, where I could be found if Congress should have any communication to make to me, but informed them at the same time that I would hold myself uncommitted as to my course if Congress should send me any bill for my action. I said the same thing to some members of Congress. I retired accordingly, accompanied by Mr. Mason and Mr.

Johnson. The other members of the Cabinet remained at the Capitol. My private secretary also remained at my request. When Mr. Johnson, Mr. Mason, and myself reached Willard's Hotel we had some refreshments, for I was exceedingly fatigued and exhausted. Mr. Johnson went to his house, Mr. Mason lay on a sofa in my parlour, and I retired to an adjoining chamber where Mrs. Polk was. About six o'clock A.M. I was called and informed that a committee of Congress were in my parlour waiting to see me. I repaired immediately to the parlour, for I had not undressed. The joint committee on enrolled bills of the two Houses of Congress presented to me for my approval and signature two bills, one being the Civil and Diplomatic Appropriation Bill and the other a bill to extend the revenue laws of the United States over California. The Civil and Diplomatic Bill did not contain the obnoxious amendment of the House of Representatives, which I had resolved to veto. The bill had been amended so as to strike out not only the House amendment in relation to slavery, but to strike out also Senator Walker's provision for the government of California and New Mexico, so as to leave the bill the ordinary annual appropriation bill for the support of the government.[3] I approved and signed the two bills, being unwilling to defeat so indispensable a measure as the Civil and Diplomatic Bill, the failure to pass which would have produced vast public inconvenience. . .

I find that I have omitted to notice the passage by Congress, after night of this day's proceedings, of a bill to establish the Department of the Interior, or Home Department. It was presented to me for my approval late at night and I was much occupied with other duties. It was a

[3] The bills for the government of California and New Mexico having failed, the stage was now set for the fierce struggle over the prohibition of slavery in these new acquisitions which was to threaten disunion, and to end only with the adoption of the Compromise of 1850. Polk had hoped to close his administration amid sectional harmony; instead, he ended it with the Northern free-soilers fiercely arrayed against the Southern followers of Calhoun.

long bill containing many sections and I had but little time
to examine it. I had serious objections to it, but they were
not of a constitutional character, and I signed it with reluctance. I fear its consolidating tendency. I apprehend its
practical operation will be to draw power from the States,
where the Constitution has reserved it, and to extend the
jurisdiction and power of the United States by construction
to an unwarrantable extent. Had I been a member of Congress I would have voted against it. Many bills pass Congress every year against which the President would vote
were he a member of that body, and which he yet approves
and signs.

Sunday, 4th March, 1849. — Having closed my official
term as President of the United States at half past six o'clock
this morning, that being about the hour at which Congress
adjourned, I attended divine service with my family, consisting of Mrs. Polk and our two nieces, Miss Hays and
Miss Rucker, at the First Presbyterian church. An excellent
sermon was preached by the Rev. Mr. Ballentine, the pastor.
At the close of the service the minister and elder members
of the church, male and female, approached and shook hands
with Mrs. Polk and myself on taking leave of us, accompanied with many expressions of their friendship and affectionate regard. The scene was an interesting and gratifying
one. We had attended worship regularly and with few exceptions almost every Sabbath during the term of my Presidency, and the congregation today seemed to realize that
they were about to part with us, and that in all probability
we should never worship with them again. The affectionate
manner in which they took leave of us made the scene a very
impressive one. We returned to our lodgings at the Irving
Hotel, and from thence I rode in my carriage to the President's House to collect some letters and manuscripts
which I left in my office on leaving it last evening. In the
afternoon I rested at the hotel, being much fatigued by the
very severe duties of the past weeks. A few friends called

in the evening and we saw them in our parlour. I feel exceedingly relieved that I am now free from all public cares. I am sure I shall be a happier man in my retirement than I have been during the four years I have filled the highest office in the gift of my countrymen.

Monday, 5th March, 1849. — Soon after breakfast this morning many of my friends called to see me and many strangers called to pay their respects. Among them were all the members of my late Cabinet and the ladies of their families. Between eleven and twelve o'clock a procession of military companies and citizens, conducted by many marshals on horseback, moved from Willard's Hotel as an escort to General Taylor, the President-elect of the United States. On reaching the Irving Hotel, where I had my quarters, the procession halted and the open carriage in which General Taylor was seated stopped immediately opposite to the hotel. In pursuance of the arrangements made by the committee of the Senate, I was conducted to the same carriage and seated on the right of General Taylor. Mr. Seaton, the Mayor of Washington, and Mr. Winthrop, the late Speaker of the House of Representatives, were seated in the same carriage. The procession moved to the Capitol. On arriving there we were met by the committee of the Senate, consisting of Senators Davis of Mississippi, Johnson of Maryland, and Davis of Massachusetts, and were conducted to the Senate chamber, where the Senate were in session. General Taylor and myself walked in together and were seated, I being on his right. My late Cabinet were seated on the floor of the Senate. After remaining a few minutes the whole body of persons proceeded to the eastern front of the Capitol, General Taylor and myself walking out together in the same manner we had entered the Senate chamber. After being there a few minutes General Taylor read his inaugural address. He read it in a very low voice and very badly as to his pronunciation and manner. The oath of office was administered to him by the

Chief Justice of the Supreme Court of the United States.
As soon as this was over I advanced to him and shook him
by the hand, saying to him, " I hope, sir, the country may be
prosperous under your administration." We were then conducted to the carriage in which we had come to the Capitol,
and proceeded along Pennsylvania Avenue, Mr. Seaton and
Mr. Winthrop being in the carriage with General, now
President, Taylor and myself, towards the President's mansion. On arriving at my lodgings at the Irving Hotel the
procession halted and I took leave of the President. He
proceeded to the President's mansion. On proceeding to the
Capitol and returning I remained covered. General Taylor
occasionally took off his hat and bowed to the people. When
not making his respects to the people he was free in conversation. On going up to the Capitol California was alluded
to, in conversation between Mr. Seaton and Mr. Winthrop
and myself. Something was said which drew from General
Taylor the expression of views and opinions which greatly
surprised me. They were to the effect that California and
Oregon were too distant to become members of the Union,
and that it would be better for them to be an independent
government. He said that our people would inhabit them
and repeated that it would be better for them to form an
independent government for themselves. These are alarming opinions to be entertained by the President of the United
States. I made no response, nor did Mr. Seaton or Mr.
Winthrop. I have entertained serious apprehensions, and
have expressed them in this diary, that if no government was
provided for California at the late session of Congress there
was danger that that fine territory would be lost to the
Union by the establishment of an independent government.
General Taylor's opinions as expressed, I hope, have not
been well considered. General Taylor is, I have no doubt,
a well-meaning old man. He is, however, uneducated, exceedingly ignorant of public affairs, and, I should judge, of
very ordinary capacity. He will be in the hands of others,

and must rely wholly upon his Cabinet to administer the government. Upon reaching my quarters at the Irving Hotel, hundreds of persons called, and among others the military company from Baltimore, who called last night, came in and I shook hands with them. I continued to receive company until ten and eleven o'clock at night, when I went with Mrs. Polk to the steamboat to take my departure by the southern route to my residence in Tennessee. All the members of my Cabinet, with the females of their families, called in the course of the afternoon. The demonstrations of kindness and respect paid to me on the eve of my departure from Washington were highly gratifying, and all that I could have desired. Mr. Buchanan, Mr. and Mrs. Marcy, and Mr. and Mrs. Mason accompanied us to the boat, though it was a wet night, where they took leave of us.

CHAPTER XIV
March 6, 1849 – April 2, 1849

DEPARTURE FROM WASHINGTON — ARRIVAL IN CHARLESTON — RECEPTION IN MONTGOMERY AND MOBILE — YELLOW FEVER IN NEW ORLEANS — VOYAGE UP THE MISSISSIPPI — ILLNESS — AT HOME IN NASHVILLE

Tuesday, 6th March, 1849. — This morning at three o'clock the steamboat left, and I was on my journey homeward. The railroad cars stopped a few minutes at Fredericksburg. A crowd was assembled to see me. I stepped to the end of the cars and bowed to them, shaking hands with some of them. At a place called the Junction, twenty miles from Richmond, I was met by a committee from that city, consisting of Robert G. Scott, James A. Seddon, and Mr. Casker, who insisted that I should spend a day at Richmond, but I declined to do so. They informed me that the General Assembly of Virginia, now in session, had passed a resolution, without distinction of party and unanimously, to receive me in their legislative capacity. On arriving at the depot at Richmond I found a large crowd of people assembled. I was met at this point by a committee of the legislature, who informed me officially of the resolution which the legislature had passed and invited me to visit that body, then in session. I did so. On being conducted into the hall of the House of Delegates, where both houses were assembled, and where a vast crowd of citizens were collected, I was addressed by the Speaker of the House in a very eloquent and complimentary speech, to which I responded, and after being introduced individually to the members, proceeded on my journey, having spent about an hour in going through the imposing ceremony. The Speaker also addressed Mr. Walker, who responded. During these ceremonies Mrs. Polk and the ladies of my party were entertained at the hospitable mansion of the Hon. James A. Seddon, where, as they informed me, they met many of the ladies of the city and partook of a splendid collation.

On arriving at Petersburg we found a large crowd assembled at the depot, and on reaching the hotel where we dined I was addressed, and made a very short response, being much fatigued and suffering from the effects of a severe cold. Mr. Walker was also addressed and responded at some length. After dinner we were conducted to the railroad cars, accompanied by many hundreds of people, and proceeded on our journey. We arrived at Weldon, N. C., in the night, and found the principal hotel and other buildings of the place brilliantly illuminated. This is a region of tar and turpentine, and bonfires (turpentine and tar barrels) were blazing in the streets.

Wednesday, 7th March, 1849. — About ten o'clock this morning the railroad cars arrived at Wilmington, North Carolina, at which place I had accepted an invitation to spend a day. I was met at the railroad depot by the authorities of the town and a large number of citizens; and was conducted through the town in an open carriage to the hotel where quarters had been provided for me. On reaching the hotel and alighted from the carriage I was addressed in a very complimentary manner by Mr. Hill (a young man) in an eloquent manner.

Friday, 9th March, 1849. — Early in the morning the steamer reached Charleston, but we did not go on shore until between eight and nine o'clock, this being the arrangement of the committees and city authorities. A large concourse of citizens were assembled on the wharf, and on being conducted on shore, I was received by a committee of citizens, and welcomed to their city by Henry W. Conner, their chairman, in a strong and very complimentary address, to which I responded. . . My reception in Charleston was most brilliant and everything connected with it was conducted with order and good taste. It was not only a warm, but an enthusiastic welcome, and every mark of distinction and respect, without regard to political divisions, was paid to me. We retired to rest at a late hour. The weather during the day had been unusually warm for Charleston for this season of the year. I had left snow and ice at Washington not four days ago, and now I found myself in the midst of summer heat. This sudden transition from cold to heat, and the great fatigue I had endured during the day made the rest of the night very acceptable to me.

Saturday, 10th March, 1849. — About seven o'clock this morning I left the hotel and went on board the steamboat for Savannah, Georgia. We were taken to the boat in open carriages, escorted by the committees, Mayor, and city authorities of Charleston, Governor Seabrook, and many citizens. On taking leave of Charleston we passed under a beautiful canopy, erected on cotton bales tastefully arranged and with the inscription, " The Old Palmetto State bids thee farewell." I proceeded on my journey in charge of the committee of gentlemen from Savannah, under a fire of a salute from the forts.

Monday, 12th March, 1849. — At an early hour this morning (before seven o'clock), after taking a cup of coffee, I left the hotel in Savannah and, under a military escort and with a crowd of citizens who had assembled at this early hour of the day, I left the hotel (being conveyed in an open carriage and accompanied by the Mayor) and proceeded to the railroad depot, where we took leave of the Mayor, authorities, and people of Savannah. Every manifestation of public respect was paid to me by all political parties at Savannah. On the departure of the cars a salute was fired. I was accompanied by a committee of gentlemen from Savannah

to the 90-mile station on the railroad to Macon. At this
place we dined and met a committee from Macon, who had
been deputed to receive and accompany me to that city.
After dinner I took leave of the Savannah committee, who
returned, and I proceeded on my journey. A large number
of persons had collected at the 90-mile station, where we
dined, to meet me. I was presented to them and shook
hands with many of them, ladies and gentlemen, old persons
and little children. At all the depots or stopping-places on
the route from Savannah to Macon persons were collected
from the surrounding country, to all of whom I made my
respects, and shook hands with many of them, during the
short period the cars stopped at each place. About sunset
we reached Macon, a distance of 180 miles from Savannah.
I was received at the depot by the authorities of the town
and many hundred persons who had assembled. We were
placed in open carriages and proceeded about a mile, under
a military escort, to a hotel where quarters had been provided for me. We had a dusty and fatiguing ride on the
railroad, and after retiring to my room for a short time I
came to the parlour and was introduced to many persons,
ladies and gentlemen. Having taken supper and continued
to receive company until ten o'clock I retired.

Friday, 16th March, 1849. — On arriving at the depot
at Montgomery I found a very large number of persons
collected. I was conveyed to the town in a splendid open
carriage drawn by six fine horses richly caparisoned. On
arriving at the hotel I was addressed and welcomed to Montgomery, to which I made a response. Though much fatigued
and suffering from violent cold and cough, the effect of the
exposure to which I had been subjected for the last two days,
I was presented to several hundred ladies and gentlemen
during the evening. The citizens of Montgomery had had
very short notice of the precise day I would probably reach
that place, and as I was desirous of proceeding on my journey on which I had been more delayed than I had antici-

pated, and had on that account declined an invitation to remain with them on tomorrow, the committee had ordered a
public supper or collation for tonight. It was near eleven
o'clock before the supper was ready and we sat down to the
day table. Regular toasts had been prepared and were
drank, one of which as a matter of course had reference to
myself. It was highly complimentary and I responded to it
in a short speech. All political parties were present on the
occasion. Many sentiments were given and speeches made,
and among others one by the Hon. Mr. Yancy, late a member of Congress. I retired at a late hour, greatly fatigued
and quite unwell.

Sunday, 18th March, 1849.— We spent this day on
board the steamer descending the Alabama River. Wherever the boat stopped to take in wood or for any other purpose, a number of people came on board to see me. I continued to be somewhat indisposed, but enjoyed the rest.

Monday, 19th March, 1849.— About ten o'clock this
morning we reached Mobile. . .   On landing I was conducted to the platform erected for the occasion and was
addressed by Col. Philips on behalf of the citizens, in an
eloquent manner, and was welcomed to the hospitalities of
the city. A dense crowd of people filled the open space on
the wharf, and every window in the vicinity was filled with
ladies. After this reception was over I was placed in an
open carriage and conducted by the committee, escorted by
the military, through the principel streets to the hotel where
quarters had been provided for me. I was conducted into
the hotel and was there received by the Mayor who was
stationed in an upper hall of the hotel with the city authorities around him. A large number of ladies were also assembled to witness the ceremony. The Mayor, who was a
Whig (Childers), addressed me, to which I responded, and
was then presented to the city councils, and to the ladies, with
whom I shook hands. A few minutes before the dinner hour
I was relieved and retired to my chamber. We dined with

the Mayor, city authorities, and a number of citizens. I met
here my old college friend, Walker Anderson, of Florida,
who had come to Mobile with his two daughters expressly to
meet me. My friend James E. Saunders, Esquire, and his
family were constantly with us and were particularly atten-
tive. After dinner there was still a round of visitors. Late
in the afternoon we took a ride of three or four miles up
the shore of Mobile Bay to the hospitable mansion of Col.
Philips. On returning to the hotel I found myself still in
the midst of a crowd of visitors. After tea, yielding to importunate solicitations, I attended the theater, to which I
had been invited. I was accompanied by Col. Philips and
his wife, some members of the committee, and my two nieces,
Miss Rucker and Miss Hays. Mrs. Polk did not accompany me. On entering the theater I found a crowded audience and was received with great applause and every demonstration of respect. I remained at the theater but half an
hour, when I returned to the hotel exceedingly fatigued and
exhausted. My reception at Mobile, and particularly the
approach to the City and the landing, was most imposing
and magnificent. The hospitality and warm cordiality of
the Southern character was displayed in an eminent degree.
On reaching the hotel I was heartily rejoiced at the opportunity of retiring for the night.

Tuesday, 20th March, 1849. — I rose this morning much
exhausted from my fatigue, and the excessively warm
weather for this season of the year, even in this climate. In
addition to this I was still somewhat indisposed. From the
moment breakfast was over I was occupied in receiving visitors, ladies and gentlemen. The cholera, I learned, was prevailing to some extent at Mobile, but was not epidemic. I
consulted Dr. Knott, an eminent physician of the place, who
prescribed for me and gave me medicines to be used in case
of an attack of cholera with any of my party. He informed
me that the disease was prevailing at New Orleans, and
advised me in my state of health to spend as little time as

possible in that city; and I resolved that when I reached New Orleans I would take the first boat bound for Nashville.

Wednesday, 21st March, 1849. — At daylight this morning the boat from Mobile reached the landing on Lake Ponchartrain, a few miles below New Orleans. I was soon called by a servant and informed that a committee from New Orleans were on board and desired to see me. I went into the cabin as soon as I could dress, etc. Two or three gentlemen met me and informed me that they had been deputed by the city authorities at New Orleans to receive me on landing at this point, and conduct me to the hotel on shore where I would be detained until nine o'clock, at which time the authorities of the city would be prepared to receive me. I informed them that my purpose was to proceed with the least possible delay up. They said that learning by letters and telegraphic despatches of my approach, the city authorities and citizens of New Orleans had made extensive preparations to give me a public reception today; that the military had been ordered out, and that the Governor of the State would participate in the ceremonies of the occasion. They assured me that the city was healthy, and that there was no danger from cholera. A few cases of the disease, they said, were occurring, but they were confined to indigent and imprudent persons, and no epidemic was prevailing. Perceiving that I could not carry out my resolution to pass immediately through the city without seeming to act rudely, I yielded to their wishes. They conducted us from the boat to the hotel, distant about a fourth of a mile. After an hour or two breakfast was announced. It was, I supposed, a sumptuous breakfast. All the dishes were prepared in the French style of cooking, and to one unaccustomed to it was difficult to tell of what they were composed. Fish of every variety and prepared in various ways constituted a large part of the repast. The table was covered, too, with every variety of light wines. I could see nothing before me that I had been accustomed to, or that I should have deemed it safe to eat in my state of health and in a cholera atmosphere. I took a cup of coffee and something on my plate to save appearances, but was careful to eat none of it. As soon as an opportunity offered I asked a servant in a low tone if he could give me a piece of cornbread and broiled ham. He dashed off in great haste and in an incredibly short time he brought me the bread and ham. Before we sat down to breakfast an additional number of the members of the committee had arrived. About nine o'clock we took the cars to the city. On arriving at the depot I found an imposing array of the military drawn up. On alighting from the cars I was met and welcomed to the city by the Mayor (Crossman) in a few words. I was glad he made no formal speech. In a few words of reply I thanked him for the honour done me. A long procession of citizens in carriages and on foot, preceded by an imposing array of the military, moved through the city. Governor Johnson, Major-General Gaines, United States Army, and many other persons of official distinction, joined in the procession. I was seated in an open carriage with the Mayor and Recorders, Genois and Baldwin. The day was warm, and the streets dusty. Though I had taken the precaution to take my umbrella in my hand I was often exposed to the rays of the sun. The procession moved slowly, frequently halting for a few minutes, through several of the principal streets of the city. I bowed constantly on the right and left to the ladies in the windows and on the balconies of the houses. I did not note the precise time but should guess it was between three and four hours from the time the procession moved from the railroad depot until I was taken to the quarters provided for me at the St. Louis hotel. I was covered with dust and perspiration. I retired to my room for an hour and changed my dress. I feared the effects of the exposure to the sun and the excessive fatigue I had endured. I dined with the Mayor and other authorities at the hotel. After night, as well as throughout the afternoon, I was called on by many acquaintances and friends, as well as many strangers, ladies and gentlemen. In the evening, I informed the Mayor and some members of the committees of the state of my health, of my great fatigue, and of my wish to proceed up the river in a boat which was to leave that night. The Mayor and the other gentlemen expressed great solicitude that I should not do so. The Mayor said they had sent out invitations to more than 250 gentlemen to attend a public dinner, which they proposed to give me on tomorrow, and that if I left it would be a source of deep regret and mortification to the citizens of New Orleans. He assured me further that if there was the slightest danger from cholera they would at once have informed me of it; for they would not on any account put my life in hazard by causing me to remain. I found myself compelled to yield, and agreed to remain and partake of the dinner on tomorrow, though I did so reluctantly and against my own wishes and judgment. I retired to rest as soon as I could do so with propriety, though it was at a late hour. Though more fatigued I do not discover that my health is worse than it was when I left Mobile.

On the Mississippi, Friday, 23rd March, 1849. — I rose this morning without being so much refreshed by a night's sleep as I had hoped to be. I was still indisposed and felt the effects of the severe fatigue which I had endured. Early in the morning an incident of thrilling interest occurred. Four or five persons in a small skiff approached the boat from the shore, and in endeavoring to come on board the boat upset and turned bottom upwards, precipitating those unfortunate persons into the angry current of the Mississippi. Great anxiety prevailed to save their lives. The boat stopped, the small boat was quickly manned and sent to their relief, and luckily they were all saved. One or two of them were white men and the others negroes. About eleven o'clock the boat reached Baton Rouge, where I was received by the firing of a salute, and by a large number of persons who had assembled on the shore. I was waited on by a committee and conducted by them to a hotel in the town where, in the presence of a large number of ladies and gentlemen, I was addressed by the chairman of the committee, and to which I responded. I remained on shore about an hour, when I returned on board. A collation had been prepared in anticipation of my arrival, but I had not time to partake of it; and indeed was glad to avoid the fatigue which I must have undergone to have done so. While I was on shore, many persons, ladies and gentlemen, visited the boat and paid their respects to Mrs. Polk. A man died on board the boat of cholera today. His body was put into a coarse, rough box, hastily nailed together and and was entrusted to some wood choppers at the wood yard to be buried. The boat proceeded up the river. In the night she stopped several hours in consequence of a dense fog in the river rendering it unsafe for her to run.

Sunday, 25th March, 1849.—My disease (a derangement of the stomach and bowels) which had from its commencement assumed a bilious type, was no better this morning. I was quiet during the day, except at a few points where the boat stopped on the river, at several of which a number of persons came on board to see me. After night a steamer from Vicksburg with a large number of persons, ladies and gentlemen, on board, met our boat, and rounding to was lashed to our boat. Two committees, the one from Vicksburg and the other from Jackson, Mississippi, were among the persons who came to meet me. They were urgent in their solicitations that I should accept the hospitalities of these towns and spend a day at each. The same reasons which compelled me to decline accepting the hospitalities of the people of Natchez compelled me to decline accepting their request. I was introduced to the whole party, ladies and gentlemen, who met me and I shook hands with them. Arriving at Vicksburg, our boat remained but a few minutes, when we proceeded on our journey. I learned from the persons I met that Senator Houston of Texas had passed down the river, and the Hon. Henry Clay of Kentucky had passed up the river this afternoon, each stopping a short time at Memphis. They told me that when the boat on which Mr. Clay was approaching Vicksburg from below, a salute which had been prepared for my reception was fired, supposing that I was on board. Mr. Clay, they told me, on learning the fact humorously observed, " I hope, gentlemen, I am not stealing Mr. Polk's thunder." To which the committee replied that they had plenty of powder for both.

Tuesday, 27th March, 1849.——The boat arrived at Memphis about daylight this morning. My two nephews, Samuel P. Walker and Samuel P. Caldwell, who reside at Memphis and who were expecting me, soon came on board. They informed me that anticipating my arrival on yesterday evening a steamer had been chartered and a large party, ladies and gentlemen, had proceeded many miles down the river, but not meeting me had returned in the night. A committee of citizens soon came on board. I endeavoured to excuse myself for declining to go on shore by pleading my state of health. As, however, I was able to receive my friends in the cabin of the boat, they insisted I was able to go on shore, and pressed me very much to do so. They insisted that as Memphis was the first point in my own State which I had touched after an absence of more than four years, and that as extensive preparations had been made to receive me, that I should go on shore if it was even for a short time. In the meantime many of my old acquaintances and friends came on board, and their importunities were so great that finally against my own judgment I yielded and went on shore with the promise that I would be detained there but a short time. I was seated in an open carriage with Judge Dunlap and Col. Watson, who had accompanied me from Montgomery, Alabama, to this place, and was conducted in procession into the town, and around and through the Navy Yard, occupying more than an hour. I was then conducted to a hotel where a large crowd of people, ladies

and gentlemen, had assembled. Before I alighted from the
carriage I was addressed in front of the hotel by the Hon.
Spencer Jarnagin, to which I responded from the carriage.
Mr. Jarnagin was lately a Whig Senator in Congress from
Tennessee. His address was liberal and kind in its tone and
could not fail to be gratifying. The leading men of both political parties were present and participated in the ceremony
of bidding me welcome back to my own State. I was conducted from the carriage into the hotel, where I was most
cordially received by hundreds of old acquaintances and
friends. I met also many ladies and many of my relations
who reside at Memphis. I felt highly honored and gratified
at the enthusiastic reception given to me, but felt exhausted
and much fatigued, and as soon as I could with propriety I
returned to the boat. I declined to remain and partake of
a collation which had been prepared for the occasion. The
boat left, and I very soon felt the ill effects of the exertion
through which I had imprudently gone. I found that the indisposition which had afflicted me for several days was increased.

Wednesday, 28th March, 1849. — I found myself no better this morning. Towards noon I was much worse and remained constantly in my stateroom. There was no physician on board. The type of my disease continued to be
bilious, a circumstance which was perhaps fortunate while I
was in a cholera atmosphere. I took medicine prepared for
me by Dr. Nott at Mobile, but not being certain that it was
the proper prescription for my case, on reaching Paducah on
the Ohio River after night, I sent on shore for a physician.
A Dr. Jones came on board. He examined my case and said
that it was not cholera, but that all diseases of the bowels
had a tendency to run into cholera when that disease prevailed, and he advised me to leave the boat. He was a man
in appearance of more than fifty years of age, and appeared
to be discreet and sensible. I requested him to accompany
me on the boat to Smithland, which was only twelve miles

up the river. He agreed to do so, and after going on shore to procure medicines he returned and accompanied me.

Thursday, 29th March, 1849.—I was in a comfortable hotel at Smithland this morning with every attention from the obliging landlord which it was possible for him to bestow. I was confined to my bed throughout the day. Dr. Jones and Dr. Saunders visited me repeatedly during the day.

Monday, 2nd April, 1849.—I was much better this morning, but was quite feeble from the effects of medicine and my indisposition. A few miles below Nashville we met a steamer having on board a committee of gentlemen and a number of my old acquaintances and friends. Among them was my brother-in-law, Dr. John B. Hays of Columbia, who, hearing of my illness and detention at Smithland, had set out to meet me. His daughter had spent the past winter in my family and was with me on her return home. On arriving in sight of the boat landing at Nashville, I discovered that the wharf was covered with people. I stood on the deck of the boat as she approached, and was enthusiastically cheered by the crowd on shore. As soon as the boat touched the shore many of my old acquaintances and friends came on board. After a few minutes I was conducted on shore and in passing from the boat to the carriage prepared to receive me I was met by the dense crowd and warmly greeted by many old acquaintances and friends, with whom I shook hands. I was seated in an open carriage with ex-Governor A. V. Brown and two other persons, and conveyed up Broad and Cherry streets and thence to the public square in front of the Nashville Inn, where I was addressed by Gov. A. V. Brown, who warmly welcomed me back to my old State and to my home. A very large number of people had turned out on the occasion; and standing in the open carriage, though feeling scarcely able to do so, I responded to his address. When I had done I was exceedingly feeble and exhausted. I was then conducted to the Verandah

House, where quarters had been prepared for me. Here again I met and shook hands with many of my friends, who were waiting at the hotel or called to see me. I was compelled very soon to retire to my room where I remained during the balance of the day. A few old and intimate friends saw me in my room. The meeting of my old friends had produced an excitement which contributed to sustain me during the day and to enable me to bear the fatigue.[1]

[1] Polk did not long survive his return to his Tennessee home. He had bought a residence in Nashville, which had belonged to his teacher in the law, Felix Grundy, and he had hoped to spend his last years in dignified retirement. But his exhaustion after the four laborious years of office and the ceremonies attending his trip home had left him ill-fitted to resist disease. An old illness shortly returned, and after a few weeks spent in looking to the improvement of his estate, on June 15 he died. He had enjoyed his freedom from the cares of the Presidency for less than four months. He was buried in a tomb before his house, but many years later his remains were removed to the State Capitol, where they now rest.

INDEX

A

Aberdeen, Lord, and the Oregon question, 15, 21, 43, 55, 73n, 109.
Abolitionists, 367.
Adams, Charles Francis, 337.
Adams, John, 221, 222.
Adams, John Quincy, 33, 34, 44, 48; and army commanders, 187, 188; 221, 222; death, 308, 309; funeral, 311, 312.
Allen, Senator William, 48, 56, 59n, 61, 67, 68, 190.
Almonte, 53.
American System, 348 ff.
Anderson, Gov. Hugh J., 60.
Annexation of Texas, retrospect of, 334.
Archer, Senator William S., 7, 31, 99, 117.
Armstrong, Robert, and military service, 232.
Art of shaking hands, 361, 362.
Arthur, T. S., 274.
Ashley, Senator Chester, 320.
Aspinwall, William H., 372.
Atocha, A. J., 50–54, 205.

B

Bagby, Senator Arthur P., 7, 132, 133, 298.
Baker, Representative E. D., 85.
Barbour, John S., 209, 210.
Baldwin, Judge Henry, 12, 37.
Baltimore Convention, 323–326.
Bancroft, George, as Secretary of the Navy, 4, 8, 13, 25, 33, 34, 40, 47, 48, 54, 58, 64, 69; opposes

war, 82; and war message, 84; as Minister to England, 135, 145; 147, 363.
Bankhead, Col. James, 231.
Baring Brothers, 20.
Barnburners, convention of 1848, 328–330, 337, 338.
Barrow, Senator Alexander, death of, 179, 180.
Baton Rouge, Polk visits, 399.
Beach, Moses, in Mexico, 217, 218; calls on Polk, 230.
Bedford Springs, Polk at, 340, 341.
Bell, John, 269.
Benton, Eliza, marriage, 103.
Benton, John Randolph, insults Polk, 273, 274.
Benton, Senator Thomas Hart, and Oregon question, 17–19, 31, 38, 39, 56, 59, 62; and Mexican affairs, 67–71; opposes war, 79 ff.; and war message, 86–89; and plan of war, 95; instructions to Taylor, 122; and tariff, 126; and the two-million bill, 131, 132; Vera Cruz expedition, 161 ff.; and command in Mexico, 163 ff.; plan of campaign, 168; recommends Scott, 170; and Polk's message, 174; and lieutenant-generalship, 175 ff.; on conduct of war, 190, 191; offered major-generalship, 199–201; declines, 202; Pierce on, 203; and son-in-law's office, 206, 227, 228; and Frémont-Kearny dispute, 254 ff., 271 ff., 274 ff.; quarrel with Marcy, 282; peace treaty, 312–314; relations with Polk, 320, 321; speech against Kearny, 336;

405

M

McCalla, Rev. William L., 156–158.
McConnell, Representative Felix S., suicide, 145–147.
McDowell, Gov. James, 62.
McDuffie, Senator George, 30, 56, 57, 60, 69, 74.
McGuffey, W. H., 345.
McKay, Representative James J., 60.
McLane, Minister Louis, 15, 43, 54, 55, 72; and the war, 91; considered for Secretary of State, 124.
McLane, Robert, 27, 28.
McVean, Charles, 344.
Macomb, Gen. Alexander, 187, 188.
Macon, Nathaniel, 236.
Madison, Mrs. Dolly, 69, 311, 374.
Mangum, Senator Willie P., 312.
Marcy, William L., as Secretary of War, 4, 8, 14, 28; and plan of war, 93, 94; troubles with Scott, 99–102; and dismissal of Scott, 103 ff.; and Frémont-Kearny affair, 227; and Frémont trial, 282; and Scott-Pillow quarrel, 288–290; and Frémont findings, 301–304; and peace treaty, 305, 306.
Marshall, John, 37.
Mason, John Y., Attorney-General, 1, 4, 5, 8, 31, 64, 69, 75; illness, 108; as Secretary of Navy, 145; remissness of, 199, on Calhoun, 214; portrait of, 233, 234; visits University of North Carolina, 234–240; and Frémont trial, 301–304; 326, 355.
Mason, Col. Richard B., 255.
Massachusetts, volunteers from, 168.
Matamoras, 6; Taylor at, 81, 83.
Memphis, reception to Polk, 401.
Mexico, relations with, passim; war declared, 83–89; army of, 94n; negotiations with, 137 ff.; rejected, 148 ff.; and blockade, 202, 203; peace negotiations, 211 ff.; terms of peace, 213 ff.; prisoners of war, 234; operations from Vera Cruz, 249 ff.; military levies on, 258, 259; new terms of peace, 261 ff.; armistice, 262, 263; rejects peace, 266, 267; revolution in, 270; export duty in, 279, 280; negotiations with Trist, 292–295; treaty of peace, 308; treaty signed, 327; designs on, 343, 344.
Mexico City, advance on, 249 ff.; occupation possible, 262, 263; Scott enters, 270.
Missouri Compromise, extension of line, 186, 190, 328, 331.
Mitchell, Elisha, 238.
Mobile, reception to Polk, 395.
Molino del Rey, battle of, 270.
Monroe Doctrine, 16, 18, 19.
Monterey, capture of, 153–156.
Montgomery, Ala., reception to Polk, 394.
Morehead, Gov. John Motley, 237.
Mormons, 47; and Mexican War, 109, 110.
Morton, Marcus, 47.

N

Nashville Union, 24n.
Nashville, reception to Polk, 403.
National Era, 319, 320.
National Intelligencer, Washington, and the war, 218.
Nauvoo, Ill., 47n.
New Mexico, 10, 66, 330, 331, 332, 336, 382–386; admission defeated, 386.
New Orleans, reception to Polk, 397.
North Carolina, University of, 234; visit to, 234–240.
Nourse, Dr. Amos, 72.
Nueces River, 5n.
Nugent, New York Herald correspondent, 310, 317.

O

"Old Defenders of Baltimore," 8.
Oregon, negotiations on, 1–75 passim; new proposals, 109 ff.; Senate advises ratification, 115; treaty ratified, 116; admission of, 330–339; too remote for Statehood, 389.

BIBLIOGRAPHICAL NOTE

THE standard and doubtless definitive life of Polk, exhaustive and able, is Eugene Irving McCormac's *James K. Polk* (1922). It quite supplants John S. Jenkins's *James Knox Polk, and a History of his Administration* (1852), a book by a Democratic admirer. On the Mexican war there are two admirable works, written from somewhat different points of view. Justin H. Smith's *The Annexation of Texas* (1911) was followed by his two volumes called *The War With Mexico* (1919). Less sympathy for the policies of Polk and the Democrats appears in George Lockhart Rives's *The United States and Mexico, 1821–1848*, also in two volumes (1913). On Winfield Scott the best work is the *Memoirs of Lieutenant-General Scott, written by himself* (1864). On Zachary Taylor we have *Letters from the Battlefields of the Mexican War*, reprinted from the originals in the Bixby collection in St. Louis (1908); and the *Life of Taylor*, by Oliver Otis Howard (1892). The best study of diplomatic affairs in this period in Jesse S. Reeves' *American Diplomacy Under Tyler and Polk* (1907), supplemented by *The Life of James Buchanan*, by George Ticknor Curtis, in two volumes (1883). On political affairs Thomas Hart Benton's *Thirty Years' View . . . 1820–1850*, in two volumes (1854–59), is indispensable. An excellent summary view of the whole period may be found in George Pierce Garrison's volume in the American Nation Series called *Westward Extension* (1906), which contains a good working bibliography.

An interesting picture of Polk's management of his two plantations is supplied by John Spencer Bassett's *The Southern Plantation Overseer as Revealed in His Letters* (1925).